RED ST★R OVER THE PACIFIC

RED ST★R OVER THE PACIFIC

China's Rise and the Challenge to U.S. Maritime Strategy

Toshi Yoshihara and James R. Holmes

NAVAL INSTITUTE PRESS
Annapolis, Maryland

Naval Institute Press
291 Wood Road
Annapolis, MD 21402

Library of Congress Cataloging-in-Publication Data
Yoshihara, Toshi.
  Red star over the Pacific : China's rise and the challenge to U.S. maritime strategy / Toshi Yoshihara and James R. Holmes.
    p. cm.
  Includes bibliographical references and index.
  ISBN 978-1-59114-390-1 (alk. paper)
  1. Sea-power—China. 2. Sea-power—United States. 3. Naval strategy. 4. Geopolitics—Asia. I. Holmes, James R., 1965- II. Title.
  VA633.Y67 2010
  359'.030951--dc22
                                        2010017443

Printed in the United States of America on acid-free paper

14 13 12   9 8 7 6 5 4 3 2

 # Contents

 # Acronyms and Abbreviations

A2/AD	antiaccess/access denial
AAW	antiair warfare
ASBM	antiship ballistic missile
ASCM	antiship cruise missile
ASUW	antisurface warfare
ASW	antisubmarine warfare
BMD	ballistic missile defense
CBSA	Center for Strategic and Budgetary Assessments
CCP	Chinese Communist Party
CMSI	China Maritime Studies Institute
CNO	chief of naval operations
CVN	nuclear-powered carrier
DDH	helicopter destroyer
EEZ	exclusive economic zone
EMP	electromagnetic pulse
ICBM	intercontinental ballistic missile
JMSDF	Japan Maritime Self-Defense Force
MAD	mutual assured destruction
MaRV	maneuvering reentry vehicles
MRBM	medium-range ballistic missiles
PLA	People's Liberation Army
PLA Navy	People's Liberation Army Navy
PRC	People's Republic of China
PSI	Proliferation Security Initiative
SLBM	submarine-launched ballistic missile
SLOC	sea lines of communication
SOSUS	Sound Surveillance System
SSBN	nuclear-powered ballistic-missile submarine
SSN	nuclear-powered attack submarines
TBM	theater ballistic missile
VSTOL	very short takeoff and landing

 **Preface**

This book represents the culmination of more than five years of collaborative research and publishing on China's seaward turn. We conceived of revisiting geostrategic analysis and sea-power theory while poring over a map of Asia in the summer of 2004 in landlocked Athens, Georgia, an unlikely place to think about affairs on the high seas. Since that brainstorming session, we have presented papers at international conferences, written numerous journal articles, and published two books on Chinese sea power and maritime strategy in Asia. Our first major work, *Chinese Naval Strategy in the Twenty-First Century: The Turn to Mahan*, was an attempt to discern an intriguing intellectual anomaly in China. In the early 2000s, we noticed that Chinese scholars were paying homage to a long-dead American sea-power theorist reviled by Maoist China. The apparent popularity of Alfred Thayer Mahan caught our attention because it signaled to us that Chinese strategists were studying and internalizing his writings in anticipation of China's entry into the nautical domain. Our thesis was that China would draw from and reshape Mahan's theories for China's unique maritime circumstances. Since then the study of Mahan has matured considerably, and policy statements from officials at the highest levels of government in Beijing bear out our contention.

We consider this book a companion volume that validates, refines, and expands upon our survey of Chinese interpretations of Mahan's theories. But it goes far beyond strategic theory. International politics is a competitive enterprise; interaction between competitors vying for important interests determines its nature. The United States needs to think seriously about its side of the interactive relationship with China if it is to sustain a strategic position that has benefited itself and Asia for many decades.

In short, we believe that China's maritime capacity—as measured not only in hardware terms but also in terms of seamanship and warfighting skill—has reached a point where Chinese strategists' theorizing will be put to the test. In other words, Beijing is on the brink of commanding the seas "with Chinese characteristics," to borrow a phrase common among Chinese officials and scholars. Why China is going to sea has been well documented. What capabilities China needs to fulfill its maritime ambitions is also a well-trodden research area. Indeed, our colleagues at the Naval War College's China Maritime Studies Institute (CMSI) publish excellent studies of the Chinese navy as a matter of routine. But *how*, specifically, Beijing will make its entry into the nautical arena remains largely unexplored. We intend to fill this gap in Westerners' understanding of Chinese sea power. In particular, this volume examines how Chinese strategy, operations, and tactics may interact with U.S. naval power in Asia, and it considers nonmilitary implements of national power likely to play a defining role in Chinese sea power in the coming years.

We employ a research methodology pioneered at CMSI, of which we are affiliate members. The chapters in this volume reference a variety of Chinese open-source literature. The sources come from the impressive collection accumulated by the CMSI library in recent years, the China National Infrastructure Knowledge online database, which houses more than 7,200 full-text journals, the Open Source Center (formerly the Foreign Broadcast Information Service), and personal purchases at bookstores in China and Taiwan. The periodicals we cite include scholarly work on international and regional affairs, writings on the intersection between strategy and operations, surveys of advanced weaponry around the world, and scientific and technical journals. We analyzed and interpreted the content of several hundred discrete articles in the course of this research. Only a small percentage of this exhaustive literature survey is cited in this book. Unless otherwise noted in the citations, all translations of Chinese works are our own, and we alone are responsible for translation errors.

Given the explosion of publishing outlets and sources in China, it is often impossible to verify the expertise and the institutional affiliation of Chinese authors. As a result, China specialists are increasingly preoccupied with quality control and managing bibliographical integrity. As such, the sources used in this study reflect a careful vetting process based on five benchmarks. First, we make a good-faith effort to identify the authors' expertise, and we rank the periodicals based on institutional credibility. For example, we give priority to publications from the Academy of Military Sciences, the Chinese Academy of Social Science, and other university-based journals. Second, articles that produce sloppy analysis or far-fetched conclusions are excluded from the analysis. If a source contains technical analysis beyond our expertise, we consult active-duty or retired naval officers with engineering backgrounds or with ample operational experience. Fortunately, such individuals are in abundant supply at the Naval War College.

Third, we use studies that seem to parrot Western, especially American, writings, so long as they are helpful in tracking the degree of original intellectual thought in China. Chinese translations of American writings are used sparingly, and only to highlight interest in a particular topic. Fourth, frequent, sustained discussions and debates on specific subjects are attractive candidates for citation and constitute the vast majority of the sources used in this study. Ongoing discourses lay down markers that let us track whether similar debates are taking place in officialdom or are being picked up by policymakers. Finally, signs of divergent thought or, more importantly, consensus on a concept or policy prescription are among the most highly prized sources in this volume. Sustained consensus suggests that an intellectual critical mass has been reached on a particular topic—which allows for strong findings and predictions.

The intent of this extensive literature survey is to gauge intellectual development and sophistication within China's naval community. We make no particular claims about the authoritativeness of the articles or the degree to which these writings influence policy decisions in Beijing. However, this bottom-up assessment of contemporary Chinese strategic thought provides a basis for capturing potential interactions and exchanges between China's chattering classes and officialdom. After all, "popular" or professional military journals in the United States, such as the U.S. Naval Institute *Proceedings*, have produced articles with deep, lasting impact on the U.S. Navy and on the Pentagon at large. We must not discount the influence that forums unaffiliated with government institutions may exert on Chinese strategic thought.

It is our judgment, furthermore, that official sources often suffer from rigid ideological correctness and unimaginative analysis, but outlets in the unofficial domain exhibit superior intellectual vitality and creativity. Indeed, we have been continually impressed with the learning, candor, and independence displayed by Chinese thinkers. Those who lump "the Chinese" together as an undifferentiated mass do themselves a disservice.

The helter-skelter change convulsing the Chinese state and society will amplify the battle of ideas in the coming years, making it harder for the government to crowd external voices out of strategy making. Nor may it see the need. Indeed, Beijing may be looking to outside sources for inspiration. Thus, we maintain that measuring the influence of external intellectual stimuli on Chinese policymakers and planners substantially benefits our understanding of how China's defense community conducts debates over strategy and operations. Such an evaluation is simply not possible without a thorough knowledge and mastery of China's burgeoning open-source literature.

Over the past five years, our work on Chinese sea power has benefited from the generosity of many friends and colleagues. We would like to extend our thanks to those who have taught and mentored us, informed our thinking, and furnished important venues for disseminating our ideas. We express our gratitude to Peter Liotta, the executive director of the Pell Center for International Relations and Public Policy at Salve Regina University, who first gave us a platform to air our ideas about Chinese maritime strategy and shepherded us through sea-power panels at two International Studies Association conferences. Geoffrey Till of King's College London and Ralph Sawyer reviewed our previous work on China's turn to Mahan and offered guidance and kind words of encouragement. Alan Wachman of the Fletcher School of Law and Diplomacy allowed us to share our research with his students. And finally, many editors opened their doors to our work.

We convey our heartfelt appreciation to John Maurer, the chairman of the Strategy and Policy Department at the Naval War College, a great boss and colleague but an even better friend who has lent our research unstinting support. Lyle Goldstein and Andrew Erickson of the China Maritime Studies Institute have generously shared CMSI's resources, in particular those of the CMSI library, home to a collection of maritime-related publications unmatched in the United States. The annual CMSI conferences at which we presented papers, moreover, offered forums crucial for developing and fine-tuning the ideas put forth here. We thank Commander William Murray, USN (ret.), for his expertise on undersea warfare, and Commander Peter Dutton, USN (ret.), our teaching partner on Chinese Statecraft, for subjecting our ideas to at-times pungent scrutiny.

Finally, we would like to thank our wives and daughters for their understanding and support. This book is dedicated to them.

RED ST★R
OVER THE PACIFIC

CHAPTER 1

Mahan's Two Tridents

In December 2006, Chinese president Hu Jintao told a group of naval officers, "We should endeavor to build a powerful people's navy that can adapt to its historical mission during a new century and a new period." The fleet should stand ready to uphold Chinese interests "at any time." "It is a glorious task," concluded Hu.[1] As the president's words attest, this is a time of flux for navies. Consider the material dimension of maritime strategy, the most easily observable, most easily quantifiable expression of strategic thought about the sea. Yale University professor Paul Kennedy observes that European and Asian navies are on opposite trajectories from a material standpoint. European governments seem resigned to letting their fleets shrink, in effect surrendering their claim to sea power. This downward drift is taking place despite the European Union's aspirations to leadership in the Gulf of Aden and the Red Sea, where piracy endangers merchant shipping critical to global prosperity.[2] For Europeans, broadly speaking, sea power is now more a matter of constabulary action than it is of armed encounters to determine who will rule the waves.[3]

Counterpiracy off Somalia is a better metaphor than the clash between enemy main fleets for contemporary European sea power. High-end naval platforms and capabilities command ebbing popular and elite support in European capitals—witness the recent decision by Britain's Royal Navy to decommission surface combatants with useful service life remaining. The Royal Navy in effect mortgaged its future to fund two midsized aircraft carriers only to see the British government consider canceling the carriers as well.[4] In November 2009, *The Guardian* of London reported that the U.K. Ministry of Defense was mulling selling one of the carriers to India.[5] What a metaphor for the eastward shift of sea power now taking place! Financial pressures and interservice rivalry have driven the British force structure inexorably downward. Indeed, the Royal Navy is now smaller than the French Navy for the first time since the 1805 Battle of Trafalgar, when Lord Horatio Nelson's fleet outdueled an allied Franco-Spanish fleet in the Mediterranean Sea.

The decline of European seafaring inverts half a millennium of maritime history. Western apathy toward traditional sea power is manifesting itself even as Asians bolt together fleets with gusto. Europe inherited its mastery of Asian waters almost by default, when Portuguese seafarers made their entry into the Indian Ocean following Hindu and Chinese rulers' abandonment of sea power. Kennedy likens the discontinuity in maritime history evident today to a similar discontinuity following the decision by China's Ming dynasty to dismantle the world's most formidable navy, Admiral Zheng He's "treasure fleet."[6] China evacuated the seas scant decades before Vasco da Gama dropped anchor along the Indian subcontinent, ushering in an age of external dominion over Asian national life.[7]

Control of maritime communications in Asia enabled European conquerors to deprive India of its independence for the only time in the subcontinent's long history, to have their way with a China in decline, and to establish bases and colonies throughout coastal Asia. Only in the 1950s, following two world wars and long decades of imperial decline, did Great Britain withdraw from east of Suez, tacitly ceding naval supremacy to the U.S. Navy. By quitting Asian waters, the Royal Navy signaled the beginning of the end of the "Vasco da Gama epoch" of Asian history.[8]

As Europeans turn their backs on conventional combat at sea, Asians have hurled themselves into the naval enterprise with aplomb, and to great fanfare. After decades of studied silence, China has at last confessed, more or less, to its aircraft-carrier ambitions. Over the past ten years, the People's Liberation Army Navy (PLA Navy) has introduced five new classes of modern conventional and nuclear submarines. High-tech PLA Navy guided-missile destroyers made their debut in the Indian Ocean, discharging counterpiracy duties. Beijing is reportedly attempting to manufacture an antiship ballistic missile that might well change the rules of the contest for maritime mastery in the Far East. President Hu's words about a powerful people's navy manifest themselves in such platforms and systems. Hu's words are more than mere rhetoric. They betoken a sharp, determined turn to the sea. His phrase has become a fixture in Chinese commentary and strategic debates about maritime matters.

China is not alone in laboring to construct a great navy. Japan, which already boasts a world-class fleet, recently put to sea what it euphemistically calls a "helicopter destroyer," or DDH. By all appearances, the DDH is a prototype for a future light carrier. Next-generation Japanese submarines equipped with air-independent propulsion—a cutting-edge technology that permits diesel boats to remain underwater indefinitely, eluding detection—have started to enter service. South Korea finds itself in the midst of an across-the-board naval modernization program. Over the next decade, Seoul will take delivery of frigates, diesel submarines, and amphibious assault ships, not to mention state-of-the-art Aegis guided-missile destroyers. Well to the south, Australia too plans to acquire Aegis destroyers. Canberra will also procure twelve diesel-electric submarines worth nearly $17 billion. The submarine project represents the most ambitious, most expensive military project in Australian history. And to Australia's northwest, India forthrightly avows its desire for a dominant navy. While Indian naval development has made fitful progress, New Delhi has inked a contract for a retired Russian aircraft carrier and cut steel on two Indian-built flattops—creating the core of a blue water fleet.

As one civilization vacates the oceans, then, another is crowding the seas and skies with ships and warplanes that bristle with offensively oriented weaponry. What the rise of Asian naval power portends for the region remains to be seen, but past maritime realignments should prompt practitioners and scholars of sea power to take notice. The interwar period, for example, saw the future belligerents fit out the navies that would pummel one another in World War II. There is little reason to believe that a similar great-power cataclysm is imminent today, or even thinkable. Even so, the material ingredients for competition and rivalry are certainly present in the tight confines of the East Asian littoral. Two Chinese analysts warn of Sino-Japanese frictions, given the close geographic proximity between two venturesome sea powers. Observe Zhang Ming and Chen Xiangjun, "Due to geo-strategic considerations, it is very difficult to contain two world-class powers along the cramped western Pacific coastline and to keep two ocean-going navies confined within the first island chain."[9]

Zhang and Chen prophesy that the potential for accidents, miscalculations, and even deliberate provocations will mount as great navies encounter one another in Asian waters. They are onto something important, and something that defies normal methods for appraising sea power. Tallying up ships, aircraft, and weaponry is only one benchmark for sea power, worthy and indeed critical though it is. The realm of ideas is admittedly more nebulous than that of net assessment, but understanding how an aspiring or established sea power thinks about strategy is indispensable to forecasting how it will fare on the high seas. If a navy's political masters and commanders incline toward offensively minded strategy, it will employ the assets at its disposal far differently from a navy predisposed to defense. Some scholarship, for instance, condemns the "cult of offense" that permeated strategic thought and military planning in Europe for helping bring on the slaughter of World War I.

Unsurprisingly, then, the material discontinuity Paul Kennedy discerns between Asia's maritime rise and the freefall of European sea power finds an intellectual parallel. Professor Geoffrey Till of King's College London expands on this point, maintaining that Europeans are entering into a "postmodern," "post-Mahanian" perspective on sea power. The postmodern approach is predicated more on noncombat missions aimed at upholding "good order at sea" in the face of nontraditional challenges than on pounding away at enemy fleets. Asians, says Till, are on precisely the opposite intellectual track. Asia is entering a "modern," "neo-Mahanian" world rather like the one inhabited by Western sea powers and Japan in the days of Mahan. If he is right, Asians will display a bloody-minded outlook toward the chances of armed conflict at sea.[10]

And indeed, Mahan is making a comeback, judging by the martial overtones of Asian commentary on marine affairs. The Asia columnist for the *Economist* magazine attended the May 2009 meeting of the Shangri-La Dialogue, which convened in Singapore under the auspices of the International Institute of Strategic Studies. As "Banyan" tells it, whenever he "prodded a military man from India or China, out leapt a Mahanite."[11] These days the name of Mahan is shorthand for fatalistic acceptance of zero-sum international competition and war on the high seas. *Atlantic Monthly* columnist Robert Kaplan stops short of such bleak predictions, but he observes that "whereas the U.S. Navy pays homage to Mahan by naming buildings after him, the Chinese avidly read him; *the Chinese are the Mahanians now*"[12] (our emphasis). Echoing Banyan, Kaplan opines that it is not just the Chinese; "his books are now all the rage" among Indians as well.[13] If the PLA Navy and the Indian Navy indeed attempt to transcribe Mahanian theory directly into naval strategy and forces, the chances of an epic fleet battle like the one America's sea-power "evangelist" or "Copernicus" seemed to preach will increase.[14]

For its part, the United States appears to be trying to straddle the neo- and post-Mahanian worlds, meeting proliferating demands with flat or declining resources. An old navy joke holds that if the sea services keep doing more and more with less and less, they will end up doing everything with nothing. Such is the lot of a nation like the United States that regards itself both as the chief custodian of free navigation in the world's sea-lanes, a function that involves upholding good order at sea, and as the protector of its own national interests and prerogatives against aspiring "peer competitors," rivals more or less equivalent to the United States by the yardsticks of diplomatic, informational and ideological, military, and economic power.

U.S. Navy operations in the Indian Ocean are a microcosm of this larger strategic phenomenon. Navy fighter/attack aircraft render close air support to troops in Afghanistan, the highest form of power projection ashore, even as billion-dollar ships track innumerable, often primitive small vessels to suppress piracy and interdict proliferation of weapons of mass destruction. At the same time, the Navy is almost certainly prepared to strike against the Iranian nuclear complex should statesmen in Washington give the order. How well the sea services handle the dual character of sea power, in which police and warfighting functions appear coequal, represents the central test of American staying power in the maritime domain. This challenge is particularly acute in Asia, where the expansion of indigenous naval power is accelerating while the U.S. presence remains stagnant.

If prognoses by Kennedy, Till, Kaplan, and the like are correct, the Asian seas are primed for a reconfiguration of maritime power. Helping the United States manage a disturbance to the regional order—to the extent possible—is our chief purpose in this book. It is no secret that China's rise is the primary challenge and, we hope, a major opportunity for the United States and its Asian allies. In a sense, the book is a "red team" exercise in which we try to anticipate future trends, helping the United States, the "blue team," start adapting its strategy and forces—keeping abreast if not ahead of change. We believe empathy with the red team is a virtue in this kind of endeavor, so we pay special attention to the human dimension of maritime strategy. Americans must avoid projecting their own assumption onto societies with vastly different traditions, experiences, and habits of mind. By knowing how competitors think, the United States will improve its prospects of responding wisely to Sino-American interactions.

CHINESE SEA POWER AND THE ANTIACCESS/ AREA-DENIAL DEBATE

Military and operational trends are the focal point for most analyses of challenges to U.S. nautical supremacy. The notion that an Asian antagonist might employ antiaccess and area-denial strategies has gained substantial currency inside the Beltway. (For simplicity's sake, we group these strategic variants together as "access denial.") Such a strategy involves taking concerted military and nonmilitary steps to (1) delay the arrival of U.S. and allied forces in-theater; (2) prevent U.S. forces from using bases in the region to sustain military operations (or, failing that, disrupt the use of these bases); and (3) keep U.S. power-projection assets as far away as possible.[15] However useful in the military sphere, we believe this one-dimensional outlook impoverishes the study of access. Another purpose of this book, consequently, is to widen our conception of access beyond the use of force.

American analysts have been hard at work attempting to project how access denial would affect a clash over Taiwan. As Thomas Ehrhard and Robert Work explain:

> PRC "anti-access operations" are defined as actions taken to deny U.S. forces from deploying to a position in theater from which they can conduct effective operations against Chinese forces. They include PRC political action to coerce regional countries into denying U.S. forces access to operational bases, and operational attacks against existing U.S. regional bases or forward deployed naval forces. PRC "area-denial operations" are actions taken within the Pacific theater of operations to deny successfully deployed U.S. forces an ability to conduct effective operations in the vicinity of Taiwan and the Chinese mainland.[16]

The authors sound a gloomy note, concluding that, *"For the first time since the late 1980s, and for only the second time since the end of World War II, U.S. carrier strike forces will soon face a major land-based threat that outranges them"*[17] (their emphasis). In other words, they rate the Chinese threat to U.S. forces in Asia on par with that posed by the Soviet and Imperial Japanese fleets, the last to challenge the United States for command of Far Eastern waters.

Unsurprisingly, considering the bleak tone assumed by influential commentators, access denial has become the prism through which policymakers in Washington survey the rise of Chinese sea power. They see the threat as real, growing, and worrisome. Their obsession with access denial is understandable, and even necessary given the ramifications for Taiwan. Conceiving of China's maritime ascent too narrowly, though, poses certain analytical dangers. We contend that China's access-denial strategy is only one facet of a broader, more sustained Chinese nautical challenge to the United States. To casually conflate access denial with China's ambitious naval project is to misread Chinese sea power entirely. This sort of myopia severely limits fore-casts of China's longer-term maritime prospects, misinforming U.S. efforts to make and implement strategy in Asia.

Assume that China's buildup of access-denial capacity, manifest in its naval modernization program, is designed solely to return Taiwan to main-land rule. If so, it is also safe to assume that Beijing will curtail its challenge to U.S. naval supremacy, or end it altogether, once it regains the island. By this logic, a satiated China will likely turn inward on the "day after Taiwan." The Communist Party regime will have retrieved the last piece of Chinese territory lost to foreign aggression, restoring national unity and dignity in the process. China will have accomplished its aims at sea while the United States will have little choice but to acquiesce in the new normal across the Taiwan Strait. Asia will return to an uneasy equilibrium between the ascendant land power, China, and the ascendant sea power, the United States. In this alterna-tive future, neither can overcome the other's comparative geostrategic advan-tages; neither has much reason to try. Relatively stable coexistence resumes.

What if this optimistic chain of reasoning is wrong? Present trends in China's naval buildup, and in rhetoric issuing from Beijing, suggest that such a benign outcome is neither inevitable nor probable. That China is already building up power-projection capabilities for the post-Taiwan future is no longer a controversial statement.[18] If so, systems under development for access denial are the precursor to a more capable, lasting Chinese presence in Asian waters. Few China-watchers have begun exploring the ramifications of such a presence. Of the few who have, even fewer have sought to estimate China's prospects of gaining more control of its maritime environs. How Beijing might establish an offshore preserve is a question that remains unanswered.

Without a firm grasp of specific factors, processes, and scenarios impel-ling China's seaward turn, Washington and its allies have little basis to plot long-term maritime strategy in Asia. We intend to plug this analytical gap.

A MAHANIAN LOGIC AND GRAMMAR OF ACCESS

As noted earlier, Western strategists tend to restrict the question of access to its military dimension, impairing their ability to envisage the future of Chinese maritime strategy. We nonetheless believe the term "access" possesses enormous analytical value. An expansive outlook toward access makes a use-ful starting point from which to chart the course of Chinese sea power, and to assess its potential effects on U.S. maritime strategy in Asia. For help reca-librating our field of view, we turn to Alfred Thayer Mahan, whose writings supply the building blocks for a holistic approach to this topic.

The sea, proclaimed the American sea captain, was a "wide common, over which men may pass in all directions."[19] "Communications," meaning secure passage through this watery medium, was "the most important single element in strategy, political or military."[20] The "eminence of sea power" lay in its ability to control the sea-lanes, along with critical geographical nodes that facilitated or impeded the flow of commercial and naval shipping. Digging a Central American canal and obtaining Caribbean bases from which to safeguard the approaches to the Isthmus obsessed him.[21] The ability to ensure communications "to one's self, and to interrupt them for an adversary, affects the very root of a nation's vigor," concluded Mahan.[22]

Military-centric definitions of access conform to these fairly familiar observations about sea power. But there is more to Mahan than that, as a thorough survey of his massive body of work shows. Mahan's works can and should be read on two levels. Prussian strategic theorist Carl von Clausewitz sheds light on the twin nature of Mahanian sea-power theory, postulating that "war is only a branch of political activity; that is in no sense autonomous." Clausewitz refutes the common idea that war suspends political interchange between the belligerents "and replaces it by a wholly different condition, ruled by no law but its own." He poses a rhetorical question: "Do political relations between peoples and between their governments stop when diplomatic notes are no longer exchanged? Is war not just another expression of their thoughts, another form of speech or writing? Its grammar, indeed, may be its own, but not its logic."[23] By this he means two things that bear on our understanding of access. War, first of all, is the pursuit of national policy with the admixture of military means. It differs from other international interactions by virtue of chance and uncertainty, the dark passions it fires, and countless other factors. Second, political interchange between belligerents does not cease when gunfire starts. Nonmilitary instruments like diplomacy, economic pressure or incentives, and alliance politics play their part during wartime.

Now apply this dual structure to Mahanian theory. Many commentators pay excessive heed to Mahan's grammar of operations and tactics, to the neglect of his larger logic—or, as historians Harold and Margaret Sprout termed it, his "philosophy"—of sea power.[24] Slighting the logic, which infuses meaning into his grammar of marine combat, limits and distorts our understanding of Mahanian sea power.[25] The naval historian vehemently denied lusting for battle on the high seas, and indeed, in *The Problem of Asia*, he insisted that "military or political force" represented an "alien element" in international relations.[26] Mahan urged navies to take the offensive should war be thrust upon them, but he never advocated naval rivalry for its own sake. In contemporary parlance, he urged sea powers to "hedge" against the likelihood of military conflict, keeping their options open.

But he also went Clausewitz one better, carrying his logic/grammar construct beyond the battlefield and into the domain of peacetime diplomacy. Naval strategy differed from military strategy, wrote Mahan, because it had "for its end to found, support, and increase, as well in peace as in war, the sea power of a country."[27] Finding and securing strategic geographic nodes was one way to bolster sea power in peacetime, as were efforts to hold open access to markets and bases. A nation intent on sea power was perpetually on the offensive, in wartime and peacetime alike. Not for nothing did German admiral Wolfgang Wegener affirm that Great Britain had prosecuted a centuries-long strategic offensive, assembling the largest maritime empire the world had known.

Naval preparedness was the sharp edge of maritime strategy, then, but it was only a means to an end. Although Mahan believed fleet actions were necessary at times, he was adamant that peacetime commerce was the true path to national prosperity and greatness. "War has ceased to be the natural, or even normal, condition of nations," he declared, "and military considerations are simply accessory and subordinate to the other greater interests" they serve.[28] Economics and commerce predominate. The "starting point and foundation" for comprehending sea power was "the necessity to secure commerce, by political measures conducive to military, or naval strength. This order is that of actual relative importance to the nation of the three elements—commercial, political, military."[29]

Scarcely could there be a clearer statement of why nations covet access to far-flung regions such as Asia. In essence, commerce is about privileged access to the means needed to generate wealth and national power. Such access is impossible without the politico-military means to protect it, and to keep others from denying commercial access. Seagoing nations shoul d lock their gaze on this overriding priority. Mahan thus advances a tripartite concept, which, given the nautical bent of his writings, we call his first "trident" of sea power. Access to sources of economic well-being—namely foreign trade, commerce, and resources—ranks first among equals within the Mahanian trident; military access, third. This cuts against the usual interpretation of Mahan's works.

The second plane on which sea-power theory functions, Mahan's grammar, is more martial and operational in nature. We call this his second trident. But even here, he assigns commerce pride of place. Indeed, trade and commerce form the interface between the grammar and logic of sea power. In his most influential work, *The Influence of Sea Power upon History, 1660–1783*, the historian portrayed sea power as founded on the three "pillars" of production, merchant and naval shipping, and overseas markets and bases. Mysteriously, he conflated markets, essential to commercial interchange, with the forward outposts needed to refuel and repair steam-propelled vessels.[30] Whatever the case, all three pillars relate directly to commerce, namely industrial production at home, the merchant marine, and foreign markets. Mahan designated the "tendency to trade, involving of necessity the production of something to trade with . . . the national characteristic most important to the development of sea power."[31]

Two pillars relate directly to naval power, namely forward naval stations and the battle fleet. If the logic of sea power dictates gaining access for commercial reasons, then the grammar means securing access through force of naval arms. "Command of the sea," maintained Mahan, meant "that overbearing power on the sea which drives the enemy's flag from it, or allows it to appear only as a fugitive; and which, by controlling the great common, closes the highways by which commerce moves to and fro from the enemy's shores."[32] Overbearing power, in the form of warships, naval weaponry, and battle efficiency, embodies the martial grammar of sea power. Both tridents must remain sharp for either to do its work.

The two-tiered nature of sea power, embodying as it does both peacetime and wartime activities, reaffirms Mahan's nuanced approach to maritime affairs. Importantly, both the grammar and the logic of sea power have access to locations (such as seaports and bases) and to physical goods (such as trade commodities and natural resources) as their end. The logic and grammar advance the same goals, but the logic governs the geopolitical and strategic aspects of sea power while the grammar supplies the rules for naval preparedness and warfare.

Defined in Mahanian terms, incorporating both economic logic and military grammar, access is a broad concept indeed. Nor is it confined to the United States, meaning simply the liberty of the U.S. military to project power into waters adjoining China. In fact, our study is about access from the Chinese perspective. Beijing too worries about access denial. Chinese leaders and commanders fret that the United States will deploy naval might to deny

China access to the commons, retaliating against some Chinese transgression or even, conceivably, on the whim of an American president. Ensuring the physical freedom of movement across the maritime commons is central to economic and military endeavors that the Chinese regime considers crucial to the nation's economic vitality and prestige.

Access, accordingly, advances strategic aims far broader than a Taiwan contingency or other short-term military objectives. Redefining access in Mahanian terms opens a window into the future direction of Chinese sea power. Peering through this window suggests that China's march to the seas will not end with Taiwan. Far larger forces are at work.

STRUCTURE OF THE ARGUMENT

While trade and commerce hold pride of place on Mahan's two tridents, we focus on the military "tine" for the purposes of this book. In grammatical terms, the martial tine is Mahan's vision of overbearing power at sea, to which so many Chinese Mahanians pay homage. We expand his vision of over-bearing power to mean China's ability to harness such power against others or to nullify the overbearing power adversaries hold in important sea areas. The narrower, military-centric concept of access denial belongs in the latter category. When he espoused a powerful people's navy, Hu Jintao was clearly speaking in grammatical terms. But imposing and nullifying overbearing power are not mutually exclusive endeavors. That is, the ability to deny sea control opens the way for the sea-denial fleet to exercise command in its own right. This understanding of access captures the dynamism typical of encounters between two maritime contestants with important interests at stake in the same waters and skies. Sino-American relations are nothing if not interactive.

One organizing principle for this volume is that geography helps delineate where access and antiaccess efforts will take place. We postulate that China will strive to achieve and ensure access for itself—and amass the capacity to deny access to others—in concentric geographic rings rippling out from the Chinese coastline. Beijing will first attempt to guarantee access to its immediate maritime periphery, which the Chinese term the "near seas." Again, we mean access as the commercial, political, and military maneuver space enjoyed by China within a particular geographic zone. Once China is confident about its freedom of action in the near seas, it will work to expand its access beyond the periphery, to what the Chinese term the "far seas." Broadly conceived, then, this quest for access gives Western observers an instrument for tracking China's maritime ascent. How closely China approaches the

Mahanian ideal of sea power (as we have interpreted it here), with commerce taking precedence over military considerations, will say much about the kind of maritime strategy Beijing will pursue.

The book surveys the access problem from a variety of standpoints. Chapters 2 and 3 set the strategic context. In Chapter 2, we examine the theoretical foundations of access in more detail. We explore how China is consulting strategic theorists and other sources of strategic thought, fairing this guidance into its maritime strategy. Mahan will figure prominently in this analysis, but China's long, rich history also offers abundant lessons on how to make and execute strategy. Specifically, we argue that Mahan furnishes the logic of Chinese sea power while Mao's "active defense" concept helps Beijing tailor the warlike grammar of sea power to China's local circumstances. Chapter 3 adopts a retrospective approach, comparing the access dilemma facing the Kaiser's Germany to China's current predicament. We examine geography, capability, and national will—the three main ingredients for attaining and expanding access in the face of a superior adversary—for both aspiring naval powers. We find that China is better positioned than Germany to turn difficult geography to its advantage.

Chapters 4 through 7 unfold loosely along geographical lines, in keeping with the near- and far-seas concepts. We probe various facets of Chinese maritime strategy, focusing first on commercial and trade imperatives close to Chinese coasts, then on China's efforts to radiate influence into more distant theaters. Chapters 4 and 5 analyze how China may leverage tactical concepts and capabilities to attain or deny access in the near seas. As China's leadership sees it, wresting some control of the nation's maritime periphery from the U.S. Navy is critical to economic vitality, and thus to the long-term welfare of the communist regime. We begin, therefore, by examining how Beijing will attempt to manage the Yellow, East China, and South China seas, the waters that wash against Chinese shores. Access-denial operations and tactics are impelling this push into the China seas. We also investigate Chinese views of and responses to sea-based missile defense in an effort to determine how the PLA will adjust its antiaccess strategy to offset this emerging U.S.-Japanese capability.

Chapters 6 and 7 examine how the political and psychological effects of China's nuclear-powered ballistic-missile submarine (SSBN) fleet and naval "soft power" could deepen and extend Chinese access, both along the nautical periphery and well into the far seas. In Chapter 6 we explore the prospects for the PLA Navy undersea deterrent, manifest in nuclear-powered submarines and sea-launched ballistic missiles. We find that undersea deterrence interacts synergistically with Chinese access and antiaccess strategy. An invulnerable second-strike capability keeps the United States at bay at the strategic level, opening up antiaccess options for the PLA in the near seas at the theater level of war. At the same time, a robust antiaccess posture raises a protective shield under which PLA Navy SSBNs can expand their deterrent patrols eastward, bringing more of North America within range.

In Chapter 7, we maintain that Beijing will apply its energies to guarding its interests in the Indian Ocean, the wellspring of much of China's economic lifeblood. Chinese leaders have laid the groundwork to exert influence in the region by integrating a sophisticated historical narrative into their regional diplomacy, casting China as an inherently trustworthy sea power. If successful, Beijing will create permissive surroundings for the PLA Navy, should Beijing decide forward deployments of hard naval power are necessary to ensure free passage through South Asian waters for Chinese merchantmen.

After this exhaustive survey of Sino-U.S. interactions at sea, we turn to U.S. maritime strategy in Asia. Chapter 8 dissects and compares the 1986 and 2007 U.S. maritime strategies, identifying relationships and tensions between the logic and grammar of sea power. Whereas the former excelled at grammar for the contest against the Soviet Navy, the latter articulates a compelling logic of sea power while saying little about grammatical matters. We examine both strategies, their merits, and their Asian and Western detractors. The comparison will help policymakers determine whether and how to adjust the current "Cooperative Strategy for 21st Century Seapower" to better its prospects for success, both in post-Mahanian enterprises such as counterproliferation and sea-lane security and in neo-Mahanian missions such as naval preparedness, deterrence, and—should Sino-U.S. relations sour—sea combat.

We close out the book by revisiting the logic and grammar of sea power, in an attempt to determine how the United States and China measure up by Mahanian standards. This is an apt note to end on, as it indicates whether each nation is on an upward, downward, or flat trajectory as a sea power. Trend analysis, we believe, will help makers and executors of maritime strategy establish whose grip on the Mahanian tridents is surer—and who is poised to reign over Asia's wine-dark seas.

CHAPTER 2

China Engages the Strategic Theorists

As seen in chapter 1, sea captain Alfred Thayer Mahan beseeched would-be seafaring nations to amass international commerce, merchant and naval fleets, and forward bases. By Mahanian standards, China is progressing swiftly toward sea power. There is no shortage of import or export trade in China, whose economy relies on a steady flow of seaborne cargoes of oil, natural gas, and other raw materials from Africa and the Persian Gulf region. It also relies on the oceans as a thoroughfare by which Chinese export wares reach foreign consumers. Chinese shipyards are turning out merchantmen at breakneck speed. Indeed, the Chinese shipbuilding industry threatens to overtake the South Korean and Japanese yards, the world's leaders, in numbers of keels laid, if not necessarily in quality.

In the realm of military shipping, similarly, the People's Liberation Army Navy (PLA Navy) has made rapid strides. Not so long ago, Western mariners and scholars deprecated Chinese naval power. An oft-heard joke held that China would have to launch a "million-man swim" to land troops on Taiwan. In 1999 Boston College professor Robert Ross held forth on the "geography of the peace" in an article for the journal *International Security*. Ross argued, elegantly, that the United States would continue to rule the Asian seas, China would remain supreme on the Asian continent, and neither power would be able to apply its power against the other.[1] The American whale and the Chinese elephant might dislike each other, then, but there was little they could do about it. In a similar vein, Brookings Institution analyst Michael O'Hanlon wrote at length on the conflict in his article "Why China Cannot Conquer Taiwan."[2] In 2001 National Defense University professor Bernard Cole maintained that the PLA Navy could not defend Chinese sea lines of communication (SLOCs) aside from "those immediately off its coast." Cole concluded, furthermore, that the Chinese navy had little need to extend its seaward reach so long as the U.S. Navy remained the trustee of Asian maritime security.[3] It could free ride on U.S. naval supremacy.

Few make such arguments these days. If anything, the PLA Navy now inspires excessive forebodings among leading officials and pundits. The Pentagon's annual *Military Power of the People's Republic of China* reports have taken on increasingly anxious overtones. The opaque nature of strategy in a closed society is responsible in part for this. Western analysts argue over whether defense spending figures released by Beijing are accurate.[4] Sinologists and officials debate the intentions that accompany China's increasingly impressive arsenal. "This situation will naturally and understandably lead to hedging against the unknown," concludes the executive summary to the 2008 Military Power report.[5] In April 2009, the PLA Navy held a naval review to mark the sixtieth anniversary of its founding. The review showcased domestically built Chinese warships, including no fewer than four indigenous submarines and its first *Yuzhao*-class amphibious assault ship.[6] And, after years of studied denials and obfuscation, the People's Liberation leadership has more or less openly stated that it wants aircraft carriers. During a meeting with Japanese defense minister Yasukazu Hamada, Chinese defense minister Liang Guanglie declared that Beijing would eventually build flattops. While Liang set no timetable for this ambitious new project, his comment represented a noteworthy departure from the standard PLA line.[7]

With regard to bases, the PLA Navy has built a base on Hainan Island capable of berthing nuclear submarines (and presumably surface units as well), extending its cruising radius toward the Strait of Malacca, the narrow sea connecting the South China Sea with resource suppliers in the Indian Ocean.[8] Top Chinese officials fret over the "Malacca dilemma" created by threats to free passage through this maritime chokepoint.[9] Chinese diplomats have negotiated basing rights throughout the Indian Ocean, giving rise to American and especially Indian worries about a "string of pearls" encircling the subcontinent from the sea.[10] One well-known analyst, Gurpreet Khurana, sees a Sino-Indian "rivalry arc" extending all the way from Japan in Northeast Asia to the Bab el-Mandeb Strait in the west.[11] If scholars such as Sir Julian Corbett or K. M. Panikkar have it right, this would place India's sea communications, and thus its national life, in Chinese hands, and it might demand that New Delhi project power into the Pacific as a riposte to Chinese encroachment in the Indian Ocean.[12] Indians remember acutely that the only time their nation lost its national independence was to a seaborne invader, Great Britain—hence New Delhi's visceral response to Beijing's pursuit of basing rights along the Indian seaboard.[13]

The material trappings of Mahanian sea power are increasingly in place for China. Does this add up to a Mahanian strategy? And, if so, what kind? The jury remains out on how, and to what ends, Beijing will apply its burgeoning naval might. It remains to be seen, moreover, how Mahanian thought will figure into Chinese strategic thought and, in turn, how it may affect Beijing's maritime endeavors. China's long, rich history and martial and philosophical traditions supply bountiful guidance, albeit from a predominantly continental perspective. To name just a few other sources of Chinese strategic thought, Confucius, Sun Tzu, Mao Zedong, Deng Xiaoping, and Liu Huaqing will exert influence on Chinese calculations. As Beijing embarks on its pursuit of command of the sea "with Chinese characteristics," to borrow the common formula used by Chinese thinkers, it will clearly consult far more sources than Mahan, and some of these indigenous sources may carry more weight than any Western theorist. Sorting through these intellectual strands is our main purpose in this chapter.

If Western sea powers are deserting the oceans while Asians go to sea, then it is a matter of considerable moment to discern what a neo-Mahanian age means for China. America's strategic longevity in the Asia-Pacific region—and, by extension, the future of the maritime order presided over by the U.S. Navy—could depend on it.

A MAHANIAN PHILOSOPHY FOR CHINA

That the Chinese even consult Mahan represents a sea change in attitudes toward marine affairs. During Mao's heyday, Mahan was reviled in China as an apostle of imperialism and colonialism, twin hobgoblins of the new China. Adherents to the land-bound doctrines of the PLA likewise rejected Mahanian sea power on ideological grounds. In an excellent book review of Mahan's *Influence of Sea Power upon History*, Ni Lexiong graphically describes past Chinese attitudes toward his work as "loathing" (憎恨) or "disgust" (厌恶).[14] Criticism and wholesale denial of the value of Mahanian theory characterized the discourse over his works.

In stark contrast, Mahan has inspired intense interest in Chinese scholarly and policy circles since Deng's opening and reform initiative a quarter-century ago. Studies parsing terms such as "command of the sea" (*zhihaiquan*, or 制海权) and "command of communications" (*zhijiaotongquan*, or 制交通权) have multiplied. Some neo-Mahanians appear spellbound by the American theorist's oft-cited description of command of the sea as "that overbearing power on the sea which drives the enemy's flag from it, or allows it to appear only as a fugitive."[15] Chinese analysts have repeated this bellicose-sounding phrase at major international conferences to highlight the value of sea power for China.[16]

For Mahan, as we have seen, trade and commerce, merchant and naval fleets, and geographic expansion—by which he meant obtaining bases or basing agreements overseas, not imposing American colonial rule on subject peoples—merged under the aegis of sea power. Commerce ranked atop his hierarchy, and he vehemently denied lusting for trials of arms. Sea war was bad for trade.[17] In a real sense, then, Mahan agreed with today's globalization proponents, who point to the high if not prohibitive costs of fighting current or prospective trading partners. Seldom is war worth the political, military, or economic cost.

Even so, his writings lent themselves to zero-sum thinking. Many of his followers resigned themselves to naval war—a Darwinian struggle that would determine which nations prospered and which shriveled and died. "Growth is a property of healthful life," opined Mahan in *The Problem of Asia*, and with it went a "right to insure by just means whatsoever contributes to national progress, and correlatively to combat injurious action taken by an outside agency, if the latter overpass its own lawful sphere."[18] Notes George Baer, "Central to the theory of sea power was the expectation of conflict. When a nation's prosperity depends on shipborne commerce, and the amount of trade available is limited, then competition follows, and that leads to a naval contest to protect the trade."[19] In Imperial Germany, a rabidly Mahanian nation, big-fleet enthusiasts even coined the term "mahanism," a saltwater variant of Social Darwinian ideas about growth, decay, and perpetual strife.[20] Inspired by a deterministic and simplistic interpretation of Mahan's writings, "naval ideology" also animated the strategic thinking of Japanese leaders during the interwar period.[21]

If Mahan indeed prized nonviolent international competition, he must have been appalled at such misuse of his theories. But many followers of Mahan, then and now, brush aside his advocacy of peaceful interchange in favor of his more bloody-minded writings—writings that evoke the glamour of the sea, fire the imagination, and promise to restore lost national majesty. Many Chinese strategists fall into that category. Mahan's appeal to economics resonates with today's China, a nation at once obsessed with economic development and increasingly reliant on seaborne shipments of oil, gas, and other commodities.[22] But so does his call for a navy capable of commanding vital waters. This suggests that China's commerce-driven maritime strategy will assume an increasingly military tincture.[23]

Unlike strategic theorists who concentrate on the mechanics of strategy and operations, Alfred Thayer Mahan explores not only functional matters but also the larger political purposes furthered by maritime strategy. In the 1940s, Harold and Margaret Tuttle Sprout observed that Mahan had articulated "doctrines of sea power and manifest destiny." He framed "a philosophy of sea power," a "theory of national prosperity and destiny founded upon a program of mercantilistic imperialism," and a "theory of naval strategy and defense" expanding upon operational and even tactical matters.[24] In Clausewitzian terms, war—a violent, interactive clash of wills—functions according to a "grammar" distinct from other human affairs.[25] But politics gives maritime enterprises their "logic," determining the ends for which mariners strive.[26] Using the metaphor we introduced in chapter 1, the logic and grammar are Mahan's two tridents of sea power.

It is possible to embrace one dimension of Mahanian theory—the logic or the grammar—while rejecting or downplaying the other. If the American theorist's grammar of sea combat has fallen into disuse with time and technological change, his sea-power philosophy remains hypnotic. Chinese naval development attests to it. The Mahanian conceit that national greatness derives from sea power beguiles many Chinese strategists. None other than PLA Navy commander Wu Shengli proclaims that China is an "oceanic nation," endowed by nature with a long coastline, many islands, and jurisdiction over a massive sea area. Admiral Wu calls on Chinese citizens to raise their collective consciousness of the seas, bringing about "the great revitalization of the Chinese nation" (中华民族伟大复兴).[27] Robust fleets roaming offshore are part of this. Mahan would have instantly recognized how Wu portrays the interplay between destiny and choice in China's maritime future.

TAKING STOCK OF THE SURROUNDINGS

We believe Beijing accepts the Mahanian logic of sea power, brandishing the American theorist's first trident while looking to indigenous traditions for guidance on the grammar of maritime strategy and warfare. Chinese Communist Party chairman Mao Zedong, who drew on earlier theorists such as Sun Tzu and Carl von Clausewitz, is the prime candidate to hand Beijing its second trident. But to understand how Mahanian and Maoist strategic traditions may intersect with Chinese maritime strategy, we must first appreciate why China is taking to the sea. Refreshing China's national greatness is a necessary but insufficient cause for Beijing to invest in a seagoing fleet. It is also crucial to discern which expanses and geographic features have captured the attention and energies of Chinese strategists. And if sea power is founded on commerce, bases, and ships, it is important to forecast where Chinese entrepreneurs will forge commerce ties, where Beijing will look for bases, and which expanses it will consider worth defending.

Why take to the seas? To start with, China increasingly has the luxury to apply its energies beyond the Asian continent. The land threats that were the bane of Chinese security for centuries have vanished. No longer must Beijing worry about parrying a Soviet land attack on the Chinese heartland or managing escalation of a Sino-Soviet clash. Lesser controversies have also subsided. Beijing has settled border disputes with Russia, the Central Asian republics, Vietnam, North Korea, and Mongolia, neutralizing much of its continental periphery. The Sino-Indian quarrel over the Indian frontier province of Arunachal Pradesh lingers, but there is little prospect of armed conflict over the impasse. In short, Beijing can now contemplate becoming a sea power without undue worry about forfeiting its interests ashore. And it can use resources formerly needed to guard China's land frontiers to amass forward naval stations and construct warships, aircraft, and munitions.

Economics, again, is the prime mover for Chinese sea power. True to Mahan, Chinese thinkers connect commercial health with naval primacy. Whether they also believe that commercial interchange should remain free of naval coercion remains a matter for debate. In the respected *Zhongguo Junshi Kexue*, Major General Jiang Shiliang invokes the American theorist to justify Chinese control of "strategic passages" traversed by vital goods. For Jiang, the contest for "absolute command" of critical waters and geographic assets is a fact of life in international politics.[28] Why the apparent militancy? With communist ideology in disrepute, Chinese leaders have staked their legitimacy on appeasing the populace and raising the standard of living for as many Chinese as possible. To fuel Chinese industry, Beijing has sought out resource suppliers in such far-flung regions as the Persian Gulf and Africa.

Economic development and energy security have riveted attentions on the Indian Ocean, the South China Sea, and the seaways passing along China's East Asian coast—sea lines of communication (SLOCs) conveying precious cargoes into Chinese seaports. Thus Chinese leaders have come to see free passage for Chinese shipping through the Yellow, East China, and South China seas as a matter of surpassing importance, if not crucial to the future of Chinese Communist rule. They balk at entrusting their most basic interest to the uncertain, perhaps transitory goodwill of the United States, the self-appointed guarantor of maritime security in East Asia. As Ye Hailin of the Chinese Academy of Social Sciences explains rather evocatively, "No matter how much China desires a harmonious world and harmonious oceans, it cannot possibly rely on other countries' naval forces to guard the safety of its SLOCs. A big country that builds its prosperity on foreign trade cannot put the safety of its ocean fleet in the hands of other countries. Doing so would be the equivalent of placing its throat under another's dagger and marking its blood vessels in red ink."[29] In Ye's eyes, China's inability or unwillingness to protect its own maritime interests would invite others to disrupt its commerce, thereby exploiting its vulnerability. Thus, the Chinese recognize that while the U.S. Navy has safeguarded Asian shipping for six decades, its benevolent posture could change radically, and it could do so almost overnight. Washington might threaten the flow of Chinese resources in times of crisis, holding the Chinese economy hostage. Chinese strategists fret over the prospect of an American naval blockade.[30]

Chinese thinkers, then, are acutely aware that geographic factors impinge on economic fitness. To China, the first island chain, which runs southward from the Japanese home islands through the Indonesian archipelago, looks like a barricade thrown up by an America intent on containing Chinese sea power. Chinese commentators recall that Secretary of State Dean Acheson delineated a U.S. "defense perimeter of the Pacific" in 1950—a defensive line that coincided roughly with the island chain.[31] Sea-power advocates are prone to view the island chain much as Acheson did—as an American rampart blocking Chinese maritime operations. The economic implications of this are plain to Chinese eyes.

Control of Taiwan, conversely, would allow the PLA to erect its own Great Wall at sea, giving Beijing some say over the exercise of foreign naval and military power in nearby seas and skies. Once PLA forces could operate at will among the islands, China in effect would have inscribed its own defense perimeter of the Pacific, turning Dean Acheson's concept outward toward the Pacific Ocean. Foreign fleets contemplating hostile entry into the China seas would think twice if confronted with Chinese forces operating from the mainland, from the China seas, or from island bases. Beijing's liberty of action would expand immensely once it recovered this defensive stronghold.

Taiwan would be a platform for offensive sea power as well. Analysts view Taiwan as the one geographic asset that can grant Chinese forces direct access to the Pacific. If the island is a guard tower in an offshore Great Wall, then its offensive value is unmatched. During World War II, Admiral Ernest King declared that the U.S. Navy could "put the cork in the bottle" of the South China Sea by wresting Formosa from Japan. That is, a nation in possession of Taiwan has the freedom to cut the sea communications connecting Northeast with Southeast Asia or, alternatively, to keep the bottle uncorked for its own use.[32] This is the essence of command of the sea. Chinese thinkers recall General Douglas MacArthur's description of Taiwan as "an unsinkable aircraft carrier and submarine tender" positioned off the Chinese coasts, bolstering the aerial and undersea components of America's containment strategy.[33] The United States stationed surveillance and nuclear-capable combat aircraft on Taiwan, which forms the midpoint of the inner island chain, until the 1970s. References to Taiwan-based "foreign forces" are commonplace even today. Bad memories linger.

Chinese analysts, then, cite Mahanian-sounding principles when appraising the value of Taiwan. They occasionally cast their gaze as far as Guam, America's naval stronghold in the second island chain, discussing it in similarly austere terms.[34] If Taipei preserves its de facto independence, the mainland will remain confined within the island chain, unable to range freely into the broad Pacific. Declares the authoritative *Science of Military Strategy*, "If Taiwan should be alienated from the mainland . . . China will forever be locked to the west side of the first chain of islands in the West Pacific." If so, "the essential strategic space for China's rejuvenation will be lost."[35] On its face, at least, China's geostrategic quandary resembles that confronted by Imperial Germany a century ago. (See chapter 3.) If America could project power inward from the island, China can project it outward. The offshore island chain at once constitutes a defensive and an offensive asset. It is no passive edifice.

CHINA'S DEFENSE WHITE PAPERS AND NAVAL STRATEGY

Beijing's biannual defense white papers, titled "China's National Defense," provide clues to how the PLA will handle the geostrategic challenges China confronts. Sinology is admittedly an inexact science. China-watchers continue to struggle with the bibliographical chore of determining which primary sources, many of them by PLA-related publishers, are more or less authoritative. Even so, the act of publishing a detailed statement that explains how China plans to cope with its security environment and has withstood thorough interagency vetting suggests that the Communist Party establishment has reached a consensus on these matters. While other governments, including Washington, routinely bemoan the lack of detail in the white papers, they nevertheless constitute the most authoritative statements of how Beijing views its strategic context and the threats that inhabit its neighborhood.

Of these documents, "China's National Defense in 2004" was perhaps the most groundbreaking in its commentary on naval matters. It hails the trend toward peace and economic development in East Asia. But it also insists that "new and profound readjustments" trouble international relations. The "balance of power among the major international players" has undergone "a fundamental realignment." The United States is "realigning and reinforcing its military presence in this region by buttressing military alliances," while Japan—whose home islands form the northern arc of the first island chain, enclosing part of China's east coast—is "adjusting its military and security policies" to reinforce its own position.

It is far from clear to Beijing, then, that geopolitical dynamics are acting in China's favor. The framers of the 2004 white paper strike an ambivalent tone vis-à-vis globalization, maintaining that "a fair and rational new international political and economic order is yet to be established," and that "struggles for strategic points, strategic resources, and strategic dominance crop up from time to time" until such an order is in place. The "military factor" thus "plays a greater role in international configuration and national security." The white paper directs the PLA to craft military forces capable of "winning both command of the sea and command of the air."[36]

This remains the starkest official statement of China's Mahanian outlook. It also represents the first mention of command of the "commons"—namely the seas, skies, space, and perhaps even cyberspace—in an official directive. "China's National Defense in 2004" orders the PLA Navy to acquire warships, aircraft, precision armaments, and information technology suitable to support its bid for *zhihaiquan*—command of the sea, or sea control—in China's environs.

For reasons unknown, the 2006 defense white paper drops the Mahanian language found in its predecessor. But it remains deeply ambivalent about the future of global politics, faithful to the offensively minded appraisal of offshore waters and airspace voiced before, and true to the 2004 edition's geopolitical bent. The report designates threats to international commerce as a major source of concern, declaring that "security issues related to energy, resources, finance, information and international shipping routes are mounting." Strikingly, of the five security issues listed in the report, three relate directly to seaborne transport, one leg of the Mahanian trinity.

The document further states, "The Navy aims at gradual extension of the *strategic depth for offshore defensive operations* and enhancing its capabilities in integrated maritime operations and nuclear counterattacks. The Air Force aims at speeding up its transition from territorial air defense to both offensive and defensive operations."[37] (our emphasis). The explicitly Mahanian terminology is missing; the notion of commanding the commons in an expanding offshore belt remains.

The 2008 defense white paper softens the harsh-sounding tone struck in the 2004 and 2006 editions. It repeats its predecessors' mandate for offshore operations but pays homage to working with other sea powers to meet non-traditional threats like piracy, humanitarian assistance and disaster relief, and, presumably, seaborne weapons proliferation. The white paper depicts this as the latest phase in an evolving, increasingly outward-looking naval posture:

> From the 1950s to the end of the 1970s the main task of the Navy was to conduct inshore defensive operations. Since the 1980s, the Navy has realized a strategic transformation to offshore defensive operations. Since the beginning of the new century . . . the Navy has been striving to improve in an all-round way its capabilities of integrated offshore operations, strategic deterrence and strategic counterattacks, and to gradually develop its capabilities of conducting cooperation in distant waters and countering non-traditional security threats, so as to push forward the overall transformation of the service.[38]

This passage captures the impressive progress the Chinese navy has made since its humble beginnings during the Maoist era and the diverse range of missions it will be expected to fulfill in the coming years. At one end of the operational spectrum, the PLA Navy will provide China with its undersea deterrent, securing Beijing's retaliatory capacity against a disarming first strike. At the other end, Chinese flotillas will help maintain good order at sea in waters deemed critical to China's energy security and commercial access. China's apparent willingness to telegraph its plans to shoulder nontraditional tasks marks a major departure from previous white papers, bespeaking growing confidence in Chinese capability at sea.

It is important to clarify the key terminologies and concepts used in the series of white papers cited here, for they provide a sound basis to properly understand the priorities the PLA Navy assigns to its current and future roles and missions. In particular, "offshore defense" remains a foundational concept for Chinese planners, but confusion about its precise meaning persists in the West. Although *jinhai* (近海) is normally translated as "offshore" in official publications, a more literal and perhaps more accurate rendering of the term is "near seas." As Nan Li explains, "Offshore is too vague to reflect the relative distance that the Chinese term intends to express."[39] "Near seas," he contends, is a better expression of a Sinocentric perspective of the nautical environment. For the purposes of this study, however, the terms "offshore" and "near seas" are used interchangeably. "Near," we maintain, is no less subjective than "offshore."

In the past, some observers concluded that "offshore" connoted the capacity to project power in terms of distance, usually measured at two hundred nautical miles. But authoritative figures and sources in the Chinese navy have weighed in definitively on the subject, and a closer look suggests that Chinese strategists do not subscribe to this narrow spatial view. In his memoir, Admiral Liu Huaqing, the founding father of the modern Chinese navy—and an officer known in the West as "China's Mahan"—set the record straight.[40] As the PLA Navy commander in the early 1980s, Liu provided the intellectual foundation for China's naval strategy under the general guidance of Deng Xiaoping. As such, Liu writes with authority. He states clearly: "'Near seas' refers to our nation's Yellow Sea, East [China] Sea, South [China] Sea, Spratly archipelago, and the waters within and beyond the Taiwan-Okinawa island chain, as well as the northern sea area of the Pacific. Just beyond the 'near seas' is the 'mid-far seas.'"[41] Liu's brief description of what the PLA Navy considers the near seas reveals several analytical insights worthy of attention. First, geographic boundaries do not necessarily dictate Chinese conceptions of the nation's maritime environs. For Liu, naval operations undertaken pursuant to offshore defense are not confined to the bodies of water enveloped by the first island chain. For instance, Liu's reference to the "northern sea area of the Pacific" may include waters well east of the Japanese archipelago. How far offshore defense goes beyond the first island chain is left unstated—perhaps deliberately, to allow future generations of PLA commanders to interpret it according to China's needs and capabilities of the moment.

Second, it is notable that Liu developed and refined the near-seas concept more than a quarter-century ago. Its longevity not only attests to the impressive long-term nature of Liu's vision for the PLA Navy, but it also speaks volumes about the conceptual flexibility of the term. Liu's insistence that offshore defense had to be disentangled from arbitrary distances ensured that the range of offshore defense could be extended commensurate with the PLA Navy's growing capabilities. Recent white papers pushing offshore defense farther and farther from the mainland coast appear to validate the malleability of the concept.

Third, Liu's definition of near seas conveys a very Sinocentric worldview and thus a highly proprietary attitude toward China's littorals. This apparent presumptuousness is unsurprising, given that major offshore sea areas were historically integral to the Chinese periphery and thus qualified as a Chinese nautical preserve. Beijing's sovereign claims in the China seas should be understood partly in this context. In this sense, offshore defense should be treated as a subcomponent of Chinese homeland defense. We should therefore expect China to attach extraordinary value to fighting and winning in the waters that fall within the near-seas construct.

The PLA Navy's official encyclopedia defines offshore defense in exclusively functional terms, encompassing four main objectives. The Chinese navy will (1) hold fast to defensive naval strategic objectives; (2) increase its maritime defensive power; (3) carry out battlefield preparations; and (4) implement active defense. According to the entry: "[Offshore defense involves] the combined use of all kinds of methods to exercise the overall effects of maritime power to preserve oneself to the maximum extent while unceasingly exhausting and annihilating the attacking enemy. It requires a sufficient grasp of mobile combat capabilities to search and destroy the enemy, gradually shift the power balance, change the strategic situation, and thereby appropriately time the transition to the strategic counter offensive and attack."[42] The entry on offshore defense concludes that "[as] the effective ranges of at-sea offensive weaponry increase, the theory and practice of offshore defensive strategy face many major reforms." It recognizes the interactive nature of maritime warfare and anticipates fighting a superior adversary that boasts greater reach and striking power. The entry was written in 1999, before the Chinese navy achieved its current stature. Like Liu Huaqing, succeeding generations of PLA Navy commanders clearly foresaw the need to expand offshore defense and adapt it to newly emerging military trends.

Writing in the prestigious *Junshi Kexue* journal, Major General Yao Youzhi and Senior Colonel Chen Zeliang argue that the ever-competitive nature of "warfare under high-technology conditions" demands the military capacity to extend and assert control over the wide commons, or what the authors refer to as the "communications battlefield" (交通战场). They declare:

> Carrying out offensive defense [*gongshi fangyu,* or 攻势防御] requires the improvement of communications battlefield construction. . . . Under the new historical conditions, the communications battlefield expands simultaneously towards the enemy and us. We must not only defend adequately our own communications battlefield, but we must seek to push the communications battlefield in the direction of the adversary. We must attack or slow down the enemy on the routes it must use. At times, the perimeter of the communications battlefield could extend from the land to the sea and air. Expanding the scope of the outward-oriented communications battlefield is essential to preparations for military struggles and to guarantee "fighting to win."[43]

This view of an enlarged and more competitive battle space across the various dimensions of the commons comports fully with the broader naval requirements set forth by successive defense white papers. For some, this more forward-leaning defense posture is consistent with the lessons of Chinese history. As Colonel Dai Xu states: "The newly formed 'sea-approaching' development direction of the Chinese military construction, compared with the long-term old-fashioned land concept, did push the line of defense a bit outward, but the nature of strategic defense remains unchanged. In the past 200 years, all the wars took place on the land or at sea near China. China deservedly has the right to push the battlefields farther away."[44] More notably, Chinese writers insist on a highly offensive operational stance to win and exercise command of communications. This offensive spirit traces its origins to China's own strategic and military traditions. While Chinese officials, mariners, and scholars draw their grand inspiration from Mahan, an American theorist, they frequently consult the politico-military writings of Mao Zedong for help with force structure, strategy, and naval doctrine. As we show in the following, references to offshore defense and offensive defense owe their conceptual existence to Maoist strategic thought. As such, it is worth revisiting his theories of warfare to appreciate the grammar of future Chinese sea power.

MAO'S ACTIVE DEFENSE STRATEGY

Mao, the founding Chinese Communist Party (CCP) chairman, imprinted his own strategic outlook on contemporary China, both through personal example and by bequeathing a massive body of work on political and military affairs. Communism may be on the wane in China, but Mao's image remains affixed to the Tiananmen Gate, at the political center of the capital city. Mao paid little heed to seagoing pursuits, keeping his attention on continental affairs. Even so, the PLA Navy's strategy of "offshore active defense" takes both its name and its basic principles from Mao's doctrine of "active defense."

Chairman Mao refined his "offensive-defensive" approach to warfighting over long decades of waging land warfare from a position of relative weakness, first to expel Japanese occupiers from China and later, during the Chinese Civil War, to defeat Chiang Kai-shek's Nationalist Army.[45] Unable to prevail by conventional means, staging a quick, decisive victory, the Red Army replied to the Nationalist campaigns by deliberately prolonging the war, wearying its enemies, and recruiting among the Chinese populace. Mao accepted much of the guidance advanced in Sun Tzu's *Art of War*, one of his favorite works of strategic theory, while tacitly ignoring Sun Tzu's warning against protracted war.

This was sheer expediency. Like today's Chinese sea-power proponents, Mao ridiculed passive defense, even while his Red Army appeared capable of little else. He foresaw that his theory of protracted war might be misread as an endorsement of passivity, so he took pains to distance himself from it. "Only a complete fool or a madman," he proclaimed, "would cherish passive defense as a talisman." Rather, active defense referred to the art of preparing the conditions for a strategic counteroffensive culminating in a decisive engagement: "As far as I know, there is no military manual of value nor any sensible military expert, ancient or modern, Chinese or foreign, that does not oppose passive defense, whether in strategy or tactics. . . . That is an error in war, a manifestation of conservatism in military matters, which we must resolutely oppose."[46] Despite the physical mismatch in favor of the Nationalist Army, the Red Army blended direct and indirect attacks (*cheng* and *ch'i*) artfully, in the best tradition of Sun Tzu.[47] Ultimately, after biding their time on the strategic defensive, the communists were able to shift the balance of forces in their favor, take the strategic offensive, and prevail.

Dexterity was essential. "Militarily speaking," Mao counseled, "our warfare consists of the alternate use of the defensive and the offensive." Strategic retreat was the right choice at the outset of a defensive campaign, but only until a powerful counterblow could be delivered. Defending forces should exploit China's vast strategic depth. They could feign weakness, falling back to tempt their enemies to overextend themselves:

> Defensive warfare, which is passive in form, can be active in content, and can be switched from the stage in which it is passive in form to the stage in which it is active both in form and in content. In appearance a fully planned strategic retreat is made under compulsion, but in reality it is effected in order to conserve our strength and bide our time in order to defeat the enemy, to lure him in deep and prepare for our counter-offensive.[48]

Mao likened Red Army forces to a "clever boxer" who "usually gives a little ground at first, while the foolish one rushes in furiously and uses up all his resources at the very start, and in the end he is often beaten by the man who has given ground." "Avoid the enemy when he is full of vigor," he advised, quoting Sun Tzu; then "strike when he is fatigued and withdraws."[49] After falling back on their base areas, concentrating force while tiring their opponents, Red Army defenders would strike back. Over time, they would assume the offensive, carrying the battle to the foe.

Mao's theory of active defense displays a pronounced geospatial component. Of the second Sino-Japanese War, he wrote that the invaders operated along "exterior lines" in a bid to envelop the defending Chinese, who operated on "interior lines." Then as now, the prospect of encirclement excited concern among Chinese leaders, prompting them to think ahead about countermeasures. According to Milan Vego,

> A force moves along *interior lines* when it runs between those of the enemy's lines of operations. Interior lines always originate from a central position. They are formed from a central position prolonged in one or more directions or they can also be understood as a series of central positions linked with one another. Interior lines in general allow concentration of one's forces against one part of the enemy force, while holding the other in check with a force distinctly inferior in strength.[50]

Relegated to the interior lines, Chinese Communist forces fought at a disadvantage, but even so, it was "possible and necessary to use tactical offensives

within the strategic defensive, to fight campaigns and battles of quick decision within a strategically protracted war and to fight campaigns and battles
on exterior lines within strategically interior lines." This maxim held true
"both for regular and for guerrilla warfare."[51] To prosecute microlevel offensives within a macrolevel defensive campaign, Mao admonished commanders
to vanquish enemy forces piecemeal. "Concentrate a big force to strike at
[and annihilate] a small section of the enemy force," he advised. Better to
cut off one of an enemy's fingers entirely than to injure them all.[52] Interior
lines, then, could be turned to the weaker party's advantage. This applies not
only to terrestrial campaigns but also to naval combat. Furthermore, Mao
mused about forging alliances around the Pacific basin, allowing China to
operate against Japanese imperialism along exterior lines. Despite the strategic encirclement of Chinese forces, an "anti-Japanese front in the Pacific area"
constituted a sort of diplomatic counter-encirclement.[53]

Maoist theory, then, informs the logic of Chinese statecraft and grand
strategy as well as its operational and tactical grammar. Mao's military writings were unambiguously offensive in character. Passive defense represented
"a spurious kind of defense" while "the only real defense is active defense."
Offensive defense was "defense for the purpose of counter-attacking and taking the offensive."[54] Defensive measures were transient, dictated by an unfavorable balance of forces. They were not the core of China's national strategy,
let alone its strategic preference.[55] For the CCP leader, clearly, resort to the
strategic defensive did not limit military strategy or tactics to the purely
defensive or passive.

Mao Zedong's strategic wisdom applies to sea as well as land combat.
Prompted by Mahan and Mao, Chinese naval strategists such as Ni Lexiong
now talk routinely of prying control of the waters within the first island chain
from the U.S. Navy's grasp.[56] They intend to surround and control these waters
by offensive means, even while the United States retains its overall mastery of
Asian waters. Many Chinese see American rule of East Asian waters as a latter-
day, nautical version of the Nationalists' strategy of encirclement and suppression—an effort to use superior firepower and numbers to suppress China's
rightful aspirations on the high seas.[57] Mao's Red Army fought back against
encirclement and suppression by means suitable for naval combat; indeed,
evidence suggests that many Chinese strategists do transpose Mao's land-warfare principles to the sea.[58] If the PLA Navy abides by Mao's strategic wisdom,
it will remain patient until it attains a position of relative strength vis-à-vis
prospective antagonists.

Mahan, then, seemingly furnishes the geopolitical logic for an offensive Chinese naval strategy while Beijing looks to the doctrines of Mao for the strategies and tactics to execute such a strategy. This represents an impressive synthesis of strategic theories from foreign and indigenous sources.

WHAT KIND OF MAHANIANS ARE THE CHINESE?

How can American observers chart trends in Chinese maritime strategic thought? Many Chinese experts read Mahan attentively, quoting him as authority for their views. But they offer few specifics about the lessons they draw from him. It bears noting that rising sea powers of the past have interpreted his writings far differently—sometimes to dismal, self-defeating effect. Fittingly, Great Britain and the United States fared best putting sea-power theory into practice. Nineteenth-century Britain's liberal maritime empire, defended by an unrivaled Royal Navy, supplied the model for Mahanian sea power. Mahan ratified what the British had been doing, flattering their sensibilities. Unsurprisingly, he was showered with accolades during his travels in the British Isles. While commanding USS *Chicago*, for example, he was presented honorary degrees at Oxford and Cambridge and delivered a speech before the venerable Royal Navy Club.[59]

Fin de siècle America greeted Mahan's works tepidly at first. Of the publication of *The Influence of Sea Power upon History*, he observed wryly, "That it filled a need was speedily evident by favorable reviews, which were much more explicit and hearty in Europe, and especially in Great Britain, than in the United States."[60] It took events to overcome the Republic's historic insularity, prompting Americans to look westward toward Asia and southward toward the Caribbean and the isthmus, its gateway to the Pacific. Mahan contended that, by defeating Spain in 1898, the United States had succeeded to Spanish duties and responsibilities in the Caribbean and the Philippines, the latter a pillar of the first standing U.S. naval presence in Asia.[61] The U.S. Navy built a twenty-battleship fleet, as Mahan urged, and it held European fleets at bay in American waters. The Navy had little need for a fleet able to outgun entire great-power navies; it merely needed enough firepower to defeat the largest contingent likely to venture into the Americas. American strategy might—but need not—culminate in a fleet encounter like Trafalgar or Tsushima.

Imperial Germany leapt at Mahanian theory. On one occasion, Kaiser Wilhelm II declared, "I am just now not reading but devouring Captain Mahan's book and am trying to learn it by heart. It is on board all my ships and

[is] constantly quoted by my captains and officers."[62] Despite German leaders' gushing, Mahan was a poor fit for Germany, a continental power shackled by disastrous maritime geography. Mahan wrote mainly for Americans, whose Navy and merchant marine enjoyed easy access to the Atlantic and Pacific. Unlike Germany, the United States faced no land threats that diverted resources from seagoing pursuits. Vessels originating in German ports must pass by the British Isles, either through the English Channel or between Scotland and Norway, to reach the broad Atlantic—and thence German possessions in Africa and Asia.[63] Royal Navy men-of-war cordoned off the "dead" North Sea, imposing a distant blockade that left German shipping to wither on the vine during World War I. (Chapter 3 examines the Imperial German case in some detail.)

Mahan reported that the Japanese were his most ardent followers. In his memoir, he recounted "pleasant correspondence with several Japanese officials and translators." That no one had "shown closer or more interested attention to the general subject" than the Japanese was obvious from "their preparation and their accomplishments in the recent war" with Russia (1904–1905). "As far as known to myself," added Mahan, "more of my works have been done into Japanese than into any other one tongue."[64] In 1902 Admiral Yamamoto Gombei offered him a lucrative teaching post at Japan's Naval Staff College.[65] Apart from its initial success, however, Imperial Japan followed a maritime strategy that miscarried badly—owing in part to the dominant Japanese interpretation of Mahan, under which Japan sought to carve out an autarkic economic zone, impose a defense perimeter along the second island chain, and build an unmatched fleet of big-gun battleships.[66] Tokyo's obsession with geographic features and force structure proved its undoing.

Like past sea powers, China now teems with Mahan enthusiasts and their critics. To date, however, Chinese commentary has seldom gone beyond familiar Mahanian principles. Judging from available literature, Mahan's more nuanced assessments of sea power have yet to sink in. Chinese analysts also tend to gravitate toward the more memorable passages of Mahan's works for their own narrow purposes, ratifying predetermined conclusions. They accept at face value, for example, the notion that Mahan's single-minded purpose was to persuade nations to build navies able to settle economic disputes through force of arms.[67] Typifying some of the more casual descriptions of Mahan's writings, Zhan Huayun states:

U.S. naval officer and historian Mahan, who created the theory of naval power, pointed out that the determining factor in the rise and fall of all empires was whether or not they had naval power and could control the seas. His theory of naval power can be considered a watershed in world naval strategy. His doctrine of the theory of naval power and theory of naval strategy arose at an historic moment, becoming the cornerstone of Western naval strategic theory and an ideological weapon in seeking hegemony.[68]

Feng Zhaokui quotes Mahan as writing, "Sea dominance embraces everything that can make a nation a great one by means of the sea or through the sea." The author then proceeds to chide Mahan for making sweeping martial claims about sea power, stating, "Instead of saying it would be enough so long as the fleets of a country were able to sail through the vast ocean, the unspoken message contained in this remark indicated that gaining control over important sea routes and acquiring overseas resources was actually the real intention of the major nations that had risen up."[69] Feng urges China to avoid the hegemonic path that Mahan laid out for ambitious maritime powers of his own day. Others directly credit Mahan with U.S. preeminence in maritime Asia, particularly its dominant military position along the first island chain, and take him to task for America's purportedly hostile intentions toward China. According to Gao Xinsheng of the Shenyang Artillery Academy:

In Mahan's famous "The Influence of Sea Power Upon History, 1660–1783," he expressed that to have the command of the sea, one must rely on powerful naval force and establish a naval base network all over the globe. . . . Under the guidance of his principle, America occupied most of the main islands in the Pacific Ocean in succession, built many important military bases on the islands, and also formed a solid military alliance with island nations in the Pacific Ocean such as Japan, Australia, the Philippines, and Singapore. This realized America's maritime expansion strategy, formed the so-called "island blockade line," and became America's important strong points to control the sea and a netlike strategic layout.[70]

Chen Zhou, a senior research fellow at the PLA Academy of Military Sciences, argues that raw geopolitical interests have always underpinned U.S.

China policy. He declares: "From the very beginning the U.S. strategy toward China had a profound geostrategic background. Exactly following the thinking of U.S. naval strategist Mahan, the U.S. occupied Hawaii, the Philippines and other important Pacific islands, making them 'stepping-stones' for marching towards Asia and China and stretching out its forces as far as 7,000 miles away from its west coast and as close as only 700 miles to China's eastern coast."[71] Both Gao and Chen draw a straight line from Mahanian sea-power theory published more than a century ago to U.S. strategy in Asia today. The linearity and causal relationship depicted by the Chinese are dubious from an analytical standpoint. That Mahan's logic resonates deeply with Chinese strategists, leading them to impute Mahanian motives to U.S. policymakers—past and present—is beyond doubt.

Nevertheless, these cursory characterizations of Mahan's theory border on caricature, and they raise the possibility that Beijing is oversimplifying and misreading the American theorist. On the one hand, a misinterpretation of Mahan could turn out to be harmless. Chinese analysts could run into an analytical dead end and move on to another theory more suitable for China's unique local conditions. On the other hand, a less benign outcome is conceivable. If the Chinese accept the martial themes underlying Mahan's arguments uncritically and pattern Chinese maritime policy on these themes, then it is possible Beijing will follow the German or Japanese path to sea power. If so, the prospects for harmony in the Asia-Pacific region will dim.

There are at least two possible explanations for this apparent superficiality, each with important implications for the development of Chinese strategic thought about the seas. First, PLA Navy thinkers are still reading and digesting his theories and considering how to apply them to Chinese foreign policy goals. The literature suggests that they are finding there is far more to Mahan than combat between symmetrical battle fleets. Since "commerce thrives by peace and suffers by war," maintained Mahan, "it follows that peace is the superior interest" of seagoing nations. Mentions of Mahan have appeared more and more frequently in Chinese discourses since the early 2000s. They have become more varied, expanding beyond *The Influence of Sea Power upon History* to encompass more geopolitically minded books such as *The Problem of Asia* and *The Interest of America in Sea Power*.

As Chinese thinkers enrich their understanding of Mahanian theory—integrating not only the operational, tactical, and force-structure dimensions but also his views of international relations—they may well modulate their attitudes toward the proper uses of sea power. The primacy of peaceful commercial competition would be a welcome addition to China's Mahanian discourses. Western analysts should monitor for signs of a deeper, richer grasp of sea-power theory.

A number of scholars in China have already demonstrated a more sophisticated comprehension of Mahan. Liu Zhongmin's three-part series on sea-power theory, for instance, exhibits comprehensive coverage of Mahan's voluminous writings, representing a discernible advance in scholarship.[72] Beijing has also been analyzing the rise and fall of past great powers, sorting through history for guidance on how to manage its own ascent. Analysts appear keenly aware that a peaceful rise demands a more modest and prudent use of sea power, lest other seafaring powers—especially the United States—seek to counterbalance China at sea.

Indeed, some Chinese neo-Mahanians urge Beijing to exercise a version of "limited sea power" (有限海权) that remains geographically circumscribed within the first island chain.[73] In their view, a genuinely Mahanian PLA Navy ought to concentrate its efforts on seaways critical to trade and on defending China's maritime sovereignty. Such a China would content itself with an adequate—but not overbearing—fleet. Still others are beginning to acknowledge the singular importance Mahan attached to peacetime commerce. They clearly recognize that Mahan never counseled naval war for its own sake.[74]

At the more concrete operational and tactical levels, some Chinese strategists openly disavow Mahanian followers who are enamored with the most bellicose interpretations of command of the sea. Rear Admiral Huang Jiang, the dean of the Naval Command Academy, offers one of the most insightful and nuanced notions of command of the sea. He counsels:

> Seizing command of the sea is not a zero-sum interaction. In sea battle, the loss of our freedom of movement does not necessarily mean that the enemy has gained freedom of movement. Similarly, preventing the enemy from attaining freedom of movement does not mean that we possess freedom of movement. It is only when one side not only immobilizes enemy freedom of movement at sea, but also enjoys unfettered ability to maneuver at sea that command of the sea has been grasped. Otherwise, command of the sea remains in a contested state, belonging to neither side.[75]

Admiral Huang is acutely aware that command is a highly uncertain and difficult undertaking. Indeed, his words hark back to Sir Julian Corbett, who maintained that an uncommanded sea, always in dispute, was the norm.[76] He recognizes that the Chinese navy will likely operate in an ambiguous warfighting environment in which sea control will be elusive and fleeting at best. Ji Rongren and Wang Xuejin of the National Defense University prophesy a fluid contest for command between China and potential antagonists. They observe:

> Command of communications does not discount the possibility of repeated gains and losses of command during a certain time period and within a certain battlespace. For any powerful military, command of communications is always a relative concept. No military could ever completely seize command of communications, the air, and the sea from beginning to end. For our military suffering from relative backwardness in equipment, this predicament is even more acute. The duration of command will be limited, the degree of control will be relative, the scope of control will be confined, and the gain and loss of command will be situational.[77]

These sober assessments are a far cry from assertions that China could and should seek "absolute" command. In practical terms, this more realistic appraisal conforms to China's offshore defense strategy, an effort to assert sea control for a finite time up to several hundred miles off the mainland's coast. Mahan, Mao, and Liu would certainly have approved. Encouraging analytical trends, then, are starting to emerge among Chinese thinkers. How much momentum this more nuanced, more accurate interpretation of sea-power theory will gain in Beijing remains to be seen.

A more worrisome alternative is that Chinese navalists are simply using Mahan to lobby for a big navy composed of expensive, high-tech platforms. They do not need to read Mahan's works widely or deeply to hype the threat to Chinese maritime interests, building the case for a strong fleet. One article urging Beijing to build an oceangoing naval fleet suggests that opportunists are indeed using Mahan as authority for their policy preference, namely a decisive shift of resources to the sea services. Reconstructing an overly simplistic history of sea power, of a sort often attributed to Mahan, Luo Yuan states:

When we look at history, we can see that whether a country is powerful or not is closely related with its naval forces. When its naval forces are powerful, then the country is strong; when its naval forces are weak, then the country is also fragile. During the 500 years from the 15th century to the 20th century, whether the strength of the main countries in Europe grew or declined and whether they won or failed in competition between different countries obviously depended on their naval forces.[78]

Other Mahanians seize on a passage from *The Problem of Asia* that alerted the U.S. leadership of a century ago to the perils of neglecting sea power. Mahan argues that a "sagacious statesman" would grasp the "national backwardness" of American sentiment toward sea power and work tirelessly to "provide the organized force—especially the naval—without which the attempted expression of national will, on emergency, becomes the clumsy and abortive gestures of a flabby and untrained giant."[79] Chinese analysts are fond of citing this evocative metaphor as a preface to their calls for a more aggressive naval buildup.[80] They, too, are attempting to telegraph an urgent message to their political masters: the Chinese navy must modernize speedily if it is to enforce Beijing's will in the international system.

By no means would the PLA Navy be the first navy to use Mahan as a rallying cry. Indeed, it remains a standard quip that U.S. Navy leaders use Mahan to justify building a big fleet but otherwise leave his books on the shelf. There is doubtless a sloganeering aspect to the PLA Navy's use of Mahan. Like other works of strategic theory—Sun Tzu's *Art of War* comes to mind—Mahan's writings are malleable. They can be put to a variety of uses, from stoking Chinese nationalism to carving out bigger navy budgets. If Chinese Mahanians cherry-pick the parts of his theory that prescribe apocalyptic fleet encounters, China's maritime rise may tend toward confrontation with fellow sea powers. That is, if the same drumbeat of Mahanian commentary persists, it will furnish a leading indicator of trouble for the U.S. Navy and its Asian partners.

It bears mentioning that even if China does interpret Mahan in warlike fashion, it need not construct a navy symmetrical to the U.S. Navy to achieve its maritime goals, such as upholding territorial claims around the Chinese nautical periphery, commanding East Asian seas and skies, and safeguarding distant sea lines of communication. (We will revisit the grammar of Chinese force structure and operations in chapter 4.) Beijing could accept

Mahan's general logic of naval strategy while seeking to command vital sea areas with weaponry and methods quite different from anything Mahan foresaw. If the much-discussed antiship ballistic missile pans out, for instance, the PLA could hold U.S. Navy carrier strike groups at a distance.[81] Medium-sized Chinese aircraft carriers could operate freely underneath that defensive shield, sparing the PLA Navy the technical and doctrinal headaches associated with constructing big-deck carriers comparable to the U.S. Navy's *Nimitz* or *Ford* classes. Beijing would fulfill its Mahanian goal of local sea control at modest cost—an eminently sensible approach, and one that Mahan would have applauded. Western observers should avoid projecting their own assumptions onto Chinese strategic thinkers.

COMPETING SCHOOLS OF THOUGHT

To be sure, Chinese strategists are not marching in lockstep on maritime strategy. Indeed, discord rather than unanimity characterizes the discourse on the future of Chinese sea power. Analysts lodge a variety of objections to the neo-Mahanian school of thought, invoking other strategic theorists to buttress their claims. Continentalists, for example, look to Sir Halford Mackinder's land-power theories for inspiration.[82] Given China's preoccupation with landward threats to its north throughout its history, Mackinder's writings enjoy a fairly large following. Moreover, land-power enthusiasts are as likely as Mahanians to caricature and oversimplify their favorite theories. Although translations of Mackinder's work differ slightly, Chinese continentalists often invoke his famous declaration that "whoever controls central Asia controls the world island [the Eurasian continent]; and whoever rules the world island controls the world," using the quotation liberally to buttress their own arguments.[83]

Unsurprisingly, their views run directly counter to those of sea-power advocates, revealing a very diverse range of thinking about Chinese geostrategy. At the same time, differences in perspective provide an ideal opportunity for a contest of ideas. In 2007, a vigorous intellectual debate over the merits of sea and land power broke out into the open. Professor Ye Zicheng of Beijing University touched off the controversy, publishing a series of articles that year denigrating the role of maritime power in propelling China's rise while touting the importance of a landward orientation for long-term Chinese strategic success.[84] Ye argues forcefully that "land power can exist without sea power, but sea power cannot exist without land power development. Hence, land power remains the most basic geopolitical form and element, and the

Eurasian continent remains the main international political stage today."[85] Mackinder would surely have applauded these words.

According to Ye, all other forms of geospatial power, including air, sea, space, and cyberspace power, should serve China's continental prowess.[86] In policy terms, a landward orientation would require China to further develop its interior territories and foster strategic partnerships with other major land powers of Eurasia, including Europe, Russia, and India. At the same time, an inward-looking posture would eschew maritime competition in the Pacific with the current naval hegemon, the United States, thus further benefiting Beijing's peaceful rise.[87]

In another prestigious journal, Ye provides some historical perspective for his hypothesis. He claims that land powers, in contrast to sea powers, tend to exhibit greater staying power in the international system. Ye contends:

> The influence of those countries that have developed mainly through land power has lasted much longer [than sea powers]. Continental space has very great cohesion; once it forms it can endure, and the fruit of land power development can permanently sustain a country's development and status. . . . The influence of China, this land power, can last intermittently for up to 1,000 years. Although China is both a sea and land power, in essence, China's natural features and history and culture have determined that it is mainly a land power. The fact that China has been divided without being separated, has not been wrecked despite weakness, and has always been a unified country for several thousand years is closely related to its land power status.[88]

Ye then offers several cautionary tales of great powers that overreached their comparative geopolitical advantages. Russia's failed attempt at sea power during the Cold War and Japan's abortive bid for continental hegemony in World War II exemplify the hazards encountered when mastering unfamiliar geospatial terrain. For Ye, American difficulties in Afghanistan and Iraq in recent years suggest that the United States, too, has "gone far beyond the strategic potential given by its natural endowment."[89] In other words, China should stick to what it knows best, that is, land power, lest it err as egregiously as previous great powers.

Liu Zhongmin similarly looks to the past for guidance, interpreting Imperial Germany's naval rivalry against Great Britain as a stark warning to the Chinese leadership. For Liu, the "moral of the story" for Beijing is clear:

"Germany is a country whose territory included both land and sea and its most important geopolitical strategic interests were more dependent on the land. By excessively worshipping and developing the sea power, Germany went against its regional advantage, and made enemies both on the land and at sea, which aggravated its disadvantage as a country whose territory included both land and sea and resulted in double injury. In the end, Germany's challenge to the British maritime hegemony was thoroughly defeated."[90] Drawing a parallel to China's predicament today, Liu believes that Beijing too is a hybrid power saddled with both landward and seaward strategic responsibilities. Given these multidirectional pressures, China is in no position to focus exclusively on building a powerful navy. As Liu states emphatically in another article, "China's comprehensive power simply cannot help China to establish U.S.-style global sea power."[91] Thus, it must avoid the fate of Imperial Germany by shunning futile attempts to challenge U.S. maritime hegemony—attempts that could trigger a needless, unwinnable rivalry.

The centrality of land power obviously carries important resource- and force-structure-related implications. Zhang Minqian acknowledges that China must devote attention to all dimensions of geospatial power, including the air, sea, space, and information domains. However, since "resource allocation in fact cannot be inputted in equal volume but must somewhat highlight the focal points, land power is the primary option for China, which has the characteristics of being mainly a land power."[92] In other words, the Chinese leadership must selectively prioritize its military investments to maximize China's geographic advantages on land.

For Cheng Yawen, Beijing should modernize its land forces to cope with internal security challenges and external threats from neighboring continental powers. According to Cheng, "the basic way of preserving land security is air mobility and joint air-land combat, which is less complex than joint land, air, and sea warfare, and in addition helps to bring into play the traditional strong points of China's armed forces."[93] In this alternative future, China would possess powerful military forces capable of prosecuting land warfare in a manner resembling the U.S. Army's Air-Land Battle Doctrine, a concept developed during the last phases of the Cold War. Architects of the doctrine envisioned using information-based precision strike weaponry lavishly to compensate for the quantitative inferiority of American and allied forces to the Soviet Army in the European theater of operations.

For some analysts, including Ye himself, Beijing would not necessarily suffer a land-bound fate even if it kept its continental orientation. A powerful land force could still effectively control events at sea, particularly littoral seas washing against the Chinese mainland. Ye argues that technological advances have greatly extended the reach and enhanced the striking power of shore-based aircraft and guided missiles while increasing the vulnerability of blue-water navies to land-based assets. Joint land, air, and sea forces could collectively "produce sufficient deterrent power to protect most of China's coastal waters and all its coastal regions." Most important of all, according to Ye, "If the land power (army, ground-based missiles, ground-based air force) on the Chinese homeland is sufficiently strong, it will suffice to control the situation in the Taiwan Strait."[94] Interestingly, this assessment conforms largely to the current Chinese military buildup across the strait.

Reflecting the tremendous intellectual ferment in China about geostrategy in general and sea power in particular, Ye's and others' works elicited an energetic riposte from critics. *Renmin Haijun*, the official outlet of the PLA Navy, published a direct rebuttal to Ye's writings. Lu Rude, a former lecturer of the Dalian Naval Academy, argues that Professor Ye's analysis is out of step with China's strategic realities. Rebuking his narrow geographic conception of sea power, Lu contends that "the establishment of sea power is the natural extension of national strategy toward the sea, and the core issue of maritime activities. It is related to multiple fields such as politics, economy, diplomacy, technology, law, and the military. It determines the rise and decline of a nation's maritime affairs and its strengths and weaknesses. It is a matter of urgent importance to a nation and not a competition between 'land power' and 'sea power.'"[95] Lu is unabashedly Mahanian in his depiction of sea power as an expression of a nation's grand strategy. More importantly, he inveighs against the notion that the choice between land and sea power is mutually exclusive. He treats this as a false choice. Ni Lexiong, one of the most prolific and vocal neo-Mahanians in China, also objects to Ye's analysis. Ni is particularly skeptical of Ye's assertion that China can dampen the geopolitical sources of competition with the United States by facing landward. For Ni, the opposite outcome is equally likely: weakness at sea could leave China open to aggression and bullying from the sea.[96]

An even more forceful repudiation of land-power proponents elevates China's seaward turn to the grand, world-historical level. Lu Ning declares sweepingly:

> The transformation of contemporary Chinese society, in terms of its viewpoint on sea power, is the evolution from an internally oriented

economic form of a traditional farming civilization to an externally oriented economic form of a modern industrial civilization relying on sea lines of communication. . . . [This transformation] is the basis of a historic about face in China, from its traditional advocacy of land power to the modern advocacy of sea power. Beyond that, it opens up a distinct, historic path by which China can achieve a national resurgence from "continental civilization" to "maritime civilization" in the 21st century.[97]

These are breathtaking claims indeed. The notion that national destiny and greatness are inextricable from sea power is unmistakably Mahanian. It is also noteworthy that the arguments put forth by competing schools of thought are often tinged with historical determinism. Whether confidence that China's future will unfold in linear fashion is genuine or mere posturing is unclear.

In a far more conciliatory analysis, Professor Li Yihu of Beijing University calls for a dual-pronged strategy that leverages both land and sea power. "In handling sea-land relations," he advises, "we should not be biased toward one and neglect the other, nor should we assign absolute equality between the two."[98] Nevertheless, he takes issue with the confidence expressed by continentalists, such as Ye, that land power is enough to safeguard China's maritime interests. Li asserts that land power alone is inadequate to protect the "main thoroughfares of the Pacific economic rim, international navigation routes, and strategic points" along the Chinese littoral. Thus, "China's economic development and national security is premised on the strategic problem of sea power development."[99] Concurring with Li, Senior Colonel Feng Liang, a professor at the Naval Command College, urges Beijing to "persist in placing equal weight on land and sea to face its security demands."[100]

CHINA'S NAVAL-INTELLECTUAL COMPLEX

Clearly, there is a lack of consensus among Chinese strategists about the place of sea power in China's overall, long-term objectives. It is equally evident that the Mahanian worldview is by no means monolithic or even mainstream in China's strategic community. But the debate itself contains considerable analytical value. First, geostrategic ideas are thriving in an intellectually competitive and honest environment in China. In 2008, a ten-year retrospective on the state of the sea-power debate by a Dalian Maritime Academy professor cites no fewer than twenty works from topflight Chinese scholars.[101] *Xiandai Guoji Guanxi*, the flagship monthly journal of the ruling State Council of the People's Republic of China, dedicated its entire May 2008 issue to the study of geopolitics, including the sea-power question.[102] Members of the academic community and the policymaking establishment frequently borrow sea-power concepts and terminology from one another. Ideas clearly matter in China.

Second, this discourse is a key indicator that sea-power theory is being "socialized" in academic and policy circles. The two communities look to each other for guidance, spurring what appears to be a virtuous cycle of intellectual interaction and advancement. The resulting improvement in the quality of strategic thought and the attendant growth in scholarship on nautical affairs promises to serve as a useful metric, helping external observers assess the extent to which sea-power theory has gained policy traction. From a historical perspective, the extensive and rigorous debate in China represents a healthy departure from the unquestioning embrace of Mahan's writings in Imperial Germany and Imperial Japan. Beijing may thus learn the right lessons, rejecting the bellicose navalism that so obsessed leaders in Berlin and Tokyo. If so, the prospects for a cooperative maritime environment in Asian waters will brighten considerably.

Third, the intellectual struggle over ideas offers insights into the often-overlooked cultural and social dimensions of strategy. In the West today, scholars pay scant attention to geopolitics, depicting the field as hopelessly outdated and irrelevant in this age of globalization and interdependence. They tend to downplay the role of geography in international politics and, in the process, to transpose their own worldviews to other powers. Yet the literature review cited here indicates that a significant portion of the Chinese academy is moving precisely in the opposite direction.

These divergent trends dovetail with the rise of a postmodern maritime perspective in the West and the emergence of a neo-Mahanian mentality in Asia, two trends aptly captured by Geoffrey Till. What this implies for the future of Western-Asian encounters at sea remains unclear. But the apparent gap between Western and Chinese assessments of geospatial affairs suggests that the potential for mutual misunderstanding and misperception is ever-present and may become more acute over time. What seems axiomatic about sea power to Western capitals may not be for Beijing. It thus behooves Western strategists and policymakers to avoid the temptation to mirror-image and to vigilantly question deeply held assumptions about the seas that may not be shared in China.

Strategic theory, in short, gives Westerners an instrument to track China's maritime rise, complementing more traditional techniques of net assessment. If the dominant school of Chinese scholars and seafarers continues ignoring the cooperative strands of Mahanian thought, mistaking his writings for (or misrepresenting them as) bloody-minded advocacy of naval battle, Chinese strategy will incline toward naval competition and conflict. Conversely, a China whose leadership accepts the deeper understanding put forth by more thoughtful analysts—and fully grasps the logic governing Mahanian theory—may prove less contentious. Western observers should keep sifting through Chinese strategic discourses and official statements in an effort to ascertain where China's Mahanian turn may lead. America's strategic longevity in Asia could depend on it.

CHAPTER 3

The German Precedent for Chinese Sea Power

In this chapter we use a past example in which a land power dominant by many measures of national power—population, natural resources, industrial potential—squared off against the preeminent sea power of its day and saw its bid for naval mastery come to grief. In this case, maritime geography and a preponderant enemy navy were too much to overcome. But we take issue with the common wisdom that holds that continental powers cannot go to sea. This is determinism. In a sense, Asian waters today offer a laboratory in which this question is being put to the test. We maintain that China could defy the fate of past continental powers by turning apparent geographic liabilities to its advantage and managing its resources wisely. Like America, China could become a composite land and sea power if its leadership and people display enough skill at shipbuilding and seafaring, and enough will to the sea. Time will tell.

In this vein, we recall Mark Twain's quip that "history doesn't repeat itself, but it rhymes." So it does. For more than a decade, Western scholars and practitioners of statecraft have struggled to chart China's long-term trajectory. Consonant with Twain's wisdom, many have looked to history to help forecast the future. European history has colored their thinking, producing both optimistic and pessimistic predictions about China's ascent to great power.[1] The fate of Imperial Germany, which rose with Prussia's triumph in the Wars of Unification (1864–1871) and fell with the Treaty of Versailles (1919), has garnered particular attention. China-watchers predisposed to optimism maintain that Beijing is pursuing a benign, low-profile grand strategy reminiscent of Otto von Bismarck's Germany. Bismarck courted amicable relations with bordering nations, soothing fears of German capabilities and intentions.[2] Those of bleaker inclinations reply that Kaiser Wilhelm II's Germany—an industrially mighty, erratic great power situated amid lesser powers—marched Europe over the precipice in 1914. A powerful, revisionist

China could do the same, deranging the Asian status quo. Enmity, conflict, and even war are the likely results if fin de siècle Europe is any guide.[3]

The Chinese themselves have consulted the Imperial German case for guidance, studying it alongside other historical case studies involving rising powers. In 2006 China Central Television, which is run by Beijing's State Council, produced a twelve-part television—and eight-part book—series titled *The Rise of Great Powers*. The series includes a particularly instructive episode on Germany, one of the nine countries it examines from the past five hundred years. Credited for securing twenty years of peace for a newly united Germany, Bismarck is held in high if not excessive esteem. The book series showers praise on Bismarck for damping the envy of Germany's neighbors, enmeshing the nation's security with that of its neighbors, and holding a vengeful France at bay.[4] This account holds wide appeal with Chinese audiences who want Beijing to act as a "responsible stakeholder" in the international order.

Accordingly, Tang Yongsheng, deputy director of the Strategy Institute at China's National Defense University, urges Beijing to pattern its peaceful rise on the Bismarckian model. "Bismarck in Germany drew up a complex geosecurity system," observes Tang, and "by building a dazzling alliance network with countries on the periphery, he eased the strategic pressure of European powers on Germany, avoided the predicament of having enemies on both sides, and successfully isolated France."[5] China, similarly, should anchor itself to a range of multilateral alignments spanning the globe "so as to establish [itself] in an unassailable position." Other Chinese strategists fervently reject comparisons to Wilhelmine Germany. One scholar deems the likeness "ridiculous" and "based on not knowing anything about China."[6] It seems clear, nonetheless, that Chinese strategists are inspecting the German case for lessons, positive or negative.

Given the manifold nautical challenges confronting China—witness Beijing's dispatch of a squadron for counterpiracy operations in the Gulf of Aden—we expect historically minded Chinese analysts and officials to heed the past successes and failures of maritime powers. The lessons they learn from history may tell us a great deal about their future behavior and the policies they will pursue, both along China's littoral periphery and on the high seas. Wilhelmine Germany, again, furnishes potentially fruitful analogies. Germany was a continental power struggling to go to sea during the age of British naval dominion, much as land-bound China is bidding for sea power in an Asia where America rules the waves. By discovering the similarities and differences between the German disaster and China's maritime endeavors, we can catch sight of effective strategic responses.

MEASURING SEA POWER

Vice Admiral Wolfgang Wegener, Imperial Germany's most gifted naval thinker, developed a formula for estimating sea power. Wegener served as a midgrade officer in the High Seas Fleet during World War I, first as a gunnery officer and later as a ship captain. He wrote three memoranda that were distributed widely in navy circles. His indictment of German naval strategy (and its framers) appeared after the war under the title *The Naval Strategy of the World War*. It ranks among the classic treatises on maritime affairs. Sea power, writes Wegener, is a product of (1) "strategic position," a geographical factor; (2) the fleet, a tactical factor; and (3) a society's "strategic will" to the sea, which "breathes life into the fleet" and applies its energies to improving the nation's strategic position.[7] The German naval leadership never sought to improve a strategic position that stifled German naval aspirations. Rather, the fleet defended waters that the enemy saw little need to contest. Apart from misdirecting its efforts, the naval command lacked the offensive spirit to carry the battle to Britain's Royal Navy. At once provocative, mercurial, and intellectually adrift, Berlin saw battle as an end in itself rather than an endeavor designed to advance German strategic purposes.

Such heresy won him few friends in the naval establishment. Admiral Magnus von Levetzow, the last Imperial German chief of naval staff, branded Wegener "a hairsplitter and a professor" obsessed with geography and passive in outlook.[8] Even so, Wegener's template offers a useful way to compare Germany then with the People's Republic of China (PRC) now. We examine the similarities and differences between German and Chinese maritime geography, take the measure of the German and Chinese navies relative to the dominant navies of their day, and evaluate the German and Chinese peoples' propensity for seafaring. This will illuminate alternative futures for Sino-American interaction on the high seas and, with any luck, will help Washington manage its relations with Beijing cordially.

Geography

It is a natural tendency to reduce geography to an abstract jumble of lines on maps and nautical charts, but strategic geography is an innately interactive field of endeavor. And, like other dimensions of strategy, it cannot be divorced from the human factor. Consequently, it is worthwhile to consider

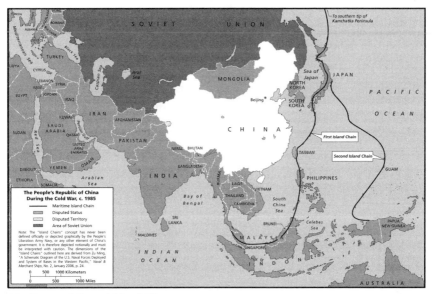

The First and Second Island Chains

how dominant sea powers of the past have sought to manage the efforts of new entrants into the circle of great powers—powers often set on reordering the prevailing maritime system to their advantage. Great Britain played the role of the preeminent sea power in turn-of-the-century Europe whereas the United States finds itself cast in this role in maritime Asia today. Any patterns of interaction between established and rising sea powers will prove enlightening.

German leaders professed fealty to the ideas of sea-power theorist Alfred Thayer Mahan. As previous chapters observed, Mahan's ideas about the interaction between human events and the sea were revolutionary—leading commentators to dub him America's "evangelist" or "Copernicus" of sea power, not to mention a leading proponent of geopolitical thought. The importance of geography was nonetheless lost on Berlin. The theories put forward in Mahan's *The Influence of Sea Power upon History, 1660–1783* found special favor with Kaiser Wilhelm II. On one occasion the Kaiser reported not just reading but "devouring Captain Mahan's book and . . . trying to learn it by heart."[9] Mahan articulated not only a theory of naval strategy, focusing on the mechanics of combat at sea, but also a "philosophy" of sea power accentuating the geopolitical motives that impel nations down to the sea in ships.[10] For him, sea power was about far more than navies and sea fights. It encompassed international trade and commerce—he regarded a people's inborn propensity to trade as the keystone of sea power—as well as forward bases to support the voyages of fuel-thirsty, steam-propelled vessels.[11]

Mahan also declared that a great seafaring nation needed one or two ready outlets to the high seas to prevent a dominant rival fleet from choking off its maritime trade and commerce.[12] The United States, Mahan's intended audience, enjoyed easy access to the Atlantic and Pacific, and unlike most continental powers, it faced no land threats that diverted resources from sea-going pursuits. Imperial Germany had no such luck. The narrow German seacoast features ports on the Helgoland Bight in the North Sea and at Kiel and Rostock on the Baltic coast, flanking the Jutland Peninsula to the west and east. But whether they originate from the North Sea or the Baltic, ships from German ports must pass under the shadow of the British Isles to reach the Atlantic seaways, and thence the modest colonial empire Germany carved out in the 1880s and 1890s.[13] Royal Navy men-of-war operating from southern ports could close the Straits of Dover with ease, while vessels based at Scapa Flow, to the far north in Scotland, could cordon off the North Sea from afar—as they did during World War I, enforcing a "distant blockade" of German shipping.

To force entry into the Atlantic against a hostile Great Britain, Germany would need a fleet able to overpower the biggest contingent the Royal Navy was likely to station in home waters. Seizing the strategic offensive was no simple matter for the High Seas Fleet. Britain already held the decisive geographic positions at the outbreak of war, and it attached unlimited value to the object of homeland defense—justifying maximum naval measures. Marveled Wegener, Britain "found herself simply in a brilliant strategic position at the outbreak of the war. The arteries of her commerce lay in the Atlantic, unreachable by the German fleet from the Elbe. The German trade routes, on the other hand, could easily be severed in the Channel and off Scotland."[14]

"England," he concluded, "was 'saturated' with command of the sea" at the outbreak of war.[15] By implication, Admiral Levetzow was shortsighted to proclaim that "victorious naval battle is . . . always *correct* and never wrong strategy—*where* at sea it will be fought against the enemy's main force is really immaterial."[16] If adopted, such a maxim would divorce operations from political purpose. The notion of battle for its own sake has beguiled military thinkers throughout history, but in a sense, this represents an un-German way of thinking. Wegener quoted Carl von Clausewitz, the quintessential German military theorist, who described strategy as the use of battles and engagements for the purpose of the war. Levetzow contradicted Clausewitz, embracing the conceit that battle was an end in itself, strategic and geographic factors aside.

Unless the German navy could outflank the British Isles, improving its strategic position, it stood little chance of furthering overall German strategic success. Tactical sorties from the Helgoland Bight did nothing beyond reinforcing German command of the North Sea, which Wegener pronounced a "dead" expanse. That is, the Royal Navy could seal it off from the high seas, in effect rendering it a strategically useless inland sea. Trying to command the Atlantic commons from the North Sea was like trying to command it from the landlocked Caspian Sea. Germany had three options:

- First, it could content itself with commanding the Baltic Sea, the conduit for Scandinavian ore and other natural resources. Maintaining dominance over the Russian navy detachment in the Baltic would have kept this lifeline open for German industry. Keeping control of the Belts, the narrow seas east of the Jutland Peninsula, would have helped Germany preserve mastery of the Baltic. This strategy, however, had a serious drawback: it would have meant forfeiting German imperial interests, with colonies such as Kiaochow, on China's Shandong Peninsula, left to wither on the vine.

- Second, the German fleet could force open the "gateway" to the Atlantic to the south. Germany could circumvent the Straits of Dover by seizing ports such as Brest and Cherbourg along the French Atlantic coast (as indeed it did during World War II). Wegener noted that the dead North Sea would have "sprung to life" if the German navy acquired Atlantic footholds. There would have been a vital sealane to contest, linking the north German ports with outposts on the Atlantic Ocean. The High Seas Fleet could have brought the Royal Navy's Grand Fleet to battle over this sea line of communication (SLOC).

- Third, the High Seas Fleet could attempt to force entry into the Atlantic by the northern route. This likely would have involved a sequential campaign, improving Germany's strategic position in stepwise fashion. The Jutland Peninsula could have been occupied or the Danish government browbeaten into granting access to its ports on German terms. This would have provided the German navy access to the northern SLOC connecting the Baltic with the Atlantic. From there German forces could have seized outposts along the southern Norwegian coast, obtaining a springboard to occupy the strategically placed Shetland or Faeroe islands, or conceivably even Iceland. Assuming that Germany could hold them against British counterattack, these island "gates" would have furnished German shipping the free access to vital SLOCs that Berlin craved. At a minimum, observed Wegener, the Grand Fleet would have been forced to fight to maintain its own strategic position, and to keep the German navy from menacing the British Isles from new points of the compass.

How willing British political leaders would be to scale back their overseas commitments to maintain an acceptable margin of superiority over the German navy—and prevent a German breakout—was one of the central questions in the Anglo-German naval arms race. The naval race saw the British government weigh the importance of colonial interests against homeland defense. Ultimately, defending home waters against a nearby threat superseded British imperial commitments in the New World and East Asia. British statesmen appeased the United States, which agreed to watch over British interests in return for a withdrawal of the Royal Navy from American waters. They struck up an alliance with Japan, supplementing the Royal Navy forces forward deployed along the Chinese coast. Diplomacy thus freed up warships to concentrate in European waters, confounding German expectations that Britain would never draw down its overseas presence for the sake of naval preponderance at home.[17]

Like Imperial Germany, China finds itself beckoned in two divergent directions by continental and maritime interests, but on a truly transregional scale. Fourteen land powers share terrestrial frontiers with China while six maritime countries together enclose the entire Chinese coastline. Of these twenty neighboring states, six rank among the world's top ten in population, eight rank among the top twenty-five in military forces, and four possess nuclear weapons. As Meng Xiangqing of the National Defense University laments, "China fronts the sea with the land on the back, yet it borders on big powers on land and is encircled by an island chain in the sea. Therefore, although it is a large country that is composed of both the land and the sea, China has never been able to enjoy any benefit from having both the land and the sea."[18] Mahan, who doubted the ability of continental powers to go to sea, would have sympathized with Beijing's plight.

When geopolitically minded Chinese strategists such as Meng gaze across the seas, many see an island barrier obstructing their nation's entry into the oceanic thoroughfare. In the eyes of Chinese analysts, the "first island chain" (第一岛链) running south from the Japanese archipelago to the Philippines compromises the mainland's long coastline, restricting Beijing's nautical activities. A map in the Pentagon's annual *Military Power of the People's Republic of China* reports helps explain the consternation that grips many Chinese thinkers when they look at the map. Japanese territory forms the northern arc of the island chain, which terminates just short of Taiwan, its midpoint and point of closest approach to the mainland coast. The island chain breaks at the Luzon Strait before resuming. It traces southward along the Philippine and Indonesian archipelagoes before looping to the north and terminating off Vietnam.[19] It is worth noting that geography is subjective. Writing in *Guofang Bao*, Jiang Hong and Wei Yuejiang depict the first island chain as sweeping all the way along the Indonesian archipelago to Diego Garcia in a single grand arc.[20] Their choice of Diego Garcia, a British-administered island commonly used by U.S. warplanes, as the western terminus of the island chain can be no coincidence. Extending the island chain into the Indian Ocean puts quite a different gloss on Chinese fears of maritime encirclement and containment.

At a casual glance, let alone the close scrutiny afforded geostrategy by Chinese analysts, it appears that nature has imposed severe handicaps on Chinese access to the sea. Given that China has been able to settle twelve of fourteen land border disputes to the mutual satisfaction of all parties involved, anxieties over perceived encirclement at sea now predominate. Writing in the prestigious journal *China Military Science*, Senior Colonel Feng Liang and Lieutenant Colonel Duan Tingzhi of the Naval Command College depict the apparent island encirclement of China in graphic terms, observing that "these islands obstruct China's reach to the sea. . . . The partially sealed-off nature of China's maritime region has clearly brought about negative effects in China's maritime security. . . . Because of the nature of geography, China can be easily blockaded and cut off from the sea, and Chinese coastal defense forces are difficult to concentrate."[21]

In a pithy summary of Beijing's dilemma, Gong Li, deputy director of the Institute of International Strategy of the Central Party School, finds the "predicament of 'having seas but not the ocean'" fundamentally intolerable for a serious maritime power such as China.[22] Drawing an explicit parallel between Imperial Germany's unenviable position and China's geographic predicament, Jiang Yu states:

The Chinese navy, in its efforts to develop a far-seas fleet, must confront the existence of the island chain as a geographic disadvantage.
If it cannot overcome the island chain blockade, even a very powerful naval force would be unable to contribute much. No matter how
strong a navy becomes, if it cannot first genuinely face the ocean
or resolve obstacles to its exits to the sea, then it is difficult for it to
be considered a far-seas navy. In coping with the problem of island
chain confinement, the Chinese navy cannot blindly develop large
fleet formations for far-seas combat. Otherwise, it can easily follow
Germany's doomed path during World War I when its High Seas
Fleet was sealed off in the near seas. As a consequence, the [German]
fleet that was built through the concentration of massive capital and
national power was unable to exercise its capabilities in the contest
for sea power.[23]

The author astutely identifies a dilemma confronting China. A powerful fleet
may be the only tool that can pierce the island barrier, or "island chain blockade," as he terms it. Yet the risk that a sizable and capable naval force—constructed at great expense—still might not be strong or battleworthy enough
to cruise beyond the island chain at will could deter Beijing from attempting
the buildup in the first place. These writings collectively bespeak an insis-
tent desire to break out of the island-chain straitjacket, ensuring unfettered
Chinese access to vital waters and frustrating what they see as an American
antiaccess strategy in the China seas.

In their search for an opening, geostrategists have fixed their attention
on Taiwan. Much as Wolfgang Wegener believed that Germany needed to
occupy the Faeroes, Shetland, or Iceland to wrench open the gates to the
Atlantic, Chinese thinkers view Taiwan, if or when it is returned to Beijing's
possession, as the lone geographic asset that would grant China direct access
to the Pacific. As Zhan Huayun observes, the East China and Yellow seas
are bounded by Japan's four main islands whereas the South China Sea is
enclosed by the nations of Southeast Asia. As such, "Taiwan's ocean facing
side on the east is the only direct sea entrance to the Pacific."[24] Dubbing the
island the "Gibraltar of the East," Li Yuping depicts it as a "critical strategic thoroughfare" and a "springboard" to the Pacific.[25] As we pointed out in
chapter 2, the highly regarded Chinese volume *Science of Military Strategy*
is emphatic about this. Gong Li graphically describes the geostrategic value
of Taiwan, proclaiming that "if the Taiwan problem is resolved, the door to

the Pacific Ocean will be opened for mainland China, thus breaking the first island chain."[26]

Lin Sixing, a professor from the Research Institute for Southeast Asian Studies at Jinan University, is even more categorical about the importance of Taiwan. Declares Lin, "A China without Taiwan will not be able to break out of the 'first island chain' and be denied entry into the Pacific, so much so that its southeastern territory will be devoid of any security."[27] The southeastern coastal provinces over which the author frets form the epicenter of China's economic miracle. Lin is clearly referring to the risk that potential adversaries, including Taiwan, might threaten Chinese sources of prosperity militarily in order to deter or coerce Beijing.

Beyond Taiwan's value as a point of entry into the Pacific, possession of the island would bestow geostrategic advantages on Beijing, ensuring access to China's historic periphery as well as safe passage for commercial shipping on which the nation's economic fortunes hinge. As Wang Wei states: "If Taiwan is returned, then it is only there that China can build *absolute control* over the adjacent sea areas. From this perspective, Taiwan would undoubtedly be the most reliable thoroughfare into the Pacific Ocean for the Chinese navy. As such, it is not difficult to appreciate the importance of Taiwan in the development of China's near-term maritime strategy"[28] (emphasis added). The notion that the People's Liberation Army Navy (PLA Navy) would attain overbearing Mahanian command by projecting power from Taiwan conforms to the thinking of many Chinese sea-power advocates, as described in chapter 2. In an article laced with terms and concepts that would have delighted Mahan, Jiang Yu describes the island chain as a "shackle" (枷锁) that poses a "serious hidden threat" (心腹之患) to the Chinese navy. He argues in surprisingly candid terms how the "return" of Taiwan to the motherland would benefit the PLA's position. He explains:

> If China can retrieve Taiwan—the mid-section of the island chain— through military or political means, then the midpoint of the entire island chain would be severed in geographic terms. The Chinese fleet and naval aviation units can then use Taiwanese bases to directly enter the Pacific, making Taiwan island a major base and a harbor of refuge favoring both the offense and the defense for China's far-seas fleet. Moreover, the sea and air combat radii from bases on Taiwan would reach the flanks of Japan and the Philippines. The mainland

and Taiwan would form a T-shaped battlefield position able to deter the periphery through semi-encirclement. Recovering Taiwan not only distinctly improves the security environment for China's littoral defense, but it would completely resolve the geographic limits set on Chinese naval power's eastern entry into the Pacific Ocean.[29]

Some observers go even further, depicting Taiwan as a platform from which to attack the U.S. position in the Pacific. They pay particular attention to the "second island chain," which stretches from the Aleutians to Papua New Guinea. Guam, a major hub for American power projection, occupies the center of this outer island chain. The flagship publication of the Chinese navy's political department declares, "Taiwan also controls advantageous routes to the interior waters of the second island chain and the quickest pathways to the open seas. Thus, if we resolve the Taiwan question, it would also represent a fundamental transformation in our ability to break through the second island chain."[30] The author presumably anticipates using Taiwan to launch offensive, perhaps preemptive, strikes against U.S. military forces based on Guam in wartime.

Hyperbole aside, what analytical or comparative value do such views hold? First, the Chinese may have painted an overly pessimistic geostrategic picture for themselves. While the first island chain looks like an imposing barrier on the map, closer examination suggests that Beijing enjoys a menu of options for breaking out of the China seas. The Luzon Strait is one prominent passageway in and out of the South China Sea that catches the eye of Chinese analysts. To Yu Fengliu, the strait represents "a maritime area with extremely high economic, military, and political value worth the weight in gold, a nautical zone boasting important strategic meaning in the Western Pacific, and also a channel for China to go past the first island chain worthy of close attention."[31]

Because the Luzon Strait is at once the largest "gap" in the first island chain and presents complex maritime terrain for the U.S. Navy to control, Yu contends that Chinese air and naval assets could sortie independently through the strait, even without shore-based cover. Such confidence speaks volumes about the strategic significance of Sanya, the newly unveiled naval base on Hainan Island. In times of conflict, it is conceivable that China would feint, staging a breakthrough along the first island chain to distract its adversaries while mounting its main effort elsewhere, perhaps well to the north. The luxury of stretching an adversary's defenses and striking at weak points—a luxury Germans certainly did not enjoy—bestows greater flexibility on Chinese strategists. Those who hype China's poor strategic position, then, are obscuring promising alternatives.

Second, unlike the North Sea, an expanse that held little value for the British, the bodies of water bounded by the first island chain are integral to the globalized order underwritten by U.S. and allied naval power. These waterways convey the lifeblood of economic vitality to all regional economies, including China's. To complicate matters, Asian allies and friends along the island chain play host to U.S. bases and facilities that are critical not only to sustainable, credible American power projection but also to efforts to deter or reverse aggression. American command of the East Asian commons, then, constitutes the sine qua non of regional stability. Indeed, Western-style economic integration and political liberalization would have been impossible across much of Asia absent the international public good of U.S.-supplied maritime security.

Free navigation cannot be sustained for long without the security guarantees that only the U.S. Navy can furnish, as it has done for more than six decades. If China were to challenge U.S. sea control, the United States would find itself compelled to choose between rising to the challenge and abdicating its long-held position. In short, Beijing can induce Washington to commit militarily in ways the Germans simply could not vis-à-vis Great Britain. Three recent events underscore China's ability to draw in the United States, whose assets operate along the Chinese littoral on a daily basis: the 2001 collision between a Chinese fighter jet and a U.S. EP-3 surveillance plane over the South China Sea, a Chinese *Han*-class nuclear attack submarine's breach of Japanese territorial seas in 2004, and Chinese vessels' "harassment" of the survey ship USNS *Impeccable* in 2009, south of Hainan Island. There is nothing dead about the China seas. They are vital to all maritime actors in East Asia.

Third, the proximity of the North Sea to British home waters guaranteed that London would pay close scrutiny to Berlin's nautical ambitions. It would have been next to impossible to separate the German naval threat from British homeland defense. Unsurprisingly, then, the British mounted a vigorous buildup of their own against Germany, maintaining an insurmountable lead in capital ships and barring the gates to the Atlantic commons. In contrast to a Britain "saturated" with sea control, American rule of Asian waters comes neither naturally nor cheaply. On the operational level, forward-deployed U.S. expeditionary forces must conquer the tyranny of geography through the complex web of mutually supporting bases, logistical arrangements, and at-sea sustainment that anchors Washington's presence in the region. Politically speaking, American voters and officials would find it hard to see a remote trend such as China's naval buildup as a mortal threat to the United States.

However imposing, the PLA Navy remains abstract to citizens occupied with daily pursuits. This makes it hard for political leaders in Washington to summon public support for an expedition to defend faraway lands of which Americans know little. Short of a Sino-U.S. cold war, then, it is difficult to imagine how Chinese naval modernization could bring forth an American response approximating Britain's feverish naval construction. This is especially true in light of the ambiguity surrounding the purposes and magnitude of Chinese sea power—ambiguity exacerbated by the vast distances involved and by Chinese efforts to calm misgivings about its maritime rise. The likely mismatch between political determination on each side of the Pacific, which favors Beijing, suggests that Washington may find it increasingly tough to keep a firm grip on the trident.

Fleet Building

Naval strategy is as interactive an enterprise as strategic geography. Germany faced a Great Britain that was not only blessed by geography—First Sea Lord Jacky Fisher christened Britons "God's chosen people" for this reason—but that deployed a "brutally superior" Royal Navy astride German maritime communications.[32] Threats consist of capabilities and intentions, but military strategists generally plan against rivals' capabilities and leave the task of judging intentions to politicians. This division of labor makes sense from combat leaders' standpoint. After all, intentions can change quickly whereas designing and building weaponry takes years in an industrial age. Admiral Tirpitz saw a dominant British Navy standing athwart German SLOCs as intolerable, despite scant evidence of British enmity toward the Reich.[33]

Shortly after assuming duties as state secretary for the navy in 1898, Tirpitz informed Kaiser Wilhelm that the military situation against Britain demanded "battleships in as great a number as possible."[34] For Tirpitz, winning Germany's rightful "place in the sun" of empire meant stationing a fleet of sixty-one capital ships at German seaports by the 1920s.[35] It meant exempting naval procurement from parliamentary oversight and continually upgrading the fleet. Tirpitz wanted automatic replacement of German capital ships after twenty-five years of service life—a figure he lowered to twenty years after 1906, when the Royal Navy commissioned the *Dreadnought*, an all-big-gun, oil-fired, turbine-driven battleship that rendered virtually obsolescent battleships that were on the vanguard of naval technology only a short time before.[36] In a real sense, the naval arms race began anew when the *Dreadnought* slid down the ways.[37]

Tirpitz calculated the optimal size of the High Seas Fleet by studying British martial traditions and the politico-military configuration of late-nineteenth-century Europe. The conclusions he reached were on the flimsy side. He postulated, first, that Germany could accomplish its purposes with a fleet smaller than the Grand Fleet that defended the British Isles. In part this was because he believed Germany could offset numerical inferiority with superior ship design, constructing vessels able to stand up to battle damage and mete out punishment better than their British counterparts.[38] And the navy secretary saw little need to match British numbers. Notes Holger Herwig, "Citing British naval history, Tirpitz argued that Britain would always be the attacker in war and, consequently, would require 33 percent numerical superiority; conversely, Germany would have to construct a fleet only two-thirds the size of the British, a 'risk' fleet . . . that London would hesitate to challenge for fear of losing its global possessions in a naval Cannae in the North Sea."[39]

Cannae was a battle from Roman antiquity in which the Carthaginian general Hannibal's army encircled and annihilated a Roman army—giving European strategic thinkers schooled in the classics part of their vocabulary for debating military affairs. A more recent, and more commonly invoked, indicator of future British behavior was the Battle of Trafalgar, the decisive 1805 clash in which Lord Horatio Nelson's outnumbered fleet crushed a Franco-Spanish fleet off the south Iberian coast. Though he seldom agreed with Tirpitz, Wegener too maintained that British mariners had been on the strategic offensive for centuries, bettering Britain's strategic position and commercial interests in wartime and peacetime alike. This was the essence of British maritime strategy. If so, it appeared reasonable to forecast that the Grand Fleet would stand into the North Sea at the outbreak of war, offering battle on German terms.

The other premise underlying Tirpitz's vision of German naval development was that fellow European powers such as France would bandwagon with Germany to escape British maritime dominance. The High Seas Fleet would form the nucleus of an "alliance fleet" that would match or surpass the Grand Fleet in numbers. But the Kaiser had systematically alienated prospective allies since dismissing Chancellor Bismarck in 1890, making him an unlikely leader for an anti-British naval coalition.[40] Worse from Berlin's standpoint, the Royal Navy supplied the international public good of maritime security, benefiting all seafaring nations. British high-handedness rankled with continental Europeans from time to time, but European leaders preferred the British devil they knew to the German devil they didn't.[41] Great Britain posed too small a menace to bind together an opposing coalition.

For an officer obsessed with a rival navy's capabilities, Tirpitz was conspicuously oblivious to the diplomatic signals his own helter-skelter shipbuilding efforts sent. Tirpitz intended to threaten the Royal Navy in home waters, so German shipwrights fitted German vessels with heavier armor, offering greater protection against British gunfire. Rugged construction added weight, consuming additional fuel and cutting their range. Since German battleships' cruising radius was too short to let them operate beyond the North Sea, it was plain to British observers that the High Seas Fleet was aimed squarely at Britain. Indeed, Paul Kennedy aptly describes the German battle fleet as a "sharp knife, held gleaming and ready only a few inches away from the jugular vein" of the premier sea power of the day.[42] This was not a force built for colonial and SLOC defense but for decisive battle in European waters. Self-defeating though such behavior was, declares Herwig, Tirpitz's strategic ideas hardened into "dogma, inviolable and sacrosanct," by World War I.[43]

Alfred Thayer Mahan hints at the dangers of obfuscating about maritime strategy. In commentary on Berlin's 1900 Navy Law, Mahan observes that the law set forth a principle that was to govern German naval development "over a term of many years," namely "that it was essential to possess a navy of such force that to incur hostilities with it would jeopardize the supremacy of the greatest naval power" of the age.[44] This was lawmakers' way of designating Great Britain as the primary foe and as the benchmark for German shipbuilding while remaining coquettish about the true purposes of the High Seas Fleet. Without "transparency" (to use today's parlance for openness in large institutions) about the motives for German naval armament, the British were forced to judge German intentions by German capabilities. A fleet of short-range, heavily gunned, thickly armored warships stationed just across the North Sea could have only one purpose: to dispute the Royal Navy's control of European waters. Net assessment, then, was the prime mover for the British naval buildup.

Today, both the United States and China are guilty of this kind of evasiveness to one degree or another. As chapter 8 will show, the American sea services steadfastly refuse to name an opponent in their 2007 "Cooperative Strategy for 21st Century Seapower," the most authoritative statement of how they see the world and the proper strategic responses to it. By agitating for a big, high-tech fleet while insisting the United States currently faces no conventional naval threat, the strategy forces Chinese naval strategists to read between the lines—and to devise their own strategy based on U.S. capabilities rather than official statements of intent.

The reverse is true. The Pentagon hectors the People's Liberation Army (PLA) ceaselessly over its lack of transparency, questioning the purposes of the impressive fleet China is assembling. And indeed, Beijing is prone to use such formulas as "a certain country" to refer to the United States, rather than frankly stating its views. Washington, too, must plan against Chinese capabilities since evidence about Chinese intentions remains nebulous. Fudan University scholar Shen Dingli frankly declares that "we compete." One could wish for more of Shen's brand of outspokenness in Sino-American relations. Theodore Roosevelt wisely advised statesmen to speak softly in diplomacy, but by that he did not mean they ought to dissemble. Candor is a virtue— even, or perhaps especially, with prospective opponents.

It is unfair to condemn German thought or actions without identifying strategic alternatives that were open to Berlin. As noted earlier, the German naval command made no effort to outflank Britain in a geographic sense, improving Germany's strategic position. Nor did the naval leadership apply much effort to developing an asymmetric strategy that employed new technology. Early on, in fact, Tirpitz ruled out the strategy of the lesser naval power championed by French thinkers since midcentury. In essence, a "*jeune école*" strategy relied on cruiser warfare overseas rather than a head-on confrontation with a superior fleet composed of "capital ships."[45] For Mahan, "the backbone and real power of any navy are the vessels which, by due proportion of defensive and offensive powers, are capable of taking and giving hard knocks."[46] That meant either battleships or battlecruisers, the battleships' faster, more lightly armored (and more vulnerable) brethren. Cruiser warfare, in short, was an asymmetric strategy that assailed an enemy's maritime traffic while avoiding that enemy's strength—a dominant battle line.

This sort of indirection was anathema to those intent on decisive fleet encounters.[47] Partisans of the *jeune école* presumably would have applauded the asymmetric means under development in various countries during the years preceding World War I. The German navy, however, did not build its first submarine until 1906, largely because Tirpitz feared that undersea warfare would siphon resources away from battleship construction. Mine warfare and torpedo boats lagged as well. As a result, Germany entered into a symmetrical arms race it could not win at acceptable cost, and it shunned unorthodox means that might have let Berlin dispute vital expanses. In short, its delay in exploring new technologies such as U-boats, mines, and torpedoes represented a major lost opportunity for the German naval command.[48]

Steeped in China's sparse maritime tradition, its weakness at sea during the post–World War II period, the legacy of Mao Zedong's guerrilla strategy, and the influence of Soviet naval doctrine, the PLA Navy embraced a minimalist posture from its inception.[49] For decades, the Chinese navy was considered a minor player against foreign invasion, at most an adjunct to the ground forces. The Chinese navy, accordingly, consisted of submarines, torpedo boats, and frigates that hugged the coast. Not until the late 1970s, amid Deng Xiaoping's reform and opening campaign, did Beijing begin to articulate a more expansive vision of sea power. Urged on by PLA Navy commander Admiral Liu Huaqing, the Chinese leadership directed the navy to develop offensive capabilities for forward defense of the mainland, both within and beyond the first island chain.

Even so, the service's brown water mentality—that is, its ingrained habit of thinking in terms of defending waters just offshore—and force structure persisted well into the early 1990s. To this day, the PLA Navy devotes substantial resources to missile boats useful for coastal defense, albeit in stealthier, more lethal forms.[50] This apparent handicap in strategy is in fact a blessing in disguise. Unlike Imperial Germany, which rushed into building a top-heavy naval force structure that still proved no match for its main antagonist, the Chinese have approached sea power in a methodical, sequential manner. Indeed, the defensive-mindedness of early PLA naval doctrine—admittedly a product of necessity rather than choice—applied a catalyst for imaginative thinking about how to beat a technologically superior foe at sea.

Chinese planners long assumed, correctly and realistically, that the PLA Navy would fight from a position of weakness should it be deployed against the United States. Accordingly, they sought to apply Chinese comparative strengths against critical American vulnerabilities, evening the odds. PLA strategists hit upon what the Pentagon terms an "antiaccess strategy," covered in detail in chapter 4. Antiaccess strategy combines military and nonmilitary measures in an effort to delay the arrival of U.S. and allied forces in a particular Asian theater of operations, preclude or disrupt the use of regional bases that are critical to sustaining U.S. military operations, and hold U.S. power-projection assets as far from Chinese shores as possible.[51]

By selectively developing inexpensive, readily available weapons systems such as submarines and cruise missiles (or purchasing them abroad), and by tailoring operational concepts to China's local circumstances, the PLA may have already put itself in position to execute an antiaccess strategy. If so, Beijing could contest American command of the commons, in effect creating a no-go zone for U.S. forces along the East Asian seaboard. Disputed command, either real or perceived, weakens American political will and forecloses certain U.S. military options. It also frees up maneuver room for the Chinese, improving the likelihood that the PLA can stage a breakout from the first island chain under the protective umbrella of antiaccess forces. Shackled by geography and relatively short-range weaponry, Imperial Germany enjoyed no such strategic option in the North Sea.

Beyond the potential operational advantages, Chinese investments in access denial promise flexibility and efficiency in terms of force structure and costs. Until very recently, Beijing eschewed an overtly symmetrical buildup of naval forces, including prohibitively expensive big-deck aircraft carriers. In contrast to Tirpitz, the Chinese seem unfazed by lopsided force ratios since antiaccess involves qualitatively different measures of effectiveness. At the same time, the PLA Navy's refusal to run a one-to-one arms race has removed the pressure from the Chinese naval command to compete numerically. This affords the navy the luxury of testing and refining its surface and subsurface combatants, producing a new ship class every few years without committing to serial production. This leisurely but fruitful process is ideal for fleet experimentation.

Strategic Will

As Carl von Clausewitz puts it, war—or, we might add, any competitive human endeavor—involves an interactive clash of wills. Drawing on British maritime history, Alfred Thayer Mahan pronounced "national character" and the "character of the government" two critical determinants of a nation's suitability for sea power.[52] For Wolfgang Wegener, the final element of sea power—the enabler for the fleet's quest for strategic position—was a nation's "strategic will" to the sea. Wegener evidently imbibed this concept from Friedrich Nietzsche's writings on the will to power. The German thinker's appraisal of British maritime culture helps explain why German shipbuilding drew forth an indefatigable response from Britons: "The English have the sea in their veins owing to their centuries-long [naval] tradition; and [sea strategy] has been instinctively ingrained in their senses, just as we have absorbed the traditions of land warfare."[53]

But "as the lost war showed," the German navy "remained intellectually a coastal navy" despite its tactical proficiency.[54] This cultural mismatch implied that Germany was unprepared to undertake an effort of the same magnitude and duration as Great Britain, which made the conscious political choice to uphold its maritime preponderance, whatever the cost.[55] And indeed, declared wartime prime minister David Lloyd George, "Every Englishman would spend his last penny to preserve British supremacy at sea." Winston Churchill, who served as first lord of the Admiralty starting in 1911, may have put it best: "With every rivet that von Tirpitz drove into his ships of war, he united British opinion throughout wide circles of the most powerful people in every walk of life and in every part of the Empire. The hammers that clanged at Kiel and Wilhelmshaven were forging the coalition of nations by which Germany was to be resisted and finally overthrown."[56] In short, Britons' will to the sea should have given German leaders pause. They should have reconsidered Alfred von Tirpitz's judgments of British operational traditions as well. German commanders' reading of British history led them to exaggerate the Royal Navy's lust for decisive battle. As we have seen, German fleet-building and strategy were predicated on Tirpitz's assumption that the British battle fleet would assume a "rigorous offensive" at the outbreak of war, sallying into the North Sea in search of an apocalyptic fleet action.

With the partial exception of the Battle of Jutland, however, the Royal Navy wisely forewent a new Trafalgar. While Germans expected a sea fight for its own sake, British commanders refused battle that did not advance British strategic purposes. The Royal Navy husbanded its assets, imposed a distant blockade on the North Sea, and exercised the sea control it already held. British commanders saw no reason to fight for what they already possessed, so the onus fell on the High Seas Fleet to challenge its nemesis for command of important waters.[57]

In short, Berlin did enough with its shipbuilding program to provoke a determined response from the British people, government, and navy, setting off a process of interaction that contributed to the outbreak of war. But the German leadership balked at the massive investment required for Germany to wrest naval superiority from Britain. The opportunity costs in terms of land defense were presumably too steep, and German commanders were curiously reticent about taking the strategic initiative at sea. A shortfall in strategic thought about the sea was partly responsible for this, as was German leaders' whimsical attitude toward sea power. If the fleet represents a flight of fancy, then dismal strategic results are apt to follow.[58]

Unlike Berlin, Beijing suffers from no such leadership deficit. China has prudently nurtured the national will and developed the naval capabilities to support its long-term naval ambitions without attracting unwanted attention or countermeasures. Faithful to Deng Xiaoping's decades-old injunction to maintain a low international profile, Beijing has framed its maritime interests and endeavors in strictly defensive terms.[59] Since its inception over a quarter-century ago, the concept of "offshore defense," which instructs the nautical services to employ highly offensive operations and tactics to obtain strategically defensive aims, has remained the cornerstone of Chinese naval doctrine.[60] In Orwellian fashion, accordingly, Quan Jinfu of the Naval Command Academy subtly couches his call for enhanced power projection into the Pacific and Indian oceans in doublespeak: "The Chinese navy . . . will inevitably develop into a formidable maritime deterrence force that possesses high seas defensive operation capabilities. This navy will be able to effectively conduct strategic defensive operations and counter-threat struggles in the vast strategic defense depths to stop or strike at any one who [dares] to invade or seize China's strategic interests."[61] How much strategic depth analysts such as Quan covet is anyone's guess. The point is that his studied understatement contrasts starkly with the reckless posturing that typified Imperial Germany. Indeed, Beijing's offshore defense doctrine has deprived the United States and China's neighbors of overt evidence of a Chinese threat, and thus of any pretext for alarm or vigorous countermeasures. For example, while Beijing defines its maritime objectives in fairly sweeping terms, in effect claiming its economic exclusive zones as territorial seas, Chinese diplomats uniformly insist that disputes be resolved by peaceful means. To date this approach has tempered the potential for overreaction in Asian capitals and Washington.

At the same time, policymakers at the highest levels of government have publicly and aggressively sought to harness Chinese national will for maritime ventures. None other than President Hu Jintao has spearheaded efforts to galvanize the PLA Navy and the public at large. At the tenth Chinese Communist Party (CCP) Congress of the PLA Navy in December 2006, Hu exhorted the service to "forge a powerful people's navy that meets the demands of carrying out our army's historic missions in the new century" and to "spur the all-round transformation of navy building in line with the demands of the revolution in military affairs with Chinese characteristics."[62]

According to three scholars at the Dalian Naval Academy, Hu is keen on "raising the offshore comprehensive operational capability of the navy within the first island chain" and "raising mobile operational capability on the distant sea."[63]

In other words, the top leadership is casting its seaward gaze much farther into the distance. In *Qiushi*, an official journal of the Chinese Communist Party's Central Committee, Admiral Wu Shengli, the commander of the PLA Navy, echoes and amplifies President Hu's directive, proclaiming that China is an "oceanic nation" whose bequest from nature includes a long coastline, many islands, and a massive sea area to protect. Wu recalls the dynastic neglect of the oceans and the century of humiliation that followed, during which Western encroachment without exception came oversea. With the resurgence of China, the admiral believes it is high time to reverse past misfortunes, achieving "the great revitalization of the Chinese nation [中华民族伟大复兴]" and fulfilling the nation's maritime destiny.[64] The interplay the admiral depicts between destiny and choice for the future of Chinese sea power would have been instantly recognizable to Mahan. Simply put, his article represents a masterful effort to reorient the national consciousness toward the seas.

China's naval capabilities are an equally impressive benchmark of national will. Over the past decade, China has purchased from abroad or produced an array of naval assets suitable for contesting sea control within and beyond the first island chain. As the PLA Navy retires obsolete submarines en masse, it has introduced three new classes of stealthy diesel-electric submarines. The sudden appearance of the *Yuan*-class submarine in 2004 reportedly took the U.S. intelligence community by surprise. China also publicly unveiled its second-generation nuclear attack boats and fleet ballistic-missile submarines, presumably as a deterrent signal. In addition to constructing new platforms, the Chinese have devoted substantial energy to honing the operational art of undersea warfare. One worrisome indicator was the 2006 incident when a *Song*-class submarine reportedly surfaced within torpedo range of the U.S. aircraft carrier *Kitty Hawk*, which was conducting an exercise. The Office of Naval Intelligence, furthermore, revealed that the rate of Chinese submarine patrols doubled between 2007 and 2008 (albeit from a low operating tempo).[65]

In the domain of surface warfare, China has commissioned four modern warship classes since 1999, including vessels equipped with advanced radars and computers reportedly comparable to the U.S. Navy's Aegis combat-systems suite, the latest in American air-defense wizardry. The PLA Navy concurrently added to its inventory *Sovremennyy*-class destroyers purchased from Russia. While tonnage is at best a crude indicator of capability, the new combatants all displace at least six thousand tons, two-thirds the displacement of U.S. *Arleigh Burke*–class guided missile destroyers. Media reports that the PLA Navy intends to construct two or more medium-sized, conventionally powered aircraft carriers—reports more or less confirmed by Chinese officials in early 2009—have spurred a flurry of international commentary.[66] Speculation about Chinese interest in fielding ballistic missiles capable of striking surface ships at sea has alarmed policymakers. Indeed, this prospect dominated discussions at a 2008 conference convened at the Naval War College to examine Chinese aerospace capabilities.[67] (We return to this subject in depth in chapter 5.)

After condescending to Chinese seafarers for decades, retired and active-duty U.S. Navy officers now pay increasing—if grudging—respect to the PLA Navy's impressive modernization program. In material terms, the Chinese are clearly on the march. What of American strategic will to the sea? Alfred Thayer Mahan fretted over his countrymen's indifference to seagoing endeavors, even during the United States' ascent to maritime prominence. He suggested that, far from following in British footsteps, the United States was a pleasant, resource-rich, continent-spanning nation that might keep its attentions fixed on North America. In this, Mahan speculated, the United States was more like France than Britain. Their strategic geography and the British Isles' poor resource endowment had driven Britons to the sea in search of trade and prosperity while Frenchmen could provide for themselves from their own resources. Or, America might be like the seventeenth-century Dutch Republic, another power that vied with Great Britain for maritime supremacy yet proved too tightfisted to fund adequate naval preparedness in peacetime.

America's seagoing culture, fretted Mahan, might be a veneer—however fundamental it was to the politics, society, and culture of the British mother country.[68] If so, public support for a vibrant U.S. Navy could prove fleeting absent an unmistakable seaborne threat. Today, as in Mahan's day, America's strategic will manifests itself in numbers of ships, aircraft, and combat systems. Rising costs have driven the size of the fleet inexorably downward. At 282 active ships, less than half the number of the (almost) 600-ship Navy of the 1980s, the U.S. Navy is the smallest it has been since World War I.[69] Few scholars or naval officers believe the Navy will manage to rebuild to the

313 ships called for in its shipbuilding plans. While individual vessels pack far more punch than their forebears, quantity still has a quality of its own—especially as prospective antagonists such as the PLA Navy begin to close the qualitative gap. It is here that the U.S. Navy is standing into danger.

Declining numbers have prodded the U.S. sea services down the intellectual pathway once trodden by Jacky Fisher and Winston Churchill. The 2007 U.S. Maritime Strategy declares that the U.S. Navy remains the two-ocean fleet it has been since World War II. But, whereas previous strategies focused on the Atlantic and the Pacific, the sea services have shifted their energies to the western Pacific and the Indian Ocean.[70] In other words, America's maritime strategic gaze is now fixed on Asia. Like Britain a century ago, the United States seems to have concluded that it must concentrate in vital theaters, scaling back secondary commitments. In the eyes of naval leaders, apparently, the Atlantic and the Mediterranean are expanses that can be entrusted to European protectors. It nonetheless remains far from clear that the United States will reach the same conscious political choice Great Britain did, continuing to invest in a predominant fleet. If not, China could find itself in a strategic position the Kaiser's Germany would envy.

CHINA'S FORTUNATE STRATEGIC POSITION

In the final analysis, the three parameters we have used to appraise China's seaward turn—strategic geography, the fleet, and strategic will to the sea—indicate that Beijing is far better positioned to fulfill its nautical aspirations than Berlin was a century ago. That the sea power, Great Britain, ultimately prevailed over the land power, Imperial Germany, is no cause for complacency. Despite the superficial similarity between Germany and the PRC, the differences between the two cases are more enlightening than the similarities. First, the seas washing against East Asian shores are worth defending for all claimants to sea power in the region. The Yellow, East China, and South China seas are not dead seas in the sense the North Sea was for Germany. SLOCs pass up and down the Asian seaboard, providing the most economical route for Indian Ocean raw materials to reach Northeast Asian seaports, and thence to power the Chinese, Japanese, and Korean economies.

Unlike the German naval command, the PLA Navy does not need to exert itself to improve China's strategic position. The initiative already rests with Beijing. It can oblige the U.S.-Japan alliance to defend freedom of navigation along the mainland. To be sure, it is important not to overplay the importance of the China seas. Some knowledgeable analysts question

Taiwan's value to China and to the United States, pointing out that the island only extends Beijing's defense perimeter roughly one hundred miles offshore and maintaining that shipping bound for Japan or South Korea can detour around it at little extra expense or inconvenience. By this reasoning, they assert that the American position in Asia would also be entirely unaffected should the mainland regain control of the island. U.S. naval operations and associated capacity to command regional waters would continue unimpeded.

Even if true, such analyses slight alliance politics. Japan is acutely sensitive to maritime security to its south. For one thing, regaining Taiwan would leave Chinese and Japanese waters adjoining each another not only in the East China Sea but also along the southern tier, where the southernmost Japanese islands are almost in sight of the northern coast of Taiwan. During the 1996 Taiwan Strait crisis, the PLA lobbed missiles into waters near Taiwan's two main ports in an attempt to influence the Taiwanese presidential election. One of the "test" missiles reportedly landed within sixty kilometers of Yonaguni, at the southern end of the Ryukyu island chain.[71]

The missile-test incident reminded Japanese policymakers how difficult it would be to disentangle Japan from any future cross-strait conflagration while also forewarning Tokyo how uncomfortably close China would be to Japanese-held territory should Taiwan fall into Chinese hands. Indeed, the "day after Taiwan" would strip Japan of a buffer zone in place since it wrested Formosa from the Qing dynasty following the 1895 Sino-Japanese War. A century-long geostrategic advantage would evanesce. For another, Beijing would presumably claim an exclusive economic zone (EEZ) around the island. If recent experience is any guide, Beijing would start asserting legal prerogatives similar to the ones it claims in other EEZs in a bid to transform these waters into de facto sovereign waters. Extending the Chinese periphery three hundred miles offshore—not one hundred—would complicate Japanese maritime defense considerably while raising costs for shippers forced to detour around Chinese-claimed seas.

To complicate matters further, the disputed Senkaku/Diaoyutai islands, to which Tokyo, Beijing, and Taipei lay claim, are sandwiched between the three contestants. Some Chinese strategists appear to believe the Senkakus would no longer be defensible for the Japanese if Taiwan fell under Beijing's control. As one analyst states: "If Taiwan is in our hands, then hostile countries would quite possibly have to reconsider their policies. If our country establishes powerful naval and air forces on Taiwan . . . then those bases would significantly increase China's combat and deterrent power. . . . Under such circumstances, it is possible that the Diaoyu island problem would develop in favor of our country."[72] This observation conforms to the notion that Chinese possession of Taiwan would enable Beijing to turn Japan's southern maritime flank. Tokyo cannot but take an interest in the islands' fate, and the transpacific alliance would embroil Washington in this reconfigured Asia as well. In other words, even if we concede (for the sake of discussion) that Taiwan is unimportant to the United States strategically or operationally, as many Sinologists insist, its centrality to Tokyo's sense of security cannot be so easily dismissed. The value Japan attaches to Taiwan will remain a major component of U.S. regional strategy unless Washington is willing to discount Tokyo's interests, gambling that Japan will greet the day after Taiwan with a shrug. Losing such a wager would likely spell the end of the U.S.-Japanese alliance, the lynchpin of U.S. preeminence in Asia for the past six decades.

Second, the United States is not "saturated" with command of the sea, to recall Admiral Wegener's evocative choice of words, to nearly the same degree Britain was vis-à-vis Germany. While its fleet remains superior for the present, the U.S. Navy cannot bar Chinese access to the high seas with the same ease as the fin de siècle Royal Navy. Neither the United States nor Japan holds positions comparable in strategic worth to the Scotland-Norway gap or the English Channel, from which it can seal off Chinese shipping from sea communications. Chinese warships enjoy ready egress into the China seas from multiple seaports along the coast. Jianggezhuang and Lushun are two bases that provide the North Sea Fleet access to the Yellow and East China seas; the East Sea Fleet is based at ports such as Ningbo and Zhoushan, and the South Sea Fleet operates out of a forward base at Sanya, on Hainan Island. These sites (and many more) easily meet the Mahanian standard for maritime access—furnishing multiple outlets to the high seas. Beijing's maritime-geographic predicament is not nearly so bleak as Berlin's.

Third, China holds the advantage (over the United States) of proximity to the theater. To borrow MIT professor Barry Posen's terms, China is ideally positioned to mount a "contested zone," leveraging nearby bases and manpower, shore-based armaments, and superior knowledge of the physical, social, and cultural terrain to do serious damage to approaching, even though superior, U.S. forces.[73] Transpacific distances attenuate not only American power but also, presumably, the value the American government and people attach to the defense of U.S. interests off Asian shores. By ratcheting up the costs of military engagements in Asia, Beijing can hope to deter or dissuade Washington from acting in ways inimical to Chinese interests.

Here, the likeness to the Anglo-German case breaks down, but the disparities are illuminating. Geography placed the antagonists close to each other during the pre–World War I naval arms race, whereas thousands of miles of ocean separate China from the United States. The U.S. territory closest to East Asia is Guam, in the second island chain; nearly five thousand miles separate Honolulu from Shanghai. From a geographic standpoint, the analogy between Japan and Britain is a far closer fit. The Japanese home islands lie some one hundred miles off the Chinese coast, depending on the latitude. Indeed, Japan constitutes the northern arc of the first island chain, meaning that the Chinese defense perimeter runs along the Japanese archipelago. And unlike China and Japan, Germany had no distant antagonist to worry about—and Great Britain no distant ally to enlist—comparable to the United States.

If Japan is playing the role of Britain and China the role of Imperial Germany, the asymmetries of power sharply favor the land power over the sea power. By the six indices of Mahanian sea power—geographic position, physical conformation, territorial extent, population, national character, and the nature of the government—it seems abundantly clear that the Japanese "whale" is not preponderant over the Chinese "elephant" in East Asia. To make the analogy between the two cases fit more closely, we must think of the U.S.-Japan alliance as a strategic unit, but even then, the strongest partner is located farthest from the arena—introducing strategic asymmetries that did not bedevil British officials and commanders formulating a rejoinder to German naval might.

Fourth, it would be a simple matter (relative to the High Seas Fleet in its heyday) for the PLA Navy to take the strategic offensive in nearby seas. If Chinese naval development keeps tracking along its upward trajectory in fleet size and quality, and if the U.S. Navy keeps dwindling in numbers, the PLA Navy may ultimately accumulate "overbearing power" within the first island chain. It will command the China seas in Mahanian terms. In the meantime, Beijing can hope to deny the U.S.-Japan alliance access to these waters for long enough to realize political goals like wresting Taiwan from its inhabitants. If so, it will be able to wring the initiative from the U.S. Navy in a way the High Seas Fleet never could, compelling America and its allies to fight for maritime access they currently take for granted.

Imagine, for example, a successful Chinese effort to push the contested zone out to the rim of the Ryukyu island chain during a cross-strait crisis or conflict. The uncomfortable proximity of a no-go area to Kadena Air Force Base, the hub of U.S. air power in the western Pacific, would impose enormous strains on U.S. and Japanese air operations carried on from Okinawan airfields. So long as the United States maintains its commitments to Japan, South Korea, and Taiwan, consequently, the strategic momentum will reside with Beijing.

Fifth, from the outset Chinese naval planners wisely took an incremental approach to fleet building, starting out with the *jeune école* approach before moving on to more advanced, more Mahanian platforms and weaponry. This was political necessity during the Mao Zedong era. The CCP chairman forbade construction of a blue water fleet and, during the Great Leap Forward and Cultural Revolution of the 1950s–1970s, purged the officer corps of much of its expertise and ingenuity in his mania for revolutionary purity. In its founding years, accordingly, the PLA Navy contented itself with lower-end capabilities such as minelayers, missile-firing patrol boats, and diesel submarines. Unlike Tirpitz, the PLA Navy command did not succumb to the allure of extravagant, budget-busting ships such as nuclear-powered aircraft carriers. By Chinese commanders' logic, a *jeune école* fleet provided a sound basis for a fleet more symmetrical with that of the United States, should Beijing someday see the need for direct naval competition.

Sixth, despite the comparatively favorable strategic setting, Chinese officials and analysts evince a will to sea power far more relentless than the on-again, off-again commitment exhibited by the erratic Wilhelmine German regime. As Mahan observed, sea power in an authoritarian state depends on the steadfastness of autocratic leaders—something in short supply in Imperial Germany but not in the People's Republic of China. Political support for the fleet can be withdrawn at any time, as it was in France under the rule of the Sun King, Louis XIV. The PRC leadership has displayed impressive determination where Kaiser Wilhelm II vacillated, and Chinese interests depend on the sea far more than German interests ever did. Nor does Beijing need the navy to bind together a new nation. Germany had no national identity or maritime heritage to speak of, so German leaders grasped at sea power as a unifying force. China has a venerable seagoing past. It can look past the neglect of the Qing Dynasty to a golden age when the China seas comprised part of a Sinocentric maritime order in Asia, and Chinese fleets roamed regional seaways at will. In all likelihood, then, the Chinese quest for sea power will have more staying power than the German bid for a place in the sun. Permissive surroundings, burgeoning resources, and strategic resolve will make China a more formidable competitor at sea than Imperial Germany ever was.

And finally, Chinese political and military leaders have demonstrated remarkable diplomatic prudence compared to the mercurial Kaiser and his lieutenants. Beijing has managed its maritime rise carefully to avoid setting in motion a cycle of naval challenge and response like the one that drove Anglo-German enmity. Chinese officials have carefully situated their nautical ascent within an inoffensive, even Bismarckian diplomatic strategy. Chinese diplomacy is replete with phrases like "peaceful rise," "peaceful development," and "responsible stakeholder," designed to convince fellow Asian powers—including the United States—that Beijing has embraced the liberal, U.S.-led maritime order. As chapter 7 will show, Beijing has tailored its message to impress upon foreign audiences that China is an inherently benevolent power. Unlike predatory imperial powers of the past, it can be trusted with a powerful navy and the geostrategic leverage a big fleet imparts.

SOME PRELIMINARY CONCLUSIONS

On the whole, the skill, resourcefulness, and fortitude with which China has managed its sea-power enterprise far outshine the clumsy efforts of Imperial Germany. This finding is at once new and startling in that it defies both optimists' and pessimists' clean-cut predictions as to whether China will follow the Bismarckian or the Wilhelmine path. That China would plunge recklessly into self-defeating naval antagonism with the United States is doubtful. But if it does take a Wilhelmine turn at some point in the future, it will have far more freedom than Germany ever did to impose strains on its seagoing rivals. And even if Beijing abides unswervingly by Bismarckian foreign policy principles, it can afford to exercise less restraint in the maritime domain than the Iron Chancellor could toward the European great powers. What we have undertaken here is clearly a thought experiment. *The Rise of Great Powers* notwithstanding, it remains far from clear whether China has distilled meaningful guidance from poring over the German experience. But the comparison is worthwhile in its own right since inquiring into the rise and fall of German sea power elucidates the challenges and opportunities facing continental nations that venture into great waters.

One final thought: It is easy to wave around the few examples in world history when great land powers failed to transform themselves into maritime powers, and thus to pronounce China's seaward experiment a failure even before the facts are in. We hope the comparative historical analysis presented here gives pause to those inclined to overly confident prophecies. Chinese maritime history may rhyme with—but will not repeat—that of Imperial Germany.

CHAPTER 4

Fleet Tactics with Chinese Characteristics

Having dwelt at some length on the more ethereal aspects of Chinese maritime strategy, accentuating geopolitics, historical precedent, and strategic thought, we now inquire into the mechanics of how China will put its strategy into practice. China's strategic surroundings provide Beijing far greater liberty than the Kaiser's Berlin to pursue a vibrant maritime strategy, even within a foreign policy premised on Bismarckian self-restraint. In the interim, the concept of sea denial furnishes perhaps the best indicator of how China will manage its nautical surroundings until it can assemble a fleet able to stand toe-to-toe with the finest fleets likely to appear in Asian waters—assuming Beijing deems the outlays needed to construct a dominant fleet worthwhile given competing priorities such as internal economic development.

A sea-denial navy frankly admits its inferiority to prospective antagonists while refusing to admit defeat. It does not flee vital expanses or resign itself to passive defense. In the late 1990s, two prominent Sinologists declared that China's innate weakness at sea forced it to shelter passively within the first island chain, waging a strategy of "protracted defensive resistance." U.S. naval supremacy was too stifling for more forceful measures to succeed.[1] We dissent. A sea-denial force works around its weaknesses and exploits such advantages as it does enjoy. Its objective is to clear rival navies out of designated waters—or to deter them from entering in the first place—for a finite interval, until the nation's strategic objectives are in hand.[2] Generally speaking, then, sea denial is a strategically defensive strategy prosecuted by inferior naval powers through offensive means. The People's Liberation Army Navy (PLA Navy) will face this strategic predicament for the foreseeable future, but it will stay on the operational and tactical offensive.

The hybrid offensive–defensive style of combat conforms philosophically both to Mao Zedong's concept of "active defense," which yokes offensive means to defensive ends, and to Alfred Thayer Mahan's dictum that even lesser navies can impose local command of important waters.[3] The Chinese military possesses, is procuring, or plans to acquire systems designed to make the seas and skies adjoining the Asian mainland no-go territory for any opponent. Beijing has lavishly purchased arms from Russia since the early 1990s. It has bolstered its domestic defense industry at the same time, allowing a variety of indigenous weaponry to be fielded. The infusion of new platforms and systems, supplemented by the advent of a more professional, more battleworthy corps of mariners, has produced a leap in offensive PLA combat power.[4]

To name a few weapons systems that have entered service in recent years, modern diesel submarines—difficult to detect, track, and target in shallow offshore waters—have slid down the ways at Chinese shipyards or been purchased from Russian suppliers in significant numbers. Destroyers equipped with sophisticated radar suites (purportedly comparable to the U.S. Aegis combat system), antiship missiles, and air-defense missiles increasingly form the backbone of the Chinese surface fleet. PLA Navy surface groups' chances of withstanding long-range missile or air bombardment are brightening. This is doubly true so long as the fleet operates within range of shore-based cover, as PLA Navy forces typically do.

The range and accuracy of shore-based assets are growing, extending the PLA Navy's combat radius commensurate with Chinese views of the importance of the offshore island chains. Indeed, China may be on the brink of rendering a strategic concept condemned by Captain Mahan—the "fortress-fleet" tethered to shore fire support—viable for the first time. Writing of the Russian Navy's dismal performance against Japan in 1905, Mahan faulted the Russian naval command for this "radically erroneous" way of conducting affairs.[5] This may no longer hold true. If Chinese land forces can hoist a protective umbrella over the near seas, PLA Navy units will be able to range freely within the waters Beijing deems important without leaving the protective cover of shore defenses.

Under this aegis, defense will increasingly blur into offense, even eastward of the first island chain. Advanced ground-based air-defense systems, capable naval fighter/attack aircraft, long-range cruise missiles, and even a ballistic missile reportedly able to find and attack vessels on the high seas are central to China's military modernization effort.[6] (Chapter 5 covers the antiship ballistic missile and its ramifications.) If the Chinese package these assets wisely and develop the requisite tactical proficiency, they will gain confidence in their ability to deter or defeat any foreign power bold enough to attempt hostile entry into nearby waters or airspace.[7]

China's continent-scale geography is an invaluable asset to the PLA Navy's sea-denial strategy, furnishing plentiful sites for coastal bases. Indeed, emerging military capabilities are explicitly designed to strike at targets in littoral sea areas from bases on the mainland. And as range improves, shore defenses can be positioned farther inland, employing China's deep continental interior as a safe haven from which to mete out punishment against intruding forces along the coastline.[8] This haven serves the purely military purpose of buffering People's Liberation Army (PLA) assets against attack. A PLA that exploits the mainland's vast strategic depth can compel enemy forces to enter the combat range of its weaponry, accepting battle on China's political, geographic, and military terms. Such a strategy would have found favor with Mao Zedong, who famously urged his followers to draw enemies deep into Chinese territory before striking a devastating counterblow.[9]

Just as important, defending from deep inland dares an opponent to act against the mainland. If U.S. forces struck at, say, Chinese antiship missile sites located well inland—especially if these sites adjoined populated areas, where collateral damage would be a risk—political sympathies would favor Beijing not only among key audiences in China but elsewhere in Asia and in the international community. The United States would risk escalating a limited naval conflict to full-blown war against China, its leading trading partner and a fellow permanent member of the UN Security Council. The repercussions of such a fight would vastly outweigh the presumably modest strategic goals at stake for Washington. The chances of Washington's climbing down from a dispute would improve—increasing the likelihood of China's winning without an actual exchange of fire. Fusing offense with defense, then, is eminently in keeping with Chinese strategic traditions. This approach constitutes the core of Chinese fleet tactics.

MASSED, DISPERSED, OR SEQUENTIAL TACTICS?

Suppose things do come to a Sino-American showdown. Captain Wayne Hughes supplies U.S. Navy mariners a primer for sea combat in Asia. As mentioned before, the PLA, America's most likely foe, is increasingly able to integrate surface, subsurface, and aerial warfare into a strong defense against seaborne threats to China.[10] The strategic environment in maritime Asia is changing at breakneck speed, and the United States must keep pace. The U.S.

armed forces must adapt their own methods and weaponry if they hope to preserve the maritime supremacy that has served U.S. interests—and those of the region at large—so well since 1945.

Hughes' *Fleet Tactics* (1986) and its successor, *Fleet Tactics and Coastal Combat* (2000) constitute a baseline for analyzing the challenges posed by Chinese antiship tactics. However useful his treatise, though, it cannot stand alone. This is no indictment. These works aspire to school tacticians in a variety of settings and against a variety of potential antagonists. Indeed, in *Fleet Tactics* Hughes describes his purpose as "to illustrate the processes—the dynamics—of naval combat" rather than to foresee how particular contingencies might turn out.[11] Thus *Fleet Tactics* is largely silent on operational and strategic matters, and it is entirely devoid of political, cultural, and strategic context. Like any good theory, it can be tailored to varying circumstances.

This is a strength and a weakness. There is a decidedly technical feel to such accounts, which are de rigueur in U.S. Navy training institutions, where warfighters learn their craft. The downside of the abstract approach to naval warfare is that, taken in isolation, Hughes' works strongly imply that technology decides the outcomes of martial encounters at sea. On the high seas, enemy fleets slug it out with volleys of precision-guided arms. Fighting close to enemy shores is a different matter. Shore defenses may fire surface-to-surface missiles at U.S. task forces, or land-based aircraft may launch antiship missiles from aloft. Quiet diesel-electric submarines may lurk below, awaiting their chance to launch torpedoes. But in both modes of fighting, the combatants hammer away with everything in their magazines, and the side that lands the first blow is the likely victor.

For Hughes, the arbiters of high-tech naval combat are (a) "scouting effectiveness," meaning the proficient use of shipboard and offboard sensors, combat systems, and computer datalinks to find enemy units; (b) "weapon range," or the ability to inflict damage at a distance; and (c) tactics, which are determined by scouting effectiveness and the range of a fleet's weaponry.[12] Hughes' account is doubtless accurate, but it is limited. Far more than missile ranges, seeker effectiveness, or detect-to-engage algorithms will shape the results of any Sino-American clash at sea. Not for nothing did Colonel John Boyd proclaim that people, ideas, and hardware—"in that order"—were the prime determinants of competitive endeavors such as warfare.[13] Or, more to the point, Mao Zedong decried "the so-called theory that 'weapons decide everything,' which constitutes a mechanical approach to the question of war. . . . It is people, not things, that are decisive."[14]

Outdistancing an opponent's sensors and weaponry is far from the only challenge any U.S. naval offensive will face. *Fleet Tactics* shares this deficit of vision with standard net assessments that tally up numbers of platforms and their technical characteristics, often scanting the human element of war and politics. A larger view is in order. Consider one datapoint from Asian maritime history: Imperial Japan, which has emerged as a model for PLA Navy development. Ni Lexiong, a leading Chinese proponent of sea power, faults China's Qing dynasty for being insufficiently Mahanian in its 1894–1895 naval tilt against Japan. Says Ni, China should bear in mind that Mahan "believed that whoever could control the sea would win the war and change history; that command of the sea is achieved through decisive naval battles on the seas; that the outcome of decisive naval battles is determined by the strength of fire power on each side of the engagement."[15]

That distinguished analysts now pay tribute to Japanese sea power, despite the bitter history of Sino-Japanese relations during the twentieth century, marks a striking turnabout in Chinese strategic thought. Beijing's willingness to consider the Japanese paradigm bespeaks increasing openness to non-Chinese, noncommunist sources of wisdom on military and naval affairs. Yet looking beyond Chinese traditions is eminently Chinese. Think about Sun Tzu's *Art of War*, an ancient text that remains a fixture in Chinese strategic discourses. The Chinese sage counsels generals to "know the enemy and know yourself; in a hundred battles you will never be in peril. When you are ignorant of the enemy but know yourself, your chances of winning or losing are equal. If ignorant both of your enemy and of yourself, you are certain in every battle to be in peril.'"[16] This is a truism, but one worth repeating. It also represents a plea for candor about the strengths and weakness of each belligerent—a candor that rejects analyses blinkered by culture or ideology.

Strategic insight, then, should be sought wherever it can be found. So, too, should American commanders heed Sun Tzu's wisdom. They need to understand U.S. forces' material and human strengths, acknowledge their shortcomings, and come to terms with the ends, ways, and means likely to guide Chinese efforts in times of crisis or war. As we showed in foregoing chapters, Mahanian geopolitical logic helps govern Chinese maritime strategy and could help goad Beijing into a trial of arms involving the United States. Our purpose here is to explain what that means in operational and tactical terms. A few propositions:

- If Mahan supplies the grand logic of maritime war, Mao Zedong's operational-level writings on land warfare will inform Chinese tactics and operational practices in any clash off Taiwan, in the South China Sea, or in hot spots elsewhere along the Asian periphery.

- The South China Sea represents the most likely maritime theater for Beijing to conduct combined-arms attacks designed to saturate and overpower U.S. task groups' defenses, fulfilling its geopolitical and strategic aims.

- PLA forces will integrate weapons systems, new and old, into joint "orthodox" and "unorthodox" attacks, executing offensive actions to attain strategically defensive goals. They will not depend on any single method or system, or solely on aerial, surface, or subsurface warfare. Multiple axes of attack, multiple weapon types, and preparedness to shift nimbly between the main and secondary efforts (and back again) will be hallmarks of the Chinese way of naval war.

- Among the three tactical scenarios Wayne Hughes posits (described below), PLA Navy planners and commanders will probably incline to dispersed attack, sequential attack, and massed attack, in that order. Unless Beijing grows so confident in its quantitative and qualitative superiority that it can simply hammer away, saturating American defenses at a single blow, it will stay with tried-and-true Chinese methods.

As Sun Tzu's theories suggest, more acute understanding of oneself and the adversary could provide the margin of victory in a test of arms with China. Now fast-forward from China's Warring States period, when Sun Tzu purportedly lived, to nineteenth-century Europe.[17] Recall that Carl von Clausewitz depicts war as "only a branch of political activity . . . that is in no sense autonomous." "Is war not just another expression of their thoughts, another form of speech or writing?" he queries before answering his own question. "Its grammar, indeed, may be its own, but not its logic."[18] By this, he means three things. First, war is the act of pursuing policy aims with the admixture of military means. The addition of violent means fires passions among the combatants—usually negative ones such as fear, anger, and hatred—while bringing chance and uncertainty to the fore. Second, nonmilitary instruments such as diplomacy and economic coercion still have a part to play after the shooting starts. And third, war—and warlike preparations—is an expression of political and strategic thought. For those schooled on Clausewitz, it is impossible to fully appreciate Chinese hardware and tactics without grasping the larger strategic, political, and cultural considerations that impart the logic to war.

Despite our bleak tone, we are not prophesying naval war in Asia. There is ample room for debate about China's intentions and its vision of its maritime destiny, and it is entirely possible that Chinese naval power will evolve in a benign direction. Indeed, one of our main recommendations is that the United States should do its best to shape conditions in favor of a maritime entente with China. As U.S. military specialists like to point out, though, hope is not a strategy. Washington cannot afford a strategy of neglect simply because it reckons the probability of a clash with China as low and wants to keep it that way. By investigating the logic and grammar of Chinese sea power, U.S. strategists can estimate how the PLA Navy would handle itself in Asian waters, mounting an integrated, offense-minded defense against U.S. Navy carrier and amphibious strike groups.

TACTICAL SCENARIOS: NEAR SHORE AND ON THE HIGH SEAS

Hughes considers two very broad categories of wartime contingencies. First, U.S. forces might close in on the coasts of an adversary that boasts considerable land-based defenses but lacks a fleet able to stand against the U.S. Navy in open waters. Second, a prospective opponent might possess a fleet able to meet the U.S. Navy in high-seas combat, operating more or less independently of land support. And, of course, the permutations between the two paradigms are endless, as Barry Posen suggests in his definition of "contested zones."

As Posen observes, a skillful though weaker adversary enjoys certain advantages when operating on its home turf, including nearby shore-based assets and manpower, short lines of communication, and familiarity with the tactical environment.[19] A savvy power can parley these advantages into distinct strategic and operational advantages over the United States, imposing costs Washington might find politically unacceptable. Even a lesser foe could impel U.S. decision makers to hesitate in times of crisis, or perhaps even to withdraw U.S. forces following a traumatic event—say, the crippling or sinking of an aircraft carrier. This dynamic—and it is worth spotlighting its pronounced psychological, nontechnical component—will characterize any near- to mid-term military encounter off Chinese coasts.

The prospects for variety in the operating environment—especially in littoral combat—should give wise tacticians pause. Bernard Brodie points out that, thankfully, "there are too few naval wars and far too few major naval battles to enable us ever to *prove* the correctness of a tactical theory"[20] (his emphasis). Even epic battles represent individual data points when evaluating a theory, and they take place too seldom to allow for rigorous trend analysis and confident findings. The U.S. Navy fought its last major engagement at Leyte Gulf in 1944; China's PLA Navy has never fought one. Furthermore, as Brodie notes, even a marginally different configuration of forces or set of tactics by one side or the other can produce a different outcome to a particular engagement—leading analysts to render a different, possibly faulty verdict about the efficacy of the tactics deployed.[21] Sobriety, it seems, is the most prudent attitude when evaluating past naval actions.

Wayne Hughes posits three representative scenarios for naval engagements on the high seas: attack by massed forces on massed forces; dispersed attack with near-simultaneous time on top of targeted forces; and sequential attack, essentially attacks dispersed in time rather than direction (see figure below).[22] Two caveats are in order. First, we are not predicting specific Chinese tactics. For the sake of simplicity, we use these three possibilities as crude indicators of how Chinese forces might respond to a U.S. naval offensive. The attacking force—"Force B" in Hughes' nomenclature—could represent a mix of Chinese shore- and sea-based missile shooters supplemented by platforms like minelayers or torpedo-firing submarines. The important question is whether Chinese strategic and operational preferences incline Chinese commanders toward massed, dispersed, or sequential attack, as depicted in figure below. A related question is, would the Chinese prefer to keep the PLA Navy closer to home, in keeping with the fortress-fleet approach favored by many continental powers, or would they feel comfortable dispatching the fleet for independent operations, beyond shore-based cover?[23]

Second, in the formulae Hughes develops to gauge the probabilities of U.S. defenses' being overwhelmed or penetrated by "leakers" (platforms or munitions that get past the battle group's layered defense), he avoids using the characteristics—ranges, warhead sizes, etc.—of specific weapons systems. For the most part, we follow suit. Capabilities change while tactical principles apply across many contingencies. Those closer to tactical questions must put the analysis and findings presented here into actual practice.In short, some composite of land and sea defenses will constitute China's contested zone in littoral sea areas. As the Chinese military extends its reach seaward, especially

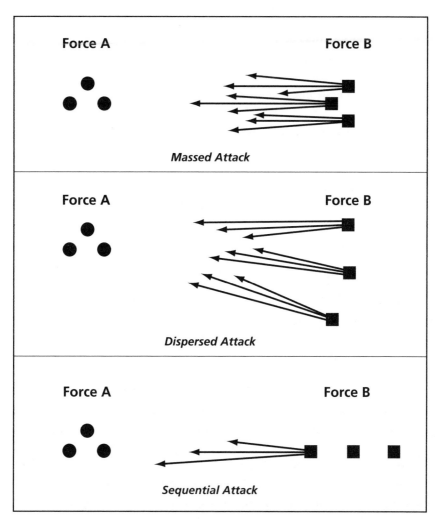

Tactics for Striking at an Approaching Naval Force. Reprinted by permission from Wayne P. Hughes Jr., *Fleet Tactics: Theory and Practice* (Annapolis, Md.: Naval Institute Press, 1986), 244.

in a post-Taiwan era, the high-seas component will naturally come to predominate. In Clausewitzian terms, as the PLA extends the range of land-based weaponry and continues building its oceangoing fleet, China will push the "culminating point of the attack" outward from Chinese coasts—improving its prospects for denying the U.S. military access to important waters and, should Beijing choose to do so, for vying for sea control. Clausewitz observes that when one state invades another, the combat power of the invading army starts to dwindle while the defending army grows stronger as the lines of communication with its bases shorten and it takes advantage of familiar surroundings. The culminating point represents the crossover point at which the defender's strength starts to surpass that of the attacker. A fleet that stands into an enemy's maritime contested zone faces the same dynamic.[24]

APPLYING MAHANIAN LOGIC TO CHINESE SEA-POWER THOUGHT

Wars are not—or should not be—fought for their own sake. Politics imparts the logic to warfare, determining the ends for which statesmen, soldiers, and mariners strive. Grammar, on the other hand, refers to the ways and means for realizing a nation's political aims.[25] As noted in chapter 2, Alfred Thayer Mahan proffered both a Clausewitzian logic of sea power premised on commerce, politics, and the military and a grammar of naval strategy, operations, and tactics. One of the conceits behind this volume is that Captain Mahan's sea-power theories now exert substantial influence on the logic of Chinese maritime strategy. While Mahan has fallen into disuse verging on irrelevance in U.S. naval circles (despite officials' occasional efforts to conjure him up to support particular initiatives[26]), his sea-power philosophy continues to beguile in Asia. Chinese naval development attests to it.

Mahan, then, furnishes both the logic and the vocabulary to argue for assertive sea power. Proponents of this school of thought write and speak in avowedly Mahanian terms, and in many cases they explicitly use his works to justify an ambitious maritime strategy. In particular, his portrayal of sea power as "overbearing power" suffuses their discourses on maritime affairs. Should the Mahanians win out among the cacophony of voices clamoring for the attention of senior policymakers, Chinese strategy will take on distinctly offensive overtones. Perhaps the most thoughtful spokesman for China's Mahanian school is Professor Ni Lexiong of the Shanghai Institute of Political Science and Law. Ni uses sea-power theory to evaluate the competing claims of the advocates of sea power and the advocates of globalization. The latter, he contends, believe that "China should not act by following the traditional sea power theory in pursuing a strong Navy, because today's world situation is different from the time of Mahan . . . the globalization of the world's economy has made various countries' interests interconnected, mutually dependent on each other to a greater degree, and that if a country wants to preserve its life line at sea, the only way to do so is to go through 'cooperation' rather than the traditional 'solo fight.'"[27] Globalization theorists, says

Ni, urge Beijing not to embark on a naval arms buildup. To do so would alert "today's naval hegemon," the United States, "making China's naval development a self-destructive play with fire," reminiscent of Imperial Germany's quixotic bid for sea power at the turn of the nineteenth century.[28] For the sake of discussion, the author stipulates that globalization theorists such as Thomas Barnett may have it right. The world may be entering an age of perpetual peace in which economic interdependence renders armed strife almost unthinkable within the advanced world. Barnett opines that the developed nations have in effect abolished war among themselves, achieving "something awfully close to Kant's perpetual peace," a realm that has transcended force as an instrument of policy.[29]

While he does not discount such a revolution in world affairs, Professor Ni rightly points out that even a pacific international system—like any domestic political order—ultimately depends on the latent or actual use of force. In either case, then, China should improve its navy. It will need a muscular PLA Navy to play its part in the "world Navy," the seagoing arm of an international police force, should such a constabulary ever put to sea. Chinese seafarers can aid the transition to a peaceful international order. Ni nevertheless believes the world remains mired in power politics, demanding that sovereign states maintain powerful military forces as a means of self-help. Thus "it is China's necessary choice to build up a strong sea power," warding off "threats to our 'outward-leaning economy' by some strong nations."[30]

By "strong nations," of course, he means the United States and its Asian allies. This is scarcely the language of someone predisposed to huddle behind an oceanic Great Wall. If Ni's Mahan-inspired brand of thinking prevails in policy circles in Beijing, Washington and its regional partners must come to grips with a newly assertive Chinese naval strategy.

APPLYING MAOIST ACTIVE-DEFENSE GRAMMAR
TO OFFSHORE OPERATIONS

Mahan's sea-power logic, then, remains persuasive. Beijing has taken up his first trident. His writings on operational and tactical matters, conversely, have a musty if not antiquarian feel about them, not only in the United States but elsewhere. He affirmed that the "offensive element in warfare" was "the superstructure, the end and the aim for which the defensive exists, and apart from which it is to all purposes of war worse than useless. When war has been accepted as necessary, success means nothing short of victory; and victory must be sought by offensive measures, and by them only can be insured."[31]

This vision of offensive battle comports with Chinese strategic proclivities, as does his advocacy of forward bases and a robust merchant marine. But Mahan's doctrine of battle between big-gun battleships offers little help designing tactics for an age of high-tech naval combat.[32] Nor do Chinese analysts draw any detailed lessons from his works beyond the injunction to mass combat power at critical points to prosecute fleet engagements. His second trident is of scant use to an ambitious China.

It comes as little shock that Mahan has fallen into disrepute in operational and tactical matters. As he admitted to Theodore Roosevelt, he made an indifferent fleet officer—"I am the man of thought, not the man of action," he confided—and more than once he came up on the short end of a technical debate.[33] He feuded with W. S. Sims, for example, on the question of whether new U.S. battleships should be fitted with all-big-gun main batteries or with a composite battery of big and lesser-caliber naval rifles.[34] Notes Richard Hough, Sims administered an "annihilating" rejoinder to Mahan's advocacy of mixed armament, upbraiding Mahan for ignoring the combat punch of Japanese 12-inch gunfire at Tsushima.[35] If Mahan fared poorly in tactical debates in his own day, it is scarcely surprising that American and foreign tacticians nowadays look elsewhere for insight.

Accordingly, Chinese officials, mariners, and scholars consult other martial traditions as they draft a grammar of marine combat. For help, they look to China's rich stock of land-warfare traditions, including the writings of Sun Tzu and, in particular, of Mao Zedong. The Chinese Communist Party's founding chairman, Mao etched his strategic outlook on contemporary China through personal example and through voluminous writings on political and military affairs. He was famously indifferent to maritime pursuits.[36] Yet, as we saw in chapter 2, China's current maritime strategy, "offshore active defense," takes both its name and its guiding precepts from the Maoist doctrine of active defense, an approach to warfighting distilled from his experiences in land campaigns against Imperial Japanese occupiers and the Chinese Nationalist Army.[37]

Mao scorned passive defense. His military writings were wholly offensive in character, even during the wilderness years when his Red Army was vastly inferior to its enemies and had little choice other than to remain on the strategic defensive. Passive defense represented "a spurious kind of defense" whereas active defense meant "defense for the purpose of counter-attacking and taking the offensive."[38] Even strategically defensive aims, then, were best attained through offensive ways and means. Distasteful and transient, passive measures were necessitated by an unfavorable balance of forces. They were not the core of China's national strategy, let alone its strategic preference.[39] This outlook lends China's quest for sea power much of its grammar.

To Chinese eyes, U.S. mastery of East Asian seas resembles the Nationalist Army's strategy of "encirclement and suppression," transposed to the East, Yellow, and South China seas.[40] The Red Army did not reply to Nationalist Army ground offensives through passive means; it used tactical offensives opportunistically to elongate the war, tire out enemy forces, and shift the balance of forces in the communists' favor. Patient action represented a precursor to a counteroffensive and, ultimately, to decisive victory. Prompted by Mao and Mahan, similarly, Chinese naval strategists talk routinely of prying control of the waters westward of the first island chain from the U.S. Navy's grasp. They intend to surround and control these waters by offensive means, even while the United States commands Asian waters. It is increasingly common for Chinese strategists to implore Beijing to take "absolute control" of the seas within the island chain.

Such commentary puts an ominous twist on Western conceptions of a passive Great Wall strategy.[41] True, Mao did warn against risking engagements in which victory was not ensured, but it is a grave mistake to equate such prudence with acquiescence in Chinese military inferiority. Again, the strategic defensive was a distasteful expedient for Chairman Mao, not a desirable or permanent state of affairs. If the PLA heeds his advice, then, its grammar of naval war should give the U.S. Navy pause. American rule of Asian waters does not render all naval battles unwinnable for Beijing. Washington must take seriously the prospect that Beijing will adopt a Mahan- and Mao-inspired naval strategy in its littoral waters, framing strategy and tactics with this prospect in mind. If so, the PLA Navy will be a force to be reckoned with.

In this context, dispersed attacks on exterior lines are becoming increasingly thinkable for the PLA, as they were for the Red Army in its struggles against the Imperial Japanese Army and the Nationalist Army. The dispersed approach confers a variety of benefits. First, Maoist preferences predispose Chinese defenders to let U.S. forces close on Chinese shores (like Mao's "foolish" boxer who "rushes in furiously and uses up all his resources at the very start"), attenuating their strength before mounting attacks from shore- and sea-based weaponry scattered around the battle zone. Nor will the PLA confine its fleet tactics to any particular warfare domain. It will unleash missile barrages complemented by submarine attack, minefields, and other tactics and systems to which China has paid lavish attention. As American forces approach Chinese coastlines, the PLA will assume the exterior lines, rendering dispersed attack possible along multiple threat axes. After falling back on land-based support, Beijing can bring the full force of its contested zone to bear, creating a 360-degree threat to U.S. expeditionary groups.

Second, PLA commanders will concentrate their efforts on individual vessels or small detachments in an effort to wipe them out. Despite the tenor of Chinese commentary and their own assumptions, U.S. commanders should not automatically assume that aircraft carriers will be the prime target for PLA action. Amphibious ships would make tempting targets in a Taiwan contingency, for example, assuming U.S. Marines attempted to land to succor Taiwanese defense forces. As we show in the following chapter, disabling or sinking one of the U.S. Navy's gee-whiz Aegis warships would give the United States pause, stirring memories of the 2000 attack on the destroyer USS *Cole* and magnifying the political impact of such a feat of arms on the American electorate. Or the PLA Navy might even assail U.S. combat logistics vessels in transit to or from the conflict zone. Despite the lower political profile of tankers and stores ships, depriving carrier or amphibious task groups of the "bullets, beans, and black oil"—to use an older generation's term for the supplies needed to sustain combat operations off enemy shores—would eventually bring the U.S. effort to a halt.

Third, and closely related, the PLA will incorporate orthodox and unorthodox methods and weaponry into its defensive scheme, conforming to Mao's and Sun Tzu's warfare precepts. Western naval analysts commonly invoke the concept of saturation attack, implying that cruise missiles will be China's sole implements, or at any rate its implements of choice. This may be true, but more likely, PLA saturation attack will involve the concerted use of missiles, aerial attack, mines, torpedo attack, and electronic warfare. Such weaponry is ideal for a contested zone, complementing more conventional means. Antiship missiles could represent not the primary, orthodox element of an active-defense campaign but the secondary, unorthodox element. For example, missile attack would compel U.S. tacticians to look skyward while *Kilo*-class diesel boats loosed salvos of wake-homing torpedoes against U.S. surface combatants. It also bears repeating that Maoist tactics are fluid, with orthodox attack morphing into unorthodox attack and back again. Distinguishing orthodox from unorthodox tactics may be difficult to impossible in the heat of battle.

And fourth, Beijing will merge nonmilitary instruments into its defensive efforts, using diplomacy to augment Maoist active defense. For instance, Beijing could impress upon Washington the lasting diplomatic and economic repercussions of taking on China over Taiwan or some other object. Its need to weigh benefits against costs could induce the United States to hesitate in wartime, improving the PLA's chances of achieving its wartime goals. Additionally, Chinese diplomats could try to weaken or pick off U.S. allies, discouraging nations such as Japan from granting the use of bases on their soil, or impressing on Australia that it will pay a price for supporting U.S. military action. This would impair America's strategic position in Asia.

Beijing would turn operational achievements of Chinese arms to propaganda advantage. Small but solid Chinese tactical victories would weary the American populace while giving Washington's allies second thoughts about supporting the United States against China, Asia's central political and economic power. Asians understand that, win or lose in a naval war, they have to live with a vengeful China. Disparate strategic views could create tensions that China could exploit—dismantling the alliance system that lets the United States operate on grand-strategic exterior lines far from North American shores.

CASE STUDY: THE SOUTH CHINA SEA
ON THE "DAY AFTER TAIWAN"

The South China Sea offers an ideal case study for future conflict off Chinese shores. While Chinese and Western strategists have commonly assumed that the Pacific Ocean is the most likely theater of twenty-first-century maritime competition between the United States and China—and indeed Admiral Liu Huaqing, the modern PLA Navy's founding father, espoused an eastward-facing strategy—the South China Sea is a more probable locus for contingencies involving the PLA and the U.S. Navy.[42]

Chinese interests rivet Beijing's attention on this expanse, its gateway to South Asia. At least four strategic challenges beckon the attention of Chinese strategists southward. First and foremost, Taiwan, along the northern edge of the sea, continues to obsess the Chinese leadership. A formal declaration of independence, or a Taiwanese breach of a Chinese redline such as constitutional reform, remains the most likely casus belli for Beijing. But the cross-strait dispute is no longer the all-consuming issue it once was. If it has not already, China will soon gain the confidence to start looking past Taiwan, to other pursuits in Southeast and South Asia. Satisfactory settlement of affairs in the Taiwan Strait will free up Chinese resources and energies, advance the cause of national unification, break through Dean Acheson's island-chain perimeter, and give the PLA its own offshore (and unsinkable, if also immovable) aircraft carrier and submarine tender. By occupying the island, moreover, Beijing can use the logic Admiral Ernest King applied to Formosa. Keeping the bottle of the South China Sea uncorked will let Chinese shipping bearing vital resources from the Middle East and the Horn of Africa reach Chinese seaports unmolested.

Second, and closely related, there is the "Malacca dilemma," or "Malacca predicament," that perplexes Chinese scholars and top officials, most prominently President Hu Jintao. Beijing fears an attempt on the part of the United States and its allies to close the Malacca, Lombok, or Sunda straits to Chinese shipping as an indirect riposte during a Taiwan conflict.[43] Ensuring free passage through the sea lines of communication linking the Persian Gulf region and Africa with Chinese seaports—in particular through the Strait of Malacca—now constitutes a matter of surpassing importance to China's communist regime.[44] The uninterrupted flow of oil, natural gas, and other raw materials across the bodies of water to the mainland's immediate south and southwest—the South China Sea and the Indian Ocean—will occupy an increasingly prominent place in China's maritime calculus. This emerging energy security imperative suggests that tracking longer-term Chinese intentions and grand strategy in southern waters constitutes an urgent task for the United States.[45]

Third, China has staked maritime-territorial claims to most of the South China Sea, making Southeast Asia a natural theater of nautical endeavor. Indeed, the National People's Congress in effect wrote China's claims into domestic law in 1992. National sentiment helps animate Beijing's goals in the region; so does the region's value for maritime communications; and so do the undersea resources supposedly to be found around the numerous islands to which China and powers like the Philippines, Taiwan, and Vietnam have lodged claims. Even cartographers have joined the fray. One laments that the landmass of China resembles a rooster, an image unworthy of China's majesty. But including the sea areas claimed by China gives the nation an appealing shape on the map—a torch. This conveys not only the region's importance for Chinese national dignity but also the interdependence between the sea and Chinese economic development. "Chinese map," proclaims the author, "you are the collected emotion and wisdom of the Chinese people, their coagulated blood and raging fire, symbolic of their power and personality, the embodi-ment of their worth and spirit."[46] Whether Beijing will attempt to enforce domestic law as its naval power grows remains to be seen—but at the very least, this is a prospect fellow seafaring states must take seriously.

Fourth, it has become apparent that undersea warfare imparts momen-tum to China's southward maritime turn. In April 2008, *Jane's Intelligence Review* disclosed that the PLA had constructed an impressive naval base com-plete with underground pens for fleet nuclear-powered ballistic-missile sub-marines, or SSBNs, on Hainan Island, in the northern reaches of the South China Sea.[47] The news prompted a flurry of speculation among strategic thinkers in the West and Asia. "Must India be anxious?" asked one Indian commentator.[48] To borrow a metaphor Chinese officials use, the Sanya base gives Beijing the first of China's "two eyes" at sea—Taiwan being the other.[49] Whimsical metaphors aside, basing SSBNs in the South China Sea would let the PLA Navy outflank U.S. and Japanese antisubmarine-warfare efforts in Northeast Asia, enabling the Chinese submarine force to operate on exterior lines. Sanya, moreover, gives the navy a forward base not only for SSBNs but also for attack submarines, aircraft, and surface units, extending its combat reach seaward in much the same way Taiwan would in the Pacific Ocean.

The South China Sea, in short, offers an ideal theater for the PLA to fight on tactically exterior lines, even while the United States operates along strategically exterior lines. The Luzon Strait, which separates Taiwan from the Philippines, will take on new prominence once operational Chinese units are stationed at Sanya. This will be doubly true once China regains Taiwan, expe-diting Chinese military access to the strait. In a day-after-Taiwan scenario, with PLA emplacements on the island, China would extend its reach seaward while gaining a commanding position opposite Luzon. This would render the logic of dispersed attack even more compelling. PLA forces could vector in attacks on U.S. Navy task forces not only from PLA Navy units at sea but also from sites on the mainland and, just as importantly, from Hainan and Taiwan—in General MacArthur's metaphor, its twin offshore aircraft carriers and submarine tenders. By forcing the United States into perimeter defense, the PLA can open up new tactical vistas for itself. It could feint in the South China Sea, for instance, stretching American defenses and situational aware-ness to the south while staging a breakout in the north, through narrow seas monitored only lightly by the U.S. and Japanese fleets since the Cold War.

Taken together, this adds up to an effort similar to the one the United States mounted in Mahan's day, when the U.S. Navy set out to establish its ascendancy over superior European navies in the Caribbean Sea and the Gulf of Mexico—expanses of comparable economic and military importance to a rising United States that had locked its gaze on Asia-Pacific markets and bases. For U.S. naval commanders, consequently, monitoring how China manages its "Caribbean" will provide important clues to Chinese capabilities and intentions.[50]

Preference #1: Dispersed Sea Denial

To return to Wayne Hughes' analytical template, what are China's strategic preferences for naval warfare? In more specific terms, how will China apply its panoply of new hardware to achieve the goal of sea denial? Using Hughes' three determinants of tactical effectiveness, Chinese defenders will attempt to disrupt U.S. scouting, outrange U.S. weaponry, and exploit defects in U.S. fleet tactics, keeping American commanders off-balance. Consonant with Mao's injunction to cut off one of an enemy's fingers rather than mash them all, PLA defenders will concentrate on individual U.S. units or small formations that find themselves remote from mutual support. By playing up tactical victories in the world press, Beijing can hope to discourage the American people and peel away ambivalent U.S. allies like Japan or Australia, collapsing the overall U.S. effort. Western analysts, then, must remain alert to inventive PLA uses of China's tactical and geostrategic advantages. Some representative weapon systems useful for dispersed but integrated attacks would include the following:

Antiship Cruise Missiles. The PLA has plowed major effort and resources into cruise-missile procurement and development. Indeed, a recent RAND report situates SS-N-22 and SS-N-27 antiship missiles at the heart of China's strategy for a Taiwan contingency, strongly suggesting that the United States would find itself on the losing end of a cross-strait encounter in 2020.[51] Antiship missiles can be fired from ships, aircraft, and surface batteries, forcing U.S. Navy antiair defenders to cope with multiple threat axes. For instance, the fast, agile SS-N-22 Moskit (known in U.S. naval circles as the Sunburn) carried on PLA Navy *Sovremennyy*-class guided-missile destroyers has excellent prospects even against the U.S. Navy's Aegis combat system, the latest in American technical wizardry and the system it was designed to penetrate.[52] Such weaponry makes an ideal candidate for orthodox antiship attack.

Antiship Ballistic Missiles. Over the past couple of years, reports that the PLA is on the brink of fielding an antiship ballistic missile (ASBM) capable of striking ships under way in the Pacific have become increasingly common. (See chapter 5 for details.) This would represent an impressive feat of weapons engineering. Such a capability is not found in even the U.S. arsenal. Fielding the capacity to strike at advancing U.S. carrier or amphibious task forces at long range (reportedly up to 2,500 km for the PLA's Dong Feng-21C missiles, which are fired from mobile launchers) would confront the U.S. military with an entirely new set of challenges. A China able to strike effectively within the second island chain with sufficient numbers of birds could hope to replicate Imperial Japanese strategy, which aimed at whittling down the U.S. battle line before a Mahanian engagement in Asian waters. It would certainly extend the range of a PLA fortress-fleet, making this concept workable for the first time. And an ASBM capability would signal China's ability to function along exterior lines against U.S. naval forces at far greater distances than once thought possible, executing a Maoist strategy on a grand scale.[53]

Antiradiation Weapons. Again, the PLA will use the raw hitting power of its antiship missiles in concert with other systems. Despite its passive nature, antiradiation weaponry makes an ideal implement for unorthodox attack. Showcased in Afghanistan, two wars against Iraq, and other conflicts of the past two decades, the modern American way of war is premised on winning the contest for information supremacy at the outbreak of war. U.S. forces have prevailed in large part because superior technology gives them a "common operating picture" of conditions in the battle space that no opponent can match. Airborne sensors detect and target multiple enemy aircraft, ships, or ground vehicles across long distances. Jammers and antiradiation missiles incapacitate enemy sensors attempting to gather data on and target U.S. assets. These tactics effectively paralyze U.S. adversaries during the opening phases of a military campaign, paving the way for an even more important battlefield condition, namely air supremacy.

Beijing's purchase of (and effort to reverse-engineer) the S-300 Russian air-defense system is instructive. An indigenous antiradiation variant of the S-300, the FT-2000, will likely be deployed near the Taiwan Strait to target Taiwanese forces and deter U.S. military intervention in a cross-strait war.[54] Reportedly nearing production, the FT-2000 is nicknamed "AWACS killer" for its mission of attacking the airborne sensors and electronic-warfare assets on which U.S. air superiority relies in wartime.[55] It homes in on radio-frequency emissions, much as U.S. aviators use high-speed antiradiation missiles, or HARM, to assault enemy air defenses in theaters like Iraq. This leaves the radiating platform no good options. It can silence its radar emissions and go blind, impairing or negating its coordinating function, or it can perform its mission and risk a missile hit. China's newest air-defense warships will be outfitted with surface-to-air antiradiation missiles comparable to the FT-2000.

In Hughes' terms, the FT-2000 could seriously degrade U.S. scouting effectiveness, one of his chief determinants of tactical success. Weapons range means little without the ability to find and target enemy forces at long distances. Since the dawn of carrier warfare, U.S. naval strategy has seen command of the air as a prerequisite for surface fleet operations. An operation near Chinese shores would be no different. If Chinese air defenses completely or partially negated the U.S. edge in information warfare, they would slow down and complicate the efforts of U.S. aircraft to establish dominance over the skies—blunting U.S. offensive action and exposing U.S. warships, including aircraft carriers, to air and missile counterstrikes. Robust Chinese air defenses would oblige U.S. commanders to devote their energy to securing the skies. Skillful use of even an inherently defensive and passive weapon such as the FT-2000, then, would open the way for PLA offensive–defensive operations in Mao Zedong's sense.

Undersea Warfare. The Chinese submarine fleet has aroused growing concern in U.S. defense circles, judging from scholarly commentary and the Pentagon's annual reports to Congress, "Military Power of the People's Republic of China."[56] Lethal, stealthy diesel-electric submarines like the Russian-built *Kilo* can prowl China's offshore contested zone while nuclear boats range farther afield, cueing PLA commanders as U.S. forces approach or launching nuisance attacks on the high seas. Armed with wake-homing torpedoes—torpedoes that find their way to surface targets by following the water turbulence churned up by the ship's propellers—even diesel boats can compel American ship drivers to attempt radical evasive maneuvers. In a very real sense, they can distract a ship's combat team while the PLA bombards the fleet with antiship cruise missiles, presenting a tough if not insoluble tactical problem.[57]

To sum up, if the PLA manages to compel U.S. forces to look toward any single dimension of the maritime threat environment—antisurface, antisubmarine, or antiair—it can then pose additional challenges in the other dimensions. Nuclear and diesel-electric attack submarines, missile-armed fast patrol boats, or "assassin's mace" systems such as minefields make good adjuncts to more traditional systems such as antiship cruise missiles and shore-based aircraft.

A well-designed Chinese force package would impose a three-dimensional threat environment on U.S. forces, and unorthodox and orthodox attacks would proceed along multiple vectors. The more stresses the Chinese can impose, the less likely U.S. forces would be to venture landward of the island chains or into the South China Sea. If China can even partially cancel out U.S. technologies that manage the fog of war, moreover, it could severely curtail U.S. forces' freedom of maneuver along Asian coastlines, access the U.S. Navy has long taken for granted. The combined effect of information warfare and kinetic measures could induce U.S. forces to operate farther from Chinese shores, helping China achieve its goal of sea denial in the China seas.

One caveat is worth stating. Despite the tone of our commentary, we do not maintain that these capabilities, alone or combined, would give China a decisive edge in littoral warfare, let alone outright military superiority over the United States. The PLA Navy remains a relative newcomer to naval warfare. The cost constraints familiar to military services worldwide burden it. It has technical hurdles to overcome. Its officers and men must gain tactical acumen by operating at sea, the only place mariners can hone their craft. When the PLA Navy will be the U.S. Navy's equal in material and human terms, if ever, remains an open question.

To offset these lingering shortcomings, the PLA will press its operational and tactical advantages, abiding by Mao Zedong's counsel. By driving up the costs of entry, Beijing can hope to deter or hamper U.S. involvement in Asian conflicts, fulfilling its defensive strategic aims. If the PLA can deny U.S. forces the ability to dictate events, it will have attained the most important goal of sea denial, imposing local dominance on the waves and aloft for long enough to realize operational and strategic goals. The approach we have posited here comports with the experiences of the past forty-plus years of naval war. From Egypt's sinking of the Israeli destroyer *Eilat* with Styx missiles in 1967, to the Argentine sinking of HMS *Sheffield* in 1982, to the Iraqi Exocet attack on USS *Stark* in 1987, to Hezbollah's crippling of the Israeli corvette *Spear* with a C-802 surface-to-surface missile in 2006, experience demonstrates that a determined yet inferior navy can hurt a superior one, forcing a change in its behavior even without scoring an outright naval victory.[58]

In each incident, a single missile hit scored a mission kill—that is, put its combat-systems suite out of action, preventing the vessel from accomplishing its mission—disabled the stricken vessel, or, in the cases of the *Eilat* and *Sheffield*, sank it altogether. The damage USS *Samuel B. Roberts*, USS *Princeton*, and USS *Tripoli* suffered from crude, cheap Iraqi sea mines during the late 1980s and early 1990s represents an even more striking example. For Chinese naval planners, then, the tactics of dispersed, multifaceted attack promise a handsome return on a modest investment. They make sense according to sound principles of naval warfare, as elaborated by Wayne Hughes, and they fit with Chinese strategic and operational traditions. It only makes sense for the PLA to employ them.

Preference #2: Cut Off the U.S. Navy's Fingers Sequentially

Chinese naval planners cannot count on defeating the United States by crippling or sinking a small, though politically significant, portion of the U.S. fleet. This might work by raising the costs of fighting China above the value Washington assigns the object at stake. But the United States has defied predictions of moral flabbiness before. One lesson of the Pacific War, the first Gulf War, and even Operation Iraqi Freedom for Chinese strategists must be not to discount the United States' will to fight. Prudence demands that Beijing think ahead and consider what to do should its sea-denial strategy fail to drive U.S. naval forces from sea areas where the PLA wants local superiority. The most obvious fallback for the PLA would be to keep doing what works. Picking off U.S. warships and formations piecemeal would eventually create a favorable environment for Chinese sea denial so long as U.S. commanders kept playing into Chinese hands, presenting a "cooperative adversary."

Successive small-scale victories at sea would resemble the numerous exterior–interior-line battles waged by Mao's Red Army against such foes as the Imperial Japanese Army and the Chinese Nationalist Army. Sequential tactics would let the PLA cut the U.S. Navy down to size over time, perhaps realizing its tactical and operational aims on the logic sketched previously. If not, it would gradually tilt the military balance toward China, enhancing the PLA's prospects for the decisive engagement that Mao foretold in land combat. To be sure, this presupposes great confidence on Beijing's part in its ability to manage escalation in an Asian maritime conflict. Keeping tabs on Chinese strategic discourses thus seems an obvious step for U.S. naval planners. Wayne Hughes' second tactical scenario, sequential attack, would likely rank second in China's hierarchy of naval tactics, dispersing defensive strikes in time as well as space.

Preference #3: Mao Zedong, Meet Alfred Thayer Mahan

In closing, it is worth pointing out that, as the PLA Navy approaches parity with the U.S. Navy, Maoist grammar will increasingly blur into the Mahanian grammar of concentrated fleet-on-fleet engagements. Hughes' third scenario, massed attack, thus merits consideration for Beijing. Some Chinese strategists look directly to Mahan for inspiration on naval strategy. One well-known pundit, Zhang Wenmu, cites Mahan's dictum that economic prosperity hinges on the deployment of naval forces at strategic locations. China, maintains Zhang, must "build up our navy as quickly as possible" in preparation for the "sea battle" that represents the "ultimate way for major powers" to resolve economic disputes.[59] One way a major fleet action might come about: a sequential PLA strategy could culminate in a Mahanian trial of arms, with the decisive clash developing by increments.

Alternatively, if the PLA felt the balance of forces favored it from the outset, its commanders might offer Mahanian battle right away. Having decided to resort to arms, that is, Beijing might seek a decision with the United States immediately rather than stay with Mao Zedong's sequential approach. Venturing everything to gain everything would not represent so dramatic a break with Mao as it appears. Mao enjoined *weaker* powers, not stronger ones, to give ground and concentrate against isolated enemy units. Once Chinese forces attain a position of parity or relative superiority, they will enjoy far more operational and tactical options, including the conventional counteroffensive Mao believed they must eventually prosecute to achieve victory. In a favorable strategic setting, there is no reason for the PLA not to proceed straight to the counteroffensive. Indeed, Mao on occasion reversed his own strategy when strategic circumstances warranted. Despite deep reservations among his comrades, Mao prevailed on them to intervene decisively in the Korean War, convinced that a massive initial blow would push UN forces off the peninsula. While this gamble failed miserably, the same type of logic and wishful thinking could again take hold of Chinese commanders. Some factors that might impel the PLA Navy to risk a fleet action include the following:

Maoist Logic–Not So Different from Mahan's After All. As noted earlier, a Mahanian engagement would be compatible with Maoist traditions under certain circumstances. Having ensnared U.S. forces deep in China's contested zone, the PLA can assume the exterior lines, applying Mao's operational logic far more broadly than he anticipated. As noted in chapter 2, the Great Helmsman himself contemplated globe-spanning exterior lines, albeit in a diplomatic—as opposed to an operational—sense. It might seem reasonable to his contemporary followers to extend his theory in other ways, pursuing a counteroffensive that promises outright naval victory.

Death Ground. In some of the contingencies foreseeable in the Taiwan Strait or the South China Sea, the Chinese Communist regime would find its survival at stake. Self-preservation is top priority for Beijing. A cross-strait war, to name the most obvious contingency, would call Chinese national unity into question, and the legitimacy of the regime with it. U.S. intervention, then, might summon forth an all-out PLA assault. If the communist regime's longevity hinged on it, self-restraint would recede in importance. Or, should the United States mount a blockade of Chinese resource shipments, a similar calculus might take hold. Clearly, all bets are off should some U.S. action place China's leadership on death ground.

Now or Never. While China often deprecates the United States' political staying power, Beijing may fear a repetition of 1941, when an Asian sea power dramatically underrated America's will and capacity to wage war across the Pacific and paid the price for it. Resigned to an armed encounter with U.S. forces, Chinese commanders might aim a knockout blow at U.S. expeditionary strike groups that venture into the China seas. Chinese strategists might fear merely disabling or sinking a small U.S. Navy contingent. By bloodying the Pacific Fleet, Beijing might provoke the kind of massive U.S. counterstroke Imperial Japan incurred after Pearl Harbor. An all-out, victorious engagement would foreclose that prospect.

Dare All to Gain All. Should the PLA offer decisive battle, the ensuing fleet action—again, assuming the PLA Navy won—would hasten China's rise to regional and world eminence and reorder the Asian and perhaps global international systems. America would not readily rebuild its navy—or regain its superpower status, which turns on supremacy in the maritime commons—following a catastrophic defeat. We find it doubtful that Beijing would risk war for this reason alone. Chinese thinkers grasp the political, economic, and military costs of great-power war. Still, the allure of a final reckoning might prod Chinese commanders to risk the fleet if they were already leaning that way for the reasons hypothesized earlier.

That Chinese decision makers could hazard a decisive fleet action does not mean they are fated to. Much will depend on how they estimate the military balance in Asia. Monitoring how Beijing sees its comprehensive national power relative to that of the United States and other rival powers thus will supply important clues to Chinese naval strategy and tactics.

CAN THE UNITED STATES PRESERVE ITS NAVAL MASTERY?

Forethought, training and doctrinal refinement for combat in Asian waters, and constant attention to the material dimension of strategy represent prudence on the part of U.S. officials, commanders, and shipwrights. Military professionals like to point out that they deal in capabilities, not intentions. How should U.S. commanders prepare for Chinese integrated attacks at sea? By embracing Wayne Hughes' prescriptions for tactical success, for one thing. Hughes urges ship designers to extend the range of U.S. missiles, improve U.S. Navy expeditionary groups' detection and targeting ability, and encourage commanders to refine their tactics to preserve or regain the advantage over prospective adversaries. Continuous work on the material dimension of strategy is crucial. So is continuous improvement in tactics such as emissions control, which manages radar and communications emissions to keep enemy forces from detecting U.S. task forces. And as we have seen, aggressive electronic warfare is central to U.S. information superiority.

Who holds the edge in weapons range and scouting effectiveness at present? If the PLA perfects its antiship ballistic missile, U.S. forces would be forced to operate within the ASBM threat envelope, assuming developments bear out the 2,500-km figure for the missile's range. That is the maximum range advertised for any U.S. land-attack cruise missile. Beyond that, the answer depends on the contingency. Until the ASBM enters service, the only vague conclusion possible is that Beijing's naval buildup is pushing the culminating point for U.S. naval action farther offshore, raising the costs of entry for the U.S. military into Asian waters. With regard to manned aircraft, the PLA Navy's J-11 fighter/attack aircraft, a derivative of the Russian Su-27 and Su-30, boasts a tactical radius of 2,000 km if refueled in flight.[60] In theory, it could hold U.S. vessels at risk up to 2,250 km distant from its base if armed with Sunburns. This pushes the engagement zone well beyond the inner island chain, supporting China's goal of sea denial in and around Taiwan and the approaches to the South China Sea.

In light of these figures, Chinese strategists are beginning to look beyond the Taiwan impasse, implying that they feel confident with their ability to deny the United States access to the waters shoreward of the first island chain. Now look at the American side. For close-in encounters such as one off Taiwan, which could involve landing U.S. Marines ashore or interdicting Chinese landing forces, U.S. forces must venture within the cruise-missile envelope and well within range of missile-armed aircraft flying from airfields on the mainland. Layered defenses will be thinner and more permeable in these cramped quarters while response times for U.S. defenders will plummet.

Shipboard defenses will take on new importance under these circumstances. The U.S. Navy's premier self-defense system, the RIM-162 Evolved Sea Sparrow Missile (ESSM), is a semiactive radar-guided missile fired from vertical launch systems or deck-mounted launchers. However accurate, its range is reported at only 45 km, which compresses reaction times for U.S. task forces against Chinese antiship weaponry such as the Sunburn, with its sea-skimming cruise altitude, maximum velocity of Mach 3, and capacity for radical evasive maneuvers in the terminal phase.[61] One study estimates the probability of a hit for a Mach 2.5 missile at 40 percent against a carrier group screened by Aegis combatants.[62] The window for multiple ESSM engagements, then, would shut quickly under battle conditions. The Close-In Weapons System (CIWS), U.S. Navy warships' point defense against aerial attack, is a radar-guided Gatling gun able to disgorge up to 4,500 penetrating rounds per minute. The range of CIWS mounts is so short, though, that their rate of fire is cold comfort for shipboard defenders against airborne threats.[63]

For the moment, U.S. warships can range Taiwan, Hainan, or coastal targets with air or cruise-missile strikes while remaining beyond the reach of shore-launched antiship missiles such as the ones examined before. Depending on the variant, the U.S. Navy's Tomahawk land-attack cruise missiles boast ranges officially reported at 1,600–2,500 km. The F/A-18 E/F Super Hornet, the mainstay of today's carrier air wings, has a combat radius of 723 km with a standard bomb load and external fuel tanks.[64] (Add another 111-plus km for the Super Hornet's standoff land-attack, or SLAM, air-to-surface missiles—278-plus km for the extended-range variant, or SLAM-ER.)[65] At extreme range, then, the F/A-18 can hit targets roughly 1,000 km away. The air-launched variant of the SS-N-22, by contrast, can strike at a reported maximum range of only 250 km. And even that figure is contingent on the PLA's ability to detect, identify, and track U.S. warships at such distances. U.S. Navy doctrine frowns on very-long-range antiship strikes for fear of hitting noncombatants. There is little reason to think the PLA Navy, which has never been tested in high-seas combat, has leapfrogged this intricate technical and doctrinal challenge. Nor is there reason to think PLA commanders would cut loose indiscriminately, heedless of the danger to civilian shipping, unless Beijing finds itself on death ground.

For now, then, the United States seems to have the advantage, but its advantage is on the wane. U.S. naval commanders should no longer expect to strike with impunity at Chinese military assets, ashore or at sea, while keeping their own high-value platforms—carriers, amphibious landing ships, Aegis cruisers and destroyers—out of harm's way. How far offshore the PLA Navy operates—a function of how widely Chinese political leaders construe their contested zone, how much risk Chinese commanders and statesmen are willing to assume, how much warfighting prowess Chinese mariners and airmen exhibit, and the technical feasibility of systems such as the ASBM—will determine when U.S. task forces will come under threat when approaching the Asian coast.

Looking ahead, we can safely say that the PLA's tactical reach already extends beyond the first island chain. It is also safe to say that Beijing will soon be able to dispute U.S. command of the waters and skies between the two island chains, if indeed it cannot already. How far offshore China's navy conducts exercises and what Chinese officers and pundits say about their doctrine will provide the best indicators available. For planning purposes, the soundest assumption is that U.S. forces will face surface, subsurface, and aerial threats along more than one threat axis, especially as they close on Chinese shores. In China's contested zone, the PLA will fight on exterior lines, mounting dispersed attacks to overpower U.S. antiair, antiship, and antisubmarine defenses. U.S. commanders, accordingly, should think in terms of mutual support, or "massing for defense," as Captain Hughes puts it.[66] Chances are, the balance will continue shifting toward the PLA in the coming years as Chinese forces expand and improve their arsenal and refine their tactics to make best use of the contested zone. In a sense, then, Mahanian grammar warrants at least a partial revival among U.S. naval planners—a point to which we return in chapter 8. Concentration of force is worth revisiting as a guide to future operations.

An additional, closely related point: it is high time for naval officers to discard their shopworn assumption that high-tech warships or carrier aviation can strike down the "archer" before he looses his "arrow" at the fleet. This is a worthy goal, to be sure, but it is not a foregone conclusion. This assumption has dominated thinking about antiair defense at least since the advent of the Aegis combat system in the early 1980s. Surface combatants have been designed around it, with thin to nonexistent armor plating to bolster their ability to stand in a fight. Past generations of naval architects designed combatants with just the opposite assumption in mind—that U.S. warships *would* suffer battle damage. Staying power was built into their very structure. Rediscovering this bleaker yet more realistic philosophy of naval architecture and taking a humbler attitude toward rising contenders befits a U.S. Navy girding itself for the rigors of sea combat in Asia.

Banishing the archer-not-the-arrow assumption means changing attitudes, a cultural task amenable to determined leadership from the top. Some of Hughes' commentary on warship design, however, cannot be speedily implemented. Improving the capacity of U.S. warships to withstand punishment would reduce the likelihood of their becoming losses or mission kills after a single enemy missile or aircraft leaked through their defenses. As mentioned earlier, staying power is in large measure a function of rugged ship construction. But, as programs such as the ill-starred DDG-1000 project show, modifying material capabilities takes time, involves steep costs, and incurs numerous uncertainties. The sooner the U.S. Navy starts hardening its fleet and reconsidering its tactical and operational practices, the better.

And finally, naval officers and civilian officials should not let themselves be entranced by net assessment—by the propensity to measure sea power by the size and technical specifications of America's or China's seagoing arsenal. U.S. analysts must continue and step up their efforts to understand how prospective adversaries such as China may wage war. Educating commanders' judgment and improving their cultural literacy is another matter. U.S. mariners must school themselves in foreign history and culture, think through prospective futures for maritime Asia, and prepare accordingly.

CHAPTER 5

Missile and Antimissile Interactions at Sea

This chapter draws on the material dimension of naval strategy to examine prospective access and antiaccess operations along the East Asian littoral. It is strongly grammatical in outlook, exploring the contours of Mahan's second trident. In particular, we focus exclusively on the role that missiles and associated systems might play in shaping Sino-U.S. maritime interactions should a competitive future come to pass. The following analysis complements the previous chapter on fleet tactics by integrating a concrete warfighting capability into our assessment of Chinese operational concepts. We have no desire to slight the other important elements of naval warfare, including such big-ticket items as warships and aircraft. We contend, however, that the missile age in the early twenty-first century could radically alter the offense–defense balance at sea, favoring those who wield missiles as a defensive instrument to blunt hostile efforts to project sea power ashore.

As such, the missile will be at the forefront, if not the weapon of first resort, in virtually all of the more vexing contingencies involving Beijing and Washington. If the missile literature in China is any indication, Chinese views of missile technologies and of their operational efficacy portend an unsettling nautical environment. Indeed, the types of missile-based maritime strike missions that some Chinese envision could be highly conducive to both horizontal and vertical escalation in times of crisis or conflict. We demonstrate in the following how seemingly unrelated antiship and anti-ballistic-missile technologies could intersect in destabilizing ways, accentuating the challenges to U.S. and allied sea-control missions in Asian waters.

WHY MISSILES?

The conviction that a single missile—a modern-day incarnation of the sling and stone David used to defeat Goliath—can inflict outsized damage on large, expensive platforms such as aircraft carriers adds force to the Chinese penchant for asymmetric strategies and tactics. The theorists the Chinese invariably consult reinforce this strategic preference. Sun Tzu proposed clever stratagems that would help the weaker side overcome the strengths of superior foes, but Mao—often mimicking Sun Tzu—wrote prolifically about how the weak could use the indirect approach to prevail over the strong. Both theorists would certainly approve of using highly asymmetric means to improve the feebler combatant's odds of success. In recent years, some Chinese analysts have taken to depicting guided missiles as an "assassin's mace" (杀手锏), a term similar to the Western concept of the "silver bullet." Missiles, then, dovetail with China's strategic traditions.

Missiles also promise concrete benefits. They are cheap. A fairly advanced long-range cruise missile costs as little as half a million dollars, a pittance even for many third world countries. Consider the lopsided financial burdens imposed on a naval power determined to force entry into waters contested by an adversary armed with shore-based antiship cruise-missile (ASCM) batteries. A single U.S. cruiser is worth around $1 billion, whereas the sums invested in one U.S. aircraft carrier would literally buy ten thousand missiles. As a weapon system, the guided missile is neither technologically novel nor difficult to manufacture. Cruise and ballistic missiles made their debut over the British Isles more than sixty years ago. Missile proliferation across the developing world demonstrates that even a modestly financed scientific and engineering community can produce effective, if crude, missiles.

In addition to cost-effectiveness and low barriers to entry, missiles designed for maritime strike are deadly and difficult to defeat. If guided accurately to its target, a missile can inflict tremendous damage on a warship. The annals of modern warfare amply demonstrate the danger to surface vessels. In the 1982 Falklands War, the Argentines sank a Royal Navy picket ship, HMS *Sheffield*, with a single French-built Exocet missile. Although the warhead did not detonate upon impact, the speed of the projectile (clocked at 700 mph) and the inferno caused by the fuel remaining in the missile's fuselage were sufficient to humble the British. The *Sheffield* came to symbolize the vulnerability of modern warships to cruise-missile attack, earning the epithet "one-hit ship." Five years later, the U.S. Navy found itself in a comparable situation while patrolling the Persian Gulf during the Iraq-Iran "tanker war." An Iraqi Mirage F1 aircraft mistakenly fired two Exocets—the same type of missile that doomed the *Sheffield*—into the frigate USS *Stark*. One-fifth of the crew perished soon after the attack. It took eighteen hours to extinguish fires that set the *Stark*'s aluminum superstructure ablaze and heated some of the disabled ship's compartments to 3,000 degrees Fahrenheit.

These disturbing examples still command attention from military strategists worldwide. For example, the battle for the Falklands remains a classic case study for military officers enrolled at the U.S. Naval War College. Chinese analysts too have carefully examined the conflict between Argentina and the United Kingdom, drawing their own lessons about antiship warfare. Describing the Exocet as a "star" in the conflict, one study credits it with compelling the British carrier task force to operate well east of the Falklands. Harrier aircraft were forced to fly longer distances to reach the islands, expending more fuel in transit and reducing their time on station.[1] As Lyle Goldstein astutely observes, China's interest in the Falklands War stems in large part from the "compelling strategic analogy between the Falklands case and a putative conflict over Taiwan."[2]

The lessons of the Falklands sea battle, particularly those related to the benefits of antiship missiles, sit well with Chinese strategists charged with putting substance into China's contested zone. The appeal of the missile provides the broader analytical context for understanding China's pursuit of a potentially revolutionary capability, the antiship ballistic missile (ASBM).

CHINA'S ANTISHIP BALLISTIC MISSILE: A GAME-CHANGER?

China's burgeoning conventional ballistic-missile force has attracted substantial Western attention since the late 1990s. Most analysts attribute the arsenal's growth to Chinese strategic requirements for a Taiwan-related contingency and for dealing with potential U.S. and allied intervention in a cross-strait crisis or conflict.[3] Observers uniformly expect that the short- to medium-range missiles fielded in substantial numbers over the past decade would be fired at politico-military targets on the island and at bases across Asia that play host to U.S. forces. Such a missile option assumes both operational and strategic importance for Beijing. Operationally, barrages or selective strikes would seek to destroy, damage, or deny access to critical warfighting as well as politically significant assets, facilities, and bases, with the aim of delaying, disrupting, or even precluding Taiwanese, U.S., and allied military operations.[4] Strategically, such attacks would be conducted to (1) signal Beijing's resolve; (2) coerce Taipei back to the status quo ante; (3) rapidly collapse Taiwan's will to resist; (4) compel host nations to deny U.S. forces access to or use of bases in the region; or (5) raise the perceived costs of U.S. intervention, creating indecision in Washington that delays a decisive American military response or deters it from ever taking place.

Unsurprisingly, Beijing continues to invest heavily in the size, accuracy, and lethality of its missile force, augmenting its strategic options as well as the force's operational effectiveness. Consequently, ballistic missiles once depicted as inaccurate terror weapons have emerged as formidable precision munitions boasting genuine warfighting capabilities. The implications for the United States and its regional allies are not lost on observers. A 2007 RAND report lists airfields; information, surveillance, and reconnaissance systems; logistical facilities; and aircraft carriers in port as the most likely targets for ballistic-missile attack.[5] The RAND authors estimate that the missiles already in China's inventory possess sufficient range to reach critical military assets deployed on Taiwan, Okinawa, the Korean Peninsula, and the Japanese home islands. In another excellent study, William Murray illustrates convincingly how a surprise long-range missile bombardment could "incapacitate much of Taiwan's navy and ground or destroy large portions of the air force" before the island's warships and fighter craft can sortie or take off.[6] That such worrisome conclusions are uncontroversial these days attests to China's growing missile prowess.

Beyond the types of challenges posed by ballistic missiles to fixed targets and platforms on land, a prospective new capability could substantially extend the seaward reach and utility of China's ballistic missiles. The future role that China's conventional missile forces might play in maritime strike missions against an adversary's surface fleet is emerging as a major topic of concern in U.S. policy circles. This intensifying interest, and alarm in some quarters, comes as little surprise: a shore-based ballistic-missile force capable of hitting ships under way at great distances from shore would furnish China with an unprecedented military tool, letting Beijing control events at sea directly from the mainland. Indeed, worries about what such a strategic turn of events might imply for the U.S. Navy's hitherto uncontested or uncontestable command of the sea have stimulated the kind of debate in Washington not seen since the rise of Soviet naval power in the 1960s and 1970s.

While serious discussions of the antiship ballistic-missile threat are a relatively recent phenomenon, speculation over China's development of such a potentially revolutionary technology dates back more than a decade. In a groundbreaking 1999 study on China's strategic modernization, Mark Stokes presciently concluded that Beijing would seek to develop enabling technologies, such as long-range precision strike, that directly threaten enemy vulnerabilities and centers of gravity while bypassing forces fielded by an adversary. In one of the earliest public statements on Chinese interest in ASBM-related technologies, Stokes claimed that China was "developing maneuverable [*jidong biangui*] reentry vehicles to complicate missile defense tracking."[7] In a 2002 study, Stokes shifted his threat assessment to the seas, asserting that "a terminally guided system with a maneuvering payload could complicate the U.S. carrier operations in the Western Pacific."[8]

It would take a few more years for Stokes' hypothesis to gain currency. In 2004, the Office of Naval Intelligence (ONI) published a study that identified an emerging Chinese interest in a maritime strike capability embodied in antiship ballistic missiles.[9] Observes ONI, "Chinese writings state [that] China intends to develop the capability to attack ships, including carrier strike groups, in the waters around Taiwan using conventional theater ballistic missiles (TBMs) as part of a combined arms campaign."[10] The 2005 issue of the Pentagon's annual report on Chinese military power mentions, for the first time, Chinese research into "the possibility of using ballistic missiles and special operations forces to strike ships or their ashore support infrastructure."[11] Successive versions of the annual report divulge additional details about the ASBM. The 2009 issue warns that an ASBM capability "would have particular significance, as it would provide China with preemptive and coercive options in a regional crisis."[12] In April 2009 the National Air and Space Intelligence Center issued its authoritative report on ballistic- and cruise-missile threats, stating that "China is also acquiring new conventionally armed MRBMs [medium-range ballistic missiles] to conduct precision strikes at longer ranges. These systems are likely intended to hold at risk, or strike, logistics nodes and regional military bases including airfields and ports. Notably, China is developing an antiship ballistic missile (ASBM) based on a variant of the CSS-5."[13] Other unofficial forums and publications on this subject indicate that the policy community now takes the ASBM challenge seriously. Since 2005, the Congressional Research Service has carefully documented the alarm expressed by official and media reports toward the ASBM threat.[14] In December 2008 the China Maritime Studies Institute at the U.S. Naval War College hosted a major conference on Chinese aerospace power, dedicating an entire panel to examining Chinese writings and debates on the potential utility of the ASBM capability. In June 2009 the congressionally chartered U.S.-China Economic and Security Review Commission held a day-long hearing titled "Implications of China's Naval Modernization for the United States," during which Paul Giarra devoted his entire testimony to Chinese development of the ASBM.[15] Andrew Erickson and David Yang published a provocative, forward-leaning article in *Proceedings*, the U.S. Naval Institute's professional journal, describing the ASBM as a potential "game-changer" for U.S. naval operations in the Pacific. The graphics accompanying the article showed a carrier in flames after a missile strike.[16]

Although the ASBM challenge has spurred a flurry of commentary, doubts over the missile's operational viability persist. A 2004 ONI report rates the employment of theater ballistic missiles for maritime strike missions as "very difficult."[17] Among the most contentious disputes surrounding the nautical application of ballistic missiles is technical feasibility. Accurately hitting a moving target operating in vast sea areas requires a complex range of intelligence, surveillance, reconnaissance, and command-and-control systems. The speed and angle of the warhead's reentry into the Earth's atmosphere, moreover, add an additional layer of targeting dilemmas unique to ballistic missiles. As such, analysts have been very careful not to overstate the feasibility of ASBMs. Even skeptics doubtful of China's ability to track and target naval vessels at sea nonetheless concede the potential operational value of antiship ballistic missiles. As Evan Medeiros states, "*If developed*, such a capability would severely complicate the U.S. ability to establish and maintain a 24-hour combat air patrol over Taiwan and the Taiwan Strait during conflict"[18] (his emphasis).

Medeiros is concerned primarily with the severe problems ASBMs might pose for U.S. naval aviation. If the United States wants to maintain an acceptable margin of air superiority over or near the Taiwan Strait, a large percentage (if not the majority) of air sorties will likely originate from carrier strike groups, especially if Beijing can stymie the use of land-based U.S. air power in Asia through politico-military means. If Chinese ASBMs boasted sufficient accuracy and lethality to disable carriers operating in Taiwan's vicinity, their successful employment could dramatically alter the strategic picture in times of crisis or conflict. Retired U.S. Navy admiral Eric McVadon asserts unequivocally:

The most important aspect of the increasing ballistic-missile threat is the prospect that within a few years China may be able seriously to threaten not only American land bases but also carrier strike groups, with maneuvering reentry vehicles (MaRVs). MaRVed missiles, with conventional warheads, would maneuver both to enhance warhead survival (defeat missile defenses) and home on mobile (or station-ary) targets. The implications for the PLAN of this prospective 2nd Artillery capability are, of course, profound; they include the ability to degrade U.S. air and missile defenses (including the Aegis systems and carrier flight decks).[19]

Similarly, the aforementioned RAND study *Entering the Dragon's Lair* concurs that "if China succeeded in overcoming [the technical challenges], its ability to threaten aircraft carriers would increase dramatically because such missiles would be extremely difficult to intercept and, given their high speeds, would extensively damage any ship they hit."[20] The potential threat to the carrier, however technically remote for many skeptics, has stimulated some serious soul-searching among U.S. analysts, inducing them to ques-tion long-standing, basic assumptions about sea power and naval warfare. Andrew Krepinevich argues: "East Asian waters are slowly but surely becom-ing another potential no-go zone for U.S. ships, particularly aircraft carri-ers, which carry short-range strike aircraft that require them to operate well within the reach of the PLA's A2/AD [antiaccess/access denial] systems if they want to remain operationally relevant. The large air bases in the region that host the U.S. Air Force's short-range strike aircraft and support craft are simi-larly under increased threat. All thus risk becoming wasting assets."[21] In short, the aircraft carrier and the forward base—the two iconic symbols of U.S. preeminence in international politics, and two of the pillars of Mahanian sea power—could face obsolescence, much as the battleship met its demise with the advent of naval aviation. Small wonder the ASBM has generated such angst in Washington.

CHINESE ASBM VERSUS AMERICAN AEGIS

The prospect of China's acquiring the technical capacity to field and employ antiship ballistic missiles, then, has fired imaginations among Chinese and American analysts alike, conjuring up apocalyptic visions of a crippled or sunk U.S. aircraft carrier in the Pacific. While the temptation to entertain night-mare scenarios is entirely understandable, the ASBM—if it reaches opera-tional status—would endanger all surface vessels of a carrier strike group. Particularly worrisome is the potential ASBM menace to Aegis-equipped destroyers and cruisers. Given that a typical carrier group relies on a few Aegis vessels to perform a wide array of countermeasures against enemy firepower, the loss of even one of these picket ships would impair the overall integrity of the task force. Defeating Aegis—densely packed as it is with weaponry to ensure that nothing gets through—is thus tantamount to undermining the survivability of the carrier itself.

As Wayne Hughes, the respected theorist on naval tactics profiled in chapter 4, observes, "Modern American firepower tends to be clumped together, striking power in a few aircraft carriers, defensive firepower in AAW [antiair warfare] missile cruisers and in the fighter aircraft aboard carriers."[22] By implication, severe harm to surface units that hoist the protective umbrella over the fleet could tip the tactical balance radically in favor of the adversary. It is conceivable that compromising shipborne AAW would either keep at bay or even turn back a strike group from a particular theater of operations without ever directly threatening the carrier. The sobering reality is that attacking secondary targets, such as Aegis-equipped cruisers or destroyers, could pay operational and strategic dividends for enemy forces. In effect, AAW pickets would become as lucrative as the aircraft carrier itself.

Intriguingly, a substantial body of Chinese analysts concurs. Their writings and statements evidence real and intensifying interest in striking Aegis combatants at sea as a part of a broader anticarrier strategy. Some of these sources point to the new anti-ballistic-missile mission assigned to Aegis warships. For them, this provides even more reason for Beijing to take aim at U.S. escort ships. The advent of Aegis technology in the early 1980s—USS *Ticonderoga*, the first Aegis cruiser, joined the fleet in 1983—restored mobility to U.S. naval plans against the Soviet Union.[23] If Beijing perfects techniques for using ASBMs against Aegis ships, it could reverse the freedom of maneuver that the United States has taken for granted for decades. As such, Chinese analysts' views of Aegis merit scrutiny. This chapter specifically examines how they assess the installation of sea-based ballistic-missile-defense (BMD) systems in Aegis warships, using their commentary as a window into Chinese strategic thought about maritime strike. We focus on seaborne BMD for four reasons. First, sea-based missile defense is a critical component of the broader U.S. missile-defense architecture. Aegis ships provide surveillance and tracking data for intercontinental ballistic-missile (ICBM) launches and have demonstrated their capacity to intercept short- to medium-range missiles during the midcourse flight phase. Second, sea-based missile defense is one of the most extensively tested defense programs ever. Third, Aegis ships with the capabilities to track, target, and intercept ballistic missiles now ply Asian waters. They monitored North Korean missile tests in July 2006 and April

2009. Finally, Japanese participation in BMD has added an allied dimension to America's missile-defense architecture, to China's consternation. For these reasons, Chinese analysts have devoted substantial attention to seaborne antimissile capability.[24] The strategic value Aegis has taken on in Chinese eyes is likely to magnify the rationale for targeting these warships with maritime strike capabilities like the ASBM in times of crisis or conflict.

CHINA SIZES UP THE AEGIS THREAT

Chinese analysts have expressed alarm at the numbers of Aegis-equipped ships operating in the Asia-Pacific region. The author of an article provocatively titled "Aegis Ships Encircle China" (宙斯盾舰合围中国) observes that Aegis deployments in maritime Asia virtually surround China.[25] According to Ren Dexin, a disproportionate percentage of the U.S. Aegis fleet is deployed in the Pacific theater. And indeed, at the time of his writing in 2007, sixteen of eighteen Aegis ships capable of intercepting ballistic missiles were stationed in Pacific waters. One commentary notes that while European navies possessed only three Aegis ships in 2007 (all in the Spanish navy), Japan, South Korea, and India collectively plan to put to sea at least seventeen Aegis ships in coming years. The article further observes that Asian navies' acquisition programs will set the stage for "Aegis inundation" (宙斯盾泛滥) along China's nautical periphery.[26] Yang Xiaowen forecasts an intense antimissile race in Asia, involving Japan, India, and South Korea, likely to position "bristling BMDs" (反导林立) along China's frontiers.[27] For Chen Lihao, the substantial presence of such ships reflects an American determination to throw an "anti-ballistic missile net" (导弹防御网) across the Pacific.[28] Given that the recipients of Aegis technology are either treaty allies of or friendly to the United States, such a conclusion is entirely understandable.

Some Chinese commentators cast their suspicions of U.S.-led seaborne encirclement in stark geopolitical terms. They see concentrations of sea-based BMD capabilities falling roughly along three lines of defense across the Pacific. One analyst describes Yokosuka as the first line of defense against ballistic missiles, while Pearl Harbor and San Diego provide additional layers.[29] Yokosuka is evocatively described as the "forward battlefield position" (前沿阵地), the indispensible front line for the sea-based BMD architecture.[30] For some Chinese, these concentric rings or picket lines of sea power appear tailored specifically to bring down ballistic missiles fired across the Pacific from locations as diverse as the Korean Peninsula, mainland China,

India, or even Iran.[31] Aegis ships in Yokosuka, Pearl Harbor, and San Diego would be positioned to shoot down a missile in its boost, midcourse, and terminal phases, respectively.[32]

Chinese observers pay special attention to Aegis deployments along the first island chain, which runs from the Japanese home islands through Taiwan and the Philippine archipelago, bounding the China seas. Some believe that Aegis ships operating in the Yellow, East, and South China seas would have the capacity to monitor the launch of any long-range ballistic missile deployed in China's interior, and perhaps to intercept the vehicle in its boost phase. Revealingly, Dai Yanli notes that rockets launched from the Xichang Satellite Launch Center usually jettison their boosters over Hunan and Guangdong provinces. From this Dai deduces that the boost phases of intercontinental ballistic missiles launched from Hunan, Henan, and Jilin would occur over the East and Yellow seas, within range of Aegis-based interceptors. He concludes, "Clearly, if Aegis systems are successfully deployed around China's periphery, then there is the possibility that China's ballistic missiles would be destroyed over their launch points."[33]

Qi Yanli from the Beijing Aerospace Long March Scientific and Technical Information Institute concurs, declaring, "If such [sea-based BMD] systems begin deployment in areas such as Japan or Taiwan, the effectiveness of China's strategic power and theater ballistic-missile capabilities would weaken tremendously, severely threatening national security."[34] Somewhat problematically, the authors seemingly assume that Beijing would risk its strategic forces by deploying them closer to shore, and they forecast a far more capable Aegis fleet than is technically possible in the near term.

The presence of Aegis combatants in maritime Asia is not the only threat that worries Chinese analysts. The October 2007 issue of *Modern Navy* published a special feature on global naval power, premised on the island-chain concept. One contributor, Bai Yanlin, depicts the U.S. BMD system in geostrategic terms. The second and third island chains, centered on the Mariana Islands and Pearl Harbor, respectively, constitute an American "sea wall" (防波堤) in the Pacific.[35] According to Bai, Aegis ships operating between the two island chains have become strategic weapons because they provide multilayered defenses on the open seas. He believes this capability undermines the strategic leverage of all states possessing ballistic missiles in the Asia-Pacific region. Similar to the analyses recounted earlier, Bai's article maintains that sea-based BMD will soon acquire the capacity to intercept long-range strategic missiles, which at the moment remains a major technical hurdle for the United States. If U.S. engineers overcome this hurdle, however, the consequences for Sino-American nuclear deterrence will be grave.

Chinese analysts also closely monitor the testing of the Aegis system, displaying acute sensitivity to reported technical breakthroughs. The destruction of a U.S. spy satellite by an interceptor launched from an Aegis ship in February 2008 set off a storm of speculation in China, yielding several dire conclusions.[36] First, the system's performance far exceeded its original design parameters, perhaps foreshadowing the capacity to intercept ICBMs.[37] Second, the satellite intercept provided convenient cover to test and showcase America's antisatellite capabilities to the world.[38] Third, the antisatellite technology and know-how will likely proliferate to Japan, a close partner of the United States in BMD development.[39] Fourth, the satellite intercept was meant as a deterrent signal to China.[40] Finally, the incident confirmed the extension of warfare to space. As Wu Qin states, "In future informatized warfare, the ballistic missile will be the lethal threat while the satellite will be the fatal weakness. A country hoping to win battlefield initiative must not only defend against the adversary's ballistic missile capability, but also interfere with and even destroy the enemy's satellite capability."[41] For some Chinese observers, the United States is seeking to hone both skills.

Perceptions that U.S. BMD presents a prospective threat to China at the strategic and the theater levels are by no means unanimous. The past decade has witnessed spirited debate in China about the efficacy of U.S. missile defense. A long line of Chinese scholars and technical experts deprecate the alarmist analyses reviewed earlier, voicing confidence that Beijing will be able to respond adequately to the American missile shield, particularly at the strategic level. Indeed, some Chinese writers profess unshakeable conviction that the offense will always be superior to the defense. In one lengthy article questioning the effectiveness of U.S. missile defense, analyst Yuan Chonghuan catalogs three grave weaknesses of sea-based BMD: (1) ICBMs launched from China's interior would remain impervious to boost-phase interceptors fired from the sea, even from Aegis vessels operating in close proximity to the mainland's shoreline; (2) China has access to too many types of countermeasures, such as decoys, for sea-based midcourse interception to succeed; and (3) basic asymmetries in cost overwhelmingly favor the offense since missiles are cheap relative to Aegis-equipped warships.[42]

Many observers, moreover, are fully aware that U.S. engineers must still surmount major technical barriers before the Aegis suite and interceptors can bring down the advanced ICBMs in the Chinese arsenal.[43] Writings that spotlight the threat of sea-based U.S. BMD have nonetheless appeared at a rapid and increasing clip in recent years.

THE JAPAN FACTOR

Perceptions of a more competitive antimissile environment along China's maritime periphery have stimulated debate over the role played by Japan in the U.S. BMD program. Many Chinese analysts assume the worst about Japanese intentions, maintaining that joint research and development on ballistic-missile defense reflect covert Japanese great-power ambitions.[44] Wang Chengyang argues that although Japan justifies its pursuit of BMD as a response to the North Korean missile threat, Tokyo is in fact seeking to become a major military power.[45] A team of authors declares that the "real motive behind Japan's development of a 'ballistic missile defense system' is to fulfill the long-standing dream of attaining political and military status equal to those of other major economic powers."[46]

In a similar vein, Wang Baofu, deputy director of the Institute of Strategic Studies at the National Defense University, asserts that Tokyo's deployment of missile defense parallels a broader Japanese effort "to break its pacifist constitution and expand military might in an attempt to become a world political heavyweight."[47] Some prophesy that "once Japan's [missile defense] capability is formidable enough to allow it to ignore the balance of power among itself, the U.S., China, Russia and the Association of Southeast Asian Nations, Japan can abandon the U.S. and act as it thinks fit."[48] For others, skepticism among the Japanese body politic over the prohibitive cost of missile defense has led the Japanese government to exaggerate Pyongyang's missile capabilities.[49] Chinese observers clearly find American and Japanese assurances that the missile shield is aimed at rogue states unconvincing.

Aside from questioning Japanese motives, the Chinese voice alarm at the potential strategic consequences of Japanese missile-defense ambitions. As U.S.-Japan BMD cooperation deepens allied interoperability, explains Luo Shanai, Tokyo will be tied increasingly into U.S. strategy toward Asia.[50] Yuan Chong believes the transpacific alignment will give rise to arms races and strategic instability in Northeast Asia.[51] Others go even further, accusing Japanese leaders of hyping the North Korean missile threat as an excuse to develop BMD for use against China.[52] For Shi Jiangyue, the primary motive behind the 2006 Pacific cruise of USS *Halsey*, the U.S. Navy's newest Aegis destroyer, was "to contain China" (遏制中国).[53] Two analysts observe that the deployment of BMD systems in Japan has "pushed forward U.S. missile defenses by several thousand kilometers, increasing warning time and expanding defensive depth. A ballistic missile launched from Asia toward the continental United States would be detected by radars based in Japan during boost phase, immediately cueing sea-based and land-based inceptors across the Asia-Pacific region to engage the threat, thus significantly increasing the chances of interception."[54] Given that China's nuclear posture is defensive and limited, they argue, the prospective U.S.-Japanese BMD system will undermine China's nuclear deterrent. In operational and technical terms, then, the Chinese fully appreciate the value of sea-based BMD relative to its ground-based counterpart.

Specifically, Aegis ships offer theater commanders a wider range of strategic options, including mobility, rapid response, flexibility, and the ability to function independently of other missile-defense systems. This is a pronounced advantage over land-based BMD.[55] Unsurprisingly, analysts have watched Japan's naval modernization closely. In particular, they are monitoring the upgrade of the Japan Maritime Self-Defense Force's (JMSDF) Aegis fleet, which by 2009 consisted of four *Kongo-* and two *Atago-*class destroyers. Most concur that two of these six highly capable vessels would be enough to "bolster warning and interception of Chinese and North Korean ballistic missiles."[56] Armed with the advanced Standard Missile-3 Block II interceptor, a faster, longer-range bird than previous SM variants, a single *Atago* destroyer could provide full coverage over the Japanese archipelago, in the judgment of some Chinese analysts.[57]

Speculation on how the Japanese might employ their Aegis fleet is perhaps the most interesting dimension of Chinese commentary. Chinese pundits, again, are deeply skeptical about U.S. and Japanese claims that the sea-based component of missile defense is exclusively defensive in nature. They foresee a blurring of the operational lines dividing defensive from offensive platforms in the coming years. One commentator asserts that Japan's sea-based BMD fleet will "extend the 'defense' spearhead ['防卫' 矛头] several hundred, even several thousand, kilometers from Japan's homeland to the Taiwan Strait and the South China Sea."[58] This analysis is consistent with prevailing Chinese suspicions that Japan's BMD capability is directed not at North Korea but at China. Wen Deyi argues that the missile shield will open up "strategic space" (战略空间) for Japan to develop more offensively oriented weapons, including its own aircraft carriers and offensive surface-to-surface ballistic missiles.[59] Consequently, even a defensive umbrella supplies the foundation for Japan to intervene militarily on the Korean Peninsula or in the Taiwan Strait—both theaters of vital Chinese interest.

Yuan Lin offers perhaps the most complete treatment of the offense–defense question. He points out that the defensive armaments of Aegis ships enable them to operate in enemy coastal waters, thus extending the reach of their offensive weapons deep into the interior.[60] Yuan cites USS *Vincennes'* inadvertent downing of Iran Flight 655 in 1987 as an example of the air threat Aegis-equipped ships operating just offshore can pose. Yuan further asserts that BMD technology supplies the basis for developing offensive capabilities. He observes, for example, that SM-2 antiair missiles on board Aegis ships have been modified to perform an antisurface function as well. Boasting a range of 275 kilometers and accuracy within 15 meters, the SM-2 represents both a defensive and an offensive weapon for Yuan.

South Korea's conversion of Nike air-defense missiles into surface-to-surface missiles offers another glimpse of the technical possibilities for modifying Aegis interceptors. Yuan concludes, "Obviously, in the future, the U.S. Navy's Aegis ships will not only serve as shields against air and ballistic-missile threats, but they will also become platforms for offensive guided missiles, while Japan's Aegis ships will naturally possess the potential capacity to conduct guided missile attacks."[61] Whether he is referring to Japan's potential for developing long-range land-attack missiles is unclear. Japan already possesses abundant supplies of capable Harpoon antiship missiles as well as a world-class industry for manufacturing space launch vehicles. As such, the value of technological spinoffs from BMD may be more marginal than Yuan maintains.

Predictably, Chinese analysts worry most about U.S.-Japanese intervention in a Taiwan Strait contingency.[62] For many years, they have fretted that Taiwan might sign on as a direct participant in the U.S.-Japan BMD program. Most analyses issued thus far have been rather abstract, but some Chinese strategists are starting to venture into more concrete territory. Wang Pengfei and Sun Zhihong, to name two, foretell that Japan will use BMD-related intelligence assets to gather information about People's Liberation Army (PLA) ballistic-missile and air forces, then transfer the data to Taiwanese authorities, either directly, or indirectly via the U.S. military. Enhanced strategic and battlefield awareness may even tempt Japan to join in air and missile-defense operations should the United States intervene in the strait.[63]

Another fascinating dimension of the Chinese discourse on sea-based BMD is the prospect of a multinational coalition centered on joint employment of Aegis ships. Some analysts argue that the United States cannot rely solely on Japan for protection against the ballistic-missile threat. Thus, they speculate, Washington wants to entice powers such as South Korea and Australia into a regional BMD architecture that makes maximum use of Asian maritime geography, in particular the island chains.[64] Others are perplexed over Australia's apparent interest in deploying its own Aegis fleet, which they fear will furnish the operational basis for a tripartite missile shield. Cao Zhigang describes how Washington might coax Canberra into an "antimissile alliance": "After the missile defense system is completed, in addition to being able to provide a security assurance for the US troops in Japan, it can also, after the technology of the defense system is upgraded, become a 'forward shield' for protecting the U.S. mainland. Moreover, the United States can use this as a 'model' to attract Australia to join its 'antimissile alliance,' thereby stepping up U.S. global antimissile capability."[65] Consequently, Ren Dexin postulates that a "U.S.-Japan-Australia anti-ballistic missile coalition" (美日澳反导联盟) may soon confront China.[66] Given the vast distances involved in defending Australia against long-range missiles, Japan and the United States would provide early warning of missile launches from mainland Asia or from submarines in the Pacific. Ren concludes that the sea-based BMD alliance would effectively erect a "protective shield" (屏障) reaching 50,000 meters above the Earth's atmosphere along the entire first island chain.

Another observer foresees a division of labor in which Japan furnishes forward defense against land-based missiles while Australia monitors for submarine launches in the Pacific.[67] Strikingly, these authors envision a far more capable missile-defense system, including the capacity to detect submarine launches, than is currently planned by the United States. The Chinese clearly impute creativity to the United States as it configures sea-based missile defenses beyond the transpacific alliance.

OPERATIONAL AND TACTICAL ASSESSMENTS

Given the central role of Aegis in bolstering the U.S. missile-defense architecture and protecting American carrier strike groups, China's naval community pays substantial attention to the combat capabilities of the *Ticonderoga*-class cruiser and the *Arleigh Burke*–class destroyer, the fleet's AAW "shotguns."[68] Many analysts believe that direct missile attacks against these Aegis-equipped vessels would compromise the overall integrity of a carrier task force. One study observes, "An aircraft carrier without the protection of the picket warships would be reduced to a live target for antiship cruise missiles."[69]

Commentary appraising tactics against Aegis combatants shows that Chinese strategists are investigating the vulnerabilities of carriers' defenses. The lessons they are learning and the conclusions they are drawing should worry naval planners in Washington and allied capitals.

For instance, Chinese observers have compared Aegis-equipped ships with other capable vessels to expose both the operational strengths and weaknesses of the U.S. surface fleet. A major conclusion from these assessments is that Aegis vessels are inferior at antisurface warfare (ASUW). A study that pits the *Ticonderoga* against Russia's *Kirov*-class nuclear-powered cruiser gives the latter a decisive edge. The author notes that the *Kirov* is designed almost exclusively for striking enemy carriers while the *Ticonderoga* must fulfill multiple tasks, including fleet air defense, that dilute its ability to contest for sea control.[70] Another article, provocatively titled "Carrier Killer vs. Carrier Bodyguard," examines the potential asymmetries between the *Ticonderoga* and Ukraine's *Slava*-class cruiser. Analyst Wang Yifeng reaches roughly the same conclusion, implying that the Aegis ship would be unable to cope with the sea-skimming cruise missiles launched from the *Slava* in a ship-to-ship engagement.[71]

Other commentators compare U.S. ships with similar platforms deployed by other Asian navies. Reporter Yi Xiang records his personal observations on board USS *Lassen*, an *Arleigh Burke*–class destroyer, which made a port call to Shanghai in April 2008. He was struck by the conspicuous absence of Harpoon antiship missiles from the *Lassen*, interpreting it as a sign of atrophy in the U.S. Navy's ASUW capability. Yi attributes this departure from the customary configuration of armaments to navy leaders' beliefs that (1) naval aviation is sufficient for sea-control missions; (2) the probability of fleet engagements on the high seas is extremely low; and (3) Aegis ships should focus on their comparative advantages in air and missile defense. In contrast, he notes, Aegis equivalents in the Japanese, South Korean, and Chinese navies are being "armed to the teeth" (武装到牙齿) with antiship missiles.[72] Although Yi does not elaborate on the operational implications of this apparent divergence among the regional navies, his observations exemplify the attention now paid to Aegis combatants' weaknesses.

Chinese analysts afford JMSDF Aegis ships the same level of scrutiny, noting that *Kongo*- and *Atago*-class destroyers are relatively feeble in ASUW missions because of competing requirements. Wen Wu contends that the emphasis placed on BMD relegates the *Atago*'s other combat capabilities, including ASUW, to afterthought status.[73] An even more critical assessment argues that the Japanese destroyers cannot maximize the operational potential of the Aegis combat system owing to U.S. restrictions on transfers of sensitive technology to Japan. Such limits have given birth to a class of surface combatants Chen Angang likens to a "deformed child" (畸形儿).[74] An unusually revealing study pits China's *Sovremennyy*-class destroyer against the *Kongo*, echoing the comparisons between the *Ticonderoga* and the *Slava* noted earlier. In a ship-to-ship matchup, Tian Ying concludes that the *Kongo* would find it difficult to defend against the *Sovremennyy*'s Sunburn cruise missiles.[75] Da Li concurs, arguing that "multiple concentrated attacks" (多发密集型攻击) with Sunburns would pose a fatal threat to the *Kongo* destroyers, and indeed to the entire JMSDF fleet.[76]

These assessments of the U.S. and Japanese surface fleets conform to the Mahanian grammar of sea power, extolling the aggressive use of offensive sea power. Indeed, some Chinese strategists conceive of operational plans against the JMSDF in terms Mahan himself might have used. Since the *Kongo* is the JMSDF's capital ship, they contend, PLA offensive operations must focus on defeating this center of gravity. As the nucleus of Japanese combat power, the *Kongo* thus may find itself the main target in wartime. Elaborating further, Hai Chao asserts: "If the adversary possesses stronger air and undersea warfighting capabilities, then penetrating the defenses of the *Kongo* class is not impossible. And, once the *Kongo* class is damaged or sunk, the overall warfighting capacity of the fleet would be severely crippled and the missile defense system that Japan had so assiduously constructed would suffer an unbearable blow."[77] This line of reasoning parallels the debate over how to counter U.S. intervention in Asian waters. Hai's finding, moreover, has operational implications for potential U.S.-Japan intervention in a Taiwan contingency. For some Chinese, attacking the weaker ally's high-value ships might yield strategic benefits by weakening coalition cohesion, demonstrating China's resolve, shoring up deterrence, and preventing escalation with the more powerful alliance partner.

Drawing upon a classical Chinese expression, Wu Hongmin explains, "The proverb, 'shoot the horse before shooting the man, capture the king before capturing the enemy' (射人先射马, 擒贼先擒王), teaches that sinking the enemy's flagship kills two eagles with one arrow: such an approach achieves the purposes of deterrence and lowers the potential for escalation."[78] Wu is presumably advocating an early, possibly preemptive, strike against JMSDF Aegis ships to knock out the Japanese fleet during a crisis or war. If successful, such a blow would indirectly shape Washington's calculus. The author does not consider the possibility that his stratagem might cause, rather than discourage, escalation. But is it clear that confrontation with Japan at sea is not far from the minds of some Chinese strategists.

In addition to ship-to-ship engagements, some of the literature examines options for defeating Aegis from aloft. One article deploring Taiwan's apparent interest in purchasing a decommissioned *Ticonderoga*-class cruiser dismisses the ship's value to Taipei's overall defense strategy. In wartime, Guan Dai argues, the Taiwan Navy would likely confront air-launched saturation attacks and "super saturation attacks" (超饱和攻击) from the mainland, instantly overwhelming the *Ticonderoga*'s air defenses.[79] In a nine-part *Modern Navy* series on the JMSDF, Zhao Yu asserts that JMSDF Aegis defenses will remain highly vulnerable unless provided land-based air support: "The current Aegis systems are unable to defend against the former Soviet Union's standard saturation attacks, particularly those involving air-launched antiship cruise missiles. The employment of Tu-22 Backfire bombers or similar types of bombers firing different types of antiship missiles, such as the integrated use of active radar guided missiles and anti-radiation missiles, would very likely tear through the layered air defense net of Aegis ships."[80] Another article, from *Naval and Merchant Ships*, estimates how many missile-armed fighters would be required to put eight Aegis ships out of action. Using reasonable figures on likely loss and failure rates, the author concludes that 150–200 Su-30s or equivalent aircraft would be needed to complete such a mission.[81] That Chinese analysts are thinking in such concrete terms about penetrating Aegis missile defenses is remarkable.

Although the commentary remains in its early stages, Chinese thinkers have begun thinking through how to use antiship ballistic missiles against Aegis-equipped platforms. Three faculty members from the Naval Aeronautical Engineering Institute penned an article in *Flight Dynamics*, a technical journal published by the China Flight Test Establishment, assessing the capacity of ASCMs and ASBMs to get past the layered defenses of a carrier strike group. The authors report that their simulations produced a 95 percent penetration rate for the ASBM.[82] Observers have also taken note of recent U.S. research on the SM-6, the next-generation interceptor that reportedly represents a direct response to the ASBM threat.[83] How the SM-6 will play into Chinese thinking remains to be seen.

Wang Xiangsui, the director of the Strategic Studies Center at the Beijing University of Aeronautics and Astronautics, explains the utility of ASBMs against the JMSDF.[84] He argues that while Japanese naval planners remain confident in their ability to defeat the Chinese fleet in a force-on-force naval engagement, the ASBM has shaken their confidence. Wang ascribes Japan's interest in joint BMD development in part to its need to defend the fleet against Chinese antiship ballistic missiles. His candid analysis reveals that some Chinese believe a viable ASBM will firm up deterrence against superior naval forces.

CHINA'S HIERARCHY OF ANTI-AEGIS TACTICS
As we showed in chapter 4, and as the commentary profiled here indicates, the PLA enjoys a range of options against foreign navies, including Aegis combatants. These alternatives are not mutually exclusive; they reinforce one another. Provided Beijing devotes the necessary resources to naval development and possesses the capacity for joint coordination, it can create a multidimensional threat environment for oncoming naval forces, mounting attacks dispersed in space and time. Combined-arms attacks involving ASUW engagements, air-launched saturation attacks, and ASBM strikes would stand a good chance of overwhelming sea-based air and missile defenses—particularly when supplemented by assassin's-mace tactics such as mine and undersea warfare.

As a thought exercise, it is helpful for American naval planners to rank the three anti-Aegis tactics by risk, cost, and geospatial and time considerations. In other words, the PLA may hold in reserve options that are risky, costly, more likely to fail, or more difficult to prosecute. In the early phases of a campaign, conversely, it would prefer to deploy tactics that hold the least risk, incur the least cost, promise a high likelihood of success, and can be used with relative ease. PLA planners, that is, may apply each capability in sequential terms in proportion to its costs and risks—thereby erecting a layered defense against approaching U.S. naval forces.

Ship-to-ship engagements are perhaps the riskiest option open to Beijing. Finding, tracking, and targeting ships on the open seas are difficult undertakings that require a range of intelligence, surveillance, and reconnaissance assets. Confrontation at sea also plays to the U.S. Navy's comparative advantages. The survivability of Chinese surface combatants in the face of U.S. Navy offensive strikes is doubtful; they would never close the range sufficiently to fire their ASCMs at the American surface fleet. Air-launched saturation attacks using over-the-horizon "fire-and-forget" missiles against the U.S. fleet would prove less costly and hold greater prospects of success than an ASUW engagement. But Chinese bombers and fighters need sufficient range and targeting capabilities to hit ships at sea. They must also contend with U.S. and allied air forces based along the first island chain before they can fire their first salvo.

This is where the value of antiship ballistic missiles becomes apparent. Launched from the Chinese mainland, the ASBM requires neither expensive warships nor manned aircraft to carry it to the target. It can vault over allied air defenses, striking directly at the U.S. fleet. In other words, the employment of such missiles does not entail the high human and material costs of fleet engagements or air attacks. And the threshold of success for ASBM strikes is low relative to ASUW or air attack. ASBMs do not need to sink or disable American vessels to complicate U.S. plans. They only need to reach the fleet's defensive envelope to compel Aegis shotguns to engage the incoming threats. This would force U.S. defenders to expend valuable rounds that cannot be easily resupplied at sea under combat conditions. Even inaccurate ASBM attacks, then, could deplete or exhaust a carrier or amphibious strike group's Standard Missile inventory, leaving it defenseless against further PLA actions. Chinese defense planners also foresee the use of warheads armed with submunitions that could be scattered across a wide geographic area to compensate for missile imprecision. For example, ASBM warheads could release antiradiation submunitions designed to home in on the radar emissions of the Aegis combat system. Similarly, electromagnetic pulse (EMP) submunitions detonated far above the U.S. surface fleet could produce devastating electrical surges that shut down the Aegis systems on board the carrier escorts. According to *The Science of Second Artillery Campaigns*, an authoritative doctrinal guide for China's strategic rocket forces, such ASBMs would be used to blind and confuse the carrier strike group. The authors assert: "Directed against the enemy's command and control system or weak links in its Aegis system, conventional missiles carrying anti-radiation sub-munitions or EMP sub-munitions can be used when enemy radar is being used and their command systems are working, with anti-radiation sub-munitions striking radar stations and EMP sub-munitions paralyzing the enemy's command and control system."[85] Senior PLA officers are thinking in astonishingly specific and imaginative ways about defeating the Aegis system with the ASBM. Used in conjunction with conventional ballistic-missile strikes against U.S. bases and other land targets across Asia—strikes that would elicit more interception attempts—ASBM raids could deprive the United States and its allies of their staying power in a sea fight.

Having weakened the invading fleet in this low-cost, low-risk manner, Beijing could then multiply the U.S. Navy's problems by launching successive waves of air and sea attacks. The PLA could unleash air-launched saturation attacks followed by undersea and seaborne cruise-missile salvos, wearing down the U.S. task force's defenses as it approached the first island chain. If planned and executed properly, a layered sequence of offensives could set the stage for some type of a breakthrough. A Chinese missile could reach its intended target, exerting unknowable strategic, political, and psychological impact on the U.S. theater commander, the U.S. political leadership, and the American populace. It is by no means unthinkable that the very possibility of a breach in the Pacific Fleet's defenses would give Washington pause when deliberating whether to intervene in a crisis. This admittedly dark scenario implies that the ASBM, if or when it becomes operational, will constitute Beijing's weapon of first resort against Aegis warships. It only makes sense according to cost–benefit analysis and Chinese strategic and tactical proclivities.

What we wrote about Mahanian massed battles in chapter 4 bears reiterating here. As the relative balance between Chinese and U.S. forces evens in terms of numbers, quality, and combat skill, PLA commanders may see less need to hold surface units or manned fighter/attack aircraft in reserve. ASUW engagements, for example, will come to seem less risky and costly; they will hold greater promise of success, even in the early stages of a campaign; and they will be easier to prosecute once the PLA stands on an equal footing with the U.S. Navy in maritime Asia. New tactical horizons will open for the PLA, letting Beijing choose its options with less fear of a disastrous military setback. PLA commanders will be able to contemplate the decisive offensive Mao Zedong urged, and it could take Mahanian form.

Nor is it likely that the United States will make the choice Great Britain did a century ago, concentrating its fleet near an adversary's shores to preserve its relative preponderance. Whereas the United States remains a remote superpower in Asia, Britain lay off German coasts, meaning that the German navy posed an immediate threat to British communications, and even to the British Isles proper. London could not look upon German naval development with equanimity. The PLA Navy will not rouse the same kind of fervor for naval preparation in twenty-first-century America that was on display in fin de siècle Britain.

And China's methodical, disciplined seaward turn (more on this in chapter 7) seems designed to avoid arousing America's latent jealousy over its mastery of the seas, and thus its competitive juices. Indeed, the ASBM dovetails with China's efforts to deflate U.S. threat perceptions. Unlike highly visible platforms like carriers, destroyers, and aircraft, which are familiar to the American public and political class, the ASBM and the operational benefits it promises are simply too esoteric to capture attention and galvanize opinion. They are nonnuclear and thus, in the popular mind, indistinguishable from the conventional missiles deployed across the Taiwan Strait. If the ASBMs are mobile, then dispersing them across the mainland would render meaningful assessments nigh on impossible. If the history of Chinese nuclear doctrine and strategic missile forces is any indication, the ASBM will be a virtual weapon, invisible to the public and impervious to scrutiny. Even the much-anticipated test of the system would pale in comparison to the Soviet and Chinese nuclear breakouts in 1949 and 1964, respectively. High-level policymakers in Washington, who oversee high politics rather than manage day-to-day affairs, probably will not consider the ASBM a game-changing weapon. Excited commentary by security specialists notwithstanding, a latter-day version of the Cold War "missile gap" debate is simply not on the horizon.

This low profile suits Beijing's strategic preferences, ensuring that Washington cannot mobilize the national will. The trend lines in force structure and capability, then, appear to favor China, making Mahanian encounters more and more thinkable for Beijing. Britons had it easy by comparison; truly difficult choices await Americans in the realm of sea power.

IMPLICATIONS

As the Chinese concentrate their attentions and energies on defeating sea-based BMD and Aegis AAW defenses, so must U.S. planners grapple with how Beijing may respond to the maritime context within which Sino-American strategic ties will unfold. What follows represents a summary of the Chinese discourses reviewed earlier and the types of missile-defense-related challenges Washington may confront in the future:

- At the strategic level, analysts who exude a greater sense of confidence about China's invulnerability to the U.S.-Japanese seaborne missile shield stand on firm ground. Their conclusion that BMD-capable Aegis ships patrolling the Asian littorals will not fundamentally undermine the deterrent value of the Chinese ICBM arsenal comports with geographic and technological realities. Taken together, China's strategic depth, the next-generation road-mobile ICBMs fielded in recent years, and the PLA Navy's emerging undersea deterrent virtually guarantee Beijing's retaliatory capacity.

- At the theater level, Chinese alarm at seaborne missile defense is not necessarily misplaced. Effective sea-based BMD could indeed erode Beijing's ability to threaten regional targets with selective, limited ballistic-missile strikes for demonstration purposes during a crisis. But this does not necessarily mean that China would be deterred from exercising its coercive option altogether.

- If Beijing concludes it must overpower the BMD system, either by launching more missiles or by targeting the Aegis ships themselves, then the potential for crisis instability and escalation will increase. In other words, the more missiles fired and the more targets acquired by China, the higher the likelihood that Beijing will trigger retaliation by its adversaries.

- In terms of alliance politics, some Chinese seem to assume that Japan will inevitably join in U.S. intervention in a Taiwan-related contingency. If Beijing does in fact view Japan as the weaker coalition partner—a partner that can be picked off through an early or preemptive strike against the JMSDF's Aegis destroyers—then escalation control could become an even more complex, more dubious undertaking.

- At the operational level, expected upgrades to the Aegis system fuel acute anxieties among Chinese analysts. The corresponding Chinese interest in antiship missions conforms to the Clausewitzian principle of interaction in war, or what he vividly describes as "the collision of two living forces." As the PLA contemplates maritime strike options against the sea-based BMD umbrella, it behooves the U.S. Navy not to treat sea control as a boilerplate mission—or, still less, as a given.

- To return to a point made in chapter 4, U.S. naval doctrine assumes that naval forces can shoot the archer, the launch platform, before he shoots his arrow. This deeply embedded American operational preference for the offense will likely come under severe strain, given that the Chinese are thinking about ways to preclude the United States from ever reaching the archer. In particular, the ASBM needs no archer; to strike at the arrow before launch, U.S. forces would have to strike at targets deep in the Chinese interior—a step with grave strategic and political repercussions. Smiting down the archer preemptively remains a worthy ideal, but it is dangerous to assume U.S. forces will always enjoy this tactical advantage.

The voluminous writings on Aegis and sea-based BMD suggest that China's interest in these topics is not ephemeral. It will not fade away any time soon. Indeed, the competitive intellectual environment in which the discourse on missile defense is taking place grants outside observers an invaluable opportunity to monitor the progress and maturation of Chinese thinking on missile and antimissile interactions. China-watchers should expect Chinese analysts to revisit these subjects in the coming years as new options, such as the prospective ASBM capability, become technically viable and ready for action.

CHAPTER 6

China's Emerging Undersea Nuclear Deterrent

This chapter broadens the conceptual scope of maritime access and antiaccess to the nuclear domain, a grammatical realm we have not yet explored at length. At first glance, nuclear strategy and nautical tactics and operations associated with access would seem unrelated because they belong to different levels of analysis. The former in part expresses the broader balance of national power and will between states while the latter pertains to in-theater encounters between opposing military forces. While these distinctions are entirely valid, we contend that sea-based nuclear deterrence and the naval contest for access are likely to intersect in unexpected ways that could bode ill for Asian maritime stability. It thus behooves policymakers in Washington and Asian capitals to better understand and appreciate the linkages between strategic- and theater-level interactions at sea.

Three analytical premises inform our analysis of China's second-generation nuclear-powered ballistic-missile submarines (SSBN), which are coming to form a major part of the military grammar of Chinese sea power. First, most Western analysts focus on whether the introduction of China's second-generation undersea deterrent will contribute to Sino-U.S. strategic stability. While we concur in general that a more survivable Chinese nuclear posture would add to stability, we intend to go beyond such abstract questions and explore more concretely the operational parameters that will guide China's planning for its submarines. Deployment is one thing. How Beijing employs its SSBNs in peacetime, crisis, or war is a qualitatively different matter that demands greater attention.

Second, the effectiveness and credibility of the emerging SSBN force are measured in large part by its ability to operate with impunity. We believe that this freedom of movement in turn will depend on the degree to which China can command the seas along its maritime periphery. As we demonstrate in the following, most conceivable submarine deployment patterns will likely fall within the range of Chinese antiaccess weapons and tactics, at least in the near to medium terms. The larger and more dangerous China's contested littoral zone becomes for unfriendly sea powers, the more likely that China's submarine force will be able to venture farther from shore, extending its striking power to hitherto unreachable target sets.

Third, Sino-U.S. strategic stability underwritten by mutually assured retaliatory undersea capability may, perversely, exacerbate theater-level instability in Asia. If SSBNs bolster Beijing's confidence that it can hold the United States at bay by precluding attempts at nuclear brinkmanship, then Beijing may feel emboldened to escalate vertically or horizontally in a limited, regional conflict under the protection of its nuclear umbrella. In other words, Chinese perceptions that the undersea fleet can blunt U.S. nuclear coercion would likely expand Beijing's antiaccess options. Thus, antiaccess and nuclear deterrence are inextricably linked.

To gain better analytical traction on the potential dynamics between sea-based deterrence and maritime access, we first examine historical precedents for Chinese ballistic-missile submarine development, revealing some parameters for China's likely future in this domain. We then review ongoing debates over Beijing's future nuclear posture, establishing a baseline for an undersea deterrent strategy. Based on these foundations, we then attempt to project the likely size and deployment patterns for Chinese SSBNs. We conclude with an assessment of potential sources of radical change to Chinese nuclear strategy.

HISTORICAL MODELS FOR CHINA'S UNDERSEA DETERRENT

Five countries have deployed undersea nuclear deterrent forces: the United States; the Soviet Union and its successor, Russia; Great Britain; France; and China. Although it may seem counterintuitive, the China of past decades is the least relevant of these historical models. For one thing, Mao Zedong scoffed at nuclear weapons, likening them to a "paper tiger," and was famously indifferent to the seas beyond China's coastal waters. For another, the purges accompanying China's Great Leap Forward and Cultural Revolution devastated the nation's scientific and engineering sectors, depriving the People's Liberation Army Navy (PLA Navy) of the expertise it needed for submarine development and construction. Accordingly, Chinese shipbuilders and weapons scientists never managed to construct the reliable fleet of ballistic-missile submarines that the nation needs to furnish an invulnerable second-strike capability.[1] For the sake of parsimony, then, we will set aside the China of the Mao era.

By examining the remaining four historical models, we can glimpse possible futures for China's sea-based deterrent.[2] The United States and the Soviet Union are obvious choices, given Beijing's much-discussed rise to world power status and the prospect that it will follow the path taken by the superpowers. At the risk of ruffling feathers, we will group the French and British cases together. Similar incentives and disincentives—notably, misgivings about the reliability of the U.S. nuclear guarantee during the Cold War—induced Paris and London to develop modest nuclear arsenals of their own and to send ballistic missiles to sea in nuclear-powered submarines. Some China-watchers, moreover, predict that Beijing will settle for regional power status in Asia, akin to the status the United Kingdom and France have enjoyed in Europe and its environs since the 1950s. This possibility commends the independent NATO-European deterrents to our attention.

United States
In the early Cold War, successive U.S. administrations concluded that the United States depended on a large nuclear force structure. The rationale for a large arsenal underwent several phases. At first, in the 1950s, this was largely a matter of exploiting the U.S. lead in nuclear weapons. The Eisenhower administration saw nuclear forces as a way to offset enormous Soviet advantages in geography and manpower, especially in the crucial NATO-European theater. President Dwight D. Eisenhower and his secretary of state, John Foster Dulles, briefly flirted with a doctrine of "massive retaliation" against any communist effort at expansion, however minor.[3] By the Kennedy years, massive retaliation had lost credibility—the notion of using nuclear weapons against, say, an insurgency in the Third World was unpersuasive—and Washington was scrambling to plug the "missile gap" that seemed to have opened with the Soviet Union's launch of Sputnik in 1957. In the 1960s and 1970s, strategists developed and refined a doctrine of "mutual assured destruction," or MAD. No sane leader on either side would risk nuclear war, maintained proponents of MAD, knowing that this would bring on an automatic, devastating second strike.[4]

And so the Western debate over nuclear strategy went. According to the scholar Lawrence Freedman, though, "the weapons never left center stage." Dominant perceptions held that a large arsenal was essential to counter an adversary that commanded overwhelming conventional supremacy and a potent nuclear stockpile of its own. Neither the vagaries of academic debate nor intermittent efforts at arms control and disarmament overcame that fundamental conviction.[5]

Hence the powerful U.S. submarine force, the core of the U.S. second-strike capability. By the late Cold War, eighteen *Ohio*-class SSBNs armed with Trident II C-4 or D-5 submarine-launched ballistic missiles (SLBMs) constituted the U.S. undersea deterrent.[6] American submariners are famously closemouthed about SSBN deployment practices, as befits their mission of keeping the nation's second-strike capability invulnerable. Telegraphing the locations of U.S. submarines' patrol grounds or their habits while on their seventy-seven-day patrols might render the submarine force vulnerable to an adversary's antisubmarine-warfare (ASW) efforts. Successive U.S. administrations have developed elaborate command-and-control procedures to guard against an unauthorized release of nuclear weapons. For instance, even a thirty-minute loss of communications with an SSBN on patrol warrants intensive efforts to restore connectivity between U.S. Strategic Command, the parent command for all U.S. strategic forces, and these crucial assets.[7] Political and military leaders are clearly mindful of the repercussions that would follow a mistaken release of SLBMs from U.S. strategic submarines.[8]

Yet they also seem comfortable allowing individual skippers to roam their patrol grounds without tight political supervision, and without the luxury of having attack submarines or land-based platforms nearby to defend them from enemy action. The U.S. approach to sea-based nuclear deterrence, then, seems offensive in nature, confident in U.S. submarines' capacity for concealment, and unfettered by geographically based conceptions that safe havens are necessary to protect American boats. If Chinese leaders follow the U.S. template, and once the supporting technologies mature, the coming years may see PLA Navy SSBNs range throughout the Pacific Ocean basin.

Soviet Union/Russia

Like the United States, the Soviet Union seemed convinced that it needed to hold a maximum number of its adversary's assets—cities or, technology permitting, military forces—at risk to ensure deterrence. Accordingly, the Soviet navy put to sea a sizable fleet of nuclear-powered submarines armed with the latest nuclear-tipped ballistic missiles. Technology—especially range limitations on the early generations of Soviet missiles—imposed constraints on Soviet SSBNs' deployment patterns, compelling Soviet commanders to send these boats into Atlantic waters, where they could threaten American cities. Indeed, U.S. naval planners worried that the presence of Soviet SSBNs in the Atlantic Ocean, a body of water crisscrossed by vital sea-lanes connecting North America with NATO-Europe, would conflate the SLOC defense and ASW missions—severely complicating the wartime tasks assigned the U.S. and allied navies.[9]

Soviet naval strategists seem to have come to the same realization, and advances in technology allowed the Soviet preference for a defensive stance at sea to reassert itself. By the 1970s, a growing body of evidence suggested that the increasingly capable Soviet navy was reverting to defensive deployment patterns. Soviet weapons engineers had improved the ranges of the navy's submarine-launched ballistic missiles while adding capabilities such as multiple, independently targeted warheads.[10] Rather than venturing into the Atlantic, Soviet SSBNs were patrolling Arctic waters, where they could still range U.S. targets while enjoying the advantages that came with proximity to Soviet naval bases.

This insight drove the thinking behind the U.S. Maritime Strategy of the Reagan years, which called on U.S. Navy task forces to seize the initiative in wartime, steaming northward into the Norwegian Sea to threaten Soviet strategic forces in their icy northern "bastions." Should Beijing follow Moscow's naval strategy of the 1970s and 1980s, PLA Navy SSBNs would shelter within such geographic redoubts as the Bohai Sea or, perhaps, the waters within the "first island chain" that parallels the Chinese coastline.[11] As the People's Liberation Army (PLA) brings new weapons systems online, notably its antiship ballistic missile, it will presumably be able to threaten enemy ASW assets beyond the inner island chain. This would let Chinese skippers extend their patrol grounds seaward, consistent with political restraints that might be imposed by the Chinese regime.

Britain/France

It is worth saying a few words about the British and French approaches to undersea deterrence, if only because they could offer a third model for a China content with regional influence and a second-strike capacity far more modest than those of the United States or the Soviet Union/Russia. London and Paris developed independent submarine deterrents out of concern that the U.S. nuclear umbrella would prove flimsy and undependable in wartime. That is, Washington might prove unwilling to expose the American homeland to a nuclear counterattack for the sake of NATO-European allies. Preserving the ability to inflict unacceptable damage on the USSR—thereby supplementing the U.S. security guarantee—helped them hedge against possible American waffling. Keeping sea-based nuclear forces modest in size was imperative in light of the meager budgets available to these middle-rank economic powers and the competing demands for preparedness in continental Europe. Asymmetrical undersea forces appeared sufficient to British and French officials in strategic as well as budgetary terms.

The United Kingdom and France, then, made do with SSBN forces dwarfed by those of the superpowers. It is worth noting that, numbers aside, SSBN deployment patterns seemingly resembled those of the U.S. Navy. The entire French SSBN force was based at the Atlantic port of Brest, but for obvious reasons, submarines based in the British Isles patrolled the Atlantic and the North Sea. Neither of these governments adopted a strategy requiring its SSBNs to stay within confined geographic regions or within range of land-based military forces for support. Should China adopt this approach, it will continue its tradition of maintaining a small nuclear arsenal but permit its submarine commanders to patrol widely in the Pacific, the South China Sea, or the Indian Ocean, subject only to staying within firing range of the targets they are assigned to threaten. Targets for Chinese SSBNs would include U.S. bases in the Pacific as well as less obvious sites in India and the Russian Far East.[12]

Recent Chinese literature exhibits keen interest in the French model in particular. Articles on the French Navy's *Le Triomphant*–class SSBNs demonstrate an impressive grasp of the technical developments and the general evolution of the French submarine force.[13] Chinese analysts note that France has gradually abandoned the philosophy of "using weakness to defeat strength" (以弱制强) that once informed its nuclear deterrent strategy while making the transition to an "effective counterattack" (有效反击) posture that connotes the capacity to conduct a more diverse range of strike missions.[14] Given that 85 to 90 percent of French nuclear striking power resides in the undersea deterrent force, some authors approvingly observe that the SSBNs are in essence the centerpiece of Paris' new strategy.[15] A few Chinese strategists find the French emphasis on "a few but top-notch" (少而精) nuclear platforms particularly appealing.[16] As we show in the following, Chinese undersea nuclear strategy may be moving in a similar direction, thus explaining Beijing's apparently outsized interest in the French experience.

Of course, it is possible that Beijing will fashion a distinctively Chinese paradigm for undersea nuclear strategy and force structure. Even so, history furnishes measuring sticks by which outsiders can track PLA nuclear developments. Judging from these Cold War historical cases, several indices are worth taking into account when appraising China's emerging submarine deterrent.

Nature of the Regime. Regimes exhibit certain distinct strategic and operational preferences. Like their authoritarian counterparts, Western liberal governments with nuclear capacity institute elaborate precautions and stringent command-and-control arrangements to prevent unauthorized releases of nuclear weapons. They nonetheless evince a fair degree of comfort with SSBN skippers operating far from their shores, in an offensive manner and beyond land-based support. Deployment patterns reflected this, with U.S., British, and French SSBNs enjoying considerable latitude to cruise independently within range of Soviet targets. By comparison, authoritarian regimes—particularly those driven by ideologies like communism, which prize military officers' loyalty to the regime and go to extraordinary lengths to enforce it—are ill-disposed to permit naval commanders this degree of control over strategic assets. As became apparent in the 1970s and 1980s, Soviet leaders preferred to keep SSBNs closer to home, under their watchful gaze. Whether Chinese leaders will incline to one of these approaches or will craft one of their own remains to be seen.

Strategic Culture. During the 1970s, Western strategic thinkers jousted with one another over whether there was a peculiarly Soviet way of thinking about and executing nuclear strategy. They formerly assumed not. But accumulating evidence indicated that, contrary to the logic of mutual assured destruction, Moscow was pursuing the capacity to fight and prevail in a nuclear conflict. Long-held assumptions among scholars and practitioners of nuclear strategy held that the same logic of nuclear deterrence governed decision making in all countries. If such assumptions were false, U.S. and Western nuclear strategy and force structures designed for MAD were dangerously misguided. Spurred by the debate over Soviet nuclear strategy, strategic thinkers began taking into account the influence of national traditions, history, and culture on the making of policy and strategy.[17]

Acknowledging such disparities did not come easy. The Soviet approach—holding SSBNs back and deploying general-purpose naval and land forces to defend them—defied offensively minded Western sensibilities. At one briefing in 1981, reports Naval War College historian John Hattendorf, Admiral Thomas Hayward, the chief of naval operations, "found the concepts of Soviet strategy so completely different that he expressed disbelief that the Soviets could possibly operate their navy in such a manner."[18] But they did, despite Hayward's disapproval. If the Soviet Union and other powers displayed distinctive styles in submarine warfare, the People's Republic of China probably will as well.

Threat Perceptions. How Beijing views the threat from prospective adversaries will shape its SSBN doctrine. Generally speaking, the historical models surveyed here involved putting to sea submarine forces able to counter a single threat. For the most part, the Soviet Union and United States sought to deter each other, keeping their opponent from gaining a nuclear advantage that would allow it to wage war without fear of a disastrous counterstrike. Britain and France tried to deter the Soviets and guard against U.S. abandonment by deploying sufficient nuclear forces. China clearly faces a more complex strategic geometry since it must worry about not only, say, a U.S. effort to knock out the Chinese intercontinental ballistic missile (ICBM) force in a Taiwan contingency but also about India, a new nuclear neighbor with which China shares a long border and a history of at-times violent competition. China and Russia also have a tumultuous past. Despite their cooperation of recent years, Russian sites will almost certainly find themselves on the target list for Chinese submarines. How these competing considerations will affect the size and operations of the PLA Navy SSBN force remains to be seen.

Technology Dependence. As seen from this survey of Cold War precedents, technology at times imposed certain constraints on SSBN deployment patterns that ran against political and culturally derived strategic and operational preferences. The Soviet Navy seemed to prefer a defensive stance leveraging geographic and land-based defenses, but early on, Soviet SSBNs were forced to venture into the Atlantic to fulfill their deterrent mission. Western submarines, similarly, were compelled to patrol in range of their targets, limiting their liberty of action. Once technological constraints eased, however, normal strategic and operational preferences grounded in political and strategic culture reasserted themselves. Soviet boats returned to geographically defined bastions while U.S., British, and French boats carried on open-ocean patrols. China will undoubtedly confront similar technical challenges as it attempts to construct and use its first effective SSBN flotilla. Once it meets these challenges, it too may pursue SSBN operations in keeping with Chinese strategic traditions and preferences.

CHINA'S NUCLEAR POSTURE:
MOVING BEYOND THE WESTERN DEBATE

The past few years have witnessed a lively debate among Western strategic thinkers over China's emerging force of fleet ballistic-missile submarines and what it portends for Beijing's overall strategy of nuclear deterrence. One influential school of thought prophesies a relatively static model for Chinese nuclear development, assuming that the rudimentary land-based missile force that served Beijing's needs in the past will continue to do so. Others dispute such benign prognoses, pointing to the introduction of next-generation, land-based mobile ballistic missiles, the rapid buildup of China's navy in general, and improvements to the navy's submarine and ballistic-missile forces in particular. If so, the coming years will see China put to sea a force more symmetrical with the U.S. Navy, both in qualitative and quantitative terms. It will abandon its traditional stance of "minimum deterrence," moreover, assuming a nuclear posture better described as "limited deterrence."

We take issue with both of these projections of Chinese nuclear strategy, doctrine, and undersea capabilities. We assess China's undersea deterrent purely at the strategic level, leaving aside other important questions such as how Beijing might use fleet submarines to support coercion against Taiwan or in other contingencies. Our chief finding: a larger, more advanced, more capable squadron of fleet ballistic-missile submarines does not necessarily signal a break with China's tradition of minimalist nuclear strategy. Indeed, a modest undersea deterrent would reinforce minimum deterrence as Beijing conceives of it.[19]

To test our hypothesis, it is necessary to assess the evolution of broader Chinese nuclear doctrine and force posture. Over the past four decades, China has carved out a rather unique niche among the five declared nuclear weapon states. Since China demonstrated its ability to fire ballistic missiles at intercontinental ranges in 1980, its nuclear posture has remained remarkably modest and resistant to change. China maintains what many Western analysts consider a doctrine of minimum deterrence, predicated on a strictly defensive posture, a small arsenal, a pledge not to use nuclear weapons first in wartime, and a commitment not to attack or threaten nonnuclear states. Official Chinese documents have repeatedly reaffirmed these minimalist principles.[20] In one clear statement of Chinese nuclear policy, China's 2006 defense white paper forcefully states: "China remains firmly committed to the policy of no first use of nuclear weapons at any time and under any circumstances. It unconditionally undertakes not to use or threaten to use nuclear weapons against non-nuclear-weapon states. . . . China upholds the principles of counterattack in self-defense and limited development of nuclear weapons, and aims at building a lean and effective nuclear force. . . . It endeavors to ensure the security and reliability of its nuclear weapons and maintains a credible nuclear deterrent force."[21]

The 2008 defense white paper reinforces the themes spelled out in its predecessor while offering more specifics about how Chinese nuclear forces will be employed. It declares:

> The Second Artillery Force [China's strategic forces command] sticks to China's policy of no first use of nuclear weapon [and] implements a self-defensive nuclear strategy. . . . In peacetime the nuclear missile weapons of the Second Artillery Force are not aimed at any country. But if China comes under a nuclear threat, the nuclear missile force of the Second Artillery will go into a state of alert, and get ready for a nuclear counterattack to deter the enemy from using nuclear weapons against China. If China comes under a nuclear attack, the nuclear missile force of the Second Artillery Force will use nuclear missiles to launch a resolute counterattack.[22]

Authorities in Beijing, then, appear unswervingly committed to key elements of China's long-standing nuclear policies. Wang Zhongchun, a professor at China's National Defense University and a senior colonel in the PLA, asserts succinctly, "China's nuclear strategy is mainly defensive, directional, passive and limited."[23] Such nuclear minimalism has exerted significant influence on China's nuclear posture, suppressing the size and readiness of the force structure. According to a 2002 RAND study: "One of the most intriguing aspects of China's nuclear weapons program has been its quantitatively and qualitatively limited nature over time. These limitations are characterized in practice by a relatively small number of warheads, technically and numerically limited delivery vehicles, an overwhelming reliance on land-based systems, persistent concerns over the arsenal's survivability, reliability and penetrability, and a limited program of research, development and testing."[24] Published in 2007, Jeffrey Lewis' analysis concurs: "China's small but effective nuclear counterattacking force—comprising around eighty operationally deployed nuclear warheads that are stored separately from their land-based ballistic missiles and intended for retaliatory missions—is significantly smaller, less diverse, and less ready to conduct actual operations than any of the arsenals maintained by the other four nuclear powers recognized under the NPT [Nuclear Nonproliferation Treaty]."[25] Nonproliferation expert Jing-dong Yuan notes: "China will continue to view nuclear weapons as largely political and psychological instruments in the contest of will, not usable weapons. Beijing will remain satisfied with the small size of its nuclear force as long as a comfortable margin of survivability of its nuclear arsenal can be assured."[26]

It is important to note, however, that minimalism or the absence of a radical departure from it does not mean that Chinese strategic thought has stagnated or that Beijing will not reconfigure its nuclear arsenal. There is clearly an ongoing, vigorous theoretical debate in China about the future of Chinese nuclear strategy. The vast majority of this discourse, however, focuses on the nuances of executing strategy rather than on the underlying, basic principles that animate doctrine and planning. The Chinese have coined a bewildering array of terms to describe their nuclear posture, including "effective defense," "limited self-defense counterattack," "counter nuclear coercion," and "counter nuclear deterrence."[27] But despite the diversity of the strategic lexicon, most analysts profess an abiding faith in the defensive, temperate nature of the Chinese approach to nuclear weapons. As Rong Yu and Hong Yuan explain, "Many concepts pertaining to nuclear deterrence theory itself are highly contested while consensus on the scale of nuclear capabilities necessary to fulfill the demands of each nation's nuclear deterrent remains elusive. For nations that have publicly declared minimum deterrence postures, the definitions of a minimum scale have all differed, and national conditions and associated perceptions of the strategic situation deeply influence those differences."[28] At the same time, qualitative advances and quantitative increases are clearly under way in China's nuclear force structure as Beijing seeks to shape and respond to a security environment in flux. In other words, change is occurring within the broader context of continuity. Sun Xiangli contends that "a limited scale in nuclear capability does not mean that the number of nuclear weapons would remain frozen in place. In reality, scale is a quantitative measure that closely correlates with the effectiveness of the nuclear arsenal. As various precision strike capabilities rapidly grow and anti-ballistic missile systems develop internationally, the minimum standards and technological benchmarks necessary for self defense must be raised accordingly."[29] In a rare public statement, General Jing Zhiyuan, the commander of the PLA Second Artillery Corps, appears to concur with these assessments. He envisions "elite effectiveness" (精干有效) and "sufficient effectiveness" (足够 有效) as the bases for his service's modernization program.[30] The emphasis on quality over quantity is unmistakable.

Beijing's efforts to define strategy, doctrine, and capabilities on its own terms supply a useful reminder to Western policymakers and academics not to project their own assumptions about nuclear strategy onto the Chinese. Indeed, some Chinese scholars openly reject Western conceptions of—and false distinctions between—minimum and limited deterrence, terming them overly simplistic, narrow, ethnocentric, and inapplicable to China.[31] They contend that distinctiveness and continuity based upon China's unique strategic circumstances and traditions will mold the future of Chinese nuclear strategy.

This analytical caveat is the premise of our assessment. Rather than speculate aimlessly about a nuclear posture not yet in existence or attempt to divine meaning from competing Chinese terminologies, we believe it is reasonable to assume that China will continue to abide by its minimalist (though continuously evolving) posture well into the next decade.[32] Such a benchmark at least provides policymakers and analysts with some basis to measure the degree of change should China decide at some point to depart from minimum deterrence.

It is within this context of apparent restraint that China's strategic calculus has come to enfold an undersea dimension. Successive defense white papers, for example, stress the need to improve nuclear deterrence at sea. Observes the 2004 issue, "Preparation for maritime battlefield [has] intensified . . . and the capability of nuclear counter-attacks [has been] enhanced."[33] Similarly, the 2006 and 2008 versions assign the PLA Navy the mission of conducting "nuclear counterattacks."[34] Beijing is clearly eyeing a larger role for its sea-based deterrent.

SUFFICIENCY GOES TO SEA

Defense planners in Beijing face several basic but crucial questions regarding the future of undersea deterrence. What types of force structures would Beijing consider viable? What factors might tend to favor a greater reliance on the nascent ballistic-missile submarine fleet? In short, how much is enough? Sizing the fleet is both an analytical exercise and an art, not least because of the political ramifications of deploying the most destructive single platform known to mankind. A large SSBN fleet would not only impose a substantial financial burden on Chinese taxpayers but could very well elicit a competitive response from potential adversaries. China thus faces a delicate balancing act that seeks to meet strategic requirements without unduly alarming fellow great powers.

An important intervening variable is Beijing's calculus concerning the proper force mix and the tradeoffs between its land-based, mobile ICBMs, the DF-31s, and the sea-based component. Each leg of the strategic dyad presents distinct advantages and disadvantages that surely influence the PRC's cost–benefit analysis. In terms of survivability, both land- and sea-based options enhance China's ability to escape a disarming first strike. The mobility of the DF-31 force will allow the PLA to exploit China's geographic depth whereas the next-generation Type 094 SSBN currently under development— in effect China's first working SSBN, succeeding the Type 092 *Xia*, which never made a deterrent patrol[35]—will impose additional targeting, tracking, and intelligence challenges on any adversary.[36] A survivable, mutually interdependent nuclear dyad would boost the versatility of China's nuclear forces immensely. If the ICBM force suffered unacceptable losses in a first strike, in other words, the Type 094s would guarantee that Beijing could still reply in kind. Even modest increases in the numbers of land- and sea-based nuclear weapons, then, go a long way toward enhancing the survivability of China's nuclear forces.[37]

Some factors unique to an undersea strategic force magnify the relative importance of SSBNs vis-à-vis their land-based counterparts. A ballistic-missile submarine distinguishes itself even from a road- or rail-mobile ICBM by its stealth and unlimited mobility and endurance, which allow it to launch from almost anywhere.[38] A Chinese study of nuclear submarines written by senior nuclear engineer Yang Daxin declares, "the ballistic missile submarine is thus far the most ideal 'nuclear weapons armory.'"[39] The author identifies three key factors that make the SSBN the ultimate weapon: survivability (as high as 90 percent), offensive power, and destructive power. The survivability of SSBNs promises to reduce the temptation for Beijing to adopt a destabilizing land-based posture that undermines crisis stability and escalation control, including increased dispersion and decentralized command and control. Jingdong Yuan concludes that a "sea-based deterrent would be less vulnerable to preemption and could reinforce China's no-first-use policy, reducing the risk of a sudden escalation to the nuclear level."[40]

In April 2009, *Naval and Merchant Ships* hosted a rare, fascinating debate in its pages over the advantages and disadvantages of putting a submarine deterrent force to sea. The journal provided the forum for a constructive dialogue that captured the readership's sharp reactions to the 2008 defense white paper's mention of a naval "nuclear counterattack" mission. Echoing Yang Daxin, Hong Hai argues that an SSBN offers (1) concealment and survivability; (2) mobility and range; (3) an offset for the limited range of ballistic missiles; (4) firepower and multivector strike; (5) flexible firing solutions and superior penetration capabilities against anti-ballistic-missile systems; and (6) independent operations far from the homeland, thus lowering collateral damage to civilians in counterforce exchanges.[41]

Lan Hai retorts that the SSBN suffers from a range of shortfalls, especially when compared to its land-based counterparts. The relative disadvantages include (1) compromises in missile accuracy; (2) the prohibitive expense of sustaining operational readiness and keeping submarines at sea; (3) difficulties in maintaining command-and-control; (4) the high impact and high consequences of damage, loss, or destruction of a submarine; and (5) very long research-and-development cycles for new platforms and exorbitant capital for ship construction and maintenance.[42] While it is beyond the scope of our analysis to judge the persuasiveness of either contention, the high quality of the arguments is fully representative of China's thinking about the seas, as assessed in chapter 2. Such analytical divergences also open a window into the discourse that is likely playing out in Beijing's policy circles.

As the debate suggests, the abstract strategic and operational benefits gained from an undersea strategic force likely will not convince the Chinese leadership to lean decisively in favor of SSBNs over ICBMs. Foremost in the thinking of any political leadership is command-and-control of its nuclear arsenal. It is unclear whether Beijing would be willing to delegate operational control of a nuclear-armed submarine to a tactical commander.[43] At the same time, the enhanced survivability that an SSBN fleet adds to China's mobile ICBM units is relative and incremental. The DF-31 represents a vast improvement over the fixed, silo-based ICBMs that have been the mainstay of China's deterrent posture for over two decades. Indeed, some Chinese scholars appear persuaded that the new land-based missiles are sufficient to maintain Sino-U.S. strategic stability.

According to Li Bin, even the United States' pursuit of strategic weaponry such as missile defense and space-based sensors would not undermine China's capacity to hit back with land-based missiles following a preemptive first strike. Nor would forward deployment of U.S. SSBNs in the Pacific render PLA ICBMs ineffective, despite the closer proximity of the firing platform to the Chinese forces being targeted.[44] In other words, China's vast territory and the DF-31's mobility would allow the ICBM force to escape a disarming attack and subsequently penetrate U.S. missile defenses in a retaliatory strike. This would nullify, or at least stay ahead of, American technological innovations and any reconfiguration of U.S. forces in Asia. If Li's confidence in the ICBM force is well founded, then the Chinese leadership must determine whether the added insurance derived from an undersea deterrent is worth the financial and political costs.

Practical considerations such as technical feasibility and steep financial costs, moreover, could impose burdens that the PRC may be unwilling to carry. The enormous technological, scientific, and engineering challenges of building an SSBN are already well documented.[45] The troubled history of the first-generation *Xia*-class SSBN is testament to the tremendous hurdles that the Chinese must overcome to master a craft that involves extraordinarily high barriers to entry.[46] In terms of costs, the price tag of a modern U.S. SSBN provides a rough sense of the financial challenges Beijing confronts. The average per-unit cost of an *Ohio*-class SSBN, measured over ten years from 1981 to 1991, came to an estimated $1.2 billion in 1994 dollars.[47] Relying on similar estimates of U.S. expenditures on SSBNs and SSNs, Chinese observers have also commented on the prohibitive costs of nuclear-powered submarines.[48] Land basing, then, still appears to have significant financial advantages.

In theory, a relatively modest number of survivable ICBMs and SSBNs should reduce the probability that "bean counting" would prompt a competitive response from the United States. In other words, Beijing will likely favor a force configuration that demonstrates restraint in order to maintain a stable deterrent relationship with Washington. However, accurately determining the number of ICBMs and SLBMs that would buttress deterrence while precluding a countervailing U.S. response is a delicate affair. Zhang Baohui observes that if China possessed four Type 094s, each carrying sixteen JL-2 ballistic missiles armed with three warheads apiece, then Beijing's undersea deterrent would boast 192 warheads.[49] If China deployed six SSBNs with six multiple warheads atop each JL-2, the number of warheads would jump to 572. These figures exclude the ongoing introduction of DF-31s and DF-31As, which could also be armed with multiple warheads. Such a dramatic increase would likely raise concerns in Washington, even assuming U.S. strategic forces continue to enjoy their commanding edge over China's nuclear arsenal in numbers and capability.[50] While a classic arms race resembling the Cold War would not ensue from a shift in the nuclear balance, U.S. defense planners would not react passively to an orders-of-magnitude increase in the Chinese nuclear inventory.[51]

The final number of second-generation Chinese SSBNs that will ultimately put to sea thus remains a subject of contention. Official and some unofficial estimates, however, appear to have settled on a range of four to six submarines. The Pentagon postulates that "up to five" SSBNs will be deployed.[52] The U.S. Navy's Office of Naval Intelligence projected that "a fleet of probably five TYPE 094 SSBNs will be built in order to provide more redundancy and capacity for a near-continuous at-sea SSBN presence."[53] While *Jane's Fighting Ships* expects as many as six boats, *Jane's Strategic Weapons Systems* predicts four to six submarines.[54]

Some parameters and assumptions embedded in the historical models set forth previously provide useful guidance for estimating the likely size of China's future SSBN fleet. First, an underlying principle of minimum deterrence is that as long as the number of surviving retaliatory weapons after a disarming first strike is not zero, then the posture is credible. As the British and French models show, the threshold for sufficiency would be quite low for China. In theory, even if all of China's land-based deterrent were destroyed in a first strike, a single SSBN armed with multiple reentry warheads would need to survive a "bolt from the blue" to conduct a retaliatory strike. One Type 094 could inflict damage unacceptable to any conceivable U.S. political leadership. Second, the only power with the capacity to inflict a disarming preemptive attack on Chinese nuclear forces on land and at sea simultaneously for the foreseeable future will be the United States. This reduces if not eliminates China's requirement to conduct deterrent patrols against lesser nuclear powers such as India, and perhaps even Russia. In other words, the SSBN fleet would only have to cope with one threat axis, across the Pacific.

Third, this study assumes that the United States' ability to degrade the survivability of an SSBN will not improve radically over the coming decade—say, by making the oceans transparent to U.S. sensors and ASW weaponry. This is a safe assumption, given the incremental advances of sonar technology and of exotic systems supposedly capable of peering into the depths. Since the end of the Cold War, furthermore, America's nuclear attack-submarine fleet and ASW aviation squadrons—the most potent counters to an undersea threat—have atrophied in numbers and proficiency at a rate that many believe will take decades to reverse. Nor is U.S. ballistic-missile defense in its current state any match for missiles launched by submerged SSBNs. Indeed, a counter-SLBM capability might be decades away from deployment. Chinese mariners can take comfort in the survivability of their undersea deterrent. Fourth, Beijing's high degree of comfort with the ambiguity surrounding the survivability of its nuclear forces, a long-standing hallmark of Chinese nuclear strategy, further reduces its need for absolute numerical guarantees.

These factors suggest that four to six submarines would suffice for China, as the Chinese and Western estimates cited before indicate. The rule of thumb—familiar to U.S. naval planners—is that three vessels are needed to keep one fully operational at sea at any given time. Of the remaining two, one will be in extended maintenance, probably in a shipyard and entirely unavailable for service. The third will be undergoing training and workups for deployment, and its combat readiness will thus be reduced. Assuming China adopts similar operating procedures, a minimum deterrent posture would not demand too much in terms of quantity. Assuming 50 percent of the at-sea SSBNs fell prey to enemy ASW—a generous estimate in view of SSBNs' capacity for concealment and quiet operations—only two Chinese SSBNs would need to be at sea at any given time to ensure that one survived a first strike. Based on the rotating deployment cycle described above, then, China would need six SSBNs at most to fulfill the basic demands of minimum deterrence.

Again, depending on the eventual technical quality, reliability, and characteristics of the Type 094, Beijing may not even need six boats. If the PLA Navy adopted an arrangement similar to the U.S. Navy's Blue and Gold crew system, which alternates crews after each deterrent cruise with a short maintenance period in between, it might make do with a two-for-one ratio between boats in port and at sea. Four fleet boats would meet China's needs under these circumstances.

POTENTIAL DEPLOYMENT PATTERNS

Beyond force sizing, China must also consider a range of possible deployment patterns. U.S. analysts have recently taken to speculating about the logic of a "bastion strategy" for China.[55] The Chinese themselves seem intrigued by the Soviet experience with this approach.[56] China could replicate the Soviet model, turning Asia's maritime geography to its advantage.[57] The bastion approach would create sanctuaries within which high-value SSBNs could operate. Beijing could, for instance, concentrate its SSBNs within the protective confines of the Bohai and Yellow seas.[58] Nuclear attack submarines, shore-based fighter aircraft, antiship ballistic missiles, and surface combatants could act as "palace guards," responding rapidly against hostile forces seeking to hold China's SSBNs at risk. Sea- and shore-based assets could presumably identify and hold at bay hostile forces operating near or in the Bohai or Yellow seas, exploiting the shallowness and complex acoustic environment of littoral waters as well as the fact that high-speed American hunter-killer submarines were designed for open-ocean operations during the Cold War. Shallow-water ASW plays neither to the strengths nor to the tactical preferences of the U.S. SSN force.

However attractive it seems, a bastion strategy entails certain risks. Keeping the PLA Navy undersea deterrent in the Bohai area would constrain patrol patterns, increasing the likelihood of detection by enemy ASW forces; forego much of the inherent stealth and mobility of the SSBN; and keep certain targets out of reach owing to the longer distances the missiles must traverse.[59] To overcome such obstacles, China would have to build large, capable naval forces to protect SSBNs lurking within the bastion, and to enable the boats to stage a breakout should hostile forces attempt to bottle them up and hunt them down in confined waters. The main risk of such an all-consuming deterrent strategy is that excessive investment in protecting SSBN forces would siphon off resources from equally high priorities like a Taiwan contingency, sea-lane defense, and secure access to overseas energy supplies.[60]

As an alternative to a Soviet-inspired bastion strategy, strategic submarines could range more freely along China's long coastline under the protective cover of air forces flying from mainland airfields or ships under way. Recent studies (such as our own) postulate that China has already embarked on an ambitious plan to create "contested zones" along its maritime periphery, using its home-team advantage to offset American advantages in numbers, hardware, and combat skill.[61] Enlisting the concept of sea denial, Beijing would exercise local superiority within the maritime belt shoreward of the first island chain that stretches from the Japanese archipelago through the Philippines, encompassing most of the South China Sea.

Under this paradigm, China might be confident enough to permit SSBN patrols along the Asian mainland, particularly in the Bohai, Yellow, East China, and South China seas and the Taiwan Strait. Given that China confronts several deterrent relationships in Asia, including vis-à-vis India, one analysis argues that the presence of SSBNs in the South China Sea would help shore up deterrence on the southern flank.[62] It would also let PLA Navy commanders stretch allied ASW defenses, threatening or staging a breakout into the Pacific through the Luzon Strait. This sort of "expanded bastion" strategy would clearly open up new options for the PLA, albeit at greater risk since some of the dilemmas associated with operating in the Bohai and Yellow seas would still pertain. As Liu Jiangping argues:

> Not only are surface areas of the near seas along coastal states within the first island chain small, but the waters are also very shallow. The conditions of such sea areas are completely inappropriate to serve as patrol grounds or attack positions for very large strategic nuclear submarines carrying out strategic nuclear deterrence. In shallow waters, nuclear submarines are unable to conceal themselves reliably and unable to escape the detection of enemy anti-submarine capabilities. In small sea areas, nuclear submarines cannot cruise freely in the confined grounds and cannot rely on high-speed mobility to shake off the tracking of enemy anti-submarine capabilities.[63]

Liu concludes that a sea-based nuclear deterrent can only reach its full retaliatory power in the open ocean. In this far more ambitious scheme, China could deploy submarines out into the Pacific in forays reminiscent of the U.S.-Soviet undersea competition during the Cold War. As a platform for such forays, one analyst speculates that China might base its SSBNs in the South China Sea, enabling them to slip into deeper Pacific waters undetected.[64] The large Sanya naval base on Hainan Island would be ideally suited to homeport the SSBNs.

Cruising farther east in the Pacific Ocean would bring far more U.S. targets within range of JL-2 missile strikes. Assuming China manages to develop very capable and, most importantly, very quiet submarines, Chinese patrols in the Pacific would pose the greatest challenges to U.S. Navy ASW defenders. Forward patrols would also oblige the United States to devote more of its attack boats to shadowing Chinese submarines in open waters—thereby diverting American SSNs that might otherwise be available for a Taiwan contingency or some other flare-up. With only fifty-three SSNs in service (as of the end of fiscal 2008), attack boats have become a very scarce resource for the Pacific Fleet.[65] Stretching U.S. defenses is wise strategy for PLA commanders.

The PLA Navy, nevertheless, would incur strategic and operational risks by permitting such free-ranging deployments. From a political standpoint, active patrols within the first island chain or in the Pacific would almost certainly provoke the United States into a competitive response. U.S. naval planners would likely see China's entry into Asian waters as a dramatic change in the threat environment, especially given the lack of Russian deterrent patrols in the Pacific since the end of the Cold War. Since the *Xia*-class SSBN never conducted a deterrent patrol, even a modestly forward-leaning deployment pattern would signal a sea change in Chinese nuclear strategy, significantly heightening American threat perceptions.

From an operational standpoint, submarine patrols along the mainland coast or in the Pacific would expose PLA Navy boats to U.S. and allied ASW measures.[66] Throughout the Cold War, the United States developed extensive, highly effective undersea detection networks—most notably the Sound Surveillance System, or SOSUS—to track Soviet submarines. In the Pacific theater, U.S. submarines aided by SOSUS monitored every movement of Soviet SSBNs in waters off the Kamchatka Peninsula. In the 1980s, American and Japanese naval forces raised ASW to an art form, working together closely to bottle up Soviet forces operating in the seas of Okhostk and Japan. These "legacy" systems and well-developed tactics lend themselves to ASW against Chinese SSBNs.

The ability of the Japan Maritime Self-Defense Force (JMSDF) to track a Chinese *Han*-class submarine that breached Japanese territorial waters in 2004 reaffirmed the JMSDF's high level of ASW readiness. Commenting on the *Han* incident, a former JMSDF chief of staff proclaimed that Chinese submarines would be unable to slip into the deep waters of the Pacific through the Ryukyu island chain, to the north or south of Taiwan, or through the Bashi (Luzon) Strait. U.S. and Japanese ASW forces would detect any egress.[67] If the Japanese boast is true, then the Sanya basing option could be problematic for the PLA Navy. The Type 094 SSBNs based there would have to pass through the Luzon Strait, sandwiched between Taiwan and the Philippines, to reach forward patrol grounds from which the JL-2 missiles could menace U.S. targets. Whether PLA Navy SSBNs can reach the broad Pacific undetected or unmolested in times of crisis or war is a key question for Chinese planners.

Given such potent risks, China will probably avoid coastal and blue water patrols, especially during the initial stages of deployment when training, tactical skills, and doctrine remain immature.[68] Additionally, Beijing simply might not have enough SSBNs to contemplate riskier, more forward-leaning options. As noted above, China may be content with two boats on patrol at any given time. If so, then secondary missions like patrolling the South China Sea to deter India could come to be viewed as a diversion from the main mission of deterring the United States. These factors suggest that

PLA Navy submarine deployment patterns will be rather constrained. Beijing will likely favor force protection over effectiveness during the early phases of SSBN deployment, and thus will content itself with some type of bastion strategy. Over time, if the vessels prove capable of extended patrols far beyond the Chinese coastline, then China might be willing to relax its protectiveness and permit more forward patrols.

The Chinese are well aware of the strategic and operational dilemmas they face. Analysts have held up the French SSBN experience during the Cold War as an analytical proxy to identify China's future challenges. According to one Chinese narrative, the limited range of first-generation French SLBMs compelled Paris to deploy its submarines in the North Sea and the Norwegian Sea, where they could range Moscow. This exposed the boats to Soviet attack submarines and other ASW assets.[69] To reduce such risks, the French Navy worked actively to extend the reach of its missiles, thereby allowing its SSBNs to patrol in safer waters. Yet even as France extended the reach of its missiles, it also had to develop advanced warhead penetration capabilities to defeat Moscow's anti-ballistic-missile systems. The parallels and analogies between Franco-Soviet interactions and the current Sino-U.S. strategic balance have clearly caught the attention of Chinese strategists. If Beijing acts on the lessons it draws from the history of the French undersea deterrent, we should expect to see continuing advances in the range of JL-2 missiles and in the types and sophistication of countermeasures fielded against U.S. ballistic-missile defense systems.

It is important to note that these deployment options—bastions, coastal patrols, and open-ocean patrols—are not mutually exclusive. It is possible that the Chinese may keep open variants of the three choices and alternate among them as security conditions change. Beijing may be content to rely on a bastion strategy during peacetime, when no immediate threat is evident. In times of crisis or conflict, China may permit more active coastal patrols, or may slip its SSBNs into open waters to signal resolve or to counter nuclear coercion by an adversary. In sum, even a small undersea deterrent gives Beijing multiple options across a spectrum of contingencies.

POTENTIAL STIMULI FOR A LARGER UNDERSEA DETERRENT

While a restrained Chinese nuclear posture is likely at present, it is nevertheless worth exploring how China's willingness to retain its minimalist posture could come under pressure in the future. For at least a decade now,

China-watchers in the U.S. policy community have speculated about the prospects of a shift in China's deterrent posture, from minimum to limited deterrence.[70] Western analysts have long predicted that China will make the transition to a more flexible capacity that allows the PLA to undertake a broader range of nuclear "warfighting" missions. Such a shift would require substantial increases in the numbers and types of nuclear weaponry. So, too, Chinese analysts and policymakers have exhibited greater willingness to question and reconsider the basic merits of minimum deterrence.

Although official policy remains firmly rooted in the status quo, three key factors could challenge the logic of minimalism. First, China's ongoing refusal to acknowledge that adversaries possess a viable nuclear first-strike option—a refusal that is central to the concept of minimum deterrence—depends in part on whether the United States submits to the logic of assured (but minimal) retaliation vis-à-vis China. Some U.S. strategists reject the option of deliberately remaining vulnerable to Chinese counterstrikes, asserting that the United States should design its ballistic-missile defenses specifically to negate the Chinese deterrent.[71] Reflecting such an attitude, one missile-defense advocate argues that should Beijing continue to exhibit hostile intent toward Washington, particularly with regard to Taiwan, then the United States "may simply have no choice" but to build defenses against China.[72] If Washington overtly seeks to deny China its retaliatory option, then Beijing will almost certainly respond by stepping up nuclear modernization—including the buildup of its undersea strategic forces.

Second, strategic technical advances or surprises would strain China's fairly leisurely approach to bolstering its nuclear posture. Should the United States field genuinely capable missile-defense systems in the coming decades, for instance, it would shake Beijing's confidence in its retaliatory options. It is conceivable—although highly improbable in the near term—that the advent of space-based lasers and other advanced capabilities could radically reshape China's outlook.[73] The missile-defense program's track record of incremental progress casts doubt on such game-changing breakthroughs, but SSBNs would provide a strategic trump card should American engineers indeed pull off a technological leap.[74]

Third, the reconnaissance/precision-strike complex boasted by the U.S. military could alter China's exclusively retaliatory stance. Major General Zhu Chenghu touched off a sensation in July 2005 when he declared to the foreign press that "if the Americans draw their missiles and position-guided ammunition onto the target zone on China's territory, I think we will have to respond with nuclear weapons."[75] He argued that if China faced the prospect of defeat in a conventional conflict over Taiwan, then Beijing would have no choice but to conduct a preemptive nuclear strike against American cities.

Similarly, in a candid assessment of how Chinese calculations might change, Shen Dingli argues that precision conventional strikes against China's nuclear forces during a Taiwan contingency could force Beijing to abandon its no-first-use pledge. He asserts that "if China's conventional forces are devastated, and if Taiwan takes the opportunity to declare *de jure* independence, it is inconceivable that China would allow its nuclear weapons to be destroyed by a precision attack with conventional munitions, rather than use them as true means of deterrence."[76]

In other words, if the effects of America's conventional attacks are indistinguishable from a disarming nuclear strike, China would be foolish to cling to its no-first-use policy.[77] Rong Yu and Peng Guangqian frame a hypothetical scenario to illustrate a similar point from a different perspective:

If the nuclear weapons of one warring party are attacked by the enemy's conventional weapons, resulting in nuclear radiation, nuclear contamination or even a nuclear explosion, could this be viewed as a nuclear first use? On the surface, this is merely a conventional attack, but in effect, its impact is little different than suffering a nuclear strike and incurring similarly heavy losses. In this case, conventional attack might also be seen as breaking the nuclear threshold, and the attacked party will find it difficult to refrain from a nuclear counterattack, which, in turn, will greatly increase the risks that either side launches a nuclear attack first.[78]

The implications for strategic stability are obvious, and the conclusions proffered by these analysts conform to China's long-standing aversion to nuclear blackmail. In this context, a much larger SSBN fleet might seem the only viable insurance policy against a disarming first strike—nuclear or conventional.

Clearly, a next-generation undersea deterrent will give Beijing the strategic option of hedging against sudden shifts in the international security environment. It is important to acknowledge, however, that SSBNs are not China's only answer to the strategic dilemmas noted earlier. Beijing is actively developing a range of alternative countermeasures to shore up the credibility of its deterrent forces. For instance, it has put in place a rather comprehensive set of programs to defeat U.S. ballistic-missile defenses.[79] The 2007 Chinese antisatellite test vividly demonstrated China's determination to accumulate multiple options, ensuring that missile defenses cannot debilitate Beijing's deterrent posture.

IMPLICATIONS

This chapter demonstrates how China can make significant qualitative and quantitative progress in its nuclear posture without fundamentally overturning the minimalism (at least at the strategic level) that typifies its nuclear strategy. Its strategy and force structure are not static, that is, even though the governing principles endure. China will possess a more effective, more credible nuclear deterrent once its Type 094s join the fleet, even though technical and doctrinal advances by the U.S. military have introduced some elements of nuclear instability. It appears, then, that China has redefined the parameters of minimalism to stay abreast of the fluid security environment surrounding it.

More importantly, our assessment underscores that the more conservative deployment patterns for Chinese SSBNs, such as the bastion and expanded-bastion options, require protective cover from land- and sea-based assets to ensure survivability. In other words, the deployment schemes favored by Chinese strategists will likely prove asset-intensive. Conversely, a bastion approach would take place in waters coinciding with those in which the PLA would undertake antiaccess tactics and operations. Submarine patrol grounds within and beyond the first island chain would benefit from the protective cover of shore- and sea-based forces. This common operational geography suggests that China's nautical contested zone will complement Beijing's evolving nuclear posture and broader strategic aims. Chinese command of the near seas, then, will yield benefits far beyond those related to Taiwan, other territorial disputes, and sea-lane security. This will be doubly true if events bear out reports that PLA naval, air, and ground arms are improving their ability to operate jointly. Closer coordination between the SSBN fleet, other components of the PLA Navy, and the air force and army is not only thinkable but would pay off handsomely for Beijing.

Finally, while the introduction of the Type 094 SSBN augurs well for overall Sino-U.S. strategic stability, it may not be conducive to stable maritime interactions on the theater level. Meaningful deterrent patrols off Chinese shores will almost certainly solidify Beijing's protectiveness over and sense of entitlement to the China seas—thereby raising the stakes for access to the East Asian littoral. If so, the net strategic outcome will be an even more competitive maritime environment in Asia.

CHAPTER 7
Soft Power at Sea

China grabbed headlines in late 2008 when it dispatched two destroyers and a combat logistics ship to the Gulf of Aden on counterpiracy duty. Over the ensuing months, the People's Liberation Army Navy (PLA Navy) demonstrated capabilities that had eluded it to date, including the capacity to replenish fuel and stores far from Chinese shores, to conduct repairs without the benefit of a nearby Chinese shipyard, and to conduct on-station relief between one detachment and its replacement. By all accounts, the Chinese flotilla coordinated its actions smoothly with the U.S.-led Task Force 151, the European Union's Operation Atalanta, and the individual naval contingents trying to hold open a transit corridor through the Gulf of Aden. In so doing, the PLA Navy compelled Western observers to revise their once-mocking estimate of Chinese aptitude for naval expeditionary operations. The deployment also laid down a marker on the prospects for a maritime entente in the Indian Ocean, contravening widespread notions—especially in India—that a Chinese presence in the region would menace regional security.

The PLA Navy is entering unfamiliar territory as its vessels cruise the Gulf of Aden, despite the seemingly inoffensive and even healthful nature of counterpiracy patrols. For the past several years, Beijing has been attempting to shape the diplomatic and strategic environment in maritime Asia, projecting an image of itself as an innately trustworthy great power. It has created a network of more than three hundred Confucius Institutes around the world to acquaint foreign audiences with Chinese language and culture.[1] The institutes also strive to popularize the philosophies of China's spiritual founder, for whom they are named, and to depict today's Chinese Communist regime as heir to the Confucian legacy. Confucius advocated a purely defensive, even pacifist approach to political interactions. In a similar vein, Beijing has retailed the story of Zheng He, the Ming dynasty eunuch admiral who voyaged to destinations throughout the South China Sea and the Indian Ocean six centuries ago, renewing the Sinocentric system of diplomacy and commerce that has characterized Asian politics for millennia. The Ming expeditions were almost wholly nonviolent—a point Beijing never fails to hammer home with Asian interlocutors.

This kind of narrative appeals to sentiment among the Chinese populace and to key audiences throughout Southeast and South Asia, where Chinese leaders may see fit to exercise naval power. An attractive vision of China, they hope, will avert the tendency of lesser powers to band together to offset Chinese power. Until now, Chinese diplomats have enjoyed the luxury to tell China's story how they want since deployments of PLA Navy forces beyond East Asia remained abstract. Beijing neither saw the need nor boasted the capacity to maintain strong forces far from Chinese shores. Despite the vast differences between the dynastic China of antiquity and today's communist China, Beijing hopes to convince key audiences it remains Confucian in outlook—and thus can be trusted not to abuse the sea power it is amassing. By depicting itself as an inherently defensive power, China has set a standard for its behavior at sea. Fellow Asian powers will hold it to this lofty standard—measuring its actions against the precepts of Confucius and the actions of Zheng He. In a sense, then, Chinese diplomats have rendered foreign analysts (like ourselves) a service, helping us track the evolution of Chinese maritime strategy.

FASHIONING A USABLE PAST

The American past offers a glimpse into China's seagoing future. Driven by its real and growing dependence on foreign supplies of oil, natural gas, and other commodities—supplies transported predominantly by sea—China has fixed its attentions on the Indian Ocean, where most of the nation's natural-resource imports originate, and on the South China Sea, China's maritime gateway to South Asia. As it does so, leaders in Beijing are busily fashioning what historian Henry Steele Commager would call a "usable past" to justify an increasingly ambitious maritime strategy to China's continentally minded populace and to ease worries such a strategy might arouse in Asian capitals. Commager explains how early Americans, starting anew in the Western Hemisphere, spun a historical narrative of their own. They crafted a heroic past for a disparate populace—deliberately stimulating nationalism to bind the new republic together. And they did so with dispatch. "Nothing is more impressive," writes Commager, "than the speed and the lavishness with which Americans provided themselves with a usable past."[2]

America's usable past manifested itself in history, legends, and heroes, not to mention artifacts like paintings and patriotic ballads. The founding generation engraved certain traits on the United States' identity, which Ronald L. Jepperson, Alexander Wendt, and Peter J. Katzenstein define straightforwardly as the nation's "basic character."[3] Whether early Americans intended it or not, the expectations generated by their identity helped foreign observers foresee how the United States would conduct its affairs. Dread of temporal or religious tyranny was central to the American temperament. Americans loathed standing armies and concentrated power. For them it was a matter of conviction that the nation had a special destiny, apart from the Old World. And they generally agreed that the United States should shun entanglements that might embroil it in foreign wars. The "great rule of conduct" framed by George Washington in his Farewell Address and Thomas Jefferson's warning against "entangling alliances" codified these views. Americans should abstain from overseas intrigues, which bore "a very remote relation" to U.S. interests; once the nation was consolidated, its leaders might "choose peace or war, as our interest, guided by justice, shall counsel."[4]

This all conveyed a dislike of foreign adventures. Despite the changes the nation underwent in ensuing decades, America's self-image as a great power that shied away from territorial aggrandizement or military dominion endured into the twentieth century. And it endured despite the United States' spasm of territorial acquisitions following the Spanish-American War, which gave the nation possession of the Philippines, its first base in Asia.[5] Burgeoning power and Americans' sometimes high-handed attitudes grated on sentiments overseas, particularly among the United States' Latin American neighbors.[6] Still, the image of a great power relatively free of land hunger outlived the end of the Cold War, which left the United States presiding over a unipolar world order. Confounding predictions from international-relations realists, no alliance or coalition has yet emerged to oppose American hegemony, despite occasional qualms about the direction of U.S. foreign policy. While America possesses the means to pose a threat, its lack of any apparent proclivity for doing so helps explain the world's muted response to American hegemony.

In short, America's identity bore the imprint of its usable history, cultural markers, and traditions. This fabricated common past not only united the American people but also signaled to foreign countries that, by the standards of past great powers, their republic had little zeal for power politics or territorial aggrandizement.[7] The new nation's identity created certain expectations about American behavior, helping assuage foreign nations' worries about the United States' rise to great power and the threats that a prosperous, continent-spanning republic might pose. Unsurprisingly, American statesmen across the political spectrum have gone out of their way to preserve this distinctive national character.[8] It sends a message.

Contemporary China has an interest in forging a benevolent, self-denying identity of its own. Beijing hopes to create a seafaring identity in order to rally public support behind maritime ventures and to mold strategic conditions in keeping with its foreign policy goals. Having seen its ideological appeal sag since the end of the Cold War, the Chinese Communist regime believes it must sustain the nation's impressive economic performance to provide the blessings of economic development. In effect, Beijing hopes to substitute prosperity for ideological fervor, bestowing new legitimacy on Communist Party rule. Economic imperatives at home, then, have riveted Chinese leaders' attentions on the security of the sea-lanes that convey the stuff of modern economic life from suppliers in the Middle East and Africa into Chinese seaports. The survival of the regime could turn on China's ability to devise a grand strategy upholding its interests on the high seas.

As it integrates a nautical element into its strategic thinking, Beijing understands that fellow Asian powers and the United States, whose Navy has ruled the Asian seas since World War II, will take a wary view of China's newly expansive grand strategy and the naval and military power that underwrites it. Calming fears that might give rise to a countervailing, perhaps U.S.-led coalition thus has become a matter of some import for the success of China's grand strategy. Accordingly, Beijing is attempting to use the past to realign the nation's identity and "strategic culture" with today's exigencies, portraying China as an intrinsically peaceful maritime power. Accentuating the feats of past Chinese seafarers such as Zheng He, who sojourned in maritime Asia without attempting military conquest, is one means to this end.

The kind of maritime identity China's leadership crafts, then, says much about how China will fit into the international order now taking form in Asia. What motivates Beijing? Prediction is a hazardous business, as Yogi Berra sagely counsels—especially when it involves the future. But at least three analytically distinct scenarios are plausible, each commanding support from eminent scholars:

- *Confucian Pacifism.* Reared on China's traditions of pacifism and aversion to the offensive use of force, Chinese leaders reflexively pursue a nonviolent grand strategy that regards military force as a last resort. John King Fairbank, a leading exponent of this view, famously depicted force as a "disesteemed," or distasteful, implement of foreign policy for Chinese leaders.[9] Chinese diplomacy seeks to propagate a maritime identity conforming to Fairbank's assessment.

- *Cultural Management.* In this view, Chinese leaders are not captives of culture but enjoy some flexibility to manipulate China's strategic culture, pursuing a grand strategy premised on realpolitik while reassuring fellow sea powers of their beneficent intentions. Although they differ—sometimes bitterly—on how strategic culture operates, Iain Johnston and Colin Gray, to name two prominent theorists, agree that action independent of culture is possible.

- *Cult of Defense.* Under this paradigm, Chinese elites sincerely believe their nation incapable of acting against its pacifist traditions—even when it uses force offensively or preemptively. Andrew Scobell writes of a "Chinese Cult of Defense," a mindset under which Chinese leaders can use force aggressively while fervently maintaining—and apparently believing—that their actions are defensive.[10] This bespeaks an extraordinary capacity to tolerate cognitive dissonance.

There is merit to all three schools of thought, but we doubt there is any one-size-fits-all model that explains Chinese strategic behavior. China's leaders, like their counterparts elsewhere, are likely driven by mixed, changeable motives. Even so, the policy implications of each scenario are quite different for the Asian nations and for the United States, making this an exercise worth undertaking. One imponderable raised by this analysis is whether China's venerable culture will prove as malleable as that of early America, which in essence gave the founding generation a blank slate on which to inscribe the nation's identity. Can political and military leaders reorient China's culture seaward without some traumatic event that disturbs the nation's cultural equilibrium, allowing a new, marine equilibrium to form? Will China's history be usable, or will it prove inescapable?

THE INFLUENCE OF IDENTITY AND CULTURE

To clarify these matters, we need to detour briefly into international relations theory. What is identity in international affairs, how does it work, and how susceptible is it to conscious manipulation by decision makers? We mingle concepts from the literature on identity freely with those taken from the literature on strategic culture, as indeed do the contributors to Peter J. Katzenstein's well-known volume *The Culture of National Security*, among them Alastair Iain Johnston, a leading specialist in Chinese strategic culture.[11] These authors differ on certain points, at times vehemently. But even discordant views enliven analyses of Chinese identity and culture, and help Asian sea powers track possible futures for China's grand strategy, identify variables that could influence these futures in one direction or another, and plot strategies for future contingencies. Scholars of strategic culture agree on the most basic point, that "the security environments in which states are embedded are in part cultural and institutional, rather than just material."[12] Security is about more than tallying up numbers and capabilities. These scholars' insights make a useful way to evaluate China's maritime identity.[13]

The first such observation is that nation-states have distinctive identities and play certain roles in the international system. This insight represents a sharp break with international-relations scholars' ingrained habit of using material, quantifiable factors to account for the behavior of states.[14] The makeup of a nation-state and the larger society derives not only from external factors but also from the traditions, attitudes, and habits of mind that are fundamental to how a society conducts its affairs. Ideas count. This is one reason we differ from the pure realist view, which explains nations' actions in terms of cost–benefit analysis—a mode of analysis presumably applicable to all societies. While it may be true that leaders and institutions think in cost–benefit terms, the fact is that there is no single way to calculate the value of a particular variable, say, the benefits or risks associated with a certain action or policy. National traditions and habits of mind color attitudes toward these goods.

The Greek historian Thucydides famously declared that fear, honor, and interest are the prime movers of states' actions.[15] Of these motive forces, interest might be susceptible to realist cost–benefit analysis, but the weight laid on fear and honor will vary greatly from society to society. To use a simple example drawn from chapter 3, geography placed Great Britain in close proximity to Imperial Germany, engaging not only British interests in free navigation and homeland defense but also fears of German militarism and naval prowess and, finally, steadfast determination to preserve the naval supremacy that was the lynchpin of British national honor. The United States, similarly, has a vital interest in free navigation in Asia, on which the global order of trade and commerce depends. But North America lies far from China, rendering any Chinese threat to the U.S. homeland remote and largely abstract in the eyes of the American populace and political class. And whether the Chinese naval buildup will engage American national honor to the same degree seen in the Anglo-German naval race remains to be seen. To our way of thinking, there is no algebraic formula that determines how human affairs unfold.

Second, a nation-state's identity is a complex thing, made up of a mélange of ideas and traditions—intellectual and emotional factors that at times may coexist uneasily or even contradict one another. Nor is identity immutable, even though many strategic-culture theorists imply that each nation-state has a more or less static "core" strategic culture that is highly resistant to change. A more supple view is in order. As Commager's notion of a *usable* past implies, elites may put history, traditions, and symbols to work, serving their own ends while etching their own ideas on the nation-state's character and the role it is perceived to play in the international system. Observes Johnston, "Traditions are constantly redefined and reinterpreted by successive generations of elites with a political interest in highlighting or downplaying particular traditions."[16] Johnston also points out that the complex interplay of geography, culture, and strategic experience can give rise to multiple strategic cultures. If so, certain traits eclipse others or recede at certain times in a society's history, depending on circumstances.[17] In effect, this offers skillful elites a menu of options, helping them draw out cultural characteristics that align with their chosen political objectives, policies, and grand strategy.

Third, as ruling elites manipulate identity and culture, they generate expectations about how the nation-state will conduct itself in domestic and international settings. In part this is because culture, though not entirely intractable, changes more slowly than political conditions—giving a nation-state's behavior a measure of predictability. This view finds support in the work of Charles Kupchan, who observes that elites can use language that resonates with the populace to summon up popular support for particular strategic choices.[18] Kupchan finds that both status quo and revisionist powers are prone to imprudent, "self-defeating behavior" toward prospective rivals—that is, to pursuing their interests in an overly cooperative or an overly competitive manner.[19] In large part, he says, this is because elites tend to rouse public demands they cannot fulfill—for prestige and influence on the part of rising powers, for preservation of existing prerogatives on the part of established powers.[20] Managing culture is no simple matter.

Kupchan defines strategic culture more narrowly than did Jack Snyder, who coined the term in the 1970s, defining it as "the body of attitudes and beliefs that guides and circumscribes thought on strategic questions, influences the way strategic issues are formulated, and sets the vocabulary and perceptual parameters of strategic debate."[21] For Kupchan, strategic culture is "the realm of national identity and national self-image," consisting of

> images and symbols that shape how a polity understands its relationship between metropolitan security and empire, conceives of its position in the international hierarchy, and perceives the nature and scope of the nation's external ambition. These images and symbols at once *mold public attitudes and become institutionalized and routinized in the structure and process of decision making.* . . . Inasmuch as strategic culture shapes the boundaries of politically legitimate behavior in the realm of foreign policy and affects how elites conceive of the national interest and set strategic priorities, it plays a *crucial role in shaping grand strategy.*[22] (our emphasis)

This definition supplies the crucial link between the abstract concepts of identity and culture and the concrete behavior of elites and governmental institutions. Kupchan finds the influence of culture especially pronounced in times of change. When elites are "faced with the need to make immediate, discrete policy choices to respond to changes in the external environment," such as shifts in the international distribution of power and influence, they are typically "guided in their allocation of military and economic resources by strategic beliefs and domestic political forces."[23]

In short, as members of the larger society, members of the elite are influenced by the prevailing strategic culture; they use concepts derived from that culture to shape public attitudes; and they find themselves working within the constraints of strategic culture—constraints they themselves help create through their advocacy on behalf of a distinctive vision of the nation-state's basic character or identity. Argues Colin Gray, a member of the founding generation of strategic-culture theorists, culture permeates ideas and behavior, providing "context" for strategy-making at all levels:

Strategic culture should be approached both as a shaping context for behaviour and itself as a constituent of that behaviour. . . . Both [people and institutions] have internalized strategic culture and in part construct, interpret, and amend that culture. In other words, the strategic cultural context for strategic behaviour includes the human strategic actors and their institutions which "make culture" by interpreting what they discern. . . . Strategic culture is not only "out there," also it is within us; we, our institutions, and our behaviour, are the context.[24]

Hence, strategic culture has a circular quality to it. Expectations flowing from national identity, traditions, and habits of mind allow ruling elites to set the terms of national discourse, but past expectations entrenched in public attitudes and institutions fetter elites' strategic options. It clearly takes effort for a nation-state's leadership to press identity and culture into the service of grand strategy. Traits anchored deeply in history, tradition, and the national psyche might not be as plastic as Charles Kupchan and like-minded scholars aver. Indeed, Kupchan himself attributes self-defeating behavior on the part of rising and established empires to elites' inability to modify strategic culture quickly enough to keep pace with change in the international system, managing the expectations they themselves have raised. Culture, then, is at once pliable and intractable.

Fourth, identity and strategic culture can make a useful adjunct to grand strategy if deftly managed. These traits hint at how the nation-state will conduct its domestic and foreign affairs, creating expectations that support elites' political objectives and strategy. This applies to routine diplomacy, just as it did for Henry Steele Commager's early Americans, who wittingly or unwittingly telegraphed the nature of the country they had founded. Consider Joseph Nye's concept of "soft power," which refers to the cultural attributes, ideas, and policies that make a nation attractive to other peoples and countries, creating an atmosphere of goodwill that helps its leaders muster support for the foreign policy enterprises they favor.[25] Popular discourse tends to reduce soft power to McDonald's and Hollywood, but America's open, democratic society and the benefits that derive from it furnish the nation a major reservoir of soft power.[26] As Asia's traditional "central" power, and with its economic and military power on the upswing, China enjoys sizable soft-power reserves of its own.[27] If the United States or China can convince fellow nations it has historically played a beneficent role in the international system and still abides by its self-denying traditions, it can reduce the system's propensity toward balancing behavior that would apply a brake on its foreign policy. Its prospects for diplomatic or military success will brighten.

In short, acting in concert with the principles, beliefs, and traditions perceived to comprise their nation-state's strategic culture lends credence to ruling elites' statements of purpose. If they can show that they have adhered to principle or have behaved in a certain manner in past interactions, then their words today will carry that much more weight. And if they issue a public commitment to take this or that action—holding themselves accountable to constituents steeped in the society's identity and culture—they can tap into an especially powerful, culturally informed variant of Thomas Schelling's "commitment tactic."[28] Going on record is a powerful thing. If leaders bind themselves publicly and then seem to relent on principle or contradict their nation's basic character, they risk discrediting themselves in the eyes of the domestic populace and foreign diplomats and soldiers. Wise statesmen appeal to their usable past sparingly.

AN ANCIENT MARINER HELPS CHINA RECAST ITS IDENTITY

Again the exigencies of economic development have beckoned the attention of China's leadership irresistibly to the seas, inducing Beijing to remake its traditionally land-based grand strategy. To unite the Chinese populace behind seagoing pursuits, China's maritime-oriented leadership must work some cultural alchemy similar to that of the American founders. The Chinese have regarded their nation as a purely continental power for centuries.[29] Mao Zedong deprecated the seas, urging the nation to continue thinking of itself in these terms.[30] For Mao, control of the waters immediately adjoining Chinese shores was enough. During the Deng Xiaoping era, however, China's most senior military officer, Admiral Liu Huaqing, urged Beijing to break with its Mao-inspired tradition of coastal defense. As noted in previous chapters, Liu commanded the PLA Navy throughout much of the 1980s, espousing a maritime strategy designed to give China control of East Asian waterways along with critical geographic nodes such as the island chains that roughly parallel China's coastline. Ultimately, around 2050, the PLA Navy would take its station as a blue water force on par with the U.S. Navy, putting to sea aircraft carriers and a full panoply of naval weaponry.[31] In early 2009, in concert with the navy's sixtieth-anniversary celebrations, defense officials more or less confirmed speculation that the PLA will construct carriers, although they committed to no particular timetable.

Admiral Liu's pleas on behalf of sea power went mostly unheard until the 1990s, however, when rapid economic growth impressed upon China's leadership the importance of secure sea-lanes to the nation's "peaceful rise" to economic development and ultimately to its bid for regional great power. With communist ideology in disrepute, the Chinese regime increasingly sought to buttress its legitimacy and appease public sentiment by promoting economic development and the physical comforts prosperity brings. China first became a net importer of oil in 1993, and its appetite for energy has only grown since then.[32] Mindful of their nation's resource needs, Chinese leaders will likely modify Liu's phased maritime strategy, if they have not done so already. They will turn their strategic gaze southward, along the sea-lanes that convey seaborne supplies of oil and gas—principally from the Middle East and Africa—rather than eastward, toward competition with the U.S. Navy in the broad Pacific.[33] Now retired, Liu doubtless agrees with this shift of geographic focus, which keeps Chinese maritime strategy aligned with vital interests. Direct competition with the United States for power and influence can wait until more immediate priorities are in hand.

Despite the nation's meager stock of maritime lore, China's strategic elites have turned to history to help cultivate an affinity among the Chinese body politic for seagoing ventures in Southeast and South Asia, mustering popular support for oceanic endeavors while striving to allay any misgivings their naval buildup might provoke among Asian maritime nations. In short, they have set out to incorporate a seagoing strain into China's identity and strategic culture. There is some basis in antiquity for a usable Chinese nautical past. Indeed, as the late Edward L. Dreyer points out, the Ming dynasty, which briefly made China the master of Asian waters, was birthed in inland naval warfare.[34] Chinese leaders have conjured up Zheng He as a partner in their diplomatic enterprise. Zheng oversaw seven voyages of diplomacy, trade, and discovery, calling at ports throughout coastal Southeast and South Asia. Beijing has made deft use of the six-hundredth anniversary of the Ming cruises, in effect conscripting Zheng He as an ambassador for its nautical ventures.

Zheng He's expeditions advanced domestic self-interests—his imperial master, the emperor Zhu Di (1360–1424), feared that the nephew he had ousted from the Dragon Throne would return from exile to seek vengeance— but the expeditions were primarily diplomatic and commercial in nature. Chinese officials have made the pacific aspects of Zheng's cruises a mainstay of their regional diplomacy.[35] Hugely popular both in China and throughout maritime Asia, the ancient mariner helps Beijing reorient Chinese citizens toward the sea, instilling in them a sense of mission. "Today we are commemorating Zheng He's voyages," editorializes the *People's Daily*, the official newspaper of the Chinese Communist Party's Central Committee, "to promote the ethos with patriotism as the core . . . to strengthen the sense of identification with Chinese civilization and . . . strengthen the cohesiveness and the attraction of the Chinese nation."[36] Adds the *Liberation Army Daily*, the influential mouthpiece of the PLA General Political Department:

> The seas are not only wide roads towards international exchange and a treasury of valuable strategic resources for sustainable human development, but are also an important field in the world strategic pattern in which large powers strengthen their strategic positions and diplomatic voices. The seas have already become "new command fields" in international competition. . . . About 600 years ago, Zheng He led a huge fleet overseas in an effort to materialize glory and dreams through the blue waves. Today the task of materializing the blue dream of peaceful use of the seas has been assigned to our generation by history.[37]

By invoking Zheng, moreover, Beijing can reach out to nations along the waterways that the Ming "treasure fleet"—so named for the valuables it carried to trade with foreign peoples—once plied. In so doing, it helps soothe jitters about China's naval ambitions and remind Asian nations that China once exerted a benign, sea-based supremacy over the region.

And this maritime posture is not merely for show. Beijing has steadily shifted its diplomatic stance since the 1980s, when it preferred to pursue bilateral relationships with its neighbors. It defied predictions by forging ties with the Association of Southeast Asian Nations (ASEAN), and it agreed to a code of conduct in the South China Sea in 2002. Though largely symbolic, the code of conduct sent a useful message. In 2004, when Malaysia and Indonesia lodged strong protests against the U.S. Pacific Command's plans to use American warships to patrol the Strait of Malacca, China worked with Japan to find an alternative strategy suiting the interests of all parties. Its dexterity in maritime relations helps Beijing build credibility.

Beijing's use of Zheng He as a diplomatic tool derives in part by the relative paucity of the country's "hard" power in southern waters. A striking example followed the December 2004 tsunami, when countries such as the United States, Japan, Singapore, Australia, and New Zealand dispatched maritime assets to Indonesia to help in recovery operations off Aceh and the Sumatran coast. Beijing demurred from deploying naval forces to aid relief efforts—underscoring its inability to use military power to influence regional and world events.[38] The goodwill generated by the U.S. Navy's exemplary tsunami relief effort was a particularly jarring episode for Beijing.

In their surprisingly unsparing appraisals, Chinese analysts vividly portray Beijing's sense of helplessness when it witnessed—from the sidelines—America's impressive conversion of its hard-edged power-projection capabilities into a humanitarian vehicle. As Qu Zhaowei laments, "Although China had long wished to give full play to its own soft power in the region, because it did not possess adequate capabilities, it could only watch the United States reverse its negative image in the Asia-Pacific region since the Iraq War."[39] According to Qu, Chinese fears that America's "overwhelming soft power influence" might negate China's engagement strategy in Asia spurred the PLA Navy to build large hospital ships as a strategic countermove. The tsunami experience, then, painfully demonstrated the harsh reality that hard power must effectively underwrite soft power. As Bruce Elleman notes, "When viewed in terms of the Confucian concept of *ren*, or 'humaneness,' Washington was able to outshine Beijing by far. China is clearly aspiring to become a regional superpower by using a whole range of government powers, including its military forces, but when put to the test its naval forces failed."[40] Beijing's lingering military weakness, inexperience in overseas environments, and deployment of forces to ensure internal security in provinces such as Tibet and Xinjiang and regain control of Taiwan have prevented the PLA from building up forces in regions of real and growing interest. These strategic impediments and pressing priorities explain the inaction in 2004.

Without hard power in these regions, Beijing has turned to Zheng He as a stopgap, deftly proliferating an admirable idea of China through its sophisticated historical narrative. This allows Chinese diplomats some say in Southeast and South Asian affairs, even while Beijing remains weak at sea. It also helps Beijing mold diplomatic conditions in the South China Sea and the Indian Ocean basin in anticipation of a future buildup of naval power in regional waters, should Chinese leaders decide their interests warrant such a buildup. And its invented soft power may give rise to an innocuous impression of China, helping make the increasing Chinese political and military presence in coastal Asia palatable if not welcome to regional governments.

History, then, influences China's outlook on maritime affairs, imbuing

Beijing's oceanic aspirations with a sense of destiny. China's leadership routinely connects its grand strategy to past endeavors while attempting to conciliate its maritime neighbors. In short, strategic culture is helping China's leaders sculpt an impressive program of public diplomacy, using the deeds of a venerated historical figure, backed by tangible signs of good faith, to summon up support for today's oceanic ventures.

BROADENING CHINA'S CULTURAL APPEAL— AT HOME AND ABROAD

Because he embodies China's heroic maritime past, then, Zheng He makes an elegant emissary for an increasingly confident, outward-looking nation, which helps Beijing transmit several messages. Chinese leaders hold up the legend of the treasure fleet to show that China by its nature is a more reliable steward of maritime security in Asia than any Western power—namely the United States, whose naval mastery in the region reaches back six decades—could be. The reinvigorated tributary system over which the Ming Dynasty presided was in considerable measure the handiwork of Zheng He, who negotiated agreements under which local potentates acknowledged Chinese suzerainty in return for certain economic and diplomatic benefits. Zheng seldom used force to uphold the system, and even then only in limited fashion. The eunuch admiral's self-restraint is a common refrain in Chinese diplomacy today, and it finds some sustenance in scholarship.

Indeed, the six-hundredth anniversary of Zheng He's first voyage in 2005 provided an opportune occasion for Chinese analysts to weigh in on the relevance of the Ming admiral's expeditions to contemporary Chinese foreign policy. Three themes that have emerged from this discourse are particularly noteworthy. First, the Chinese analysts uniformly assert that Zheng He set a unique historical precedent for a harmonious international order. They observe that, despite the military superiority of the Ming fleet, Admiral Zheng refrained from coercion and conquest in Southeast and South Asia while engaging exclusively in peaceful commercial and cultural exchanges.[41] By implication, China's naval rise today does not portend a more competitive future in the Asian littorals. As one Chinese article declares, "During the glorious era when Zheng He went on his western expedition, China did not seek hegemony: today and in the future, China will rise peacefully and will still not seek hegemony."[42]

Second, Chinese commentators evince belief that Zheng He's peaceful encounters with other trading partners are attributable to China's unique civilization and culture. Analysts boast that a much stronger China exhibited "peaceful benevolence" (和平宽容) toward weaker, smaller Asian neighbors.[43] The presumption is that Beijing today would replicate the Middle Kingdom's benign foreign relations. Others credit China's Confucian traditions for Zheng He's restrained behavior.[44] Invariably, they draw a sharp contrast between the Chinese expeditions and Western colonization of those same lands that the Ming admiral visited. As Xiao Yaocheng concludes: "Zheng He's peace is the product of peaceful interaction based on civilization. . . . Zheng He's distant voyages are an embodiment of the Chinese people's peaceful relations with the outside world . . . and it is deeply rooted in the soil upon which the survival of our Chinese civilization depends."[45] While some of the sweeping claims are likely hyperbole or the rhetorical flourishes commonly found in the Chinese literature, the widely shared sense of Chinese exceptionalism among the authors is still quite remarkable. It is hard to imagine, for example, Japanese commentators writing about the future of Tokyo's foreign policy with similar triumphalism.

Third, the Chinese see Zheng He as the symbol of China's current openness to the world and to the seas. Indeed, some view his achievements as an important precursor to Deng's transformative economic reform and opening movement. For Cai Yiming, the implications for Beijing's future are clear:

> History proves that: "To face the sea is to invite rejuvenation while turning the back to the sea is to precipitate decline." Oceanic development and the reform and opening are inextricably linked. We must learn from the seafaring spirit of Zheng He's expedition to the western seas. At the same time, we must face squarely the long-standing paucity of an oceanic consciousness in China's historical traditions and the harmfulness of the shortsighted land power thinking to the civilizational progress of modern China."[46]

In other words, China's long-term strategic success depends upon the type of peaceful, maritime commercial relations that Zheng He promoted six centuries ago. More importantly, such success will require a concerted national effort to reject the insular, landward orientation of the past.

This embrace of Zheng He as an archetypal figure for Chinese foreign policy is not an exclusively Chinese phenomenon. Some Western observers compare the hierarchical arrangement of the Ming years favorably to the European balance-of-power system, noting that the resort to arms was relatively rare during the era of Chinese dominance, as opposed to the blood-shed common in European international relations.[47] David Kang goes further by arguing that the return of a hierarchical order in Asia centered on a rising China would be conducive to future stability in the international system. Kang states: "East Asia from 1300 to 1900 was economically and politically important, and it was more stable and hierarchic than the European system. . . . There is a logic of hierarchy that can lead, and has led, to a stable, relatively peaceful hierarchic international system under (early) modern conditions."[48] While it is beyond the scope of this analysis to judge the theoretical validity of Kang's claims, it is clear that the notion of a Sinocentric regional order premised on Chinese exceptionalism in international affairs retains wide appeal. To some, then, great-power politics will not always be tragic. The popularity of this strain of thought in some Western academic circles suggests that the Zheng He narrative has found a receptive audience far beyond China's shores.

Similar to Kang's logic of hierarchy, Chinese officials at the highest levels of government openly declare that their nation is intent on a peaceful rise to regional eminence, or, in Beijing's latest formula, on achieving "peaceful development."[49] Chinese officials thus use Zheng's expeditions of commerce and discovery to portray China as a beneficent, nonthreatening power. Chinese power, they suggest, is intrinsically self-denying, and history proves it. In a speech delivered in South Africa, President Hu Jintao asserted that Zheng He's armada "brought to the African people a message of peace and goodwill not swords, guns, plunder or slavery."[50] Premier Wen Jiabao, while visiting the United States, declared that Zheng "brought silk, tea and the Chinese culture" to foreign peoples, "but not one inch of land was occupied."[51]

Guo Chongli, China's ambassador to Kenya, proclaimed that while "Zheng He's fleet [was] large . . . his voyages were not for looting resources"—code for Western imperialism—"but for friendship. In trade with foreign countries, he gave much more than he took," fostering "understanding, friendship and trade relation[s] between China's Ming Dynasty and foreign countries in southeast Asia, west Asia and east Africa."[52] The *People's Daily* agrees that Zheng's expeditions gave "full expression to the Chinese spirit of 'harmony,'" as expressed in Confucian teachings, whereas Columbus and his successors "opened up a large group of colonies" in the Americas, bent on "a typical predatory rise."[53] A commentary published in the official *China Daily* is even more explicit about comparing China to the West: "Unlike many of its latter-day European counterparts, which sailed across the great oceans to conquer other nations by force, the Chinese fleet brought to those foreign lands tea, chinaware, silk and craftsmanship. They gave the rest of the world peace and civilization and never occupied any foreign land, an achievement symbolizing the ancient kingdom's sincerity to increase exchanges with other nations."[54] The message to countries wary of Beijing's ambitions is that despite China's mounting political, economic, and military power, it can be counted on to refrain from territorial conquest or Western-style military dominion.[55] China's identity and strategic culture will restrain its ambitions on the high seas, just as it did in the days of the treasure fleet. Banding together to balance a resurgent China is unnecessary. As the ruling State Council proclaims in a white paper titled *China's Peaceful Development Road*,

> It is an *inevitable choice based on China's historical and cultural tradition* that China persists unswervingly in taking the road of peaceful development. . . . The spirit of the Chinese people has *always* featured their longing for peace and pursuit of harmony. Six hundred years ago, Zheng He . . . [reached] more than 30 countries and regions in Asia and Africa. . . . What he took to the places he visited were tea, chinaware, silk and technology, but did not occupy an inch of any other's land. What he brought to the outside world was peace and civilization. . . . Based on the present reality, China's development has not only benefited the 1.3 billion Chinese people, but also brought large markets and development opportunities for countries throughout the world. China's development also helps to enhance the force for peace in the world.[56] (our emphasis)

China's maritime rise, then, is not only harmless but also qualifies as a positive international public good benefiting the region at large. During his keynote speech at Cambridge University, Premier Wen returned to this historical and cultural dimension of contemporary Chinese foreign policy. Wen once again invoked Zheng He to highlight China's allergy to power politics and dominion. He proclaimed:

> The cultural tradition of valuing harmony has nurtured broad-mindedness in the Chinese people. As the earth can bear all things, our people exercise great tolerance; as the heavens work with vigor, our people display justness. . . . During the 15th century, the famous Chinese navigator Zheng He made seven voyages to western seas, and went to 30 countries. He took with him Chinese tea, silk, and

porcelain. He also helped some of the countries along his route to eradicate piracy. He truly spread benevolence and friendly relations.

The idea that a strong country must be a hegemon does not sit well with China. Hegemonism is at odds with our cultural tradition, and it runs counter to the wishes of the Chinese people. China's development harms no one, nor does it threaten anyone. China wants to be a great country of peace, a great country of learning, a great country of cooperation, and China exerts effort on building a harmonious world.[57]

Chinese spokesmen have also sought to assuage Asian nations' fear of China's naval buildup in sweeping historical terms. "The essence of Zheng's voyages does not lie in how strong the Chinese Navy once was," declared Xu Zuyuan, the Chinese government's vice minister for communication, "but in that China adhere[d] to peaceful diplomacy when it was a big power. . . . Zheng He's seven voyages to the West [explain] why a peaceful emergence is the inevitable outcome of the development of Chinese history"[58] (our emphasis). Chinese officials intimate that, had the Ming Dynasty not outlawed naval pursuits after Zheng He's final voyage, Asian history might have taken a different—and presumably more humane—course under Chinese supervision. Chinese officials, then, are seeking to propagate the notion that China represents a qualitatively superior, pacifying force in world history.

China's leadership also uses the treasure expeditions to add luster to China's reputation as a seafaring nation, skilled in navigation, shipbuilding, and—though Beijing plays down this aspect of maritime affairs, staying on message—naval combat. Zheng He's cruises in effect made China the first country to station a naval squadron in the Indian Ocean.[59] The treasure fleet was a technological wonder by the standards of his day. Chinese ships had been equipped with compasses since the Song dynasty. Navigators knew how to determine latitude and could plot and follow a course to a predetermined destination using charts accurate enough that many of them remained in use in the eighteenth century.

Zheng's *baochuan*, or treasure ships—essentially giant seagoing junks, some outfitted with as many as nine masts—featured technical innovations that did not make their way into Western naval architecture until the nineteenth century.[60] If a treasure ship suffered hull damage from battle or heavy weather, for instance, the watertight bulkheads that subdivided the interior of the vessel limited the spread of flooding, helping it resist sinking.[61] If battle loomed, the *baochuan* were equipped with incendiary weapons like the cat-apult-thrown gunpowder "grenades" the treasure fleet used to overawe and defeat a pirate armada near the Strait of Malacca, then as now a critical artery for seaborne trade and commerce.[62] Reporting on the efforts of Yao Mingde, the official in charge of organizing activities to commemorate the treasure voyages, the official news service Xinhua observed that "Zheng He's fleet sur-passed all other marine navigators of his time in scale, sophistication, technol-ogy and organizational skills in his seven sea trips, which were a great event in the world's navigation history."[63] Such boasts of China's nautical prowess abound in Chinese commentary.

Zheng allows Beijing to indulge in one-upmanship at Western expense, furthermore, by playing up Chinese seamanship and technology. On one trip to Europe, for example, Premier Wen reminded audiences that the Chinese explorer had "sailed abroad earlier than Christopher Columbus."[64] Chinese spokesmen invariably contrast the size and technical sophistication of Zheng's vessels with the relatively backward fleets put to sea in fifteenth-century Europe, including not only Columbus' flotilla but also that of Vasco da Gama, who dropped anchor along the Indian subcontinent in 1498.[65] Da Gama's voyage ushered in centuries of European dominion in Asia, giving Beijing a point of reference for its Zheng He narrative.

Chinese officials also point out that China was a power in maritime Asia first, owing to Ming seamanship.[66] In 2003, for instance, President Hu Jintao depicted Zheng He's expeditions as a historical basis for the Sino-Australian relationship, telling the Australian parliament, "Back in the 1420s, the expe-ditionary fleets of China's Ming Dynasty reached Australian shores," bring-ing "Chinese culture to this land" and "contributing their proud share to Australia's economy, society and its thriving pluralistic culture."[67] Hu's claim that Chinese seafarers settled in Australia during the Ming years is whimsy, but his central message is spot on: China's presence and power in maritime Asia far antedate those of Europeans.[68] And since maritime Asia is resuming course to a preferable future, Hu implies, China's nautical ascendancy ought to be welcomed rather than feared.

Such rhetoric makes an excellent focal point for Chinese exceptional-ism and nationalism. However, like many national legends—to return to the American example, one thinks of Parson Weems' fanciful account of George Washington chopping down the cherry tree—Beijing's Zheng He narrative rates so-so marks as history. For one thing, the nature of the ruling regime matters, in China as elsewhere. The communist regime in Beijing can scarcely claim to be a direct descendant of the Ming dynasty (or any other imperial dynasty). Indeed, Mao's regime went to extreme lengths to purge China of its traditional culture and traditions, which communists saw as a barrier to revolution. Contrary to Chinese diplomacy, therefore, events of antiquity make an unreliable predictor of Chinese behavior today.[69] For another, Zheng's voyages spanned only a brief interval in China's long history. It would be rash to extrapolate from Zheng's generally peaceful yet short-lived endeavors, concluding that China has no penchant for military dominance today.

Had the Ming dynasty not retreated from the seas—dismantling its formidable navy and ultimately outlawing the construction of seagoing vessels—it might indeed have resorted to arms to uphold the tributary system, more or less in Western style. Edward Dreyer makes no bones about labeling Zheng He's voyages an exercise in power projection, designed to overawe lesser Asian societies—to the extent that using force was seldom necessary to impose Chinese emperors' political will.[70] But the treasure fleet occasionally did use force to support kings loyal to the Dragon Throne. In 1411, for example, Chinese marines intervened in an internal war on Ceylon, quelling an insurrection led by the Buddhist chief Alakeswara and asserting Ming sovereignty over the island.[71]

Still another factor clouding Chinese maritime diplomacy: it was precisely the Confucian suspicion of profit-making that prompted the Ming court to pull back from the seas and disband Zheng He's fleet. Seagoing trade and commerce may not coexist as comfortably with Confucian precepts as Chinese diplomacy suggests. China's version of history is a bit too neat to fit the facts. These problems with the narrative of an intrinsically peaceful, benign China determined to supply the region with international public goods should give pause to outsiders examining Beijing's Zheng He diplomacy. In short, China might not be quite so unique a great power as it advertises.

CHINA'S MARITIME SOFT POWER AND THE COUNTERPIRACY OPERATION

China's turn to its usable past has intersected with real events at sea. Until very recently, Chinese diplomats have had the luxury to wax lyrical about their nation's inoffensive, even stabilizing entry into the maritime domain since the PLA Navy has remained relatively close to home. China's neighbors had little basis to judge Beijing's invocation of history and cultural traditions since its lofty rhetoric far outstripped its material capabilities and the naval activities it has prosecuted in the region. As a result, Asian officials have tended to wave away China's reassurances as either posturing or as a temporary disguise for raw realpolitik thinking. Beijing's sincerity can now be put to the test. The PLA Navy's antipiracy operations in the Gulf of Aden offer an important empirical case study for evaluating the Zheng He narrative.

Several questions guide the following effort to measure the efficacy of Chinese maritime soft power and to assess the extent to which Beijing has matched words with deeds. Have the Chinese explicitly linked the escort mission to Chinese foreign policy principles, and its objectives to Zheng He diplomacy? How have the recipients of China's soft-power message in the Indian Ocean basin responded to the presence of Chinese naval power? To what degree will Chinese maritime soft power pay off over the longer term? Some preliminary answers to these questions will highlight both the utility of and limits to Chinese soft power at sea.

China's naval operations in Somali waters were not conceived overnight or in a policy vacuum. For at least a decade, Chinese policymakers have anticipated the need to cope with nontraditional security threats, which encompass drug and human trafficking, piracy, terrorism, humanitarian disasters, arms smuggling, cybercrime, international economic and financial crime, and pandemics. Analysts contend that active efforts to combat such challenges not only fulfill China's responsibilities as a rising great power but also accrue soft power over time. Wu Weixing explains: "As China's international influence grows and experience in resolving hotspot problems accumulate, the international community's calls for China to shoulder big power responsibilities have increased day by day. To exhibit a responsible great power image to the international community not only benefits China's peaceful development, but also benefits the construction of a harmonious world."[72] The notion that contributing to international security burnishes Beijing's image on the world stage and telegraphs China's peaceful rise clearly resonates with Chinese strategists. At the same time, Wu depicts an international environment that is highly receptive to China's exercise of its power, commensurate with its emerging status.

Discussions of the military's role in dealing with nontraditional security threats date back to the late 1990s. Similar to the term "military operations other than war" used in U.S. military circles, the Chinese have coined the phrase "non-war military operations" (非战争军事行动) to describe the range of military activities conducted below the threshold of conventional conflict. Zhu Zhijiang defines nonwar military operations as actions that prevent war, dampen confrontation, promote peace and stability, achieve the objectives set by the political authorities that cannot be attained by ordinary military means, and meet the standards of international law and relevant laws of war.[73] In the maritime context, some consider peacetime, multinational naval exercises as a form of nonwar military operation designed to signal military strength, fortify deterrence, and thereby buoy up stability.[74]

This broader intellectual work and policy debate about nontraditional threats and associated nonwar responses directly inform Chinese strategic thinking about counterpiracy. The PLA Navy leadership fully embraces "good order at sea" as a major nonwar military mission. Admiral Su Shiliang, the chief of staff of the PLA Navy, states: "In the recent period, such nontraditional security threats as piracy, terrorist activities, serious disasters and pandemics, and the global financial crisis occurred frequently, causing increasingly stern challenges to our maritime transportation, resources development, fishery production, and overseas interests, and have become major threats to our national security and development."[75] Su forcefully calls upon his service to "strengthen targeted preparations for maritime non-war military actions" while still honing its capacity to fight and win more conventional battles at sea. Su's directive to the Chinese Navy to fulfill a more diverse range of roles and missions is the most authoritative and comprehensive to date.

China's naval leaders explicitly portray the naval expedition as a concrete expression of China's responsible great-power status. Admiral Wu Shengli, the commander of the PLA Navy, declares that the success of the first escort mission "fully demonstrated the fine behavior of our country as a responsible large country, demonstrated the fine image of our armed forces as a mighty and civilized force for peace, [and] demonstrated the perfect military and political quality of the People's Navy."[76] Wu's nod to the virtues of Chinese civilization bears a remarkable resemblance to the praises lavished on Zheng He's maritime feats.

Numerous writings concur with Admiral Wu that the flotilla in the Indian Ocean augments China's "image as a responsible great power" (负责任的大国形象).[77] In one of the clearest expositions of Chinese maritime outreach and Beijing's reputation abroad, Shan Dong and Wang Liwen argue:

> The high seas escort mission is a breakthrough point for China to discharge its great power responsibilities. As China's comprehensive national power increases daily, the international community will

demand that China shoulder more great power responsibilities. For a long period, China was always a free rider upon the sea lines of communication. Where China will head after its rise and whether China would be willing to fulfill its corresponding great power responsibilities, providing relevant public goods to the international community, have been a focal point of concern for many. The fight against Somali piracy provides a perfect opportunity for China to clearly demonstrate our willingness to make our own contributions to the security of international maritime routes.[78]

The view that narrow self-interest no longer exclusively animates Chinese foreign policy enjoys substantial weight in Chinese policy and academic circles. Chinese analysts' rejection of China's free-rider status vis-à-vis the U.S. Navy, and their call for Beijing to furnish international public goods at sea, suggest that they have internalized important concepts from international relations theory. Indeed, theorists of global economic interdependence would applaud the authors' conclusions, endorsing as they do an active Chinese role in safeguarding seagoing commerce, the lifeblood of the global economy.

Zheng He, too, features prominently in many commentaries on the antipiracy operation. Geographic parallels to the Ming admiral's forays in the Indian Ocean have not gone unnoticed.[79] The first PLA Navy detachment, two guided-missile destroyers and a combat logistics ship, arrived off Somalia in January 2009. The flotilla was promptly dubbed the "modern Zheng He fleet."[80] Historical coincidences dovetail with Beijing's exceptionalist claims about its stabilizing foreign policy. In particular, the Chinese naval command clearly grasps the soft-power implications of its convoy effort. In a speech to twenty-nine naval delegations commemorating the sixtieth anniversary of the PLA Navy's founding, Admiral Wu Shengli drew a straight line from Zheng He's voyages to China's current seaward turn:

> The Chinese people actively put the notion of a harmonious ocean into practice. . . . More than 600 years ago, Zheng He, the famous Chinese navigator of the Ming Dynasty, led the then world's strongest fleets to sail to the western seas seven times, reaching as far as the Red Sea and the eastern coast of Africa, and visiting more than 30 countries and regions. They did not sign any unequal treaty, did not claim any territory, and did not bring back even one slave. They wiped out pirates for the countries along their route, broadly

disseminated benevolence to friendly nations, brought China's tea, silk cloth, chinaware, and Eastern civilization to the countries they visited, brought back other people's trust and friendship toward the Chinese nation, and created a world-level example of peaceful and friendly maritime exchanges.[81]

Admiral Wu's rendition of the Zheng He narrative reflects a high degree of confidence in the power of the past to shape contemporary attitudes toward and perceptions of Beijing's maritime ascent. His speech was clearly meant to support President Hu Jintao's foreign policy vision of a "harmonious world." Wu's soothing references to the beneficent qualities of Chinese civilization and thinly veiled swipes at Western imperialism are virtually indistinguishable from the messages of his political masters, as quoted earlier. The apparent alignment of naval means with broader strategic aims suggests that Beijing has managed to synchronize its grand strategy better than many Sinologists believed it could.

Policymakers, academics, and senior military officers clearly embrace Beijing's interpretation of Zheng He's voyages. They treat it as a diplomatic vehicle to export a positive image of China's rise. Their use of maritime history as a metaphor for China's future is not a passing, ephemeral phenomenon but has been on display for the past decade, since the six-hundredth anniversary of Zheng's journeys started approaching.[82] But while Chinese leaders have provided ample commentary on China's maritime past, it remains to be seen whether their message is having much effect on the demand side of the equation—among important audiences in the Indian Ocean region. How recipients of Chinese diplomacy respond to the Zheng He narrative constitutes a critical test of the value of China's appeals.

TESTING CHINA'S SOFT POWER AT SEA: THE INDIAN RESPONSE

The PLA Navy has acquitted itself well off Somalia, rendering useful service from a public-good perspective. The Chinese navy has shown that it is no longer a coastal defense force, short on the capacity to replenish fuel, arms, and stores at sea or relieve deployed forces on station. It has been experimenting with a more ambitious fleet. That fleet is now making its debut. While it is clear that China's leaders have leapt at the opportunity to match their words with deeds, the strategic effects of the counterpiracy mission remain to be seen. Yet some Western commentators have already drawn some ominous, somewhat breathless conclusions about China's charm offensive and its geopolitical fallout. They speculate, for instance, that China might use its newfound influence to exclude outside powers from Asia. Forecasting the fate of Southeast Asia under China's spell, Joshua Kurlantzick postulates: "Perhaps, as a young United States once did in the Western Hemisphere, China could make the region its own—a Chinese Monroe Doctrine for Southeast Asia would make Beijing the major influence over regional affairs and reduce US alliances in the region."[83] But such an outcome is far from preordained. Even in nearby Southeast Asia, where states are relatively small and weak, and where both elites and ordinary citizens appear receptive to the Zheng He narrative, China's appeals may not decisively sway governments toward Chinese proposals. While analysts such as David Kang confidently assert that a hierarchical order resembling the Sinocentric tributary system resuscitated by Zheng He will reemerge, history rarely repeats itself exactly.[84] Southeast Asian bandwagoning behavior, however troubling, is neither unconditional nor graven in stone. Southeast Asian states in fact tend to pursue more subtle, sophisticated strategies than many observers allow, eschewing overt alignments. They navigate carefully among great powers, choosing not to choose sides.[85]

China's gravitational pull, moreover, does not exert its tug evenly across different regions and nations. As China turns its gaze from East Asia toward the Indian Ocean, its soft power is encountering recipients not primed to accept its message. Beijing is likely to meet the fiercest resistance to its exceptionalist diplomacy in South Asia, where—ironically—China has put the most effort into supplying maritime public goods. The source of this resistance comes primarily from the most important, most powerful state in the region: India.

Chinese maritime soft power needs Indian acquiescence if it is to pay dividends in the Indian Ocean basin. Yet vocal members of New Delhi's strategic community do not view the Chinese naval entry into its backyard with equanimity. Indeed, some of the more alarmist, at times almost panicky, Indian commentary suggests near-deafness to China's soothing overtures. Leaders of the Indian foreign policy and defense establishments voice deep ambivalence about China's antipiracy mission in the Gulf of Aden.

Many of them depict the operation as China's first step onto a slippery slope toward a permanent naval presence in the Indian Ocean—the kind of outcome that might have come to pass in fifteenth-century South Asia, had the Ming dynasty not withdrawn from the sea, and instead kept Zheng He's treasure fleet on station. One skeptic puts it bluntly: "'Antipiracy operations' have given China the best excuse to penetrate the Indian Ocean and station forces there permanently. Chinese naval ships would gain experience in long-distance maritime combat operations in preparation for the establishment of an ocean-going aircraft carrier fleet."[86] New Delhi is also convinced that Beijing intends to militarize the "string of pearls," or network of basing rights it has negotiated with South Asian states. Retired vice admiral P. S. Das warns starkly:

> China is not yet on the scene but given the pace of its naval modern-
> ization, energy interests and quite clearly articulated goals, *it is inevi-
> table that it will seek to be an IO* [Indian Ocean] *player before long.* Its
> port building activities at Gwadar in Pakistan, at Sittwe in Myanmar
> and at Hambantota in Sri Lanka can be harbingers of what may lie
> ahead. It already has listening posts in Coco Islands, in immediate
> proximity of the Andaman Islands, which it is seeking to modernize.
> We have to watch these developments carefully.[87] (our emphasis)

One well-known analyst extends the "string of pearls" metaphor, sketching a Sino-Indian "rivalry arc" that stretches all the way from Japan, along the first island chain, and through the Indian Ocean—terminating in the Gulf of Aden. In vivid geographic terms, Commander Gurpreet Khurana, joint director of the Indian Navy's Maritime Doctrine and Concept Center, explains: "As emerging powers, their [China and India's] vital security interests have been dilating from their immediate peripheries to regional extremities (and even beyond). In other words, while their immediate security imperatives lie in the western Pacific Ocean and Indian Ocean respectively; their strategic spheres have begun to overlap in both areas. This is leading them to stretch their maritime-strategic 'footprint' across the entire Asian region."[88] Notably, Khurana revised the 2004 Indian Maritime Doctrine statement, in effect the navy's strategic concept, publishing a new Indian Maritime Doctrine in 2009. For some influential Indians, then, signs of Chinese naval skill and proficiency portend future trouble—trouble that might require India not only to augment its own naval might but to project power into the Pacific in response, if the notion of a rivalry arc is any guide. An Indian countermove in China's nautical backyard would certainly do much to inflame Sino-Indian naval rivalry.

Further, given that India prides itself on being the foremost power in the Indian Ocean, evidence that Beijing might challenge New Delhi's regional preeminence would likely spur an energetic riposte. Just as Chinese navalists view the China seas as Beijing's own preserve, Indian strategists are equally zealous about what they consider their nation's rightful prerogatives in the Indian Ocean. A former chief of naval staff, Admiral Arun Prakash, captures this attitude, concluding that "whether we like it or not, the onus for ensuring strategic stability in the IOR [Indian Ocean Region] is going to fall, substantially, on India's shoulders. In order to rise to this challenge, India has to not just bolster its economic strength and capabilities, but more importantly, craft viable partnerships across the region. Above all, she must remain sensitive to changing geo-political realities, and react with vision, resolve and alacrity."[89] This sense of urgency—the sense that India must respond now to China's naval ascent—promises to become more acute as confidence in U.S. staying power wanes. For Ambassador M. K. Bhadrakumar, the rationale for Indian alertness is straightforward: "The U.S.'s naval dominance is declining. On the other hand, China's navy may have more warships than the U.S.'s in the coming decade."[90] Mahanian-sounding logic, then, animates the thinking of many Indian strategists.

Indian analysts are keenly aware of—and follow closely—the Zheng He narrative.[91] Yet, unlike their Southeast Asian counterparts, they draw little comfort from the Ming admiral's exploits. Thomas Mathew, the deputy director-general of the Institute for Defense Studies and Analyses, claims that "not many were convinced" by the "harmonious ocean" theme put forth by President Hu Jintao and Admiral Wu Shengli during the April 2009 international naval review in Qingdao.[92] Some Indian analysts have even turned the Zheng He narrative on its head. Striking a note similar to Edward Dreyer's, G. Parthasarathy describes Zheng's fleet as "an expeditionary force" and accuses Beijing of "reviving the imperial ambitions of the Emperors of the Ming Dynasty." If India responds too feebly to this effort to replay unpleasant history, warns the author, then "it will be strategically marginalized and outflanked by an assertive and expansionist China."[93] Vice Admiral Arun Kumar Singh, a former chief of the Eastern Naval Command, also inverts the Chinese interpretation of the Ming voyages, portraying them as an ominous forerunner to a Chinese deployment of attack submarines to the Indian Ocean.[94] If Beijing is selling a soothing message, many Indians clearly are not buying.

Given the limited inroads made by the Zheng He narrative in the Indian strategic community, three issues associated with Chinese maritime soft power deserve closer scrutiny. First, under certain circumstances, some states may stubbornly resist China's power of attraction, even if Beijing furnishes international public goods in the process. Beijing may find that South Asian leaders smile and nod at the Chinese Confucian and Zheng He narratives in public but decline to act on this supposed era of good feelings. It may be that soft power effectively eases suspicions of a nation's actions but that it applies too little motive force to prompt the target nation to take positive action. Refraining from overtly opposing Chinese actions is easy; expending national resources on behalf of Chinese-led ventures can be hard, not to mention politically hazardous.

Second, Walter Russell Mead has argued that nations' appeal is seldom universal, observing that not every people feels the tug even of America's open, democratic society.[95] Certain countries may hold radically different assumptions about their counterparts or possess divergent worldviews that render them immune to the intended effects of soft power. Evidence emerging from the Indian Ocean, where China already faces an unsympathetic audience in New Delhi, suggests that Mead has it right. China's charm offensive seems destined to meet with some combination of enthusiasm, indifference, skepticism, and even outright hostility.

Third, it is a relatively simple matter to sustain an attractive image when that image remains an abstraction, uncluttered by messy realities. When a power pursues specific foreign policy objectives, however, its pursuit of these goals manifests itself in concrete action, often working at cross-purposes with the strategic narrative its leadership wishes to put forth. As it begins to apply hard naval power in theaters such as the Indian Ocean, Beijing will likely find that what appeals to one foreign audience may not appeal to another, and that its soft power declines—or at least requires painstaking maintenance—as it acts in its own national interests.

China's admittedly attractive civilization, then, is no guarantee of diplomatic and military success. If Beijing (or any other government) sees soft power as a talisman to be brandished in the face of stubborn challenges, its efforts are apt to be frustrated. It remains to be seen whether China will persist with its Zheng He narrative should segments of India's strategic community persist in rebuffing Beijing's message. China could well stay the course in the hopes of persuading New Delhi through unswerving consistency in word and deed. A change in Beijing's communication tactics may be an indicator that Chinese leaders have reassessed the value of their Ming-era story line. Outside observers and Asian capitals would do well to monitor how Beijing manages its maritime outreach efforts.

The potential limits to Chinese maritime soft power raise questions about the future of Sino-Indian nautical interactions. First, is the Zheng He narrative simply a nonstarter for New Delhi? Will this charm offensive invariably fall on deaf ears, and thus fail to advance China's national purposes vis-à-vis India? Second, why is India impervious to China's comforting message? How widespread is this immunity in India's strategic community? Is it attributable to differences in basic worldviews, power asymmetries, institutional biases, or personal beliefs? And finally, to what extent will Beijing need to fine-tune or even overhaul its message as it exercises influence in the Indian Ocean? How much effort is promoting China's image worth if it means foregoing the perhaps-necessary use of hard power? Will Beijing experience diminishing returns on its investment in the Zheng He narrative? Some answers to these questions would be of value to both policymakers and academics alike.

IMPLICATIONS FOR THE UNITED STATES

Given the uncertainties surrounding China's maritime soft power, the United States should refrain from overreaction. Washington should cautiously accept some of Beijing's claims to leadership in Asian waters, conditioning its approval on China's willingness to participate in regional maritime activities such as the Proliferation Security Initiative, which in theory should advance mutual political aims. Recent military-to-military contacts between the two powers suggest that the U.S. political leadership, old and new, welcomes a constructive Chinese role in upholding good order at sea. At the same time, the United States must remain wary of any efforts on China's part to restore its supremacy in the region. If China's ancient mariner supplies Beijing a way to apply soft power, he also provides the United States with a measuring stick for China's intentions. Assuming the United States wants to preserve its own preeminence in Asia, it must watch for signs that China is deviating from the beneficent purposes embodied in its Zheng He diplomacy. Thus far, the antipiracy mission conforms nicely to Beijing's message, auguring well for broader Sino-U.S. maritime cooperation.

Nevertheless, Washington confronts a more competitive environment for influence in South and Southeast Asia. It must devise a more coherent grand strategy of its own in the region, lest it find itself less and less able to influence Asian affairs or, in the worst case, shut out of Asia altogether.[96] A forward military presence, in the form of ships, aircraft, and missiles, is no substitute for vigorous diplomacy. But the United States has supplied the international public good of free navigation—long taken for granted—for six decades now, asking little in return. Zheng He's era was fleeting by contrast, his endeavors occurred in a century long past, and in any event the Chinese Communist Party can scarcely claim credit for the Ming dynasty's short-lived seafaring exploits.

The tangible security benefits provided by U.S. maritime power since World War II offer a solid foundation for an American soft-power counteroffensive. Washington must build on this foundation, lest its regional primacy go into decline.

CHAPTER 8

U.S. Maritime Strategy in Asia

The concept of the commons remains as compelling in the United States as in China, finding its way into official documents such as the National Defense Strategy and the Quadrennial Defense Review (QDR). Indeed, Undersecretary of Defense Michèle Flournoy published an essay on the contested commons in concert with the release of the 2010 QDR. Observes Flournoy, "The architecture of the modern international system rests on a foundation of free and fair access to a vibrant global economy that requires stability in the global commons. Alfred Thayer Mahan was perhaps the first strategist to coin the term, describing the world's oceans as 'a great highway . . . a wide common' in his classic 1890 work, *The Influence of Sea Power Upon History*."[1]

Unsurprisingly, the concept is a fixture in statements pertaining to U.S. maritime strategy, but this chapter is not specifically about the "Cooperative Strategy for 21st Century Seapower," the directive published in October 2007. Nor do we intend to chronicle the history of U.S. maritime strategy in any comprehensive manner. Rather, we intend to compare and contrast two past efforts at strategy making: the Reagan administration's Maritime Strategy, published in 1986, and the Cooperative Strategy itself. We believe this retrospective approach has the virtue of parsimony while effectively illuminating the challenges, opportunities, and tradeoffs confronting American strategists and tacticians today. Roughly speaking, we use the 1986 strategy as a proxy for devising strategy for "neo-Mahanian" strategic surroundings in the loose sense that "Mahanian" connotes antagonism, naval rivalry, and combat. In Clausewitzian terms, it is a grammatical document, spelling out how the Cold War navy intended to cope with a peer competitor should a clash of arms ensue. And it is executable, specifying the sorts of platforms and weaponry needed for a high-intensity fight with a specific foe, the Soviet navy. Small wonder that naval officers, an intensely practical lot, tend to favor the 1986 strategy over its distant 2007 descendant.

By contrast, the "Cooperative Strategy for 21st Century Seapower" elaborates a logic of sea power while saying next to nothing about grammatical matters—hence the oft-heard complaint that the strategy is not a strategy at all but a public relations venture. And indeed, by contrast with the 1986 Maritime Strategy, it is less an actionable document than a statement of principle. In Geoffrey Till's words, the Cooperative Strategy is designed for a "post-Mahanian," "postmodern" world in which sea combat recedes—though not disappearing entirely—and police actions such as counterpiracy, counterproliferation, and different varieties of antitrafficking come to the fore. It sets forth the sea services' vision of a world closer to Norman Angell's ideal, in which economic interdependence exerts a palliative effect on international relations, raising the costs of armed conflict to almost unbearable levels.[2] In such a world order, protecting the system of seagoing trade becomes a matter of mutual concern for all industrial nations, warranting combined action. Because it is a document premised on naval diplomacy and strategic communications, however, the Cooperative Strategy has an ethereal feel to it that discomfits many practitioners of naval operations.

The Mahanian and post-Mahanian paradigms are not mutually exclusive, nor are the missions they embrace anything new. Take piracy. Thucydides relates how King Minos of Crete founded the first Greek navy to combat piracy before the days of Homer. Julius Caesar was once taken captive by pirates only to return and exact vengeance. Ming dynasty admiral Zheng He defeated a pirate fleet off Malacca six hundred years ago. The Barbary Wars gave new life to a U.S. Navy at risk of being dismantled to cut federal expenses. The U.S. Navy performed police functions during the Cold War, albeit as a "lesser included" element of its strategy. The current strategy, founded on international partnerships to shore up globalization, declares that the sea services remain ready to wage fleet actions and discharge other warfighting missions should the need arise. There is little new under the sun. That both traditional and nontraditional challenges persist is why uncertain surroundings confound one-size-fits-all solutions.

STRATEGY FOR A MAHANIAN WORLD: THE 1986 MARITIME STRATEGY

To get some purchase on the 2007 Maritime Strategy, it is worth reviewing the development, tenets, and critiques of the James Watkins–John Lehman strategy of the 1980s—the last official maritime strategy document.[3] Unveiled in a supplement to a 1986 issue of the U.S. Naval Institute *Proceedings*, the

Maritime Strategy was a product of interaction, reassessment, and adaptation during preparations for war—a phase that encompassed the entire Cold War. The debate over the nature of the Soviet threat and proper U.S. strategies to meet that threat remained largely abstract. Thucydides proclaims that war is a violent teacher. But without actual war at sea between the West and the Soviet Union, the U.S. Maritime Strategy and the strategic concepts on which it was founded were never put to the test of actual combat. Still, the 1980s effort to make maritime strategy for an uncertain environment inhabited by a "peer competitor" and characterized by heavy fiscal constraints illustrates perennial themes.

Crafting strategy is an iterative process. That is, efforts to match ends with means inevitably undergo many phases as new ideas are offered, accepted, rejected, or modified. As Carl von Clausewitz and Michael Handel point out, strategy involves two belligerents jockeying for comparative advantage. Clausewitz contends that "war consists of a continuous interaction of opposites," making it inherently unpredictable.[4] Handel adds that the "interaction of the warring states, each searching for a comparative advantage, *defines the unique nature of each war*"[5] (his emphasis). Interaction, reassessment, and adaptation were continual throughout the Cold War—as they will be in Asia, the principal locus for U.S. maritime endeavors under the 2007 Maritime Strategy.

The U.S. Navy performed a variety of functions from 1945 through 1970. It imposed a blockade during the Cuban Missile Crisis, projected power ashore in Korea and Vietnam, deterred Soviet military aggression, and undertook routine naval diplomacy, showing the flag in key regions. Significantly, it fought no fleet actions during this time. Its last major fleet-on-fleet engagement took place in October 1944, when it met the Japanese Combined Fleet in Leyte Gulf. In a classic article on the "Transoceanic Strategy," Samuel Huntington observed that the postwar epoch left the U.S. Navy without a great-power competitor. During the 1950s and 1960s, while the Soviet navy remained anemic, the lack of Leyte-type engagements freed the Navy for missions remote from command of the sea.[6] In one sense, perversely, the United States was a victim of its wartime success, deprived of a rival fleet around which to structure its strategy and forces.

The rise of an oceangoing, capable Soviet navy following the Cuban Missile Crisis changed all that. The Soviet navy was traditionally a homeland defense force. Josef Stalin had ordained the construction of a Mahanian battle fleet before World War II, but Moscow's Mahanian ambitions came up empty, frustrated by a backward shipbuilding industry and the competing demands of land defense.[7] Stalin had fretted over the likelihood of North Atlantic Treaty Organization (NATO) amphibious assaults along the Eurasian periphery, but his successors took a more relaxed view of the maritime threat. They let the surface fleet languish. By the time of the Cuban Missile Crisis, the Soviet navy was unable to dispute U.S. and Western sea control beyond Warsaw Pact coastal waters.

Moscow, consequently, found itself unable to contest the U.S. maritime exclusion zone—a blockade in all but name—imposed around Cuba in 1962. The Cuban debacle exposed Soviet maritime weaknesses, jolting Moscow into action. Grand Admiral Sergei Gorshkov, the father of the Soviet blue water fleet, superintended the effort to renovate Soviet naval strategy and build a fleet able to execute it. Like China, Russia is traditionally a land power. Its most recent foray into sea power had ended disastrously in 1905, when the Japanese Combined Fleet commanded by Admiral Tōgō Heihachirō sent the Russian Baltic Fleet to the bottom of the Tsushima Strait, the narrow sea separating Korea from Japan.

Russian and Soviet maritime history, then, offered the West little help charting the future of Soviet sea power. Official statements and writings were unreliable guides to Soviet strategy, colored as they were by Marxist-Leninist theory, the national interest, alliance politics, and even the whims of top political leaders. Shipbuilding patterns likewise represented a crude indicator of Soviet strategy and intentions. In the Soviet Union, as elsewhere, ships performed a variety of missions, some far removed from those for which they were designed. As in other attempts at Kremlinology, divining the principles and purposes behind Soviet maritime strategy was an exercise in conjecture.

One concept that molded Soviet thinking about maritime matters was the "blue belt of defense."[8] The blue belt was a geographically defined off-shore zone within range of land-based air and sea assets. Like contemporary China's way of thinking about the China seas, the Soviet concept envisioned enclosing and defending vital expanses, much as armies sought to do on land. Russian and Soviet strategists, then, applied land-warfare concepts to the nautical domain. Much as Stalin and his advisers wanted to ring Soviet borders with friendly or neutral states, creating a buffer against overland invasion, Gorshkov and his disciples wanted to erect a defensive barrier against advancing NATO fleets.

Alfred Thayer Mahan lambasted the Imperial Russian Navy for its concept of the "fortress-fleet," which in effect reduced the navy to a seaward appendage of shore fortifications.[9] Even so, the fortress-fleet concept persisted in Soviet naval thought. New technologies such as antiship missiles and antisubmarine warfare (ASW) could expand the blue belt outward, denying the United States and its allies control of seas washing against Warsaw Pact shores. This was sound logic. Europe is in effect a large peninsula jutting out of Asia—a peninsula that lets a dominant navy roam freely around the periphery, setting the terms for naval action. Huntington's work on the transoceanic strategy urged the U.S. Navy to think of the Mediterranean as an inlet in Eurasia, a platform from which to project power into the Soviet bloc. Holding off Western power projection required vying with NATO for control of this inlet. Gorshkov never said how wide a defensive belt he foresaw. Presumably it should be as wide as Soviet naval capabilities could make it— hence the swift quantitative and qualitative buildup from the 1960s onward.

In the realm of hardware, undersea warfare was central to the Soviet naval buildup. The Soviet navy deployed fifty nuclear-powered ballistic-missile submarines (SSBNs) by the early 1970s, along with some three hundred nuclear-powered attack submarines (SSNs). It is important not to overrate the submarine fleet, despite its numbers, for all Gorshkov's (and before him Stalin's) claims that quantity has a quality all its own. Quality lagged. A retired American submariner jokes that, for sonar operators, detecting early classes of Soviet submarines was like listening for two skeletons making love inside a metal trash can. The acoustic problem rendered Soviet numbers largely moot in the early days. Compounding the problem for Soviet submariners, the short range of early submarine-launched ballistic missiles (SLBMs) compelled Soviet SSBNs to patrol far forward if they were to range American cities. Soviet strategic preferences had to give way under prevailing circumstances.

By the early 1970s, Soviet navy operating practices showed that Moscow was gaining confidence in its ability to dispute waters the U.S. Navy had ruled since 1945. For example, the Soviets executed an impressive series of exercises dubbed *Okean* (Ocean) during the 1970s. In 1970 Moscow deployed fleets in traditional U.S. Navy preserves such as the Mediterranean and the North Atlantic while also venturing into the Norwegian Sea and the Indian Ocean. No longer was American sea control a given. The exercises even cast doubt on whether the United States could count on using Atlantic sea-lanes to reinforce NATO-Europe during a land war. The 1973 Arab-Israeli war reinforced the impression of an increasingly offensive-minded, blue water Soviet navy. Indeed, the Soviet Mediterranean Squadron outnumbered the U.S. Sixth Fleet during the conflict—sending a shock through the U.S. naval leadership and the Nixon administration. The growing mismatch in numbers was hard to dismiss, throwing the disparity between U.S. and Soviet shipbuilding rates and budgets into stark relief.

Certain anomalies became apparent. Despite the enormous effort and resources allocated to Gorshkov's blue water fleet, the Soviet navy was not symmetrical with the U.S. Navy. First, there was no obvious push to construct big-deck aircraft carriers comparable to U.S. flattops. Second, the naval leadership displayed little urgency about moving from sea denial to sea control. The Soviet surface fleet evidently considered ASW a secondary concern, even though guarding against undersea attack has always been essential to effective sea control. Third, as naval technology matured, extending SLBM ranges, Soviet SSBNs started operating closer to home. They could strike at American targets without venturing beyond shore support. In short, strategic preferences of centuries' standing reasserted themselves as the Soviet navy improved its combat capacity.

These patterns defied Western assumptions. In 1981 Admiral Thomas Hayward, the chief of naval operations (CNO), reportedly voiced disbelief that the Soviets would operate a great navy in such a manner. The disparity between Soviet platforms apparently designed for offense and defensive operating patterns baffled Western analysts, who debated whether the Soviets even had a naval doctrine. They debated the degree to which Soviet leaders distinguished between nuclear and nonnuclear warfare, having planned to use tactical nuclear weapons during a European land war during the 1960s. And, perhaps most importantly, the question arose whether possessing an imposing navy would generate new intentions and strategic preferences on Soviet leaders' part. If Moscow possessed a hammer, challenges might start to look like nails.

The leadership's words furnished one indicator. Admiral Gorshkov was a prolific writer. His book *The Sea Power of the State* contradicted Mahan, proclaiming that the Soviet Union was at once a mighty land power and a mighty sea power. Naval war was important, but defeating the imperialists' seagoing "big stick"—not wresting sea control from the West—was Moscow's chief goal. Defeating Western efforts at coercion would grant Moscow new freedom of action, something statesmen and commanders crave. Gorshkov lauded SSBNs for their survivability while insisting they were best patrolling waters within range of land-based support. In fact, he predicted the United States would take the same approach with its Trident SSBN fleet, mirror-imaging U.S. Navy deployment practices.[10]

As it upgraded the fleet's capabilities, the Soviet navy also shifted its center of buoyancy to the east, reestablishing a serious presence in East Asian waters for the first time since the Battle of Tsushima. Based at Vladivostok, the Pacific Fleet allowed the Soviet navy to diversify its nuclear deterrent. SSBNs now cruised an eastern bastion in the seas of Okhotsk and Japan. The eastern presence also enabled the navy to perform functions such as coercive diplomacy around the Asian periphery, shadowing forward-deployed U.S. Navy assets while opening up new options vis-à-vis an increasingly hostile China. The Pacific Fleet was a serious force, comprising more ships than the Northern Fleet. Thirty percent of the total Soviet fleet, or some ninety surface combatants, were based in the Far East.

It was unclear whether the United States still ruled the waves, faced by such an adversary. But by the 1970s, Kremlinologists and naval strategists were rethinking the nature of the Soviet maritime challenge. An emerging consensus held that the U.S. Navy had an opportunity to regain the initiative at sea. It appeared, for example, that Soviets had abandoned hopes that capitalism would collapse under its internal contradictions. Nor did they seem intent on giving capitalism a push, toppling it. It these premises were correct, nuclear escalation was not a foregone conclusion in wartime. The Soviet regime may have mellowed, much as George F. Kennan had famously prophesied.[11] And strains on the Soviet economic system were starting to show, especially once Moscow's invasion of Afghanistan began siphoning off resources that might have gone to naval power.

If the Soviet Union was indeed reverting to the defensive, the United States might be able to use its central geographic position—its ability to reach out across the Atlantic and Pacific—to regain its accustomed maritime supremacy. By acting boldly at the outset of a conflict with the Soviet bloc, the United States could blunt some of the advantages the Soviets had built up in the previous decade. How it should go about this was the question.

George Baer observes that effective strategy requires a threat, a focal point. Accurately estimating the Soviet threat was central to adapting U.S. strategy to new realities. Numbers and types of platforms were never far from the minds of American naval strategists. Whether aircraft carriers should remain the centerpiece of U.S. naval power, as they had been since World War II, ranked foremost among these. But even if the carrier remained king, it was doubtful whether it was politically thinkable to risk the nuclear-powered flattops then building in a showdown with the Soviet navy off Eurasian shores.

Different chiefs of naval operations had different ideas about these questions, although the overall trend was toward retaking the offensive. Admiral Elmo Zumwalt, who had the mixed fortune to serve as CNO in the late Vietnam years, believed the U.S. Navy should refocus its strategy on sea control. The Korean and Vietnam wars had allowed the Navy to project power onto Asian shores with little fear of enemy interference. That was no longer true with the rise of a Soviet navy that could put more than two hundred ships to sea around the world simultaneously, as it had during the *Okean-70* exercise. There existed a threat to NATO sea lines of communication (SLOCs) for the first time. Sea control, maintained Zumwalt, would ensure the United States the ability to surge men and materiel across the Atlantic at the outbreak of war.

Admiral Zumwalt instigated a long-overdue discussion of U.S. naval strategy, missions, and platforms. He also admitted that painful tradeoffs lay in store should the Navy rededicate itself to sea control. Most controversially, he insisted that the Navy must accept a smaller force structure in the short term to free up funds for new construction for the longer term. This involved risk. Zumwalt espoused a fleet founded on a "high/low mix," blending a large number of inexpensive, less capable platforms—the *Oliver Hazard Perry* frigates were the best example—with costly, high-end platforms like *Nimitz*-class nuclear carriers and cruisers and destroyers outfitted with the gee-whiz Aegis combat system. For Zumwalt, who served during the economic malaise of the 1970s, this was simple reality.

The CNO pushed a quantitative approach oriented more toward acquisitions than strategy. Policy and strategy largely disappeared. For example, Project 60, a Zumwalt-sponsored planning effort, dwelt almost entirely on fleet numbers, technological innovations, and new platforms and weapons systems such as the *Perry*-class FFG, the Sea Control Ship—a sort of low-cost carrier that could be risked more easily than an expensive CVN—and the Harpoon antiship cruise missile. The analytical shortfalls of Project 60 and similar initiatives convinced many officers they needed to rejuvenate the sea services' tradition of strategic thought. Zumwalt's critics contended that a high/low mix would leave the Navy a defensive force, able to exercise sea control but unable to win it in the first place. Higher-end ships and platforms, that is, would likely be too few and pack too little punch to win a Mahanian victory that would let the lower-end platforms do their job. They insisted in effect that the best defense was a good offense, and that the U.S. Navy was abandoning the offensive.

Zumwalt also exaggerated the rationality of the budget process in Washington. Congress gleefully pocketed the savings the Navy offered by decommissioning old ships, but lawmakers felt no obligation to reciprocate, funding replacements in sufficient numbers.[12] Shipbuilding rates plummeted by some two-thirds from the mid-1960s through the early 1970s, dragging the fleet size inexorably down. The fleet dropped from nearly nine hundred ships in 1965 to just more than five hundred in 1980. Quality improved on a ship-for-ship basis as the Navy phased out aged vessels. But quality was not everything against a numerically superior Soviet navy.

Admiral James Holloway, Zumwalt's successor as CNO, commissioned several studies to examine the repercussions of dwindling force structure.[13] "With the continuing decline in our naval force levels," Holloway told Congress, the service "had become a one-ocean navy." The Pacific Ocean was now a zone of American neglect.[14] Analysts reached likewise dismal findings. One study in effect argued that a five-hundred-ship fleet would stand little chance of prevailing in critical waterways such as the Atlantic SLOCs on which NATO strategy relied; the Mediterranean, the inlet where Huntington had insisted a transoceanic navy needed liberty to operate; and the western Pacific, a region inhabited by key allies like Japan. The naval leadership voiced confidence that an eight-hundred-ship fleet could discharge all missions assigned it.

Such findings stunned the civilian and uniformed leadership. Still, in 1978 alone, the rate of new construction fell by half. President Jimmy Carter and his secretary of defense, Harold Brown, proposed reducing carrier numbers, halting construction of new nuclear-powered carriers. Carter and Brown proposed building less expensive VSTOL (very short takeoff and landing) carriers such as those operated by smaller navies around the world. Admiral Thomas Hayward, who succeeded Holloway in 1978, publicly deplored the trend toward a "Third World strategy."[15] Not to be outdone, Secretary of the Navy Graham Claytor worried that the administration would reduce the navy to a nautical "Maginot Line."[16] Claytor doubtless chose his historical analogies carefully, implying that such a navy courted abject defeat.

However sensible Navy leaders' lobbying on behalf of a bigger force, however, they were out of step with reigning views of foreign policy and maritime power. The 1970s was a heyday of arms control and disarmament, not only for the Carter administration but also for its Republican predecessors. The Strategic Arms Limitation Treaty, the Nuclear Non-Proliferation Treaty, and the Anti-Ballistic Missile Treaty were only some of the treaties and accords negotiated in the Nixon, Ford, and Carter years. Those who think in terms of arms control assume that parity—not superiority or victorious battle—is the goal of military strategy and forces. It probably seemed natural for elected officials to think in terms of naval parity, not commanding the sea.

Nor was it obvious that the Navy had much role to play in a NATO-European war. NATO's doctrine of "Flexible Response" posited that the Alliance would use tactical nuclear weapons early in a war on the Central Front, halting a Warsaw Pact ground offensive. The matter would be decided, one way or the other, before naval power came to bear. In short, the U.S. Navy took a back seat to other instruments of national power for policymakers of the 1970s. Diplomacy was the option of first resort, naval power the last. Secretary of Defense Brown simply made this explicit, relegating the Navy to lesser missions such as convoy duty and presence functions. Self-isolating the Navy from national policy is a perilous business, whatever the merits of service leaders' arguments.

But the Navy did so. Already in the Carter years, various new studies and strategic concepts were under development, bearing names like Sea Plan 2000 and Project Sea Strike.[17] Several common themes emerged within the Navy, and among academic experts at the Center for Naval Analyses and other think tanks. First, naval proponents took to declaring that Mahanian command of the sea was the prerequisite for all other naval missions, and thus that offense should be the entering assumption for debates over strategy. The U.S. Navy should reassert its maritime supremacy. Second, experts claimed technological advances were again making Mahanian command feasible. New systems such as Aegis, improved ASW hardware and software, and cruise missiles would let the surface fleet survive and thrive, even in a high-intensity threat environment. In short, battle groups could project power, even against a Soviet navy using combined arms to defend its offshore blue belt.

Third, the U.S. fleet should seize the initiative at the outbreak of war, carrying the fight to the enemy around the Eurasian periphery. Peripheral operations would compel the Soviets and their allies to defend everywhere rather than concentrate their efforts in Germany. Maritime operations around the margins, that is, could shape the battle space ashore. Naval analysts accordingly concluded that the Carter administration should abandon plans to "swing," or transfer, ships from the Pacific Fleet to the Atlantic Fleet in times of crisis. The administration should concentrate the Atlantic Fleet to support its Europe-first strategy while the Pacific Fleet should hold the Soviet Pacific Fleet and its Pacific submarine bastion at risk—menacing the Soviet oceanic periphery. Opening a Pacific theater would force Moscow to expend scarce resources defending the Far East, thereby relieving the NATO-European theater.

The upshot was that the U.S. Navy should pierce the Soviet blue belt all around the Eurasian periphery, giving Moscow more to think about than prosecuting a ground war in Europe. A dominant navy, not one made up of a high/low mix of ships, could turn the blue-belt concept inward against the Soviet navy, making offshore waters a zone of peril for Soviet mariners. Admiral Hayward's successor as CNO, Admiral James Watkins, and his civilian superior, Secretary of the Navy John Lehman, saw fit to codify this strain of strategic thought in a formal statement of maritime strategy. The strategy was briefed to numerous different audiences in classified forums and underwent numerous refinements. It went public in 1986 in the U.S. Naval Institute *Proceedings*.

Watkins and Lehman bragged that the Maritime Strategy put the Navy and Marines on the "same set of sheet music" with the national leadership for the first time in years, if not decades.[18] It rejected claims that any NATO–Warsaw Pact war would automatically go nuclear, negating naval power as a warfighting instrument. It insisted that the United States could wage cumulative naval operations around the Soviet periphery, protracting the war and driving up costs to an unbearable level for Moscow. Indirection would allow the United States to end the war "on favorable terms."[19]

The strategy had its detractors. Critics questioned its framers' assumptions about the nature of the war. They doubted the strategy would drain resources from Warsaw Pact ground and air forces in Europe, where the main effort would take place, and they depicted it as a venture in scriptwriting and "brochuresmanship." Some of the most telling criticism came from University of Chicago political scientist John Mearsheimer, who presented a paper at the Naval War College in 1985 and later published it in the journal *International Security*. Mearsheimer roundly condemned the strategy for employing naval power to shift the nuclear balance in a conventional war. Striking at the Soviet undersea fleet during a conventional conflict, that is, would face Moscow with a use-it-or-lose-it quandary vis-à-vis nuclear weapons. Moscow might turn loose a barrage of SLBMs rather than lose its SSBN fleet to U.S. naval attack.[20]

There is no need to refight these debates here, nor is the outcome especially important for our purposes. The important point is that, however imposing a foe the Soviet navy presented, the intellectual challenge of confronting it was relatively straightforward. The existence of a discrete threat reduced the strategy-making process to a discrete set of questions, setting the parameters for debate—much as the Imperial Japanese Navy concentrated American efforts during the interwar years, when naval planners thrashed out the famous color-coded war plans for war in the Pacific. For instance, could aircraft carriers survive naval action in the Barents Sea, where the Soviet navy fought under cover of land-based weaponry? How many ASW assets did the U.S. Navy and its allies need to cover the large yet technologically backward Soviet submarine force?

And there was something to the claims of brochuresmanship. For strategic-communications purposes, an imposing rival fleet simplified the task of rallying the American government, electorate, and military behind a forward-leaning maritime strategy. Mahan himself recalled ruefully how difficult it was to persuade nineteenth-century Americans to demand naval preparedness. The nation's "dead apathy" following the traumas of the Civil War consigned the Navy to an "almost incredible" age of stagnation. He ascribed this "inertness" in large measure to "the paralysis of idea, of mental development corresponding to the movement of the world." Absent public or government support, the U.S. Navy fell into "the habit of living from day to day on expedients, on makeshifts."[21]

It was entirely reasonable, for instance, for the likes of Mahan and Theodore Roosevelt to accentuate the great-power threat to the Caribbean. But abstract arguments lack heft unless real, compelling evidence backs them up. Only war with Spain, wrote Mahan, could bring "the abstract conceptions of theorists and extremists, as they then seemed, down to earth in very concrete realization." The Spanish-American War wrought a radical change in the American worldview. It prompted citizens to look outward across the Pacific—particularly toward the Philippine Islands, now an American naval beachhead off the China coast. "What once were visions," concluded Mahan, "are now accepted as solid present matters of course by our very practical nation." The Republic rethought its venerable but outdated "Bible of American political tradition."[22] A Mahanian strategy, it seems, demands Mahanian threats to focus public discourse.

MAKING STRATEGY FOR A GLOBALIZED WORLD

Mahan would probably sympathize with the current sea-service leadership. First, like the Navy in the post–Civil War years, today's Navy confronts strategic surroundings in which traditional naval competition or conflict is a real prospect, but the threat has not fully taken form. Debates over maritime matters remain largely abstract and speculative. Second, Mahan confined his strategic analyses primarily to the Caribbean Sea and the Gulf of Mexico, urging the United States to safeguard its "gateway" to the Asia-Pacific. Today's sea services confront challenges of worldwide geographic sweep—and will do so as long as the United States remains the self-appointed guardian of maritime security. Third, while no nontraditional challenge is as menacing as a strong enemy fleet, challenges such as piracy or proliferation demand ships, aircraft, and surveillance assets in large numbers simply to provide adequate coverage of sea areas beset by these scourges. Capital ships are unnecessary to combat pirates or weapons traffickers, who have neither the need nor the ability to command the sea. The maxim that quantity has a quality all its own is especially apt for navies and coast guards embarking on police duty.

The dilemma for a nation such as the United States, which regards itself both as the trustee of the sea-lanes and as defender of its own interests and prerogatives against rival sea powers, is to allocate scarce resources wisely. It must preserve adequate combat capacity while fielding sufficient numbers to exercise sea control. This is not a new debate. *Harper's* editor and anti-imperialist Carl Schurz foreshadowed Norman Angell's works in 1897, pronouncing as self-defeating Theodore Roosevelt's martial-sounding maxim that "no triumph of peace is quite so great as the supreme triumphs of war." Schurz rebuked Roosevelt's "combative ardor," scoffing at the notion that great powers menaced American security. "Jingo talk" like Roosevelt's or Mahan's represented "the veriest balderdash." Peace would come about "by our geographical position, by the well-known abundance of our resources, and by the ever-vigilant jealousies of other powers among themselves." Far removed from great-power strife, the United States "should have a smart little navy enabling us to do our share of police duty on the seas." Aside from that, the American people should enjoy the blessings of "an unarmed peace."[23]

Now as then, there is a peculiar duality to Washington's predicament. Threats like piracy are now a matter of course in expanses like the Strait of Malacca or the Gulf of Aden, but they are remote from the daily lives of people and governments. Conversely, the threat that would impinge on daily life—the emergence of a near-peer competitor that strives with the United States for maritime dominance—has not yet emerged, if indeed it ever does. A serious Chinese threat remains years off, and it may prove a mirage. It remains an abstract conception, to borrow Mahan's phrase, magnifying the dilemma for statesmen, strategists, and force planners.

We have also seen that China has used astute diplomacy to ease worries about its return to regional eminence and depict its rise as an international public good, benefiting all Asians. Chinese leaders want to keep any naval threat to the United States or its Asian allies abstract, precisely to avoid supplying an excuse for Washington to rebuild its force posture in the region. Beijing has made good use of the drift among Western scholars and practitioners of international affairs. Westerners increasingly agree with Norman Angell that the world has largely transcended power politics. If so, realpolitik implements such as battle fleets have been rendered moot.[24] Unless Beijing egregiously aggravates matters in the Taiwan Strait or the South China Sea, no stimulus comparable to the Spanish-American War, Pacific War, or Cold War will crystallize American thinking about naval strife.

Sir Julian Corbett's wisdom bears on this strategic problem. Corbett vouchsafes that an uncommanded sea is the normal state of affairs. The blanket coverage Mahan envisioned with his notion of "overbearing power" that sweeps enemy fleets from the sea is too resource-intensive to sustain for any meaningful period of time.[25] Former CNO (and subsequently Joint Chiefs chairman) Admiral Mike Mullen evidently concluded as much in 2005, surveying a strategic setting characterized by flat or declining resources and multiplying operational demands. The key to protecting shipping is having the ability to scatter forces over wide expanses while concentrating them at vital points— much as Corbett implored navies that wanted to approximate command of the sea to work toward "elastic cohesion" on the high seas.[26] For Admiral Mullen, coaxing allies and partners into an informal "1,000-ship navy," or seagoing coalition, looked like the best way to realize Corbett's ideal. The thousand-ship navy—since renamed the "Global Maritime Partnership" after foreign officials objected to the term "navy," claiming it implied they must submit to U.S. command—represented the only way to apply sufficient resources in vital waters and airspace.[27]

Enter the 2007 Maritime Strategy, unveiled at the Naval War College to great fanfare. Some one hundred chiefs of navies and coast guards from around the world traveled to Newport in October 2007 to debate the merits and drawbacks of the strategy. The "Cooperative Strategy for 21st Century Seapower" is a concise statement of aims consigned by the service chiefs of the U.S. Navy, Marine Corps, and Coast Guard. If we accept Corbett's depiction of maritime strategy as the art of determining the relations between ground and sea forces, then the Cooperative Strategy qualifies as the United States' most genuinely "maritime" strategy, encompassing not only warfighting but also police functions.

The strategy document rightly boasts that "never before have the maritime forces of the United States—the Navy, Marine Corps, and Coast Guard—come together to create a unified maritime strategy."[28] In reality, the 1986 Maritime Strategy was a naval strategy, published in unclassified form in *Proceedings* articles authored by the chief of naval operations, Admiral James Watkins, and the Marine commandant, General P. X. Kelley. Ensuing strategic documents such as ". . . From the Sea" (1992) and "Forward . . . from the Sea" (1995) were cosigned by the secretary of the navy, the chief of naval operations, and the Marine commandant, purporting to embody the sea services' consensus strategic vision.[29]

While it is important not to read too much into the reasons behind why this or that official signed a certain document, it is instructive to speculate. Again, the 2007 Maritime Strategy is the first to incorporate the U.S. Coast Guard, signifying the sea services' embrace of counterpiracy, counterproliferation, and other operations resembling law enforcement. It is signed solely by the three service chiefs. No political appointee affixed his signature, in contrast to previous documents approved by secretaries of the navy. Why not? First, there is a pragmatic reason. Unlike previous strategies, the 2007 strategy extends to bodies beyond the Department of Defense, specifically the U.S. Coast Guard, now a component of the Department of Homeland Security. Issuing a joint document would have set in motion interagency negotiations common within the U.S. government. By taking ownership of the strategy, the service chiefs skirted the intricate, perhaps prolonged and fractious process of getting two cabinet departments with very different worldviews and cultures to agree on purposes and principles.

Second, the document probably constituted an effort to influence opinion beyond the George W. Bush years, molding attitudes not only beyond American shores, with governments capable of augmenting (or obstructing) U.S. maritime strategy, but within whatever administration followed Bush in 2009. Secretary of the Navy Donald Winter would depart the Pentagon a bit over a year after the strategy was published. If Winter had acted as the final approval authority for the Maritime Strategy, he might have foreshortened the document's shelf-life. Presidential administrations distance themselves from policies created by their predecessors, putting their own stamp on policy. This is especially true when the White House changes hands between parties, and perhaps even more so given the controversial nature of the outgoing Bush administration. The service chiefs probably believed their strategic views would endure into a new administration if they kept the Bush administration's fingerprints off the Maritime Strategy.

This helps explain the service chiefs' decision to publish the strategy in 2007, in the waning months of the Bush presidency. They hoped to help set a new tone after the perceived confrontational stances taken by Washington during the first Bush term, and to codify the more consensual approach the second Bush administration deemed wise. And indeed, the framers of the Cooperative Strategy have laid the groundwork for an enduring strategic approach. The strategy's principles of defending the global system, preserving a healthy quotient of combat power, and shifting the sea services' gaze to Asia conform to the inclinations of the Barack Obama administration, despite some possible variations in emphasis. There is no escaping the persistence of both power politics and systemic problems.

So much for the origins of the 2007 Maritime Strategy. The authors point out that, unlike past strategies drafted behind closed doors, the Cooperative Strategy was developed in the full glare of publicity, with a sea-service delegation soliciting public input during "Conversations with the Country" carried on while barnstorming the United States.[30] The public response indicated that the American people wanted their armed forces to remain strong, to work with foreign partners to prevent war, and to concentrate on defending the homeland. What does this imply about the staying power of the Maritime Strategy, and of the United States as the world's preeminent sea power?

Alfred Thayer Mahan worried that the character of the American people and their government might inhibit sea power. The United States spanned a continent; like France, it boasted a pleasant climate and abundant resources. America's ability to provide for itself tended to distract attention from seafaring pursuits. French humiliation in the recurrent naval competition with Great Britain offered a cautionary tale for the United States "in this our period of commercial and naval decadence."[31] This made a sharp contrast with hardscrabble conditions in the British Isles, which drove Britons to the sea in search of trade and prosperity.[32] Or, suggested Mahan, Americans might come to resemble the Dutch during their golden age of sea power. Ruled by merchants reluctant to raise taxes, Amsterdam "would not pay" for a navy able to sustain Holland's position vis-à-vis an avaricious England.[33]

Americans might mimic the French or Dutch examples, losing out in the struggle for sea power through sheer neglect. By Mahanian indices, there is some cause for concern today. "If sea power be really based upon a peaceful and extensive commerce," he contended, "aptitude for commercial pursuits must be a distinguishing feature of the nations that have at one time or another been great upon the sea."[34] Despite the global financial crisis, the United States continues to enjoy robust commerce, buoyed by the international economic system it helped create after World War II. Hawaii and Guam are American soil, giving the U.S. military a stronghold in the second island chain. Projecting power into the first island chain, however, is a matter of adroit alliance management with nations like Japan and South Korea. With regard to shipping, the U.S. Navy and Marine Corps remain the world's foremost seagoing force, but the U.S.-flagged merchant fleet is little more than an afterthought. The vast bulk of American goods travels in foreign-flagged hulls. The outlook for U.S. staying power in the Asia-Pacific is decidedly mixed.

The Maritime Strategy, consequently, handles strategic communications toward Asian audiences delicately. The strategy's drafters shied away from naming an enemy, and indeed China is conspicuously absent from the document. The sentiment is understandable. If the strategy is a statement of principle intended to last for the next decade and a half, then singling out a particular competitor might run counter to its concept of tightening old partnerships and seeking out new ones. Beijing has remained aloof from the Proliferation Security Initiative (PSI), for instance, and targeting it as the next great antagonist would probably foreclose any efforts at PSI courtship.

Nor is the Maritime Strategy necessarily the right forum to profile a Chinese threat in any event. The Pentagon publishes annual reports to Congress on the military power of the People's Republic of China that update estimates of the PLA's military potential and evolving strategy on an ongoing basis. Chinese naval power today and over the next decade is not likely to match the global reach and capabilities that the Soviets amassed in the 1970s. The Gulf of Aden antipiracy mission, for example, pales in comparison to the *Okean* naval exercises in 1975, which showcased Moscow's blue water prowess. Unless or until Chinese actions bring the naval threat into focus, sea-service leaders will see little need to risk creating a self-fulfilling prophecy. Avoiding self-defeating behavior was central to the framing of the Cooperative Strategy.

The downside of assuaging Chinese sensibilities is that U.S. allies in Asia, particularly Japan, worry that Washington will take conciliation too far.

Tokyo long ago tethered its national security to the United States under the U.S.-Japan Security Treaty. Declares a recent defense white paper, "Defense of Japan 2009," "it would be practically impossible for Japan to ensure its national security by solely independent efforts given its population, land and economy"; thus, "Japan maintains an alliance with the world's dominant military superpower," the United States. The transpacific alliance constitutes a "central pillar of Japan's national defense."[35] Having bound their fortunes inextricably to America, Japanese leaders monitor shifts in U.S. policy and strategy carefully, looking for signs of abandonment.

But Japan's strategic community is deeply conflicted about the future of China, and about Tokyo's long-term relationship with its giant neighbor. By no means is Japanese ambivalence about Chinese ascendancy unanimous. Those who advocate continued engagement with China were probably relieved to find that explicit references to China were absent from the Maritime Strategy. They rightfully fear that a provocative document that set its U.S. ally on a maritime collision course with China would substantially increase the risk of entrapment for Japan. If a nautical rivalry emerges as a result, Tokyo could find itself compelled to distance its policy from Washington while striving for a more independent policy toward Beijing. Washington in turn needs the alliance to anchor its military presence in the region, and thus to sustain its preeminence. Similarly, querulous Southeast Asian leaders count on the United States to counterbalance Chinese pretensions in their home region. Excessive deference or hostility to Beijing, then, could corrode the maritime order presided over by the U.S. Navy since 1945. Striking a delicate balance in any policy initiative for Asia is no easy feat.

Several aspects of the Maritime Strategy warrant special scrutiny. The authors start by taking note of the interconnected nature of the globalized world. They side firmly with those, such as Harvard scholar Joseph Nye or long-dead British diplomat Eyre Crowe, who portray defense of the system as an international public good, something that benefits all seafaring nations.[36] By providing for maritime security over the past six decades, the U.S. Navy has legitimized American rule of the seas, much as the Royal Navy legitimized British supremacy before. It comes as little surprise that the Maritime Strategy displays the imprint of international relations theory, given its origins in the research wing of the Naval War College.[37] While the document makes no mention of Mahan, moreover, it is consistent with his writings on the primacy of commerce, as outlined in chapter 1, and thus with his grand logic of sea power:

The security, prosperity, and vital interests of the United States are increasingly coupled to those of other nations. Our Nation's interests are best served by fostering a peaceful global system comprised of interdependent networks of trade, finance, information, law, people and governance.

We prosper because of this system of exchange among nations, yet recognize it is vulnerable to a range of disruptions that can produce cascading and harmful effects far from their sources. Major power war, regional conflict, terrorism, lawlessness and natural disasters—all have the potential to threaten U.S. national security and world prosperity.[38]

Wars, large or small, may persist according to the service chiefs, but the Maritime Strategy portrays them primarily as disruptions to the system, not as direct threats to U.S. maritime preponderance. It also folds war into a list of ills that includes not only threats—that is, challenges that join capability to the deliberate intent of a living opponent—but also natural disasters, the uneven advance of economic liberalization, and other phenomena that are not products of human action. And the strategy's talk of preventing second- and third-order effects of these phenomena opens up the possibility of acting in a myriad of contingencies. Tracing "cascading and harmful effects" to their source, attacking that source, and doing so without serious, unforeseen consequences is no simple matter.

Clearly, this is quite a different perspective on strategy than the enemy-centric one advanced during the Reagan administration, and that is no accident. The Cold War divided the world up into rival camps. The 2007 Maritime Strategy sends the message that all nations are stakeholders in the system and should help preserve it, jointly supplying the public good of free navigation. In the process, combined action at sea will "build confidence and trust among nations through collective security efforts that focus on common threats and mutual interests in an open, multipolar world." Building the habits of trust and cooperation on functional matters, proclaims the Maritime Strategy, will foster a healthier world system. The key passage in the document assigns the maritime services six "strategic imperatives":

Where tensions are high or where we wish to demonstrate to our friends and allies our commitment to security and stability, U.S. maritime forces will be characterized by regionally concentrated, forward-deployed task forces with the combat power to limit regional conflict, deter major power war, and should deterrence fail, win our Nation's wars as part of a joint or combined campaign. In addition, persistent, mission-tailored maritime forces will be globally distributed in order to contribute to homeland defense-in-depth, foster and sustain cooperative relationships with an expanding set of international partners, and prevent or mitigate disruptions and crises.[39]

Loosely speaking, this means that the sea services must at once preserve their battle readiness, guarding against traditional military conflict, and hone their proficiency at police functions, nation building, naval diplomacy, and the like. The Maritime Strategy suggests a neat partition of functions, with combat and constabulary forces designated according to their skills and capabilities. More likely, U.S. Navy, Marine, and Coast Guard units will find themselves pressed into service in either capacity. This has been the case since antiquity, when Greek navies fought one another on the high seas, attacked or defended merchant shipping, or struck at pirates, as ordained by their political masters.

What of the means to these expansive ends? The Maritime Strategy directs the maritime services to pursue six "expanded core capabilities," including forward presence, deterrence, sea control, power projection ashore, maritime security, and humanitarian assistance and disaster response. To realize these capabilities, the Navy, Marines, and Coast Guard are directed to improve interoperability among themselves and with foreign allies and partners, bolster maritime domain awareness and intelligence, surveillance, and reconnaissance capacity, and prepare their people for the intensely interactive strategic environment they will encounter in the Indian Ocean and the western Pacific. The chiefs are blunt about sea control:

> There are many challenges to our ability to exercise sea control, perhaps none as significant as the growing number of nations operating submarines, both advanced diesel-electric and nuclear propelled. We will continue to hone the tactics, training and technologies needed to neutralize this threat. We will not permit conditions under which our maritime forces would be impeded from freedom of maneuver and freedom of access, nor will we permit an adversary to disrupt the global supply chain by attempting to block vital sea-lines of communication and commerce. We will be able to impose local sea control *wherever necessary,* ideally in concert with friends and allies, *but by ourselves if we must.*[40] (our emphasis)

The document strikes a martial note, evoking Mahan's grammar of naval strategy, and it focuses squarely on Asia. The specific mention of potential enemy capabilities, namely submarines, is particularly noteworthy. China is the only naval power in the world that has amassed undersea power prodigiously in both the conventional and nuclear domains. Since the 1990s, the PLA Navy has introduced three new classes of advanced diesel-electric boats (the *Kilo*, the *Song*, and the *Yuan*) and two classes of second-generation nuclear-powered subs (the *Jin* SSBN and the *Shang* SSN). This is unrivaled anywhere. The passage above is perhaps the closest the Maritime Strategy ever comes to identifying China's naval modernization as a major challenge to the U.S. Navy's sea-control mission. If the threat to American command of the sea is measured in terms of an adversary's capacity to sortie and operate large numbers of modern submarines, then China will likely rank atop or near the top of the list.

"Critical to this notion [of sea control]," insists the Cooperative Strategy, "is the maintenance of a powerful fleet—ships, aircraft, Marine forces, and shore-based fleet activities—capable of selectively controlling the seas, projecting power ashore, and protecting friendly forces and civilian populations from attack." This is a function of forward-deployed naval power. "Credible combat power will be continuously postured in the Western Pacific and the Arabian Gulf/Indian Ocean to protect our vital interests, assure our friends and allies of our continuing commitment to regional security, and deter and dissuade potential adversaries and peer competitors."[41] Such language would have been instantly familiar to Mahan in his most warlike moods.

Beyond that, the Maritime Strategy says little about force structure, and this is by design. The sea-service chiefs had their gaze squarely on Mahan's first trident, as befits the document's cooperative nature. As noted before, the strategy intends to set forth a logic of sea power predicated on U.S. leadership, and its primary audiences reside in foreign capitals and the international community. Advocating a particular makeup for the national fleet would serve little purpose in such a document, especially given the unsettled conditions it foresees in an unevenly globalizing world and given the need to frame a message convivial to overseas observers. Still less could it predict in advance which foreign partners would join in which specific endeavors. The service chiefs, it seems, are content to let debates over the grammar of maritime strategy and forces sort themselves out elsewhere. In all likelihood, Mahan's second trident will change its shape from contingency to contingency, depending on the kind and magnitude of foreign support Washington can round up.

CRITIQUES OF THE COOPERATIVE STRATEGY

When reviewing expert commentary on the 1986 and 2007 strategies, an interesting dichotomy emerges. The most acute critics of the 1986 strategy, a decidedly grammatical document, were academics such as John Mearsheimer and MIT's Barry Posen. To date the sharpest commentary on the 2007 strategy, a statement of sea-power logic, has come from current or former practitioners such as retired sea-service officers Robert Work and Jan van Tol. Why? The 1980s theorists were presumably concerned about the impact of operational endeavors on the geometry of deterrence, an intensively theoretical topic and a subject of academic inquiry since the dawn of the nuclear age. When practitioners complain that the 2007 strategy is not a strategy at all, they mean that it provides little to no guidance vis-à-vis doctrine (akin to the 1986 strategy's mandate to strike at the Soviet navy in its home waters), resource allocations, or specific ship and aircraft numbers. The 2007 edition contains no counterpart to the six-hundred-ship navy of the Reagan years.

Robert Work is a vice president of the Center for Strategic and Budgetary Assessments (CSBA) who in May 2009 was installed as undersecretary of the Navy. It is reasonable to suppose that he gained this influential post in the Obama administration in part on the strength of his critique of the Maritime Strategy. In 2008, he and Jan van Tol, a senior fellow at CSBA, depicted the strategy as the navy's latest search for a "naval holy grail" to replace the Mahanian one "genetically encoded" in naval officers during the interwar era but lost following the defeat of Imperial Japan, which deprived U.S. strategists of a maritime antagonist to plan against. The Navy refurbished its Mahanian tradition of offensive strategy in the 1980s only to witness the demise of the Soviet navy.

The authors propose three metrics to gauge the effectiveness of any successor strategy: it must furnish guidance to those seafarers who will execute it; it must provide a standard around which to rally public and elite support and resources; and it must be "accepted, if not outright applauded and supported, by U.S. naval allies." By those standards, say Work and van Tol, the Cooperative Strategy rates mixed reviews. Pundits such as Robert Kaplan and many governments overseas have acclaimed it while the response from the services, Congress, and the American people has been tepid.[42]

Work and van Tol first ask whether the Maritime Strategy is a strategy at all. Tellingly, they frame their analysis using the definition of strategy set forth in a Pentagon publication—Joint Publication 1-02, the "DOD Dictionary of Military and Associated Terms"—rather than one of the great works of strategic theory. They credit the Cooperative Strategy with spelling out the ends and ways of strategy but conclude that "the strategy suffers the same general weakness that [infects] many US strategy documents, which are often long on lists of laudable goals, sub-goals, and core capabilities, but short on *how* these goals and sub-goals might be achieved" (their emphasis). Worse, "it is the lack of any substantive discussion on the means necessary to accomplish its ways and ends, or how resources will be diverted toward its implementation priorities, that cause it to fall short as a true strategy. Indeed, the new strategy steers completely away from delving into its specific resource implications."[43] By failing to elucidate resource requirements, matching ends with means, the strategy falls short. Work and van Tol concede the importance of the "Cooperative Strategy for 21st Century Seapower," but they describe it not as a strategy but as a maritime "strategic concept." In Samuel Huntington's words, a strategic concept is a "description of how, when, and where the military service expects to protect the nation against some threat to its security."[44] Without a governing concept, a service finds itself intellectually, morally, and materially rudderless.

As such, Work and van Tol find that, on the "macro level," the strategy "stacks up quite well" with the cooperative themes articulated in documents such as the 2005 Quadrennial Defense Review and the 2006 National Defense Strategy.[45] They take the Maritime Strategy to task for remaining silent on a number of significant topics, notably the rise of Chinese sea power: "most readers of the document would likely deduce that the concept's authors discount the rise of China as a potential maritime competitor and have concluded that no counterstrategies for this potential outcome are necessary." The laudable goal of avoiding making Beijing an enemy does not "excuse the leaders of the three Sea Services from failing to acknowledge that the United States and China are clearly on the edge of a maritime competition."[46] Absent any discussion of China or the kinds of wars the United States may wage, they conclude, the sea services and Congress will find it impossible to set priorities or allocate resources—especially when, by objective measures, nontraditional threats in the maritime domain are at low ebb.

The CSBA analysts hint at but do not fully flesh out a problem Washington may encounter while prosecuting the Maritime Strategy. They point out, reasonably enough, that classified planning may add the specifics they criticize the strategy document for omitting. The Navy leadership, by contrast, insists there is no classified version of the Maritime Strategy. This is no doubt true in a strict sense. But it also finesses reality, for classified directives such as the

Navy Operating Concept or the Navy Strategic Concept address controversial subjects such as how to fight China. Foreign leaders worry about signing onto the Global Maritime Partnerships initiative simply because they fear agreeing to a division of labor in which the U.S. military dedicates itself to combat readiness while relegating its foreign partners to police duty. Should that come about, their governments fear they would be complicit in American misdeeds, real or perceived. There are pitfalls to diplomatic documents that compel readers to read between the lines. There they may discern meaning the drafters never intended to include.[47]

Sea-service officers and officials have not analyzed the Maritime Strategy in these terms, but there is a pronounced Clausewitzian tenor to the debate. Specifically, is it possible to orient a people, their government, and their military absent a tangible threat to plan around? This is not a new observation; it came up during the 1990s' debate over "capabilities-based planning," which abstracted U.S. military capabilities from the threats these capabilities would be used to counter. If sea-service leaders studiously avert their gaze from China's rise, are they not tacitly admitting that the United States does not need a dominant battle fleet? Active-duty officers in particular fear diffusing the rationale for a vibrant fleet, and being caught flatfooted should a peer competitor emerge. They understand it is easy for an adversary to change its intentions, and it is hard for navies to rebuild capabilities allowed to atrophy amid a seeming era of good feelings. This is a basic fact of life in an industrial age.

REGIONAL RESPONSES TO THE MARITIME STRATEGY

How has the Cooperative Strategy played with key audiences in the primary theaters, the Indian Ocean and the western Pacific? Consonant with the diplomatic nature of the strategy, Japanese, Chinese, and Indian officials and scholars have responded in measured terms. Tokyo has reacted in typical muted fashion, despite the fact that the Maritime Strategy in effect codifies the cooperative approach that underpins the Proliferation Security Initiative, to which Japan has acceded, and other important enterprises such as joint U.S.-Japan missile-defense cooperation. The Maritime Self-Defense Force's Indian Ocean refueling mission in support of Operation Enduring Freedom (now lapsed) and its counterpiracy efforts in the Gulf of Aden speak volumes about Japan's willingness to fulfill the principles set forth in the document.

At the same time, however, Japanese officials fret that the strategy makes no mention of China's rise or of the fundamental importance of the

U.S.-Japan alliance. To them, the strategy looks suspiciously like a precursor to Washington's conciliating Beijing. They fear this could mean downgrading its relationship with Tokyo or, in the extreme case, disengaging from the alliance altogether.[48] The Maritime Strategy, then, pulls Japan in two divergent directions. On the one hand, the document's emphasis on good order at sea dovetails with Tokyo's increasing enthusiasm for what Japanese policymakers call "international peace support operations." On the other hand, its conspicuous silence on China seemingly confirms long-standing Japanese concerns that Washington is too sanguine about one of Tokyo's most nettlesome regional security challenges.

Generally speaking, commentators in what Andrew Erickson calls China's "public intellectual complex" have praised the Maritime Strategy document while reserving judgment about American sincerity. For the most part, pundits such as Su Hao of China Foreign Affairs University agree that the strategy marks a new strategic direction for the United States, they hail its emphasis on preventing war, and they acclaim its acknowledgment of noncombat missions—a mode of operations embraced by Beijing in recent years, as discussed in chapter 6.[49] But skepticism lingers. National Defense University researcher Wang Baofu traces the U.S. sea services' persistent "maritime hegemonic mentality" to Mahanian thought. U.S. maritime strategies have come and gone, says Wang, but the services have never disavowed the Mahanian approach to naval strategy.[50]

Wang is clearly thinking in grammatical terms, imputing bloody-minded acceptance of sea combat to American mariners. He also acknowledges the strategic-communications aspect of the strategy but interprets this in the worst light, alleging that "some people and military industrial interest groups" have fabricated "a 'Chinese naval threat theory' or 'Russian maritime threat' argument" to lobby on behalf of bigger naval budgets.[51] Agrees Lu Rude of the Dalian Naval Vessel Academy, cooperative ventures are all very well, but it is up to the United States to live up to the principles enunciated in the strategy. Lu points to the mission of "deterring potential competitors," which he—rightly—interprets as code for China. Lu denies that the Maritime Strategy has altered underlying realities: "Obviously, "A Cooperative Strategy for 21st Century Seapower" has not changed the [U.S.] strategic goal of dominating the world's oceans. The United States still attempts to rely on its formidable sea power to control the world's oceans, carry out global deployments, [and] continue to brandish military force to 'deter wars between great powers,' thus maintaining its domination of the world's oceans."[52] He also appears to project Chinese assumptions onto the framers of the Maritime Strategy, editorializing that Washington has "implemented island chain defense" under the strategy and intends to "contain" the nameless strategic competitors of which it speaks.[53] As previous chapters showed, the island chain and the legacy of containment are freighted concepts for Beijing, evoking the nation's past maritime impotency. Chinese analysts tend to draw a straight line from Dean Acheson's "defense perimeter of the Pacific" to U.S. strategy today, inferring continuity where none may exist.

Indeed, this ambivalence about U.S. maritime intentions predates the unveiling of the Maritime Strategy. Chinese analysts, for example, inferred ulterior motives from Admiral Mullen's call for a thousand-ship navy in 2005 (much as Indians read the worst into the PLA Navy counterpiracy operation today). Du Chaoping levels a sweeping charge at the American maritime services: "After the end of the Cold War, the U.S. military's appetite for hegemony grew larger and larger. But the combat operations in Afghanistan and Iraq produced an acute awareness that the absence of allied cooperation and support makes it difficult to fill this unceasingly expanding appetite while laboring under limited resources. Through the establishment of the 'thousand-ship navy,' it can strap its allies onto a single warship, thus benefiting its own pursuit of the anti-terror war."[54] Respected military analyst Li Jie lists four possible motives for promoting the thousand-ship-navy concept. For Li, the U.S. Navy is attempting to (1) leverage the power of other navies, easing its own financial burden; (2) exploit regional players' situational awareness of and familiarity with the intricacies of their maritime environs; (3) extract detailed data from its partners about the hydrology and meteorology of local waters, aiding U.S. naval operations in peacetime and conflict; and (4) enhance information sharing and establish joint command systems, speeding up U.S. responses to shifts in regional affairs.[55]

Chinese observers find especially persuasive the notion that financial concerns are driving this burden-sharing project. For example, they compare the Pentagon's plan for a "hundred-satellite constellation" for its NATO allies unfavorably to the thousand-ship-navy construct, branding it a crude scheme to spread the financial pain of developing new space technology.[56] Some Chinese, then, see weakness rather than strength in U.S. cooperative initiatives. There is an object lesson here: what Washington hopes to convey can depart completely, and unhelpfully, from how recipients of the message want to interpret it.

How do Indians size up the "Cooperative Strategy for 21st Century Seapower"? In 2008 one Indian naval officer told CNO Admiral Gary Roughead that the Indian Navy hierarchy had parsed the document and found "not a word out of place."[57] No doubt this overstates things, but Indian officials and pundits have generally hailed the Maritime Strategy. Commander Gurpreet Khurana, formerly a research fellow at the Institute for Defense Studies and Analyses, New Delhi, also renders a favorable verdict while hinting at problems that could emerge.[58] The document's stress on surmounting threats to global networks of trade, commerce, and transportation prompts applause in the Indian naval establishment, the main guardian of New Delhi's interests at sea. Also welcome is the clause stating that the U.S. sea services will station credible combat power in the Indian Ocean region for the foreseeable future—presumably the next fifteen years, judging by the intended life span of the Cooperative Strategy. The forward deployment, believes Khurana, will reassure friends and allies of America's commitment while dissuading prospective opponents from harmful actions. Furthermore, combined maneuvers such as the Malabar exercises help New Delhi generate strategic deterrence vis-à-vis Beijing.

And the trouble signs? While India has repeatedly espoused a multipolar world, "it realizes well that this [will] not happen any time soon," and thus it greets Washington's effort to project a benign image. For the time being, perpetuating U.S. power is "necessary for global and regional security." But Washington must beware of creating a "hegemonic impression" of itself— that is, conveying the impression that it is willing to bully lesser powers. This would have "a spillover effect on India's own image in the region." A backlash could result from some action that damaged America's standing in the region, eroding Indian soft power and by extension U.S.-Indian amity and cooperation. "Dissonance" could separate the two sea powers under certain circumstances. Even seemingly innocuous ventures such as counterpiracy could conceivably cause problems if, say, the United States decided to carry the fight ashore in Somalia and its action created hardships for the Somali people.

On balance, concludes Khurana, "the U.S. strategy connects very well" with "present Indian thought" about sea power and its uses. It may represent the foundation on which a durable seagoing partnership can be erected. Keeping up the United States' good name in the region, managing controversies that might strain diplomatic relations with India, and remaining patient while India sorts through the politics and operational details of maritime partnership will be central to success. While the logic of maritime cooperation embodied in the Maritime Strategy is sound, occasional disagreements over the grammar may give New Delhi pause.

The rough consensus in Asia, then, seems to be that Asian maritime history is undergoing an interim phase. The United States still rules the seas, but its margin of qualitative and quantitative superiority over prospective rivals is on the decline. Tokyo worries that the maritime order may indeed be in transition, with the U.S. security guarantee becoming increasingly flimsy. For India, the U.S. sea services are an agent of stability, helping maintain great-power equilibrium in the Indian Ocean. New Delhi appears grateful for the strategic holiday granted it by U.S. predominance. This interlude lets the Indian military amass sea power at leisure, without launching itself into a crash naval arms program that might interfere with economic development, the top priority for all emerging great powers.

Beijing, too, seems to have resigned itself to U.S. preponderance in East Asia—for now. This has its advantages for China, as for India. As long as the U.S. Navy remains the steward of maritime security, the PLA Navy can continue fleet experimentation, tailoring its fleet and strategy to Chinese interests. It seems imperative for Washington to reinforce its strategic position in Asia—and to be seen doing so—if it hopes to forge a lasting partnership with India, work with China where interests coincide, and reassure Japan that the security guarantee remains the mainstay of the transpacific relationship.

A TALE OF TWO STRATEGIES

What guidance can we distill from all of this? What do the likenesses and disparities between the 1986 and 2007 maritime strategies say about making and adapting strategy in an increasingly competitive Asian nautical environment today? First, the two strategies are written on two different analytical planes. The 1986 document speaks primarily to operational-level commanders, corresponding to the Clausewitzian grammar of sea power, or to Mahan's writings on fleet tactics. The 2007 document is pitched at the grand-strategic level, corresponding to Clausewitzian logic, to Mahan's sea-power philosophy, and to Huntington's definition of a strategic concept. As we demonstrated in chapter 6 when we examined the interactions between undersea deterrence and maritime antiaccess, there is considerable interplay among the operational and strategic levels. The Watkins–Lehman strategy envisioned modifying the nuclear balance in America's favor even in a conventional conflict, as the strategy's critics pointed out. This lent grand-strategic import to a vision of offensive naval warfare. And, even though it remains silent on operations and tactics, the Cooperative Strategy is clearly intended to govern these matters. This is another facet of interaction that strategists should bear in mind, lest they incur unintended consequences.

Having an adversary to impart focus, and having a leadership willing to be frank about identifying and planning against that adversary, simplifies the intellectual challenge before strategists. That was the case during the formulation of the 1986 strategy. But there are vast differences between the strategic contexts then and now. The Soviet naval threat had been real and compelling for well over a decade by the time Watkins and Lehman began pushing their new approach. The drafters of the 2007 strategy had no such luck. The Cooperative Strategy could itself help shape the nature and magnitude of a Chinese threat—or even determine whether a threat emerges at all. Think of how the 1986 strategy would have influenced strategic debates in Moscow had it been released in, say, 1960—before Admiral Gorshkov embarked on his fleet-building enterprise, and before the Soviet navy was more than a nuisance. In all likelihood, a declaratory strategy proclaiming that the U.S. Navy intended to sink its Soviet antagonist in its home waters would have strengthened Gorshkov's hand in internal quarrels with the army and air force over strategy and resources.

Warlike talk from the U.S. Navy and Marines might have prompted Moscow to take a far more offensive stance at sea, overriding the Soviets' strategic preference for fighting within their blue belt of defense. This would have magnified and complicated the strategic challenge before Washington. The same logic applies to the case of China. Updating the 1986 strategy for the early decades of the twenty-first century would doubtless have been counterproductive in Asian waters. As we showed in chapter 7, the Chinese have assiduously cultivated a pacific image of China in the region. A bellicose U.S. document would have undermined the policy agenda of the top Chinese leaders, Hu and Wen, who have thus far exhibited a preference for moderation and conciliation while strengthening the hand of hardliners in the Chinese government. As Andrew Erickson noted shortly after the Maritime Strategy's release, "some elements in the People's Liberation Army . . . may already believe that U.S. sea power and ambitions remain fundamentally unchanged, and continue to challenge China's interests."[59]

It is possible, then, that a grammatically driven approach to U.S. maritime strategy would have not only reinforced the proclivity of key elements of the Chinese foreign- and security-policy establishment to assume the worst about the United States but also politically sidelined those more open to engagement with Washington. Whether Sino-U.S. enmity would have resulted is not clear, but a China-driven document premised on warfighting functions would surely have foreclosed prospects for cooperation at sea. While we should always be skeptical of casual claims that forthrightness with China will induce a self-fulfilling prophecy, giving rise to rivalry and antagonism, a revival of the 1986 strategy would have darkened the maritime environment in Asia, alarming allies and undecided powers alike.

Under certain circumstances, then, strategy statements themselves become part of strategic interaction with adversaries, allies, or bystanders. Careless phrasing is tantamount to self-defeating behavior. Both the 1986 and 2007 maritime strategies constituted exercises in strategic communication. The audiences for strategic communication correspond to the Clausewitzian trinity—roughly speaking, the government, the people, and the armed forces—for each party to an interactive relationship, plus international bodies like the UN Security Council or the North Atlantic Treaty Organization that take an interest in oceanic affairs. Clearly, the strategic-communications geometry becomes more and more complex as the number of parties increases. The geometry of the 1986 Maritime Strategy was relatively straightforward, encompassing the American trinity, the Soviet trinity, and the NATO allies. By aiming to draw all seafaring nations into a maritime consortium, the 2007 Maritime Strategy attempts a far more difficult feat. Because it elaborates principles without going into specifics, the 2007 strategy may be more durable than its predecessor was, and better fitted for regions like Asia where the configuration of power and interests remains fluid.

The upshot: candor matters, but it also has its pitfalls. Theodore Roosevelt was fond of invoking the West African proverb, "Speak softly and carry a big stick; you will go far." But speaking softly is not the same thing as dissembling about uncomfortable subjects such as Sino-American naval rivalry. Soft-pedaling the chances for traditional naval conflict undercuts the case for expensive platforms such as carriers and Aegis destroyers, and it does so while fanning speculation in Asia about what U.S. leaders *really* think, given the undeniable reality of a rising, militarily strong China. This is the worst of all possible worlds for strategic communicators. History primes Chinese officials and scholars to be skeptical about American sea power, no matter what Washington says. As a general rule, it is better to speak softly—but also forthrightly—about the proper uses of maritime power.

CHAPTER 9

Who Holds the Tridents?

I n August 2009 the RAND Corporation published a monograph profiling the military balance in the Taiwan Strait. Using wargaming models, the volume postulates a high-intensity invasion scenario to illustrate the relative balance of forces in the cross-strait standoff. The report is worthy of attention because it represents an honest, thoroughgoing reassessment of a previous RAND work completed nearly a decade ago. Three of the new volume's five authors are from the same team that compiled the original study, providing a sound basis for tracking changing views and attitudes at one of the United States' preeminent research institutions. Based on quantitative and qualitative analysis, the team's refreshingly clear findings represent a major reconsideration of China's military options and operational effectiveness against Taiwan.

The RAND report warns that China's large, modern missile and air forces are likely to pose a virtually insurmountable challenge to Taiwanese and American efforts to command the air over the strait and the island. The analysts believe that massive ballistic-missile salvos launched against Taiwan's air bases would severely hamper Taipei's ability to generate enough fighter sorties to contest air superiority. They state, "As China's ability to deliver accurate fire across the strait grows, it is becoming increasingly difficult and soon may be impossible for the United States and Taiwan to protect the island's military and civilian infrastructures from serious damage."[1] As a result, the authors observe, "China's ability to suppress Taiwan and local U.S. air bases with ballistic and cruise missiles seriously threatens the defense's ability to maintain control of the air over the strait."[2] They conclude, "The United States can no longer be confident of winning the battle for the air in the air. This represents a dramatic change from the first five-plus decades of the China-Taiwan confrontation."[3] These are stark, sobering conclusions.

And they represent a break with past wisdom. For years, U.S. strategists insisted that Taiwanese air superiority was the ultimate trump card against

Chinese invasion and coercion. Without air cover, the People's Liberation Army's (PLA) surface fleet and amphibious assault forces would be completely vulnerable to attack from above, making any cross-strait invasion a risky if not suicidal endeavor. While Chinese air dominance by no means guarantees military success against the island, it shifts the odds dramatically in Beijing's direction. The study's findings thus overturn key assumptions about the defense of Taiwan. Indeed, the RAND authors admit that "this is clearly a much less optimistic picture than was painted by our 2000 assessment and it poses hard strategic, operational, and programmatic decisions to both Washington and Taipei. It obviously does not bode well for the future stability of the situation along the Taiwan Strait."[4] Beyond the short-term operational implications of Taiwan's deteriorating position lie even more fundamental questions about U.S. policy and strategy toward the cross-strait stalemate. The report seems resigned to the conclusion that the geographic distance separating the United States from the theater of operations, combined with the ease and swiftness with which China could strike regional targets across Asia, might render the defense of Taiwan untenable. The report states quite plainly: "This geographic asymmetry [between China and the United States], combined with the limited array of forward basing options for U.S. force—and China's growing ability to mount sustained and effective attacks on those forward bases—calls into question Washington's ability to credibly serve as guarantor of Taiwan's security in the long run."[5]

Compare the bleak verdicts issued in this study to those of its predecessor nearly ten years ago. Forecasting a cross-strait war five years from the time of publication in 2000, the report envisaged a far more favorable position for Taipei. The same analysts argued that "Taiwan could, if proper steps were taken, have a reasonable degree of confidence in its ability to defeat a Chinese air offensive and thereby prevent a successful invasion."[6] Their broader findings conformed to the prevailing conventional wisdom at the time, namely that the overall military balance still favored Taiwan. They asserted: "Any near-term Chinese attempt [around 2005] to invade Taiwan would likely be a very bloody affair with a significant probability of failure. . . . The PLA cannot be confident of its ability to win the air-to-air war, and its ships lack adequate antiair and antimissile defenses. Provided the ROC [Republic of Taiwan] can keep its airbases operating under attack . . . it stands a relatively good chance of denying Beijing the air and sea superiority needed to transport a significant number of ground troops safely across the strait."[7] Again, the analysis reaffirmed how critical air superiority would be during the early phases of any campaign against Taiwan. Without it, follow-on PLA naval forces would become easy targets for Taiwanese aerial bombardment. The RAND report thus concluded: "Beijing would be imprudent to resort to massive air and missile attacks or an invasion of Taiwan as a means of compelling unification. Our results show an incredibly costly war that the PLA should have serious doubts about winning. The odds against the mainland appear to increase still further if the United States gets actively involved—*even minimally*—in Taiwan's defense"[8] (our emphasis).

One of the most troubling insights from this comparison concerns the role of the United States. For more than a decade, it was considered virtually axiomatic that with American intervention on Taipei's behalf, Taipei would decisively defeat PLA forces. Indeed, the 2000 RAND study apparently believed that relatively token U.S. military assistance would frustrate Chinese attempts to mount a credible invasion or coercive campaign against the island. The fact that U.S. policymakers can no longer count on a margin of superiority long presumed uncontestable attests to the dramatic leap in Chinese military power.

While this volume's analytical value does not hinge exclusively on the Taiwan question, we believe that the apparent end to a cross-strait military balance favorable for Taipei and Washington represents a much larger geostrategic trend that conforms to our analysis. Military modernization designed for a Taiwan scenario could be applied to broader Chinese ambitions should Beijing choose to pursue a more expansive foreign policy. As the 2009 report asserts, "A China that is conventionally predominant along the East Asian littoral could pose a direct, difficult, broad, and enduring challenge to the U.S. position as guarantor of regional stability and security, a challenge that could extend well beyond Taiwan."[9] We have argued throughout this study that China's ability to contest access within the first island chain opens up additional strategic avenues in the Asian littorals and beyond. Antiaccess by definition bestows on the denier some capacity to gain access for itself and to assert control over a confined area for a limited period of time. Even circumscribed PLA command of the Chinese littorals could alter the regional configuration of power. At the same time, a more secure hold over the commons would enable Beijing to bolster its other strategic aims, including its undersea deterrent posture, while instilling greater confidence in the Chinese leadership. Command of the commons would embolden Chinese statesmen to look farther from shore in their quest for access. We have in essence identified both the incremental dividends (ease of access) and the sequential dividends (scope of access) likely to accrue from investments in forcibly settling the Taiwan question.

Equally important, the RAND reassessment provides an opportunity to address some of the methodological challenges associated with studying the PLA. In so doing, we hope to anticipate some critiques our study is likely to summon forth, and to persuade those inclined to doubt Chinese military power not to dismiss the persistent maritime challenges we posit in this volume. The 2009 RAND study does not stand alone in its basic reassessment of China's military prowess. Prominent scholars, too, have rethought both Beijing's naval power and Chinese options against Taiwan. In 2001 Robert Ross argued that Taipei's qualitative military superiority would keep the Chinese at bay, even absent American help. Ross held forth on the potency of Taiwanese tactical aircraft: "Taiwan's purchase of 150 F-16s and 60 Mirage 2000 jets and its domestic production of the Chingkuo fighter nearly guarantee it air superiority over the Taiwan Strait, denying the mainland the ability to sustain offensive operations against it. The mainland still lacks the amphibious capabilities required to occupy Taiwan against the island's coastal defenses. Taiwan's assets alone could enable it to frustrate a mainland effort to occupy the island."[10] He concurred with the 2000 RAND study, adding that the United States would almost certainly come to the island's rescue and that, if so, its intervention would probably decide the matter: "Overwhelming U.S. superiority means that the strategic, economic and political costs to China of U.S. military intervention would be astronomical. U.S. conventional superiority and its strong political commitment to Taiwan mean that the credibility of the U.S. threat to intervene is very high. In an insecure world, the U.S. deterrent posture in the Taiwan Strait is an unusually secure one."[11]

Yet, within a span of five to six years, Ross substantially revised the premise of his argument. In 2006, he concluded that "Beijing's growing land-based missile and air capability in the Taiwan Strait provides an assured capability to inflict high costs on Taiwan in a cross-strait war . . . . For the first time since the first U.S. commitment to defend Taiwan in 1950, China's military can critically undermine the Taiwan economy and its democracy, regardless of the level of U.S. military intervention."[12] One year later he declared, "The United States can no longer defend Taiwan. It cannot help Taiwan deal with mainland retaliatory sanctions and it cannot defend Taiwan from the mainland's aircraft and missiles."[13] This reversal from a sanguine to a rather fatalistic attitude toward the cross-strait balance was among the sharpest analytical turns among China specialists. Ross was prescient, foreshadowing the more specific operational findings furnished by RAND.

The unhinging of the cross-strait equation is not the only subject that has induced an about-face among China specialists. In the naval realm, too, Western observers have recast their previous assessments, as the PLA modernization program far exceeded what they once considered unreachable. Bernard Cole, author of a pioneering volume on the Chinese navy, argued in 2001 that

> The PLAN [People's Liberation Army Navy] is a long way from being the dominant naval power in East Asia, however, even apart from the U.S. maritime presence. The JMSDF [Japan Maritime Self Defense Force] is certainly superior to the PLAN, and the ROKN [South Korean Navy] would be a difficult opponent. Even the Taiwan Navy would not be a pushover for the PLAN. Clearly, a wise maritime strategist in Beijing would not, in the event of a conflict, pose the PLAN "one-on-one" against any of these modern naval forces.[14]

In a 2003 analysis of the Chinese navy's capacity to cope with a Taiwan contingency, Cole remained rather upbeat about Taipei's defense. He asked, and then answered: "Is the PLAN currently and will it in 2005 be a threat to Taiwan's security? Yes, but not in terms of a navy-on-navy contest with even the Taiwan navy, and certainly not if the United States intervenes."[15] By 2007, however, Cole offered two quite pessimistic, though slightly different, forecasts for the Taiwan Strait balance ten years hence. In one study, the author revised his previous estimate, asserting that the Taiwan navy could no longer win a contest on its own. By this time, Cole had judged that only U.S. assistance could stave off Taiwanese naval defeat. He prophesied that China would be "clearly superior to Taiwan in naval strength below, on, and above the ocean's surface by 2016," and that, should present trends persist, "only successful U.S. intervention in a Taiwan contingency would alter this calculus."[16]

In his second analysis, Cole reached even more sweeping conclusions. His findings are worth quoting at length to capture the magnitude of his turnabout in judgment. He claimed:

By 2016–17, China will have available as an instrument of national power a Navy capable of carrying out ambitious assigned missions. The Taiwan imbroglio may still head that list, but the PLAN a decade hence [from 2007] will also be capable of denying command of the East and South China Seas to another power, and of commanding those seas for discrete periods. . . . The PLAN of 2016–17, at three times its present size will dominate East Asian navies, with the possible exception of the JMSDF . . . and will offer a very serious challenge to the U.S. Navy when it operates in those waters. . . . *By 2016–17, present trends indicate that the Chinese Navy will allow Beijing to exert hegemonic leverage in maritime East Asia."*[17] (our emphasis)

While Cole did not define the term "hegemonic leverage," his estimate was a far cry from the earlier belief that China would remain inferior to even second-rank regional navies. A hegemonic PLA Navy would presumably permit Beijing the dominant say not only in the strait but also in events elsewhere off the Asian seaboard.

We do not present this review of the literature to disparage fellow China specialists. Prediction is an inherently hazardous business. We review the literature because it is remarkable that leading analysts were compelled to jettison reasonable, accurate findings about China's military within a few short years. We believe this analytical excursion is a useful reminder of the difficulties intrinsic to studying military affairs in China, a closed society, and it says much about the industry with which Beijing has applied itself to its maritime enterprise. By exploring these lessons learned, we hope to encourage China-watchers to keep an open mind about the prospects of Chinese sea power, neither discounting nor overstating Beijing's naval potential.

OLD THINKING ABOUT CHINESE SEA POWER

A retrospective look at Western scholarship since the 1989 Tiananmen crisis provides a baseline for identifying analytical shortfalls, helping explain the lag in assessments of the PLA in general and of the Chinese navy in particular. Twenty years ago, Western specialists on Chinese naval development could be counted on one hand. Many of them underestimated the scale and pace of Chinese naval modernization while denigrating the competence of Beijing's scientific and engineering community, which was decimated during the Great Leap Forward and the Cultural Revolution. When Deng Xiaoping ordered the military to crush the pro-democracy movement in June 1989, the People's Liberation Army became the butt of jokes throughout the West. The mainstream view held that the Chinese military remained an insular, poorly equipped, land-bound organization trapped in the Maoist dogma of people's war.

Less than two years after the Tiananmen crackdown, the spectacular display of U.S. military might against Saddam Hussein seemingly offered further proof of the Chinese military's utter inadequacy in an age of high-tech warfare. Many experts prophesied confidently that the PLA would remain backward in professional and hardware terms well into the twenty-first century. Westerners were equally dismissive of the Chinese navy. Typifying attitudes commonplace during the post-Tiananmen period, the 1990 issue of the authoritative *Jane's Fighting Ships* pronounced the PLA Navy "a technically backward and operationally immature navy with rudimentary command and control systems and little high seas experience."[18] Subsequent studies throughout the 1990s dovetailed with this appraisal.

In 1994 an article in the journal *International Security* cataloged a litany of deficiencies plaguing the PLA Navy. Most prominent among them were the lack of modern ships and submarines, shortages in funding, and weaknesses in research-and-development capacity. The author, Michael Gallagher, was particularly harsh in his forecast for Beijing's industrial-military complex: "The PLA faces the high probability of merely being locked into a higher level of technological obsolescence than is now the case."[19] In other words, Chinese military might fall even further behind the West in the 1990s. Similarly, a 1996 monograph by the Center for Naval Analyses discounted China's ability to field a regional navy, even by 2010. Tellingly, the report was titled "People's War at Sea." After considering domestic production, reverse engineering, and foreign acquisitions as potential avenues for modernization, the author found that none, alone or together, would give the PLA Navy a capable regional fleet by 2010. The report foretold instead that a "regionally oriented Chinese Navy" would remain implausible until 2020.[20]

Such judgments persisted as the new century dawned. Declarative statements that "China is a second-rate military power"[21] and "China's military is simply not very good"[22] constituted the conventional wisdom among PLA-watchers. As noted earlier, observers voiced confidence that Taiwan would hold its own against the Chinese navy for many years. Leading defense analysts contended that Taipei's superior air and naval forces, formidable geographic features favoring the defense, and Beijing's limited military options made Taiwan an impregnable island fortress. As Michael O'Hanlon asserted in one provocative essay, "China cannot invade Taiwan, even under its most favorable assumptions about how a conflict would unfold. Nor will it be able to do so for more than a decade, if not much longer."[23] Worse, the flippant remark that China had little coercive option aside from "a million-man swim" across the strait echoed through the halls of think tanks throughout Washington.[24]

As we now know, these verdicts were far off the mark. It would be unfair, however, to write them off completely. The authors were writing at a time when open-source materials were fewer and far more restricted than today, when analysts find themselves deluged by the vast amounts of information available in the United States as well as in China. It is important to acknowledge, then, that they were right in certain important areas. They should be credited with identifying obstacles and constraining factors that are likely to endure for the next several years.

First, the overall growth in the PLA Navy force structure is certainly real, but it does not portend a radical shift in the regional balance of sea power. For the surface fleet in particular, the Chinese seem to have undertaken a methodical experimentation process. The PLA Navy typically builds a few hulls in each ship class, then evaluates the performance of the class as a basis for technical improvements to subsequent classes. The naval command evidently has not yet settled on a ship design for serial production. The West, accordingly, should watch for signs that Beijing is laying down much larger groups of nearly identical destroyers or frigates. These will be the PLA Navy's future surface combatants, with which the U.S. Navy and allied fleets will have to contend, and they may be built at a rapid clip.

Second, as Mao counseled, people, not hardware, are the true determinants of victory. The Chinese navy still has a long way to go in "software" areas such as training, education, seamanship, and the myriad of other skills that comprise battle readiness. More importantly, the PLA Navy has never confronted the rigors of modern naval warfare. It is a common refrain among PLA-watchers that China has not fought a major war for thirty years, since the Sino-Vietnamese border clashes. The PLA Navy has never fought one. How the Chinese fleet will fare under real wartime conditions against a capable regional navy, let alone the U.S. Navy, is anybody's guess. The navy's persistent reluctance to engage in serious combined operations with fellow navies (beyond superficial port calls and exercises) betokens a lack of confidence, a penchant for secrecy, or both.

Third, the geographic scope of Chinese naval power remains rather limited, especially when compared to the global reach of the U.S. Navy. The PLA Navy remains preoccupied with sea-denial missions designed to contest American command of the seas along the East Asian seaboard. It still lacks the capacity to assert sea control in a blue water environment. However, as chapters 4 and 5 demonstrated, the PLA Navy is already in position to impose its will on critical transport routes that run through the China seas, conveying the lifeblood of the global economy. With apologies to Thomas Christensen, China possesses the nautical tools to cause the United States and its allies severe problems without ever catching up in symmetrical terms.[25]

On balance, nevertheless, China-watchers missed many critical indicators that the Chinese navy, and Chinese sea power more generally, were poised at the threshold of a major transformation. Sanguine conclusions and condescending attitudes persisted for years, even when the evidence pointed elsewhere. It is thus worth asking some tough questions. To borrow a phrase from Bernard Lewis, what went wrong? Why was there such a chasm between earlier predictions and actual developments in Chinese naval power? Why did it take so long to revise outdated estimates? It behooves policymakers in Washington and Asian capitals to answer these uncomfortable questions, lest they misread Chinese naval developments again to the detriment of regional maritime stability.

EXPLAINING THE ANALYTICAL BLIND SPOTS

As a first, modest step toward solving this puzzle, we venture some propositions. First, Western analysts are too cavalier about using China's past as a guide to the present and the future. Among the most oft-heard historical observations is that China's lack of maritime traditions deprives it of a foundation for sea power. As Cole observes, "Naval planners face China's lack of maritime tradition: voyages half a millennium ago do not constitute a useful heritage when the intervening centuries have been devoted to introspective nationalism."[26] But this is a narrow reading of Chinese history. Contemporary writings on Chinese maritime history suggest that dynastic encounters with the sea were far richer and much more intense than once thought.[27] The tie-in between maritime tradition and sea power, moreover, is correlative rather than causal. One obvious Asian example: maritime tradition cannot explain the rise of Japanese sea power, in total or in part, since the archipelago's inward-looking inhabitants lacked seafaring experience for centuries prior to the Meiji Restoration. By 1898, thirty years after the Meiji Restoration, the Imperial Japanese Navy had defeated a materially superior Qing dynasty fleet and was girding itself for the 1904–1905 showdown with the Imperial Russian Navy—a showdown that left two Russian fleets at the bottom. A determined people can build a great navy with remarkable dispatch.

We showed in chapter 3 how superficial similarities between Imperial Germany nearly a century ago and China today do not tell the whole story. The failure of one continental power to transform itself into a sea power does not necessarily mean another will meet the same fate. Indeed, geostrategic conditions will likely aid China's seaward turn, helping the PLA pose a much broader, more sustained challenge to U.S. staying power than anything the German High Seas Fleet managed vis-à-vis the Royal Navy.

To other observers, the history of modern China represents another indicator of Beijing's meager prospects at sea. The Qing dynasty's abortive naval modernization during the nineteenth century and the naval defeats China suffered at the nadir of Qing dynastic rule are considered auguries for Beijing's current maritime enterprise. Lamenting the poor state of China's military-industrial complex, Cole states: "Today's PLAN is being modernized the same way Li Hongzhang tried to create a Chinese Navy more than a century ago, by following three different approaches: indigenous production, purchases abroad, and reverse engineering foreign systems. It did not work particularly well then, and is not likely to work any better in the twenty-first century."[28] But the Qing navy used these three approaches to create a fleet that was considered modern and capable. Its failings had more to do with seamanship, the lack of offensive-mindedness in the officer corps, and the superior élan and skill of its opponents than with material shortcomings. As noted in previous chapters, Chinese analysts today look to the Imperial Japanese Navy, not the Qing navy, as a paradigm for command of the sea. Imperial China is a negative example for them.

Still others point to the chaos and associated legacies of the Maoist period as an ever-present impediment to China's industrial capacity and scientific and engineering ingenuity. After surveying China's efforts from the 1950s through the 1980s, one analyst found that China spent an average of fifteen years reverse engineering each foreign technology for serial production. Extrapolating from patterns that date back four decades, he concludes that this desultory performance will endure well into the twenty-first century. But contemporary China is neither a dynasty decaying from within nor a revolutionary state wracked by radical ideological movements. While the lingering influence of China's Maoist and imperial past should not be discounted, other national experiences in Asia have given rise to sudden technological advances. These experiences are more apt and should be in the analytical mix as we contemplate historical precedents. Again, sloppy historical parallels can skew analysis.

Second, some of the arguments denigrating future Chinese sea power have a straw-man feel to them. They contend that since a global, blue water navy remains entirely aspirational for Beijing, Chinese ambitions and Chinese threats to U.S. interests will remain minimal. As Anthony Cordesman and Martin Klieber argue, "It has become commonplace to equate the procurement of modern naval vessels, especially those for blue-water capabilities, with expanded geopolitical ambitions."[29] The mantra might be summarized as no carrier, no threat. We disagree. Discerning intentions (as opposed to capabilities) is a problematic exercise fraught with tautology and circular reasoning.

More critically, as we have demonstrated throughout this volume, China does not need to compete symmetrically or across the globe to pose a severe challenge to U.S. staying power in Asia, the main theater. That Beijing cannot fight the United States in a one-on-one contest in the Pacific says little about the numerous strains that the PLA Navy can impose on U.S. naval forces short of a Mahanian sea battle. Mahan himself exhorted the United States to focus its naval exertions on the Caribbean and the Gulf, where local preponderance over European fleets was thinkable and necessary. We detailed in chapter 4 how Beijing conceives of sophisticated fleet tactics that could prove as deadly to U.S. naval forces as a Mahanian force-on-force engagement—despite the complete absence of carriers and comparable weaponry. Carrier development is an unreasonably demanding standard for Chinese maritime prowess.

The same problem afflicts debates about the scope of future Chinese power projection. As some would have it, Beijing's ability (or lack thereof) to extend sea control out to the second island chain casts doubt on China's naval aptitude. That is, since the PLA exhibits limited capacity to command the seas beyond even the first island chain, Beijing's maritime ambitions and capabilities warrant little attention. This is another straw man. Compelling, permanent Chinese maritime interests vector Beijing's attention to the south and southwest—toward the Indian Ocean, rather than the middle of the empty Pacific. Chapter 7 detailed Beijing's efforts to cultivate a permissive environment in the Indian Ocean, a maritime region on which the Chinese economy relies for natural resources. There is little reason to expect China to forego pressing geopolitical interests in South Asia in order to seize control of distant waters to its east. Prudence dictates expending finite resources on matters of vital importance.

True, Chinese strategists fret over the prominent place Guam has assumed in U.S. regional strategy, as the locus of American military power and as a jumping-off point into China's maritime environs. But Beijing has displayed little interest in projecting overbearing power against Guam, and it has eschewed futile efforts at fighting sea battles on American terms. In the spring of 2009, U.S. Pacific Command chief Admiral Timothy Keating revealed that a senior PLA Navy officer had proposed partitioning the Pacific basin between China and America.[30] The Chinese officer may have been only half joking, but both the logic and the grammar of Chinese sea power point to adjoining Chinese and U.S. spheres of interest, with the dividing line somewhere around the second island chain. Furthermore, as we demonstrated in chapter 2, China would prefer to "lure the enemy in deep," near or within the first island chain, before dealing out decisive blows using operational concepts derived from Mao's active-defense doctrine.

Third, some of the commentary rests on dubious assumptions. Projecting American conceptions of effectiveness and efficiency onto Chinese naval development is a recurring pattern. For instance, assumptions that the PLA Navy would need to more or less replicate a U.S. *Nimitz-* or *Ford*-class nuclear-powered carrier (CVN) to fulfill its aims have led some to conclude—prematurely—that the enterprise is prohibitively costly and far too complex for China. While it makes superficial sense—it might take some time for Chinese shipwrights to construct CVNs, seeing as they are the product of decades' worth of U.S. experience with carriers—this line of reasoning is nonetheless off the mark. If it perfects the antiship ballistic missile (ASBM), the PLA can hope to hold off U.S. task forces venturing into Asia, erecting a defensive shield beneath which even smaller, less capable Chinese flattops could do their work around the Asian periphery. They would have little need to risk a lopsided engagement with 100,000-ton American behemoths. They would have other functions to perform, such as coercive diplomacy, showing the flag, and the like. Fleet actions need not be in their portfolio provided shore-based forces keep the U.S. Navy carrier fleet at a safe distance.

And even if it did opt for big-deck CVNs, Beijing could make do with fewer carrier strike groups than Washington deploys, unless or until it opts for a global maritime strategy comparable to that of the United States. That is the advantage of being the defender in a contested zone. With fewer and smaller sea areas to roam, the PLA Navy could probably make do with a two-to-one ratio between combat-ready vessels and those in work-ups, as opposed to the three-to-one ratio that governs the U.S. training, maintenance, and deployment cycle. Chinese vessels would probably spend more time pierside, much as Zheng He's fleet returned to East Asia periodically, having reminded the inhabitants of Southeast and South Asia of the Dragon Throne's suzerainty. If Beijing displays a similar outlook in the coming decades, the PLA carrier fleet simply will not incur the same wear and tear and the same need for periodic overhauls, and its ships will be in port when such maintenance is required. The simple act of confining PLA Navy operations to Asia will cut back on the expense and technical demands of sustaining carrier operations. In all likelihood, Beijing will not impose comparable operational demands on the PLA Navy and thus will not need a force equal in numbers to the U.S. carrier fleet.

The debate over Chinese ballistic-missile submarines (SSBNs) bears on the carrier controversy. As we argued in chapter 6, American assumptions about the makeup of a sustainable undersea deterrent may not apply to China's operational requirements. A more modest SSBN fleet than the fourteen-boat U.S. Navy fleet may be enough to guarantee a credible second-strike capability as Beijing conceives of it. Mirror imaging, we believe, has exerted a baleful influence, discouraging creative thinking about how China might offset its relative quantitative and qualitative inferiority while exploiting such advantages as it does possess.

U.S. analysts have also casually superimposed the behavior and capabilities of past American foes on the Chinese. Observers have cast doubt on China's prospects for deploying ASBMs, for instance, basing their objections primarily on abortive Soviet attempts to develop similar weaponry during the Cold War. A former director of U.S. naval intelligence argued that the Soviets abandoned the ASBM out of technical difficulties, fears of nuclear escalation, and the availability of alternative platforms for launching antiship missiles.[31] By implication, China will run into the same roadblocks and opportunity costs and will thus be dissuaded from fielding ASBMs.

Leaving aside the facts that almost four decades have passed since Moscow gave up on its ASBM program and that technologies now available would have been unthinkable in the 1970s, the historical parallel cannot withstand close scrutiny. Technical barriers to entry are insufficient in themselves to account for all strategic choices. It is plausible that the Soviets would have opted out of the ASBM even had the technological challenges proved surmountable. Nonmaterial factors such as operational and strategic preferences may have prompted them to do so. Different values and proclivities, conversely, may impel the Chinese to pursue the ASBM doggedly, regardless of inefficiencies or potential tradeoffs in operational effectiveness. We contended in chapter 5 that unique qualities of the ASBM not directly associated with warfighting, including its relatively low political profile, magnify the appeal of the technology for Chinese planners. What makes a weapon system "good enough" is almost always in the eye of the beholder.

Fourth, analysts' habit of underrating Chinese naval potential is rivaled only by their habit of inflating U.S. combat capacity in Asia. Even as many China specialists have begun voicing alarm about the American strategic position in the region, and despite his newfound despair about the U.S. armed forces' ability to succor Taiwan in wartime, Robert Ross insists that the U.S. Navy will stay well ahead of any challenge China can mount. Despite conceding that the U.S. Navy "can no longer guarantee the security of a carrier," Ross contends that the United States is developing adequate countermeasures, assuring its capacity to project power into Asian waters. With regard to antisubmarine warfare, he declares: "Due to better funding, improved technologies and peacetime surveillance of Chinese submarines, the American carrier strike group's ability to track them and the U.S. Navy's antisubmarine capabilities are constantly improving. The U.S. strike group's counter-electronic-warfare capabilities can also interfere with the PLA Navy's reconnaissance ability."[32] Consequently, while U.S. naval forces would have to "maintain a greater distance from China's coast," Professor Ross reassures the reader that "such [undersea] complications to U.S. operations do not significantly degrade Washington's ability to project superior power into maritime theaters."[33] We imagine Chinese strategists—avid students of the Falklands War, which saw British carriers struggle to keep up the same sortie rate from greater range—would dissent from this statement.

We take issue with Ross' prognosis in several ways. If the United States cannot operate near Chinese shores at will, then by definition Chinese anti-access capabilities and strategies have already achieved a measure of success vis-à-vis a supposedly predominant foe. If we take "a greater distance" from China's shores to mean remaining clear of sea areas within and beyond the first island chain—essentially, all of the bodies of water that constitute the East Asian littoral—then it is unclear what maritime theater is left for the U.S. Navy to project power into. The Navy has not deployed carrier attack aircraft or other weaponry with enough reach to let carrier strike groups place the same ordnance on target from greater standoff distances. Quite the opposite. Long-range, heavy-payload A-6 Intruder attack aircraft were retired years ago. U.S. Navy and Marine F/A-18 E/F Super Hornet warplanes, the core of any carrier air wing, represent a step back from previous generations of attack aircraft in terms of combat radius. The carrier has seen its striking range foreshortened, meaning that it must venture closer to shore to fulfill the same missions. Its combat punch has diminished commensurately while its vulnerability is now more acute than ever.

If the U.S. Navy can no longer provide for its flattops' defense, the PLA Navy is already on the brink of sea denial in nearby waters while local sea control is coming into sight for Beijing. Nor does the wider naval community share Ross' confidence in the U.S. Navy's capacity to enforce sea control in Asia. His admission that the United States cannot ensure the survivability of its carriers, a mission verging on sacrosanct, comes as cold comfort to theater and fleet commanders entrusted with managing events in the western Pacific. Our analysis in chapter 8 underscored the dilemmas faced by sea services committed both to high-end conventional missions and to constabulary functions, all against the backdrop of declining budgets. To borrow a phrase from Robert Kaplan, how the U.S. Navy manages its "elegant decline" will be central to the future of American maritime strategy in Asia.[34]

Finally, timing is everything. Naval and military modernization programs are extraordinarily capital-intensive. The life cycles of big-ticket defense items like warships—from research and development to serial production to regular service life to deactivation—are measured in decades. As such, many of the Chinese assets that joined the PLA operating forces after the turn of the century must have undergone development during the 1990s, when Western observers were forced to depend on spotty open sources. In effect, these programs were invisible to outsiders. The rate at which the PLA introduced major weapons systems over the past decade suggests that they were developed in parallel, conveying the impression that the Chinese military had managed to leapfrog forward in weapons technology.

Unbeknownst to them, then, analysts writing in the late 1990s and early 2000s were doing their work at an inflection point in the trajectory of Chinese military modernization. It was easy to remain complacent about Chinese military might then, before the PLA's investments and labors had borne fruit. This explains why institutions such as RAND started revising their estimates only around 2005, when the bow wave of Chinese naval modernization started to crash. We make no claim to be above such analytical traps and fallacies. The only prediction we feel entirely safe making is that some of our insights will not stand the test of time. When thinking ahead, it is worth bearing in mind Michael Handel's portrayal of war—and, we might add, all competitive human affairs—as a continual process of interaction between belligerents jockeying for comparative advantage.[35] Foresight is a fine thing to strive for, but sobriety is the best attitude to take toward international relations in Asia, arguably the most dynamic region of all.

This short survey of the debate over China's maritime rise reveals, yet again, that it is perilous to accentuate the Mahanian grammar of sea power to the exclusion of its governing logic. True, it is possible that, as in the Germany and Japan of Mahan's day, the grammar of sea battle will win out in Chinese strategic deliberations, deflecting Chinese maritime strategy onto an ominous course. By no means would the Chinese be the first to fall under the spell of gee-whiz weaponry or maritime derring-do. But we should not assume this will be the case, and in any event, the possibility of an inversion between the logic and grammar of maritime strategy gives us yet another way to track the development of Chinese strategy. If Chinese discourses depart from the logic of access, coming to center on weapons systems for their own sake, this will be a trouble sign for the United States and its allies.

Until then, the safest assumption is that the logic of sea power, not the technical specifications of this or that naval weapon, will determine China's nautical destiny. Bringing Mahan's first trident of commerce, politics, and military power into the debate, alongside his second trident of sea fights, will enrich the Western discourse on Chinese sea power immensely—and those Americans and Asians who go down to the sea in ships will be better off for it.

 **Notes**

CHAPTER 1. MAHAN'S TWO TRIDENTS

1. David Lague, "China Airs Ambitions to Beef Up Naval Power," *New York Times*, December 28, 2008, http://www.nytimes.com/2006/12/28/world/asia/28iht-china.4038159.html.

2. Paul Kennedy, "The Rise and Fall of Navies," *New York Times*, April 5, 2007, http://www.nytimes.com/2007/04/05/opinion/05iht-edkennedy.1.5158064.html.

3. Author discussions with European officials and scholars; and Conference on "Pioneering for Solutions against Piracy," Netherlands Institute of International Relations, July 8, 2009, http://www.clingendael.nl/cscp/events/20090708/.

4. Jasper Gerard, "Ministers Accused of 'Sea Blindness' by Britain's Most Senior Royal Navy Figure," *Telegraph*, June 12, 2009, http://www.telegraph.co.uk/news/newstopics/politics/defence/5517833/Ministers-accused-of-sea-blindness-by-Britains-most-senior-Royal-Navy-figure.html.

5. Tim Webb, "MoD May Sell Aircraft Carrier to India to Limit Cuts," *The Guardian*, November 15, 2009, http://www.guardian.co.uk/politics/2009/nov/15/mod-may-sell-carrier.

6. Kennedy, "Rise and Fall of Navies." For more background, see Bruce Swanson, *Eighth Voyage of the Dragon: A History of China's Quest for Sea Power* (Annapolis, Md.: Naval Institute Press, 1982), esp. 28–43; and Louise Levathes, *When China Ruled the Seas: The Treasure Fleet of the Dragon Throne, 1405–1433* (London: Oxford University Press, 1994).

7. Julian S. Corbett, *Some Principles of Maritime Strategy*, intro. Eric J. Grove (1911; repr., Annapolis, Md.: Naval Institute Press, 1988), 94; K. M. Panikkar, *Asia and Western Dominance: A Survey of the Vasco da Gama Epoch of Asian History, 1498–1945* (New York: Day, 1954); and K. M. Panikkar, *India and the Indian Ocean: An Essay on the Influence of Sea Power on Indian History* (New York: Macmillan, 1945).

8. Nicholas Evan Sarantakes, "The Last Days of the Royal Navy: Lessons from Britain's Strategic Retreat from the Pacific," in *Asia Looks Seaward: Power and Maritime Strategy*, ed. Toshi Yoshihara and James R. Holmes (Westport, Conn.: Praeger, 2007), 32–45. See also Panikkar, *Asia and Western Dominance*.

9. 章明　陈向君 [Zhang Ming and Chen Xiangjun], 太平洋的碰撞: 浅论新世纪中日两国海上力量的发展及可能出现的冲突　["Collision in the Pacific: Assessing the Development of Sino-Japanese Maritime Power and Possible Confrontation in the New Century"], 舰载武器 [*Shipborne Weapons*] (November 2005): 19.

10. Geoffrey Till, "Maritime Strategy in a Globalizing World," *Orbis* 51, no. 4 (Fall 2007): 569–575; and Geoffrey Till, *Seapower* (London: Frank Cass, 2003).

11. "Chasing Ghosts," *Economist*, June 11, 2009, 48, http://www.economist.com/displayStory.cfm?story_id=13825154.

12. Robert D. Kaplan, "America's Elegant Decline," *Atlantic*, November 2007, http://www.theatlantic.com/doc/200711/america-decline.

13. Robert D. Kaplan, "The Revenge of Geography," *Foreign Policy*, May/June 2009, http://www.foreignpolicy.com/story/cms.php?story_id=4862&print=1.

14. Margaret Tuttle Sprout, "Mahan: Evangelist of Sea Power," in *Makers of Modern Strategy: Military Thought from Machiavelli to Hitler*, ed. Edward Meade Earle (Princeton, N.J.: Princeton University Press, 1943), 415; Robert Seager II and Doris D. Maguire, eds., *Letters and Papers of Alfred Thayer Mahan*, vol. 2, *1890–1901* (Annapolis, Md.: Naval Institute Press, 1975), 342.

15. For a definition of antiaccess, see Roger Cliff, Mark Burles, Michael S. Chase, Derek Eaton, and Kevin L. Pollpeter, *Entering the Dragon's Lair: Chinese Antiaccess Strategies and Their Implications for the United States* (Santa Monica, Calif.: RAND, 2007), 11.

16 Thomas P. Ehrhard and Robert O. Work, *Range, Persistence, Stealth, and Networking: The Case for a Carrier-Based Unmanned Combat System* (Washington, D.C.: Center for Strategic and Budgetary Assessments, 200), 137–138.

17. Ibid., 195.

18. Mark Cozad, "China's Regional Power Projection: Prospects for Future Missions in the South and East China Seas," in *Beyond the Strait: PLA Missions Other Than Taiwan*, ed. Roy Kamphausen, David Lai, and Andrew Scobell1 (Carlisle Barracks, Carlisle, Pa.: Strategic Studies Institute, 2008), 287–325.

19. Alfred Thayer Mahan, *The Influence of Sea Power upon History, 1660–1783* (1890; repr., New York: Dover, 1987), 25.

20. Alfred Thayer Mahan, *The Problem of Asia* (1900; repr., Port Washington, N.Y.: Kennikat Press, 1970), 124.

21. Alfred Thayer Mahan, *The Interest of America in Sea Power, Present and Future* (1897; repr., Freeport, N.Y.: Books for Libraries Press, 1970), 65–83, 277–292.

22. Mahan, *Problem of Asia*, 124.

23. Carl von Clausewitz, *On War*, ed., trans. Michael Howard and Peter Paret (Princeton, N.J.: Princeton University Press, 1976), 605.

24. Harold Sprout and Margaret Sprout, *The Rise of American Naval Power* (Princeton, N.J.: Princeton University Press, 1939), 203, 217–222.

25. James R. Holmes, "China's Way of Naval War: Mahan's Logic, Mao's Grammar," *Comparative Strategy* 28 (2009): 1–27.

26. Mahan, *Problem of Asia*, 33.

27. Mahan, *Influence of Sea Power upon History*, 22–23.

28. Alfred Thayer Mahan, *Retrospect & Prospect* (Boston: Little, Brown, 1902), 246.

29. Ibid., 246.

30. Mahan, *Influence of Sea Power upon History*, 71.

31. Ibid., 53.

32. Ibid., 138.

CHAPTER 2. CHINA ENGAGES THE STRATEGIC THEORISTS

1. Robert S. Ross, "The Geography of the Peace: East Asia in the Twenty-first Century," *International Security* 23, no. 4 (Spring 1999): 81–118. See also Andrew J. Nathan and Robert S. Ross, *The Great Wall and the Empty Fortress: China's Search for Security* (New York: Norton, 1998).

2. Michael O'Hanlon, "Why China Cannot Conquer Taiwan," *International Security* 25, no. 2 (Fall 2000): 51–86.

3. Bernard D. Cole, *The Great Wall at Sea: China's Navy Enters the Twenty-first Century* (Annapolis, Md.: Naval Institute Press, 2001), 181.

4. See Keith Crane, Roger Cliff, Evan Medeiros, James Mulvenon, and William Overholt, *Modernizing China's Military: Opportunities and Constraints* (Santa Monica, Calif.: RAND, 2005), 91–134.

5. U.S. Department of Defense, "Annual Report to Congress: Military Power of the People's Republic of China" (Washington, D.C.: Department of Defense, 2008), http://www.defenselink.mil/pubs/pdfs/China_Military_Report_08.pdf.

6. "China's Navy: Distant Horizons," *Economist*, April 23, 2009, http://www.economist.com/world/asia/displaystory.cfm?story_id=13527838.

7. Wang Jianfen and Nie Ligao, "Japan Defense Minister's China Visit a Sign of Warming Relations," *China Daily*, March 23, 2009, http://www.chinadaily.com.cn/china/2009-03/23/content_7607571.htm.

8. "Secret Sanya—China's New Nuclear Naval Base Revealed," *Jane's Intelligence Review*, April 21, 2008, http://www.janes.com/news/security/jir/jir080421_1_n.shtml.

9. Ian Storey, "China's 'Malacca Dilemma,'" *China Brief* 6, no. 8 (April 12, 2006), http://www.jamestown.org/programs/chinabrief/single/?tx_ttnews%5Btt_news%5D=31575&tx_ttnews%5BbackPid%5D=196&no_cache=1.

10. Bill Gertz, "China's Pearls," *Washington Times*, January 1, 2009, http://www.washingtontimes.com/news/2009/jan/01/inside-the-ring-84163751/.

11. Gurpreet Khurana, "China-India Maritime Rivalry," *Indian Defense Review* 23, no. 4 (July–September 2009), http://www.indiandefencereview.com/2009/04/china-india-maritime-rivalry.html.

12. Julian S. Corbett, *Some Principles of Maritime Strategy*, intro. Eric J. Grove (1911; repr., Annapolis, Md.: Naval Institute Press, 1988), 94.

13. K. M. Panikkar, *Asia and Western Dominance: A Survey of the Vasco da Gama Epoch of Asian History, 1498–1945* (New York: Day, 1954); and Panikkar, *India and the Indian Ocean* (New York: Macmillan, 1945).

14. 倪乐雄 [Ni Lexiong], 海权的昨天，今天和明天—读马汉"海权对历史的影响" ["Sea Power Yesterday, Today, and Tomorrow—Reading Mahan's *The Influence of Sea Power upon History*"], 中国图书评论 [*China Book Review*], no. 8 (2006): 23.

15. Alfred Thayer Mahan, *The Influence of Sea Power upon History, 1660–1783* (1890; repr., New York: Dover, 1987), 138.

16. "Asia's Maritime Rivalries," *Economist*, June 11, 2009, http://www.economist.com/displayStory.cfm?story_id=13825154.

17. Alfred Thayer Mahan, *The Problem of Asia* (1900; repr., Port Washington: Kennikat, 1970), 38.

18. Ibid., 29–30.

19. George W. Baer, *One Hundred Years of Sea Power: The U.S. Navy, 1890–1990* (Stanford, Calif.: Stanford University Press, 1994), 12.

20. V. R. Berghahn, *Germany and the Approach of War in 1914* (New York: St. Martin's Press, 1973), 35.

21. See Sadao Asada, *From Mahan to Pearl Harbor: The Imperial Japanese Navy and the United States* (Annapolis, Md.: Naval Institute Press, 2006).

22. See, for instance, David Hale, "China's Growing Appetites," *The National Interest* 76 (Summer 2004): 137–147.

23. On the buildup of China's merchant fleet, see David Lague, "The Making of a Juggernaut," *Far Eastern Economic Review*, September 18, 2003, 30–33. "Mahan is alive and well and living in Beijing," declares Lague, pointing to the rapid growth of the Chinese merchant fleet. Some news outlets have taken account of the Taiwan focus of the Chinese naval buildup. See, for example, Edward Cody, "With Taiwan in Mind, China Focuses Military Expansion on Navy," *Washington Post*, March 20, 2004, A12.

24. Harold Sprout and Margaret Sprout, *The Rise of American Naval Power* (Princeton, N.J.: Princeton University Press, 1939), 203, 217–222.

25. Carl von Clausewitz, *On War*, ed., trans. Michael Howard and Peter Paret (Princeton, N.J.: Princeton University Press, 1976), 605.

26. Michael I. Handel, *Masters of War: Classical Strategic Thought*, 3rd ed., repr. (London: Frank Cass, 2004), esp. 119–134.

27. Wu Shengli and Hu Yanlin, "Building a Powerful People's Navy that Meets the Requirements of the Historical Mission for Our Army," *Qiushi* 14 (July 16, 2007), FBIS- CPP20070716710027.

28. Jiang Shiliang, "The Command of Communications," *Zhongguo Junshi Kexue*, October 2, 2002, 106–114, FBIS-CPP20030107000189.

29. Ye Hailin, "Safe Seas," *Beijing Review* 13 (April 2, 2009), FBIS-CPP200904 30716005.

30. Bruce Elleman, "A Comparative Historical Approach to Blockade Strategies: Implications for China," in *China's Energy Strategy: The Impact on Beijing's Maritime Policies*, ed. Gabriel B. Collins, Andrew S. Erickson, Lyle J. Goldstein, and William S. Murray (Annapolis, Md.: Naval Institute Press, 2008), 365–386.

31. Dean Acheson, "Remarks by the Secretary of State (Acheson) before the National Press Club, Washington, January 12, 1950," in *Documents on American Foreign Relations*, vol. 12, *January 1–December 31, 1950*, ed. Raymond Dennett and Robert K. Turner (Princeton, N.J.: Princeton University Press, 1951), 431.

32. Quoted in Samuel Eliot Morison, *The Two-Ocean War: A Short History of the United States Navy in the Second World War* (Boston: Little, Brown, 1963), 476.

33. Quoted in Courtney Whitney, *MacArthur: His Rendezvous with History* (New York: Knopf, 1956), 378–379.

34. See 展华云 [Zhan Huayun], 出海口 走向世界的战略通道 ["Oceanic Exits: Strategic Passageways to the World"], 当代海军 [*Modern Navy*] (April 2007): 28; 李玉平 [Li Yuping], 台湾地缘战略的海权解读 ["Interpreting Sea Power through Taiwan's Strategic Geography"], 现代舰船 [*Modern Ships*] (April 2004): 5; 白炎林 [Bai Yanlin], 岛链与中国海军 ["Island Chains and the Chinese Navy"], 当代海军 [*Modern Navy*] (October 2007): 18; and Lu Baosheng and Guo Hongjun, "Guam: A Strategic Stronghold on the West Pacific," *Jiefangjun Bao*, June 19, 2003, FBIS-CPP20030619000057.

35. Peng Guangqian and Yao Youzhi, *The Science of Military Strategy* (Beijing: Military Science Publishing House, 2005), 443.

36. State Council, "China's National Defense in 2004," December 2004, Federation of American Scientists Web site, http://www.fas.org/nuke/guide/china/doctrine/natdef2004.html.

37. State Council, "China's National Defense in 2006," December 2006, http://www.china.org.cn/english/features/book/194485.htm.

38. State Council, "China's National Defense in 2008," January 2009, National Defense University Web site, http://merln.ndu.edu/whitepapers/China_English2008.pdf.

39. See Nan Li, "The Evolution of China's Naval Strategy and Capabilities: From 'Near Coast' and 'Near Seas' to 'Far Seas,'" *Asian Security* 5, no. 2 (2009): 145.

40. Jeffrey B. Goldman, "China's Mahan," U.S. Naval Institute *Proceedings* 122, no. 3 (March 1996): 44–47.

41. 刘华清 [Liu Huaqing], 刘华清回忆录 [*Liu Huaqing Memoir*] (Beijing: Liberation Army Press, 2004), 434.

42. 中国海军百科全书编审委员会 [Editorial Board of the Chinese Navy Encyclopedia], 中国海军百科全书 [*Chinese Navy Encyclopedia*] (Beijing: Haichao Publishers, 1999), 1154.

43. 姚有志 陈泽亮 [Yao Youzhi and Chen Zeliang], 高技术战争交通战场建设初探 ["Initial Exploration of Communication Battlefields in High-Technology Wars"], 中国军事科学 [*China Military Science*] 15, no. 3 (2002): 61.

44. Dai Xu, "Rise of World Powers Cannot Do without Military Transformation," *Huanqiu Shibao*, March 15, 2007, FBIS-CPP20070326455002.

45. For an account of China's naval efforts during the Cold War, see John Wilson Lewis and Xue Litai, *China's Strategic Sea Power: The Politics of Force Modernization in the Nuclear Age* (Stanford, Calif.: Stanford University Press, 1994); Alexander Chieh-cheng Huang, "The Chinese Navy's Offshore Active Defense Strategy," *Naval War College Review* 47, no. 3 (Summer 1994): 9–18; and Jun Zhan,

"China Goes to the Blue Waters: The Navy, Sea Power Mentality, and the South China Sea," *Journal of Strategic Studies* 17, no. 3 (September 1994): 180–208.

46. Mao Zedong, "Strategy in China's Revolutionary War," in *Selected Writings of Mao Tse-Tung*, vol. 1 (Beijing: Foreign Languages Press, 1966), 207, 224.

47. Sun Tzu, *The Art of Warfare*, trans. Roger T. Ames (New York: Ballantine, 1993); Mao, "Strategy in China's Revolutionary War," 217–218.

48. Mao, "Strategy in China's Revolutionary War," 220, 234.

49. Ibid., 208, 211, 217, 234.

50. Milan N. Vego, *Naval Strategy and Operations in Narrow Seas* (London: Frank Cass), 85–88. For the U.S. Army's definition of interior lines, see Headquarters, U.S. Department of the Army, Field Manual 3-0, *Operations* (Washington, D.C.: U.S. Army, June 2001), 5-7–5-9, http://www.dtic.mil/doctrine/jel/service_pubs/fm3_0b.pdf.

51. Mao Zedong, "Problems of Strategy in Guerrilla War," in *Selected Writings of Mao Tse-Tung*, vol. 2 (Beijing: Foreign Languages Press, 1966), 83.

52. Ibid., 82–84.

53. Mao Zedong, "On Protracted War," in *Selected Works of Mao Tse-tung*, http://www.marxists.org/reference/archive/mao/selected-works/volume-2/mswv2_09.htm.

54. Mao, "Strategy in China's Revolutionary War," 207, 224.

55. The offensive mindset "does not mean, however, that when we are already locked in battle with an enemy who enjoys superiority, we revolutionaries should not adopt defensive measures even when we are hard pressed. Only a prize idiot would think in this way." Ibid., 208.

56. Admiral Liu is credited with coining the phrase "offshore active defense." He urged China to adopt a phased strategy to wring control of the waters within the first island chain from the U.S. Navy before turning its attention to the waters within the "second island chain," farther out in the Pacific, and ultimately to global competition for maritime supremacy. See Cole, *Great Wall at Sea*, 165–168; Goldman, "China's Mahan"; Jun, "China Goes to the Blue Waters," 189–191; and Huang, "Chinese Navy's Offshore Active Defense Strategy," 18.

57. References to U.S. "encirclement" and "containment" are ubiquitous in the Chinese press. See, for example, Willy Wo-Lap Lam, "Hu's Central Asian Gamble to Counter the U.S. 'Containment Strategy,'" *China Brief* 5, no. 15 (July 5, 2005), 7–8.

58. Mao, "Strategy in China's Revolutionary War," 205–249.

59. Alfred Thayer Mahan, *From Sail to Steam: Recollections of Naval Life* (1907; repr. New York: Da Capo, 1968), 313–316.

60. Ibid., 302.

61. Alfred Thayer Mahan, *Retrospect & Prospect: Studies in International Relations, Naval and Political* (Boston: Little, Brown, 1902), 8–10.

62. Robert K. Massie, *Dreadnought: Britain, Germany, and the Coming of the Great War* (New York: Random House, 1991), xxiii–xxiv. See also Margaret Tuttle Sprout, "Mahan: Evangelist of Sea Power," in *Makers of Modern Strategy: Military Thought from Machiavelli to Hitler,* ed. Edward Meade Earle (Princeton, N.J.: Princeton University Press, 1943), 415–445.

63. Wolfgang Wegener, *The Naval Strategy of the World War* (1929; repr., Annapolis, Md.: Naval Institute Press, 1989), 22.

64. Mahan, *From Sail to Steam,* 303.

65. Shinohara Hiroshi, *Kaigun sōsetsu shi* [*History of the Navy's Establishment*] (Riburopōto, 1986), 409–13; David C. Evans and Mark R. Peattie, *Kaigun: Strategy, Tactics, and Technology in the Imperial Japanese Navy, 1887–1941* (Annapolis, Md.: Naval Institute Press, 1997), 67–71.

66. Sadao, *From Mahan to Pearl Harbor.*

67. For a sample of an excessive focus on the more bellicose dimensions of Mahan's writings, see 刘新华 秦仪 [Liu Xinhua and Qin Yi], 现代海权与国家海洋战略 ["Modern Sea Power and National Maritime Strategy"], 社会科学 [*Journal of Social Sciences*] (March 2004): 73.

68. Zhan Huayun, "Strategic Uses of the Sea—Knocking at the Door of a Grand Strategy," *Dangdai Hiajun,* May 1, 2007, 17–19, FBIS-CPP20070626436011.

69. Feng Zhaokui, "China's Rise Cannot Rely Only on Heading towards the Sea," *Huanqiu Shibao,* March 23, 2007, FBIS-CPP20070402455001.

70. Gao Xinsheng, "Islands and China's Coastal Defense in the New Century," *Guofang,* December 28, 2006, FBIS-CPP20061228478003.

71. 陈舟 [Chen Zhou], 美国对华战略演变与中国和平发展 ["The Evolution of U.S. Strategy toward China and China's Peaceful Development"], 和平与发展 [*Peace and Development*], no. 4 (November 2008): 9–13.

72. See 刘中民 [Liu Zhongmin], 地缘政治理论中的海权问题 ["The Question of Sea Power in Geopolitical Theory," Parts 1–3], 海洋世界 [*Ocean World*], May–July 2008.

73. 王素娟 [Wang Sujuan], 全球化时代与中国海权 ["Globalization Era and Chinese Sea Power"], 赤峰学院学报 [*Journal of Chifeng College*] (February

2007): 87; and 张文木 [Zhang Wenmu], 生存发展海权 ["Survival, Development, Sea Power"], 当代军事文摘 [*Contemporary Military Digest*] (July 2006): 30.

74. See 蒲瑶 [Pu Yao], 地缘政治理论的历史现况与发展趋势 ["The History, Current State, and Development Trends of Geopolitical Theory"], 社会学家 [*Social Scientist*] (June 2008): 144.

75. 黄江 [Huang Jiang], 论现代制海权 ["On Modern Command of the Sea"], 中国军事科学 [*China Military Science*] 16, no. 2 (2003): 25.

76. Corbett, *Some Principles of Maritime Strategy*, 91.

77. 纪荣仁　王学进 [Ji Rongren and Wang Xuejin], 试析制交通权与制空权，制海权的关系 ["Assessing the Relationships between Command of Communications, Command of the Air, and Command of the Sea"], 中国军事科学 [*China Military Science*] 15, no. 4 (2002): 114. For a very similar description of command of the sea, see Liu Yijian, "Theory of the Command of the Seas and Its Trend of Development," *Zhongguo Junshi Kexue*, January 2005, FBIS-CPP20050427000217.

78. Luo Yuan, "Call from Blue Sea to Protect Development Interests of Country," *Liaowang*, February 9, 2009, FBIS-CPP20070621436010.

79. Mahan, *Problem of Asia*, 190–191.

80. For the various Chinese uses of this particular passage by Mahan, see 李义虎 [Li Yihu], 海权论与海陆关系 ["Sea Power Theory and the Sea-Land Relationship"], 太平洋学报 [*Pacific Journal*], no. 3 (2006): 21; 刘江平　追月 [Liu Jiangping and Zhui Yue], 世纪经略海洋—中国海军将何去何从? ["Ocean Planning in the 21st Century—What Course for the Chinese Navy?"], 当代海军 [*Modern Navy*] (June 2007): 8; and Liu Jiangping, "Chinese Navy Should Use Asymmetric Operations to Fight Against Sea, Air Threats," *Huanqiu Shibao*, June 4, 2009.

81. Andrew Erickson and David D. Yang, "On the Verge of a Game Changer," U.S. Naval Institute *Proceedings* 135, no. 5 (May 2009): 26–32.

82. See 刘从德　吴晓波 [Liu Congde and We Xiaobo], 不变的公式? 哈尔福德麦金德对 "心脏地带" 理论的三次论证 ["An Unchanging Formula? The Three Tests of Halford Mackinder's 'Heartland' Theory"], 华中师范大学学报 [*Journal of Central China Normal University*] 40, no. 5 (September 2001): 52–56; and 吴征宇 [Wu Zhengyu], 重新认识 "心脏地带理论" 及其战略涵义 ["Reacquainting 'Heartland Theory' and Its Strategic Meaning"], 现代国际关系 [*Contemporary International Relations*], no. 3 (2005): 55–61.

83. See Yu Sui, "Rice's Trip Highlights Central Asia Hot Spots," *Liaowang*, October 15, 2005, 45–47, FBIS-CPP20051021510020; and Yang Danzhi, "Asia-Europe

Meeting Poses No Threat to Anybody," *Jiefangjun Bao*, October 27, 2008, 5, FBIS-CPP 20081027710009.

84. For his earlier critique of sea-power advocates, see 叶自成 幕新海 [Ye Zicheng and Mu Xinhai], 对中国海权发展战略的几点思考 ["A Few Thoughts on China Sea Power Development Strategy"], 国际政治研究 [*Studies of International Politics*] (August 2005): 5–17.

85. 叶自成 [Ye Zicheng], 中国的和平发展: 陆权的回归与发展 ["China's Peaceful Development: The Return and Development of Land Power"], 世界经济与政治 [*World Economics and Politics*] (February 2007): 24.

86. Ibid., 29.

87. Ibid., 31.

88. 叶自成 [Ye Zicheng], 从大历史观看地缘政治 ["Examining Geopolitics from the Perspective of Grand History"], 现代国际关系 [*Contemporary International Relations*] (June 2007): 2.

89. Ibid., 4.

90. Liu Zhongmin, "Argument about China-U.S. Sea Battle Misleading," *Huanqiu Shibao*, March 12, 2008, 11, FBIS-CPP20080407587002.

91. Liu Zhongmin, "Some Thoughts on the Issue of Sea Power and the Rise of Great Nations," *Shijie Jingji Yu Zhengzhi*, December 2007, 6–14, FBIS-CCP20080111590002.

92. Zhang Minqian, "Geopolitical Changes and China's Strategic Choices," *Xiandai Guoji Guanxi* [*Contemporary International Relations*], May 20, 2008, 18–19, FBIS-CPP20080724508001.

93. Cheng Yawen, "The Eurasian Continent Is the Center of Gravity of China's Interests," *Huanqiu Shibao*, November 15, 2007, FBIS-CPP20071211587001.

94. Ye Zicheng, "China's Sea Power Must Be Subordinate to Its Land Power," *Guoji Xianqu Daobao*, March 2, 2007, FBIS-CPP20070302455003.

95. Lu Rude, "Former Naval Lecturer Argues China Needs Strong Navy," *Renmin Haijun* [*People's Navy*], June 6, 2007, 4.

96. 倪乐雄 [Ni Lexiong], 从陆权到海权的历史必然 ["The Historical Inevitability of the Transition from Land Power to Sea Power"], 世界政治 [*World Politics*] (November 2007): 31.

97. Lu Ning, "Merging into 'Maritime Civilization,' China Should Havean Aircraft Carrier Battle Group," *Dongfang Zaobao*, March 24, 2009, FBIS-CPP20090325066002.

98. 李义虎 [Li Yihu], 从海陆二分到海陆统筹—对中国海陆关系的再审视 ["From Sea-Land Division to Sea-Land Integration—Reexamining China's Sea-Land Relations"], 现代国际关系 [*Contemporary International Relations*] (August 2007): 6. See also Li Yihu, "Changes in the Entity of Geopolitics," *Xiandai Guoji Guanxi*, May 20, 2008, 6–7, FBIS-CPP20080718508008.

99. Li, "From Sea-Land Division," 6.

100. Feng Liang and Duan Tingzhi, "Characteristics of China's Sea Geostrategic Security and Sea Security Strategy in the New Century," *Zhongguo Junshi Kexue*, January 2007, 22–29, FBIS-CPP20070621436010.

101. Shi Chunlin, "A Commentary on Studies of the Last Ten Years Concerning China's Sea Power," *Xiandai Guoji Guanxi*, April 20, 2008, 53–60, FBIS-CPP20080603590001.

102. See the editorial note in Wang Zaibang, "The Globalization Process and Evolution of the Geo-strategic Pattern," *Xiandai Guoki Guanxi*, May 20, 2008, 1–2, FBIS-CPP20080715508001.

CHAPTER 3. THE GERMAN PRECEDENT FOR CHINESE SEA POWER

1. Aaron Friedberg, "Will Europe's Past Be Asia's Future?" *Survival* 42, no. 3 (Autumn 2000): 147–159.

2. Avery Goldstein, *Rising to the Challenge: China's Grand Strategy and International Security* (Stanford, Calif.: Stanford University Press, 2005), 204–219.

3. "Statement of Dr. Arthur Waldron, Full Committee Meeting on the Strategic Intentions and Goals of China," House Armed Services Committee, June 21, 2000, http://armedservices.house.gov/comdocs/testimony/106thcongress/00-06-21waldron.html. Similarly, former leading policymakers from Democratic and Republican administrations have used Imperial Germany's experience as a cautionary tale. Even so, they have taken pains not to suggest that China's future is fated. See Zbigniew Brzezinski, "Living with China," *National Interest* 59 (Spring 2000): 11, and Paul Wolfowitz, "Remembering the Future," *National Interest* 59 (Spring 2000): 42.

4. 中国中央电视台 [China Central Television], 大国掘起 德国 [*The Rise of Great Powers: Germany*], 北京 中国民主法制出版社 [Beijing: China Democracy and Law Publisher, 2006], 137.

5. Tang Yongsheng, "Construct a Solid Geostrategic Prop," *Xiandai Guoji Guanxi* [*Contemporary International Relations*], May 20, 2008, 20–21.

6. See Qiu Huafei, "The Development Trend in Sino-U.S. Strategic Relations in the New Century," *Shehui Kexue* [*Social Science*], February 20, 2006, 18–26.

7. Wolfgang Wegener, *The Naval Strategy of the World War* (1929; repr., Annapolis, Md.: Naval Institute Press, 1989), xxvii, 96–100.

8. Holger H. Herwig, "Introduction," in ibid., xxviii, xxxvi, xxxix–xli.

9. Quoted in Robert K. Massie, *Dreadnought: Britain, Germany, and the Coming of the Great War* (New York: Random House, 1991), xxiii–xxiv. See also Margaret Tuttle Sprout, "Mahan: Evangelist of Sea Power," in *Makers of Modern Strategy: Military Thought from Machiavelli to Hitler*, ed. Edward Meade Earle (Princeton, N.J.: Princeton University Press, 1943), 415–445.

10. Holger H. Herwig, "The Influence of A. T. Mahan upon German Sea Power," in *The Influence of History on Mahan*, ed. John B. Hattendorf (Newport, R.I.: Naval War College Press, 1991), 70–71.

11. Mahan, *Influence of Sea Power upon History*, 71.

12. The *Times* of London likened the revolution wrought by Mahan's works to that "effected by Copernicus in the domain of astronomy." Gregory Weeks, "Mahan, Alfred Thayer," in *Encyclopedia of Historians and Historical Writing*, vol. 2, ed. Kelly Boyd (Oxford: Routledge, 1999), 754.

13. Wegener, *Naval Strategy of the World War*, 22.

14. Ibid., 14.

15. Ibid.

16. Herwig, "Introduction," xxxix–xli.

17. Paul M. Kennedy, *The Rise and Fall of British Naval Mastery* (London: Ashfield, 1986), 205–218.

18. Meng Xiangqing, "When the Periphery Is Stable, China Is at Peace," *Huanqiu Shibao* [*Global Times*], April 4, 2007, FBIS-CPP20070420455004.

19. Department of Defense, *Annual Report to Congress: Military Power of the People's Republic of China, 2007* (Washington, D.C.: Department of Defense, 2007), 16.

20. Jiang Hong and Wei Yuejiang, "100,000 US Troops in the Asia-Pacific Look for 'New Homes,'" *Guofang Bao*, June 10, 2003, 1, FBIS-CPP20030611000068.

21. Feng Liang and Duan Tingzhi, "Characteristics of China's Sea Geostrategic Security and Sea Security Strategy in the New Century," *Zhongguo Junshi Kexue* [*China Military Science*], January 1, 2007, 22–29.

22. Quoted in Ma Haoliang, "China Needs to Break through the Encirclement of First Island Chain," *Ta Kung Pao*, February 21, 2009, FBIS-CPP20090221708020.

23. 江雨 [Jiang Yu], 岛连与中国海军向远洋的发展 ["Island Chain and Far Seas Development of the Chinese Navy"], 舰载武器 [*Shipborne Weapons*], no. 12 (2008): 30–31.

24. 展华云 [Zhan Huayun], 出海口 走向世界的战略通道 ["Oceanic Exits: Strategic Passageways to the World"], 当代海军 [*Modern Navy*], April 2007, 28.

25. 李玉平 [Li Yuping], 台湾地缘战略的海权解读 ["Interpreting Sea Power through Taiwan's Strategic Geography"], 现代舰船 [*Modern Ships*], April 2004, 5.

26. Quoted in Ma, "China Needs to Break." See also Peng Guangqian and Yao Youzhi, *The Science of Military Strategy* (Beijing: Military Science Publishing House, 2005), 443.

27. Lin Sixing, "Sino-North Korean Relations Are Indestructible though Not Stable," *Yazhou Zhoukan,* no. 32 (August 13, 2006), OSC-CPP20060814720006.

28. 王伟 [Wang Wei], 台海战略随想 ["Thoughts on Taiwan Strait Strategy"], 舰载武器 [*Shipborne Weapons*], no. 11 (2005): 79.

29. Jiang, "Island Chain and Far Seas Development," 31.

30. 白炎林 [Bai Yanlin], 岛链与中国海军 ["Island Chains and the Chinese Navy"], 当代海军 [*Modern Navy*], October 2007, 18.

31. 俞风流 [Yu Fengliu], 进出太平洋的最佳海上要道 巴士海峡 ["The Best Sea Lane In and Out of the Pacific: Strait of Luzon"], 当代海军 [*Modern Navy*], May 2007, 20.

32. Wegener, *Naval Strategy of the World War*, 11.

33. Paul M. Kennedy, "The Development of German Naval Operations Plans against England, 1896–1914," in *The War Plans of the Great Powers, 1880–1914*, ed. Paul M. Kennedy (Boston: Unwin Hyman, 1979), 171.

34. Paul G. Halpern, *A Naval History of World War I* (Annapolis, Md.: Naval Institute Press, 1994), 2.

35. Holger H. Herwig, *"Luxury" Fleet: The Imperial German Navy, 1888–1918* (London: Allen & Unwin, 1980), 95–110; and James R. Holmes, "Mahan, a 'Place in the Sun,' and Germany's Quest for Sea Power," *Comparative Strategy* 23 (2004): 27–61.

36. V. R. Berghahn, *Germany and the Approach of War in 1914* (New York: St. Martin's, 1973), 25–42.

37. Alfred von Tirpitz, *My Memoirs*, vol. 1 (New York: Dodd, Mead, 1919), 142–165.

38. Ibid., 170–177.

39. Herwig, "Introduction," xviii.

40. Holger H. Herwig, "Imperial Germany: Continental Titan, Global Aspirant," in

China Goes to Sea: Maritime Transformation in Comparative Historical Perspective, ed. Andrew S. Erickson, Lyle J. Goldstein, and Carnes Lord (Annapolis, Md.: Naval Institute Press, 2009), 172–174.

41. Eyre Crowe, "Memorandum on the Present State of British Relations with France and Germany, January 1, 1907," in *British Documents on the Origins of the War 1898–1914*, vol. 3, *The Testing of the Entente, 1904–1906*, ed. G. P. Gooch and Harold Temperley (London: His Majesty's Stationery Office, 1927), 402–417.

42. Paul M. Kennedy, "Tirpitz, England and the Second Navy Law of 1900," *Militärgeschichtliche Mitteilungen* 8 (1970): 38.

43. Herwig, "Introduction," xviii.

44. Alfred Thayer Mahan, *Armaments and Arbitration: Or, the Place of Force in the International Relations of States* (New York: Harper, 1912), 57.

45. Theodore Ropp, "Continental Doctrines of Sea Power," in *Makers of Modern Strategy: Military Thought from Machiavelli to Hitler*, ed. Edward Meade Earle (Princeton, N.J.: Princeton University Press, 1943), 446–456.

46. Alfred Thayer Mahan, *The Interest of America in Sea Power, Present and Future* (1897; repr., Freeport: Books for Libraries Press, 1970), 198.

47. Tirpitz, *My Memoirs*, 57–62.

48. Herwig, "The Influence of A. T. Mahan," 72–73.

49. See David G. Muller, *China as a Maritime Power* (Boulder, Colo.: Westview, 1984), 44–56, 111–116.

50. Ting Yu, "Complete Remake or 'Old Medicine in New Bottle'? A Brief Discussion of the Role and Application of the Type 022 Stealth Missile Boat," *Xiandai Bingqi* [*Modern Weaponry*], September 2, 2008, 35–43.

51. Roger Cliff, Mark Burles, Michael S. Chase, Derek Eaton, and Kevin L. Pollpeter, *Entering the Dragon's Lair: Chinese Antiaccess Strategies and Their Implications for the United States* (Santa Monica, Calif.: RAND, 2007), 11.

52. Mahan, *Influence of Sea Power upon History*, 50–89.

53. Wegener, *Naval Strategy of the World War*, 95.

54. Ibid., 96.

55. On the deepening rivalry, see Paul M. Kennedy, *The Rise of the Anglo-German Antagonism, 1860–1914* (London: Ashfield, 1980), 410–431.

56. Winston S. Churchill, *The World Crisis* (New York: Scribner, 1923), 115.

57. Wegener, *Naval Strategy of the World War*, 11.

58. Howard K. Beale, *Theodore Roosevelt and the Rise of America to World Power* (Baltimore, Md.: Johns Hopkins, 1956), 36–38.

59. For a brief explanation of Deng's "24-character" strategy, see U.S. Office of the Secretary of Defense, *Annual Report to Congress: Military Power of the People's Republic of China, 2007*, http://www.defenselink.mil/pubs/pdfs/070523-China-Military-Power-final.pdf, 7.

60. Information Office, State Council of the People's Republic of China, *China's National Defense in 2008*, January 2009, 31, GOV.cn Web site, http://english.gov.cn/official/2009-01/20/content_1210227.htm.

61. Quan Jinfu, "The Innovations and Development of the Chinese Navy's Strategic Theory in the New Century," *Journal of PLA Nanjing Institute of Politics*, March 3, 2004, 81–85.

62. Cao Zhi and Chen Wanjun, "Hu Jintao Emphasizes When Meeting Deputies to 10th Navy CPC Congress," *Xinhua*, December 27, 2006.

63. Fang Yonggang, Xu Mingshan, and Wang Shumei, "On Creative Development in the Party's Guiding Theory for Naval Building," *Zhongguo Junshi Kexue* [*China Military Science*], August 20, 2007, 66–77.

64. Wu Shengli and Hu Yanlin, "Building a Powerful People's Navy that Meets the Requirements of the Historical Mission for Our Army," *Qiushi* 14 (July 16, 2007), FBIS-CPP20070716710027.

65. The ONI report was obtained by the Federation of American Scientists under the Freedom of Information Act. Hans Kristensen, "Chinese Submarine Patrols Doubled in 2008," Federation of American Scientist Strategic Security Blog, http://www.fas.org/blog/ssp/2009/02/patrols.php#more-731.

66. "Aircraft Carrier Project," GlobalSecurity.org, http://www.globalsecurity.org/military/world/china/cv.htm.

67. Andrew S. Erickson and David D. Yang, "On the Verge of a Game-Changer," *U.S. Naval Institute Proceedings* 135, no. 5 (May 2009): 26–32.

68. Mahan, *Influence of Sea Power upon History*, 35–42.

69. Naval Vessel Register Web site, http://www.nvr.navy.mil/nvrships/FLEET.HTM; and James W. Crawley, "Navy Has Fewest Ships since before World War I," *San Diego Union-Tribune*, October 2, 2003, GlobalSecurity.org Web site, http://www.globalsecurity.org/org/news/2003/031002-usn.htm.

70. U.S. Navy, Marine Corps, and Coast Guard, *A Cooperative Strategy for 21st Century Seapower*, October 2007, http://www.navy.mil/maritime/MaritimeStrategy.pdf.

71. Yoichi Funabashi, "As a Maritime Nation, the Seas Await Japan," *Asahi Shimbun*, February 2, 2004.

72. Bai, "Island Chains and the Chinese Navy," 17.

73. Barry R. Posen, "Command of the Commons: The Military Foundation of U.S. Hegemony," *International Security* 28, no. 1 (Summer 2003): 22.

CHAPTER 4. FLEET TACTICS WITH CHINESE CHARACTERISTICS

1. Andrew J. Nathan and Robert S. Ross, *The Great Wall and the Empty Fortress: China's Search for Security* (New York: W. W. Norton, 1997), 24–26.

2. See, for instance, J. Noel Williams and James S. O'Brasky, "A Naval Operational Architecture for Global Tactical Operations," in *Globalization and Maritime Power*, ed. Sam J. Tangredi (Washington, D.C.: National Defense University Press, 2002), http://www.ndu.edu/inss/Books/Books_2002/Globalization_and_Maritime_Power_Dec_02/29_ch28.htm.

3. Mahan had in mind the ability of the U.S. Navy to impose command of the sea on the Gulf of Mexico and the Caribbean Sea, astride the approaches to the isthmian canal, despite its overall inferiority to European navies. His most exhaustive geopolitical analysis of these waters came in two essays: "The Strategic Features of the Gulf of Mexico and the Caribbean," which appeared in *Harper's* in 1887, and "The Isthmus and Sea Power," which appeared in *The Atlantic* in 1893.

4. Martin Andrew, "The Dragon Breathes Fire: Chinese Power Projection," *China Brief* 5, no. 16 (July 19, 2005): 5–8.

5. Alfred Thayer Mahan, *Naval Administration and Warfare* (Boston: Little, Brown, 1908), 155–156.

6. Keith Crane, Roger Cliff, Evan S. Medeiros, James C. Mulvenon, and William H. Overholt, *Modernizing China's Military: Opportunities and Constraints* (Santa Monica, Calif.: RAND, 2005).

7. James R. Holmes and Toshi Yoshihara, "The Influence of Mahan upon China's Maritime Strategy," *Comparative Strategy* 24, no. 1 (January–March 2005): 53–71; and Lyle Goldstein and William Murray, "Undersea Dragons: China's Maturing Submarine Force," *International Security* 28, no. 4 (Spring 2004): 162–194.

8. Of the Japanese invasion of China, Mao wrote, "Japan, though strong, does not have enough soldiers. China, though weak, has a vast territory, a large population and plenty of soldiers." Even if strong enemy forces seized key urban areas and communication nodes, then, China would retain "a general rear and vital bases from which to carry on the protracted war to final victory." Mao Zedong, "Problems of Strategy in Guerrilla War," in *Selected Writings of Mao Tse-Tung*, vol. 2 (Beijing: Foreign Languages Press, 1966), 158.

9. Mao Zedong, "Strategy in China's Revolutionary War," in *Selected Writings of Mao Tse-Tung*, vol. 1 (Beijing: Foreign Languages Press, 1966), 220, 234.

10. Wayne P. Hughes Jr., *Fleet Tactics and Coastal Combat*, 2nd ed. (Annapolis, Md.: Naval Institute Press, 2000). This work is a lightly revised version of Hughes' classic *Fleet Tactics: Theory and Practice* (Annapolis, Md.: Naval Institute Press, 1986).

11. Hughes, *Fleet Tactics*, 266.

12. Hughes, *Fleet Tactics and Coastal Combat*, 268–274.

13. Chester W. Richards, "A Swift, Elusive Sword: What If Sun Tzu and John Boyd Did a National Defense Review?" presentation at Boyd Conference, Marine Corps Base Quantico, Virginia, Fall 2001, Center for Defense Information Web site, http://www.cdi.org/mrp/swift_elusive_sword.rtf.

14. Mao Zedong, *On Protracted War*, in *Selected Works of Mao Tse-tung*, http://www.marxists.org/reference/archive/mao/selected-works/volume-2/mswv2_09.htm.

15. Ni Lexiong, "Sea Power and China's Development," *Liberation Daily*, April 17, 2005, 5, U.S.-China Economic and Security Review Commission, http://www.uscc.gov/researchpapers/translated_articles/2005/05_07_18_Sea_Power_and_Chinas_Development.pdf.

16. Sun Tzu, *The Illustrated Art of War*, trans. Samuel B. Griffith (1963; repr., Oxford: Oxford University Press, 2005), 125.

17. Samuel B. Griffith, "Introduction," in Sun Tzu, *Illustrated Art of War*, 17–30.

18. Carl von Clausewitz, *On War*, ed., trans. Michael Howard and Peter Paret (Princeton, N.J.: Princeton University Press, 1976), 605.

19. Barry R. Posen, "Command of the Commons: The Military Foundation of U.S. Hegemony," *International Security* 28, no. 1 (Summer 2003): 5–46.

20. Bernard Brodie, *A Guide to Naval Strategy*, 3rd ed. (Princeton, N.J.: Princeton University Press, 1944), 252.

21. Ibid.

22. Hughes, *Fleet Tactics*, 244.

23. Mahan deplored fortress-fleets, or fleets that operated purely in support of land fortifications (and within range of land-based fire support). Writing today, however, he might amend his analysis. The reach of shore-based weaponry would allow a fortress-fleet to roam far more widely than in Mahan's day, diminishing the distinction between an independent fleet and one dependent on land-based fire support. Russian commanders' reluctance to challenge Togo's Imperial Japanese Navy too far from Port Arthur sparked his ire, but a PLA Navy backed

up by, say, antiship ballistic missiles able to strike at enemy warships 2,500 km away would be a far different creature. Alfred Thayer Mahan, "Retrospect upon the War between Japan and Russia," in *Naval Administration and Warfare* (Boston: Little, Brown, 1918), 133–173.

24. Clausewitz, *On War*, 528. See also James R. Holmes, "Roosevelt's Pursuit of a Temperate Caribbean Policy," *Naval History* 20, no. 4 (August 2006): 48–53, which describes Theodore Roosevelt's attempt to mount a contested zone in the Caribbean Sea and Gulf of Mexico.

25. Michael I. Handel, *Masters of War: Classical Strategic Thought*, 3rd ed., repr. (London: Frank Cass, 2004), esp. 119–134.

26. Donald C. Winter, "Navy Transformation: A Stable, Long-term View," Heritage Lecture no. 1004, February 7, 2007, Heritage Foundation Web site, http://www.heritage.org/Research/NationalSecurity/hl1004.cfm.

27. Ni, "Sea Power and China's Development," 2. For a more exhaustive look at Mahan's influence in Beijing, see Holmes and Yoshihara, "Influence of Mahan," 53–71.

28. Ni, "Sea Power and China's Development," 1–2. On Germany's quest for sea power, see James R. Holmes, "Mahan, a 'Place in the Sun,' and Germany's Quest for Sea Power," *Comparative Strategy* 23, no. 1 (January–March 2004): 27–62.

29. Thomas P. M. Barnett, *The Pentagon's New Map: War and Peace in the Twenty-first Century* (New York: G. P. Putnam's Sons, 2004), 62, 108, 152, 169.

30. Ni, "Sea Power and China's Development," 4.

31. Alfred Thayer Mahan, "Considerations Governing the Disposition of Navies," *National Review*, July 1902, 706.

32. Mahan saw battleships as the embodiment of offensive strategy: "the backbone and real power of any navy are the vessels which, by due proportion of defensive and offensive powers, are capable of taking and giving hard knocks." Mahan, *The Interest of America in Sea Power, Present and Future* (Boston: Little, Brown, 1919), 198.

33. Richard W. Turk, *The Ambiguous Relationship: Theodore Roosevelt and Alfred Thayer Mahan* (New York: Greenwood Press, 1987), 1–6, 101–107.

34. W. S. Sims, "The Inherent Qualities of All-Big-Gun, One-Caliber Battleships of High Speed, Large Displacement, and Gun Power," U.S. Naval Institute *Proceedings* 32, no. 12 (December 1906): 1337–1366; and Hughes, *Fleet Tactics and Coastal Combat*, 69–70.

35. Richard A. Hough, *Dreadnought: A History of the Modern Battleship* (New York: Macmillan, 1964), 34–37.

36. For an account of China's naval efforts during the Cold War, see John Wilson Lewis and Xue Litai, *China's Strategic Sea Power: The Politics of Force Modernization in the Nuclear Age* (Stanford, Calif.: Stanford University Press, 1994).

37. Alexander Chieh-cheng Huang, "The Chinese Navy's Offshore Active Defense Strategy," *Naval War College Review* 47, no. 3 (Summer 1994): 9–18; and Jun Zhan, "China Goes to the Blue Waters: The Navy, Sea Power Mentality, and the South China Sea," *Journal of Strategic Studies* 17, no. 3 (September 1994): 180–208.

38. Mao, "Strategy in China's Revolutionary War," 207, 224.

39. Mao was no doctrinaire on operational matters. The offensive mindset "does not mean . . . that when we are already locked in battle with an enemy who enjoys superiority, we revolutionaries should not adopt defensive measures even when we are hard pressed. Only a prize idiot would think in this way." Ibid., 208.

40. References to U.S. "encirclement" and "containment" are ubiquitous in the Chinese press. See, for example, Willy Wo-Lap Lam, "Hu's Central Asian Gamble to Counter the U.S. 'Containment Strategy,'" *China Brief* 5, no. 15 (July 5, 2005): 7–8; and Mao, "Strategy in China's Revolutionary War," 205–249.

41. Jiang Shiliang, "The Command of Communications," *Zhongguo Junshi Kexue*, October 2, 2002, 106–114, FBIS-CPP20030107000189.

42. Bernard D. Cole, *The Great Wall at Sea: China's Navy Enters the Twenty-first Century* (Annapolis, Md.: Naval Institute Press, 2001), 165–168; Jeffrey B. Goldman, "China's Mahan," U.S. Naval Institute *Proceedings* 122, no. 3 (March 1996): 44–47; Jun, "China Goes to the Blue Waters," 189–191; and Huang, "Chinese Navy's Offshore Active Defense Strategy," 18.

43. Bruce Elleman, "A Comparative Historical Approach to Blockade Strategies: Implications for China," in *China's Energy Strategy: The Impact on Beijing's Maritime Policies*, Gabriel B. Collins, Andrew S. Erickson, Lyle J. Goldstein, and William S. Murray, eds. (Annapolis, Md.: Naval Institute Press, 2008), 365–386.

44. Some 80 percent of China's oil imports, which accounts for 40 percent of total Chinese oil consumption, passes through the strait, giving rise to the "Malacca dilemma." Office of the Secretary of Defense, *Military Power of the People's Republic of China, 2005* (Washington, D.C.: U.S. Department of Defense, 2005), 33. On China's demand for petroleum, see David Hale, "China's Growing Appetites," *National Interest* 76 (Summer 2004): 137–147.

45. You Ji, "Dealing with the Malacca Dilemma: China's Effort to Protect Its Energy Supply," *Strategic Analysis* 31, no. 3 (May 2007): 467–490.

46. Xu Zhiliang, "Clearly Delineate PRC Territorial Waters in Map Making," *Nanfang Ribao*, April 26, 2001, FBIS-CPP20010427000033.

47. "Secret Sanya—China's New Nuclear Naval Base Revealed," *Jane's Intelligence Review*, April 21, 2008, http://www.janes.com/news/security/jir/jir080421_1_n.shtml.

48. Gurpreet Khurana, "New 'Revelations' on China's Nuclear Submarine Base at Hainan: Must India Be Anxious?" *South Asia Defense & Strategic Review* 2, no. 4 (July–August 2008): 28–29.

49. Author discussions with U.S. scholars, Newport, R.I., September 2008.

50. James R. Holmes and Toshi Yoshihara, "China's 'Caribbean' in the South China Sea," *SAIS Review of International Affairs* 26, no. 1 (Winter–Spring 2006): 79–92.

51. Wendell Minnick, "RAND Study Suggests U.S. Loses War with China," *Defense News*, October 16, 2008, http://www.defensenews.com/story.php?i=3774348&c=ASI&s=AIR.

52. "Hangzhou Type 956 Sovremennyy," GlobalSecurity.org, http://www.globalsecurity.org/military/world/china/haizhou.htm.

53. Ted Parsons, "China Develops Antiship Missile," *Jane's Defense Weekly*, January 18, 2006, http://www.janes.com/defence/naval_forces/news/jdw/jdw060118_1_n.shtml; and Wendell Minnick, "China Developing Antiship Ballistic Missiles," *Defense News*, January 14, 2008, http://www.defensenews.com/story.php?i=3307277.

54. For details about the FT-2000, see James C. O'Halloran, ed., *Jane's Land-Based Air Defense* (Surrey, U.K.: Jane's Information Group, 2004), 109–110.

55. According to one of the Pentagon's annual reports on Chinese military power, a brochure promoting the FT-2000 at the September 1998 Farnborough Air Show boasted that the system was an "AWACS killer." See U.S. Department of Defense, *Annual Report on the Military Power of the People's Republic of China* (Washington, D.C.: Department of Defense, July 2003), 30.

56. To browse through any of the Pentagon reports published since 2002, see "Annual Report to Congress: Military Power of the People's Republic of China," Department of Defense Web site, http://www.defenselink.mil/pubs/china.html.

57. For more on the Chinese undersea fleet, see Andrew S. Erickson, Lyle J. Goldstein, William S. Murray, and Andrew R. Wilson, *China's Future Nuclear Submarine Force* (Annapolis, Md.: Naval Institute Press, 2007), esp. 59–76, 359–372.

58. Andrew Hind, "The Cruise Missile Comes of Age," *Naval History* 22, no. 5 (October 2008): 52–57; and Lloyd de Vries, "Israel: Iran Aided Hezbollah Ship Attack," CBS News, July 15, 2006, http://www.cbsnews.com/stories/2006/07/15/world/main1807117.shtml?tag=contentMain;contentBody.

59. Zhang Wenmu, "China's Energy Security and Policy Choices," *Shijie Jingji Yu Zhengzhi* 5 (May 14, 2003): 11–16, FBIS-CPP20030528000169. See also Zhang Wenmu, "Sea Power and China's Strategic Choices," *China Security* (Summer 2006): 17–31.

60. "J-11 [Su-27 FLANKER]; Su-27UBK/Su-30MKK/Su-30MK2," GlobalSecurity.org, http://www.globalsecurity.org/military/world/china/j-11.htm.

61. "RIM-7/-162 Sea Sparrow/ESSM," *Jane's Strategic Weapon Systems*, February 8, 2008; and Joris Janssen Lok and Richard Scott, "Navies Face Choice Questions for Defense of Surface Combatants," *International Defense Review*, February 1, 2005.

62. The study was supervised by Wayne Hughes. Chase D. Patrick, *Assessing the Utility of an Event-Step ASMD Model by Analysis of Surface Combatant Shared Self-Defense* (Monterey, Calif.: U.S. Navy Postgraduate School, September 2001), 51–54.

63. "MK 15 Phalanx Close-In Weapons System (CIWS)," GlobalSecurity.org, http://www.globalsecurity.org/military/systems/ship/systems/mk-15-specs.htm.

64. "F/A-18 Hornet," GlobalSecurity.org, http://www.globalsecurity.org/military/systems/aircraft/f-18-specs.htm; and "BGM-109 Tomahawk," GlobalSecurity.org, http://www.globalsecurity.org/military/systems/munitions/bgm-109-specs.htm.

65. "AGM-84 Harpoon; SLAM [Stand-Off Land Attack Missile]," GlobalSecurity.org, http://www.globalsecurity.org/military/systems/munitions/agm-84-specs.htm.

66. Hughes, *Fleet Tactics*, 247.

CHAPTER 5. MISSILE AND ANTIMISSILE INTERACTIONS AT SEA

1. 严伟江 [Yan Weijiang], 1982: 海航第二中队战纪 ["1982: The War Record of the Second Naval Aviation Squadron"], 世界展望 [*World Outlook*], February 2003, 75.

2. Lyle Goldstein, "China's Falklands Lessons," *Survival* 50, no. 3 (June–July 2008): 65.

3. See Bates Gill, James Mulvenon, and Mark Stokes, "The Chinese Second Artillery Corps: Transition to Credible Deterrence," in *The People's Liberation*

Army as an Organization, ed. James Mulvenon and Andrew Yang (Santa Monica, Calif.: RAND, 2002), 555.

4. Roger Cliff, Mark Burles, Michael S. Chase, Derek Eaton, and Kevin L. Pollpeter, *Entering the Dragon's Lair: Chinese Antiaccess Strategies and Their Implications for the United States* (Santa Monica, Calif.: RAND, 2007), 11.

5. Ibid., 81–90.

6. William S. Murray, "Revisiting Taiwan's Defense Strategy," *Naval War College Review* 61, no. 3 (Summer 2008): 24.

7. Mark A. Stokes, *China's Strategic Modernization: Implications for the United States* (Carlisle Barracks, Carlisle, Pa.: Strategic Studies Institute, U.S. Army War College, 1999), 89.

8. Mark A. Stokes, "Chinese Ballistic Missile Forces in the Age of Global Missile Defense: Challenges and Responses," in *China's Growing Military Power: Perspectives on Security, Ballistic Missiles, and Conventional Capabilities*, ed. Andrew Scobell and Larry M. Wortzel (Carlisle Barracks, Carlisle, Pa.: Strategic Studies Institute, U.S. Army War College, 2002), 114.

9. *Jane's Defence Weekly* was first to report on the ONI's finding. See Ted Parsons, "China Develops Antiship Missile," *Jane's Defence Weekly*, January 17, 2006.

10. Office of Naval Intelligence, *Worldwide Maritime Challenges* (Suitland, Md.: Office of Naval Intelligence, 2004), 22.

11. Office of the Secretary of Defense, "Annual Report to Congress: Military Power of the People's Republic of China, 2005," 33, available at http://www.defenselink.mil/pubs/china.html.

12. Office of the Secretary of Defense, "Annual Report to Congress: Military Power of the People's Republic of China, 2009," 21, available at http://www.defenselink.mil/pubs/china.html. The 2009 issue even features a graphic depicting the flight trajectory of an antiship ballistic missile, drawn from an authoritative 2006 article published by the Second Artillery Engineering College.

13. National Air and Space Intelligence Center, *Ballistic and Cruise Missile Threat*, Wright-Patterson Air Force Base, April 2009, NASIC-1031-0985-09, 14.

14. Ronald O'Rourke, *China Naval Modernization: Implications for U.S. Navy Capabilities* (Washington, D.C.: Congressional Research Service, October 8, 2008), 2–4.

15. See Paul S. Giarra, "A Chinese Antiship Ballistic Missile: Implications for the USN," U.S.-China Economic and Security Review Commission, June 11, 2009, http://www.uscc.gov/hearings/2009hearings/written_testimonies/09_06_11_wrts/09_06_11_giarra_statement.pdf.

16. See Andrew Erickson and David D. Yang, "On the Verge of a Game-Changer," U.S. Naval Institute *Proceedings* 135, no. 5 (May 2009): 26–32.

17. ONI, *Worldwide Maritime Challenges*, 21.

18. Evan S. Medeiros, "'Minding the Gap': Assessing the Trajectory of the PLA's Second Artillery," in *Right-Sizing the People's Liberation Army: Exploring the Contours of China's Military*, ed. Roy Kamphausen and Andrew Scobell (Carlisle Barracks, Carlisle, Pa.: Strategic Studies Institute, 2007), 173.

19. Eric McVadon, "China's Maturing Navy," *Naval War College Review* 59, no. 2 (Spring 2006): 96.

20. Cliff et al., *Entering the Dragon's Lair*, 92–93.

21. Andrew F. Krepinevich Jr., "The Pentagon's Wasting Assets: The Eroding Foundations of American Power," *Foreign Affairs* 88, no. 4 (July/August 2009): 23.

22. Wayne P. Hughes, *Fleet Tactics and Coastal Combat* (Annapolis, Md.: Naval Institute Press, 2000), 305.

23. Lisle A. Rose, *Power at Sea: A Violent Peace* (Columbia: University of Missouri Press, 2007), 216–218.

24. For general overviews of the U.S. ballistic-missile defense system since 2006, see 王树斌 荣祥胜 [Wang Shubin and Rong Xiangsheng], 美国弹道导弹防御系统的历史演变过程 ["The Historical Evolution of the U.S. Ballistic Missile Defense System"], 江苏航空 [*Jiangsu Aviation*], no. 3 (2007): 30–31; 朱伟 [Zhu Wei], 美四维一体导弹防御系统逐渐成型 ["The Gradual Formation of a Four Dimensional Integrated Missile Defense System"], 国防科技 [*National Defense Science and Technology*] (January 2007): 49–51; 温德义 [Wen Deyi], 建天网: 美国现今忙些啥? ["Building a Sky Net: What Is the United States Busy Doing These Days?"], 环球军事 [*Global Military*], no. 124 (April 2006): 38–39; and 温德义 [Wen Deyi], 美国部署导弹防御计划新动向 ["The New Trends in U.S. Missile Defense Deployment Plans"], 国防科技工业 [*Defense Science and Technology Industry*] (April 2006): 59–60. For a translation of an article by Rear Admiral Alan B. Hicks, program director of Aegis Ballistic Missile Defense, see 石江月 [Shi Jiangyue], 美国海基弹道导弹防御系统 ["U.S. Sea-Based Ballistic Missile Defense System"], 现代舰船 [*Modern Ships*] 4A (2007): 16–19. The citation for the original article is Alan B. Hicks, "Extending the Navy's Shield: Sea-Based Ballistic Missile Defense," U.S. Naval Institute *Proceedings* 133, no. 1 (January 2007): 56–59.

25. 任德新 [Ren Dexin], 宙斯盾舰合围中国 ["Aegis Ships Encircle China"], 舰船知识 [*Naval and Merchant Ships*] (September 2007): 12.

26. 17艘宙斯盾围绕中国 ["Seventeen Aegis Vessels Surround China"], 晚霞 [*Sunset*] (July 2007): 18.

27. 杨孝文 [Yang Xiaowen], 反导: 中国周边上演 "三国演义" ["BMD: 'Three Kingdoms' Is Being Performed on China's Periphery"], 环球军事 [*Global Military*], no. 1 (2008): 11.

28. 陈位昊 [Chen Lihao], 宙斯盾舰成功拦截中程导弹 ["Aegis Ship Successfully Intercepts Medium-Range Ballistic Missile"], 国际展望 [*World Outlook*], no. 531 (January 2006): 9.

29. 任德新 [Ren Dexin], 太平洋的宙斯盾反导系统 ["Aegis Anti-Ballistic Missile System in the Pacific"], 当代军事文摘 [*Contemporary Military Digest*] (October 2007): 18–19.

30. 海研 [Hai Yan], 军事重镇—横须贺军港 ["Strategic Military Site—Yokosuka Naval Base"], 当代海军 [*Modern Navy*] (September 2006): 59.

31. 刘江平 [Liu Jiangping], 太平洋上的宙斯盾反导战舰群 ["Aegis Anti-Ballistic Missile Fleet in the Pacific"], 当代海军 [*Modern Navy*] (June 2008): 29.

32. 任德新 程健良 [Ren Dexin and Cheng Jianliang], 宙斯盾反导系统在太平洋的部署及使用 ["The Deployment and Use of Aegis Anti-Ballistic Missile System in the Pacific"], 舰船知识 [*Naval and Merchant Ships*] (July 2007): 17.

33. 戴艳丽 [Dai Yanli], 我周边宙斯盾舰的运行及威胁 ["The Functioning and Threat of Aegis Ships on Our Periphery"], 舰船知识 [*Naval and Merchant Ships*] (September 2007): 18.

34. 齐艳丽 [Qi Yanli], 美国海基中段防御系统 ["The U.S. Sea-Based Midcourse Defense System"], 导弹与航天运载技术 [*Missiles and Space Vehicles*], no. 3 (2005): 61.

35. 白炎林 [Bai Yanlin], 岛连上的世界海军 ["World Navies along the Island Chains"], 当代海军 [*Modern Navy*] (October 2007): 14.

36. See 吕德胜 [Lu Desheng], 美国反导, 走向何方? ["America's BMD, Which Way Is It Going?"] 中国民兵 [*China Militia*], no. 3 (2008): 50–51.

37. 烽火 [Feng Huo], 极限拦截—标准-3击毁卫星分析 ["Extreme Interception: Analysis of the Standard Missile-3 Destruction of Satellite"], 现代舰船 [*Modern Ships*] 4A (2008): 16.

38. 火木 [Huo Mu], 美国用海基导弹摧毁失控卫星真实意图何在? ["What Is the Real Intention behind the U.S. Use of Sea-Based Ballistic Missile to Destroy an Out-of-Control Satellite?"], 当代海军 [*Modern Navy*] (April 2008): 23; Wu Ganxiang, "The New Space Threat?" *Beijing Review*, March 20–March 26, 2008, CPP20080401715024; and Li Daguang, "What Is the Significance behind US

Decision to Down a Satellite by Missile?" *Banyue Tan*, April 1, 2008, 85–87, CPP20080501436001.

39. Hong Yuan, "US 'Ulterior Motives' in Destroying Satellite with Missile," *Xinjing Bao*, February 28, 2008, CPP20080222050001.

40. 戴艳丽 [Dai Yanli], 且谈美国海基反导系统拦截卫星 ["Discussion of U.S. Sea-Based Anti-Ballistic Missile System's Interception of Satellite"], 兵器知识 [*Ordnance Knowledge*], no. 4 (2008): 39.

41. 吴勤 [Wu Qin], 美国太空战的矛与盾 ["The Spear and the Shield of U.S. Space Warfare"], 现代军事 [*Contemporary Military*] (May 2005): 47.

42. 袁崇焕 [Yuan Chonghuan], 全球导弹防御系统—能否真的有效保护美国自身安全? ["Global Ballistic Missile Defense System: Can It Really Effectively Protect America's Own Security?"], 国外科技动态 [*Recent Developments in Science and Technology Abroad*], no. 4 (2006): 38–48.

43. 郭利松 刘志春 宋刘非 张蕊 [Guo Lisong, Liu Zhichun, Song Yifei, and Zhang Rui], 美国海军导弹防御系统的发展分析 ["Analyzing the Development of the U.S. Navy's Ballistic Missile Defense System"], 舰船电子工程 [*Ship Electronic Engineering*], no. 6 (2007): 53; and 许黎明 李汛 [Xu Liming and Li Xun], 标准-3独臂支撑海军战区弹道导弹防御 ["Standard Missile-3 Singlehandedly Supports the U.S. Navy's Theater Ballistic Missile Defense System"], 现代舰船 [*Modern Ships*] 7A (2005): 37.

44. 彭灏 张素梅 [Peng Hao and Zhang Sumei], 日本导弹防御系统面观 ["A View of Japan's Ballistic Missile System"], 飞航导弹 [*Winged Missiles*] 1 (2007): 22.

45. 汪成洋 [Wang Chengyang], 日本试射新型海基拦截导弹标准-3 ["Japan Test Fires New Standard Missile-3 Sea-Based Ballistic Missile Interceptor"], 当代海军 [*Modern Navy*] (May 2006): 15.

46. 林国利 朱竞成 杨海荣 [Lin Guoli, Zhu Jingcheng, and Yang Hairong], 日本导弹防御系统发展透视 ["A Perspective on Japan's Ballistic Missile System Development"], 国防科技 [*National Defense Science and Technology*] (December 2005): 35.

47. Wang Baofu, "Why U.S., Japan Speed Up Missile Shield Deployment?" *Renmin Ribao*, July 17, 2006, CPP20060717701001.

48. Shen Hung and Liang Yu-kuo, "Japan Seeks Hegemony under Pretext of 'Missile Defense,'" *Ta Kung Pao*, July 6, 2006, CPP20060712715004.

49. 陈家光 五振学 陈浩 [Chen Jiaguang, Wu Zhenxue, and Chen Hao], 日防卫白皮书对别国说三道四 ["Japan's Defense White Paper Makes Irresponsible Remarks to Other Countries"], 环球军事 [*Global Military*], no. 155 (August 2007).

50. 罗山爱 [Luo Shanai], 日本用啥保卫东京? ["What Does Japan Use to Protect Tokyo?"], 环球军事 [*Global Military*], no. 118 (January 2006): 17. For similar commentary, see 林炎 [Lin Yan], 日本首次海基弹道导弹拦截分析 ["An Analysis of Japan's First Sea-Based Ballistic Missile Interception"], 当代海军 [*Modern Navy*] (February 2008): 17.

51. 袁冲 [Yuan Chong], 日本加快部署反导步伐 ["Japan Accelerates Steps to Deploy Anti-Ballistic Missiles"], 国际资料信息 [*International Data Information*], no. 4 (2008): 39.

52. 周晓光 陈永红 [Zhou Xiaoguang and Chen Yonghong], 日本海军战略的新 动向 ["New Trends in Japan's Naval Strategy"], 当代海军 [*Modern Navy*] (July 2006): 64.

53. 石江月 [Shi Jiangyue], 美国加速提升太平洋军力瞄准谁? ["Who Is America's Accelerated Increases in Pacific Military Power Directed At?"], 现代 舰船 [*Modern Ships*] 10A (2006): 11.

54. 王鹏飞 孙志宏 [Wang Pengfei and Sun Zhihong], 联合美台,BMD即将建成 日本反导系统介入台湾 ["Joining U.S. and Taiwan, BMD Will Soon Enable Japan's Anti-Ballistic Missile System to Intervene over Taiwan"], 国际展望 [*World Outlook*], no. 18 (2007): 55.

55. For Chinese descriptions of the operational advantages of sea-based BMD, see 孟昭香 [Meng Shaoxiang], 21世纪的宙斯盾 ["Aegis of the Twenty-First Century"], 情报指挥控制系统与仿真技术 [*Information Command Control System and Simulation Technology*], no. 6 (December 2005): 3; and 钟建业 [Zhong Jianya], 日本的导弹防御系统 ["Japan's Ballistic Missile Defense System"], 中国航天 [*Aerospace China*], no. 10 (October 2005): 38.

56. 候健军 [Hou Jianjun], 日本海上自卫队的新战略与新装备 ["The New Strategy and New Equipment of Japan's Maritime Self-Defense Forces"], 当代 海军 [*Modern Navy*] (February 2006): 20; and 吕修顺 [Lu Xiushun], 点评日 韩最新型宙斯盾驱逐舰 ["Comments on Japan's and South Korea's Newest Aegis Destroyers"], 舰载武器 [*Shipborne Weapons*] (July 2007): 64.

57. 高山 [Gao Shan], 对付中国—日本未来主力舰艇发展构想 ["Coping with China—The Conceptual Development of Japan's Future Capital Ships"], 现代 舰船 [*Modern Ships*] 2A (2006): 31; 李杰 [Li Jie], 日韩新一代宙斯盾驱 逐舰 ["Japan's and South Korea's New Generation Aegis Destroyers"], 当代海 军 [*Modern Navy*] (May 2007): 33; and 雷锡恩公司将进行标准-3 Block 2A 的开发 ["Raytheon Corporation Will Soon Develop Standard Missile-3 Block 2A"], 飞航导弹 [*Winged Missiles*], no. 9 (2006): 9.

58. 博慧军 [Bo Huijun], 日本:加速向军事强国迈进 ["Japan: Forging Ahead Rapidly to Become a Great Military Power"], 环球军事 [*Global Military*], no. 120 (February 2006): 59–60.

59. 温德义 [Wen Deyi], 盾与刀—日本加速建立弹道导弹防御系统及影响 ["The Shield and the Sword—The Influence of Japan's Accelerating Development of Ballistic Missile Defense System"], 现代兵器 [*Modern Weaponry*] (January 2006): 12.

60. 远林 金琳 [Yuan Lin and Jin Lin], 防御导弹的奥秘在攻 ["The Subtlety of Ballistic Missile Defense Is in the Offense"], 当代军事文摘 [*Contemporary Military Digest*] (June 2006): 64.

61. 远林 [Yuan Lin], 导弹防御系统以攻为守 ["Ballistic Missile Defense System Relies on Offense for Defense"], 中国新闻周刊 [*China Newsweek*], January 23, 2006, 87.

62. 李瑞 [Li Rui], 美日加快军事一体化对台海安全态势的影响 ["The Influence of Rapid U.S.-Japan Military Integration on Taiwan Strait Security"], 科教文汇 [*The Science Education Article Collects*] (December 2007): 124–125.

63. Wang and Sun, "Joining U.S. and Taiwan," 55.

64. 李杰 [Li Jie], 宙斯盾为啥齐聚亚太? ["Why Are Aegis Ships Gathering in the Asia Pacific?"], 当代海军 [*Modern Navy*] (November 2007): 26. For an analysis of South Korea's potential participation in the U.S.-Japan BMD architecture, see 梁峰 观天下 [Liang Feng and Guan Tianxia], 韩国海军为何急造宙斯盾战舰 ["Why Is South Korea in a Hurry to Build the Aegis?"], 当代海军 [*Modern Navy*] (July 2008): 45. The authors argue that South Korean membership in a trilateral BMD arrangement would stimulate a competitive Russian response.

65. Cao Zhigang, "US, Japan Suffer from 'Missile Allergy,'" *Jiefangjun Bao*, July 19, 2007, 5, CPP20070719710015.

66. Ren, "Aegis Ships Encircle China," 15.

67. 杜朝平 [Du Chaoping], 东经135°的网—日本和澳大利亚军事合作走向 ["The Net at East Longitude 135 Degrees 的网—The Direction of Japanese-Australian Military Cooperation"], 现代舰船 [*Modern Ships*] (May 2007): 10–11.

68. For an overview of the evolution of the Aegis system, see 施征 [Shi Zheng], 美国海军的保护伞—宙斯盾系统 ["The U.S. Navy's Protective Umbrella—The Aegis System"], 海洋世界 [*Ocean World*], no. 8 (2006): 40–46.

69. 丁光超 吕卫民 彭瑾 刘冬 [Ding Guangchao, Lu Weimin, Peng Jin, and Liu Dong], 反舰导弹对航母编队突防策略研究 ["A Study of Antiship Cruise Missile Penetration Tactics against Carrier Formations"], 飞航导弹 [*Winged Missiles*], no. 10 (2008): 37.

70. 肖鹏 [Xiao Peng], 近看两种现代巡洋舰龙虎斗—提康德罗加 VS 基洛夫 ["A Close Look at Competition between Two Types of Modern

Cruisers—Ticonderoga vs. Kirov"], 当代世界 [*Contemporary World*], no. 4 (2007): 58.

71. 王逸峰 [Wang Yifeng], 航母杀手 VS 航母守护神—简评光荣级与提康德罗加级 ["Carrier Killer vs. Carrier Guardian—A Review of the *Slava*-class and the *Ticonderoga*-class"], 舰载武器 [*Shipborne Weapons*] (May 2005): 17.

72. 一翔 [Yi Xiang], 细品宙斯盾 ["A Close Look at Aegis"], 现代兵器 [*Modern Weaponry*] (August 2008): 7.

73. 闻舞 [Wen Wu], 爱拓级 VS KDX-3—东北亚宙斯盾大比拼 ["*Atago*-class vs. KDX-3—Aegis Competition in Northeast Asia"], 当代海军 [*Modern Navy*] (July 2007): 73.

74. 陈安刚 [Chen Angang], 点击日本宙斯盾战舰 ["Opening Up Japan's Aegis Warship"], 现代舰船 [*Modern Ships*] 10A (2006): 22.

75. 天鹰 [Tian Ying], 剑与盾—东亚水域的现代与金刚 ["The Sword and Shield—The *Sovremenny* and the *Kongo* in East Asian Waters"], 舰载武器 [*Shipborne Weapons*] (March 2007): 44.

76. 达砾 [Da Li], 小 "白蛉" 能吞大航母 ["Small 'Moskit' Can Swallow Big Carrier"], 太空探索 [*Space Exploration*], no. 10 (2008): 49.

77. 海潮 [Hai Chao], 日本铸造海上防空盾牌—日本金刚级宙斯盾驱逐舰的性能演变 ["Japan Forges an Air Defense Shield at Sea—The Evolution of the Performance of Japan's *Kongo*-class Aegis Destroyer"], 舰载武器 [*Shipborne Weapons*] (August 2005): 56.

78. 吴红民 [Wu Hongmin], 目标—金刚 虚拟战场 ["Target—*Kongo* Fictitious Battlefield"], 舰载武器 [*Shipborne Weapons*] (June 2004): 87.

79. 管带 [Guan Dai], 提康德罗加巡洋舰对台湾的影响 ["The Influence of the *Ticonderoga* Cruise on Taiwan"], 现代舰船 [*Modern Ships*] 2A (2005): 22.

80. 赵宇 [Zhao Yu], 全景扫描日本海上军事力量—海军海上作战力量 ["Comprehensive Assessment of Japan's Naval Power—The Navy's Combat Power"], 当代海军 [*Modern Navy*] (September 2005): 58.

81. 中国航空兵如何突破宙斯盾合围 ["How China's Air Arm Can Penetrate Aegis Encirclement"], 舰船知识 [*Naval and Merchant Ships*] (October 2007): 18.

82. 许诚 李永胜 孙锦 [Xu Cheng, Li Yongsheng, and Sun Jin], 基于MARKOV过程的反舰导弹突防舰艇编队能力评估 ["An Assessment of Antiship Missile Penetration Capabilities against Fleet Formations Based on the MARKOV Process"], 飞行力学 [*Flight Dynamics*] 27, no. 2 (April 2009): 95.

83. 陈娜 [Chen Na], 无限打击之刃—盘点美国未来舰载作战系统 ["Unlimited

Striking Power of the Sword—Taking Stock of America's Future Shipborne Combat Systems"], 国际展望 [*World Outlook*] 24 (2007): 53.

84. Wang is accompanied by Wu Guifu from the China Institute for International Strategic Studies and Yang Chengjun from the Second Artillery Army Institute in this summary of a conference hosted by Qinghua University's Institute of International Studies. 武桂馥 杨承军 王湘穗 [Wu Guifu, Yang Chengjun, and Wang Xiangsui], 21世纪初的航天科技与新军事变革 ["Aerospace Technology and the Transformation of New Military Affairs in the Early Twenty-first Century"], 太平洋学报 [*Pacific Journal*], no. 3 (2006): 14.

85. Yu Jixun, ed., *The Science of Second Artillery Campaigns* (Beijing: People's Liberation Army Press, 2004), 402.

CHAPTER 6. CHINA'S EMERGING UNDERSEA NUCLEAR DETERRENT

1. John Wilson Lewis and Xue Litai, *China's Strategic Sea Power: The Politics of Force Modernization in the Nuclear Age* (Stanford, Calif.: Stanford University Press, 1994).

2. On the technical aspects of operating ballistic-missile submarines during the Cold War, see Robert G. Loewenthal, "Cold War Insights into China's New Ballistic-Missile Submarine Fleet," in *China's Future Nuclear Submarine Force*, ed. Andrew S. Erickson, Lyle J. Goldstein, William S. Murray, and Andrew R. Wilson (Annapolis, Md.: Naval Institute Press, 2007), 286–303.

3. John Foster Dulles, "The Evolution of Foreign Policy," *Department of State Bulletin* 30 (January 25, 1954).

4. For an excellent snapshot of the debates over U.S. nuclear strategy, see Lawrence Freedman, "The First Two Generations of Nuclear Strategists," in *Makers of Modern Strategy from Machiavelli to the Nuclear Age*, ed. Peter Paret (Princeton, N.J.: Princeton University Press, 1986), 735–778.

5. Ibid.

6. See, for instance, "SSBN-726 Ohio Class FBM Submarines," GlobalSecurity. org, http://www.globalsecurity.org/wmd/systems/ssbn-726.htm; and "Trident II D-5 Fleet Ballistic Missile," GlobalSecurity.org, http://www.globalsecurity.org/ wmd/systems/d-5.htm. *Ohio*-class boats can carry up to twenty-four Trident SLBMs, which can strike at targets more than 4,600 miles distant and can carry MIRV'd warheads.

7. Interview with a U.S. submarine officer, Newport, R.I., February 15, 2008.

8. U.S. Department of Defense, *Soviet Military Power: Prospects for Change, 1989*, Federation of American Scientists Web site, http://www.fas.org/irp/dia/product/

smp_89.htm. For a collection of primary documents detailing U.S. thinking about SSBNs' role in U.S. naval strategy (as well as a range of other topics), see John B. Hattendorf, *U.S. Naval Strategy in the 1970s,* Newport Paper no. 30 (Newport, R.I.: Naval War College Press, 2007).

9. John B. Hattendorf, *The Evolution of the U.S. Navy's Maritime Strategy, 1977–1986,* Newport Paper no. 19 (Newport, R.I.: Naval War College Press, 2004), 23–36.

10. See, for instance, "R-39M/*Grom* [Bark]/RSM-52V/SS-N-28," GlobalSecurity. org, http://www.globalsecurity.org/wmd/world/russia/r39m.htm; and http://www.globalsecurity.org/wmd/world/russia/r39m-specs.htm. This advanced SLBM boasted a range of more than five thousand miles and could carry as many as ten MIRV'd warheads.

11. Hattendorf, *Evolution of the U.S. Navy's Maritime Strategy,* 23–36.

12. Also worth consulting is Avery Goldstein, *Deterrence and Security in the 21st Century: China, Britain, France, and the Enduring Legacy of the Nuclear Revolution* (Stanford, Calif.: Stanford University Press, 2000), 139–216.

13. See 董其峰 [Jin Qifeng], 收官之作—法国可畏号战略核潜艇 ["The Last Work—The French Le Terrrible Strategic Nuclear Submarine"], 现代舰船 [*Modern Ships*] 5A (2008): 17–20; and 齐耀久 [Ji Yaojiu], 法国胜利级弹道导弹核潜艇 ["The French *Le Triomphant*-Class Ballistic Missile Nuclear Submarine"], 现代舰船 [*Modern Ships*], no. 1 (2004): 27–28.

14. 夏立平 [Xia Liping], 法国核政策与核战略的特点与影响 ["The Characteristics and Influence of French Nuclear Policy and Nuclear Strategy"], 和平与发展 [*Peace and Development*], no. 2 (May 2008): 56.

15. 查长松 惊涛 张龙富 [Cha Changsong, Jing Tao, and Zhang Longfu], 新世纪的法国海基战略核力量 ["French Sea-Based Strategic Nuclear Power in the New Century"], 现代军事 [*Contemporary Military*] (April 2005): 56.

16. 孙晔 [Sun Ye], 法国核武,唯海独尊 ["French Nuclear Weapons, Standing Tall at Sea"], 环球军事 [*Global Military*], no. 7 (2008): 50.

17. With regard to naval affairs, observes Hattendorf, Americans "tended to view the new Soviet capabilities in terms of mirror-imaging and refighting World War II." Jack Snyder of the RAND Corporation disputed the notion that people from all societies make strategy in the same manner. Snyder coined the term "strategic culture," giving rise to a debate that rages on today. Hattendorf, *Evolution of the U.S. Navy's Maritime Strategy,* 23; and Jack Snyder, *The Soviet Strategic Culture: Implications for Nuclear Options* (Santa Monica, Calif.: RAND, 1977), 9.

18. Hattendorf, *Evolution of the U.S. Navy's Maritime Strategy,* 33.

19. Terms ascribed to China's nuclear posture, including "minimum deterrence," are highly contested in the West. Moreover, the Chinese policy community does not employ terms and concepts that correspond to those in the Western lexicon. For purposes of terminological clarity, we use the term "minimum deterrence" somewhat loosely, connoting high confidence in the ability to inflict modest damage that is nonetheless unacceptable to an adversary.

20. See, for example, Information Office of China's State Council, "China's Endeavors for Arms Control, Disarmament and Non-Proliferation," September 1, 2005, http://www.china.org.cn/english/features/book/140320.htm.

21. Information Office of China's State Council, "China's National Defense in 2006," December 29, 2006, available at http://www.defenselink.mil/pubs/china.html.

22. Information Office of China's State Council, "China's National Defense in 2008," January 20, 2009, available at http://www.defenselink.mil/pubs/china.html.

23. Wang Zhongchun, "Nuclear Challenges and China's Choices," *China Security* (Winter 2007): 60.

24. Bates Gill, James Mulvenon, and Mark Stokes, "The Chinese Second Artillery Corps: Transition to Credible Deterrence," in *The People's Liberation Army as an Organization: Reference Volume v 1.0*, ed. James C. Mulvenon and Andrew N. D. Yang (Washington, D.C.: RAND, 2002), 536.

25. Jeffrey G. Lewis, *The Minimum Means of Reprisal: China's Search for Security in the Nuclear Age* (Cambridge, Mass.: MIT Press, 2007), 52.

26. Jing-dong Yuan, "Effective, Reliable, and Credible: China's Nuclear Modernization," *Nonproliferation Review* 14, no. 2 (July 2007): 276.

27. For an excellent summary of the terminological evolution, see Liu Bin, "China's Nuclear Strategy: Adapting to Change," *Nanfang Zhoumo*, June 17, 2009, OSC-CPP20090622682003. For "effective defense," see Wei Guoan, "What Nuclear Strategy Should China Maintain?" *Huanqiu Shibao*, March 6, 2009, OSC-CPP20090309710002. For "limited self-defense counterattack," see 蒋铁峰 [Jiang Yifeng], 新战略导弹部队强化中国核防力量 ["New Strategy Ballistic Missile Force Strengthens China's Nuclear Defense Power"], 报刊荟萃 [*Baokan Huicui*] 7 (2008): 72; and 孙快吉 [Sun Kuaiji], 解读我国自卫防御核战略 ["Interpreting Our Nation's Self Defensive Nuclear Strategy"], 时事报告 [*Shishi Baogao*], no. 2 (2007): 58–60. For "counter nuclear coercion," see 李彬 [Li Bin], 中国核战略辨析 ["An Analysis of Chinese Nuclear Strategy"], 世界经济与政治 [*World Economics and Politics*], no. 9 (2006): 17. For "counter nuclear deterrence," see 荣予 洪源 [Rong Yu and Hong Yuan], 从反核威慑战略到最

低核威慑战略：中国核战略演进之路 ["From Counter Nuclear Deterrence Strategy to Minimum Nuclear Deterrence Strategy: The Evolutionary Path of China's Nuclear Strategy"], 当代亚太 [*Journal of Contemporary Asia-Pacific Studies*], no. 3 (2009): 122.

28. Rong and Hong, "From Counter Nuclear Deterrence Strategy," 130.

29. 孙向里 [Sun Xiangli], 中国核战略性质与特点分析 ["An Analysis of the Characteristics and Distinguishing Features of Chinese Nuclear Strategy"], 世界经济与政治 [*World Economics and Politics*], no. 9 (2006): 26.

30. 靖志远 彭小枫 [Jing Zhiyuan and Peng Xiaofeng], 建设中国特色战略导弹部队 ["Constructing the Strategic Missile Force with Chinese Characteristics"], 求是 [*Seeking Truth*], no. 3 (2009): 54.

31. For Chinese critiques of Western assessments, see Rong and Hong, "From Counter Nuclear Deterrence Strategy," 120–122; and Li, "An Analysis of Chinese Nuclear Strategy," 16–17.

32. This assumption does not impute any permanence to China's strategic nuclear posture. Should circumstances (such as a radical reordering of the international security environment) warrant, China would certainly harness the necessary political will and resources to depart from minimum deterrence.

33. Information Office of China's State Council, "China's National Defense in 2004," December 27, 2004, available at http://www.defenselink.mil/pubs/china.html.

34. State Council, "China's National Defense in 2006," and "China's National Defense in 2008," available at http://www.defenselink.mil/pubs/china.html.

35. Hans M. Kristensen, Robert S. Norris, and Matthew G. McKinzie, *Chinese Nuclear Forces and U.S. Nuclear War Planning* (Washington, D.C.: FAS/NRDC, November 2006), 89.

36. The ability of ICBMs to fully exploit China's strategic depth would depend on whether the country's road networks are extensive enough and robust enough to support the size and weight of the DF-31.

37. Paul Godwin calls this qualitative and quantitative mix "assured minimum deterrence." His assessment dovetails with conclusions drawn by Gill, Mulvenon, and Stokes (cited earlier) that the second-generation strategic weaponry would finally (after decades of "incredible" deterrence) endow China with a credible retaliatory capability. Paul H. B. Godwin, "Potential Chinese Responses to U.S. Ballistic Missile Defense," in *China and Missile Defense: Managing U.S.-PRC Strategic Relations*, ed. Alan D. Romberg and Michael McDevitt (Washington, D.C.: Henry L. Stimson Center, 2003), 66–67.

38. The only effective response to a capable Chinese SSBN is the employment of traditional antisubmarine-warfare assets, particularly SSNs.

39. 杨连新 [Yang Lianxin], 走进核潜艇 [*Exploring Nuclear Submarines*] (Beijing: Ocean Press, 2007), 120.

40. Jing-dong Yuan, "Do China's New Submarines Signal a New Strategy?" *WMD Insights*, July/August 2007, 4.

41. 红海 [Hong Hai], 中国应该发展海基核力量 ["China Should Develop Sea-Based Nuclear Capabilities"], 舰船知识 [*Naval and Merchant Ships*], no. 4 (2009): 24–26.

42. 蓝海 [Lan Hai], 中国发展海基核力量的疑问 ["Doubts About China's Development of Sea-Based Nuclear Capabilities"], 舰船知识 [*Naval and Merchant Ships*], no. 4 (2009): 27–29.

43. For an assessment of the command-and-control challenge, see Andrew S. Erickson and Lyle J. Goldstein, "China's Future Nuclear Submarine Force: Insights from Chinese Writings," *Naval War College Review* 60, no. 1 (Winter 2007): 69–70.

44. 李彬 聂宏毅 [Li Bin and Nie Hongyi], 中美战略稳定性的考察 ["Exploring Sino-U.S. Strategic Stability"], 世界经济与政治 [*World Economics and Politics*], no. 2 (2008): 15–17.

45. Lewis and Xue, *China's Strategic Sea Power*.

46. For a brief history of the *Xia*-class development, see 红旅 [Hong Lu], 人民海军的海基核威慑—中国核潜艇研制纪实 ["The Sea-Based Nuclear Deterrent of the People's Navy—A Record of the Development of China's Nuclear Submarines"], 舰载武器 [*Shipborne Weapons*], no. 1 (2004): 31–34.

47. This study acknowledges cost differentials between two very different economies, including calculations of purchasing power parity. But the figures are suggestive. Ted Nicholas and Rita Rossi, *U.S. Weapons Systems Costs, 1994* (Fountain Valley, Calif.: Data Search Associates, April 1994), 6–10. This figure does not include the costs of research, development, training, and education and the price of SLBMs prior to and during construction of each SSBN.

48. According to an anonymous PLA naval officer interviewed for a report, the cost of a nuclear submarine is simply too high for China. He observes, "The price of one nuclear submarine can buy several, even more than ten, conventional submarines. . . . As a developing country, our nation's military budget is still quite low, and thus the size of the navy's nuclear submarine fleet can only be maintained at a basic scale" (jiben gueimo [基本规模]). See 钢铁鲨鱼 ["Gangtie Shayu"], 三联生活周刊 [*Sanlian Shenhuo Zhoukan*] 20 (May 19, 2003): 29–30.

49. Zhang Baohui, "The Modernization of Chinese Nuclear Forces and Its Impact on Sino-U.S. Relations," *Asian Affairs* 34, no. 2 (Summer 2007): 92. Open-source photos of the Type 094 reveal only twelve launchers on board the submarines. Nevertheless, the arithmetic associated with multiple warheads is instructive.

50. For instance, Washington's unwillingness to cut its nuclear arsenal more deeply in part reflects a fear that China may seek to "race to parity."

51. Despite U.S. nuclear superiority over China, Washington remains acutely aware of the PRC's nuclear modernization program and has provided explicit policy guidelines to put the Chinese deterrent at risk. See excerpts from the 2002 Nuclear Posture Review, GlobalSecurity.org, http://www.globalsecurity.org/wmd/library/policy/dod/npr.htm. Indeed, America's evolving nuclear posture suggests that defense planners are looking to attain "absolute security" in deterrent relations with Russia and China. According to a RAND study, major technological advances combined with the anticipated U.S. nuclear force structure suggest that the United States will be increasingly capable of executing a "war winning" strategy premised on devastatingly effective preemptive nuclear strikes to disarm major powers. The report states, "What the planned force appears best suited to provide beyond the needs of traditional deterrence is a *preemptive counterforce capability against Russia and China.* Otherwise the numbers and the operating procedure simply do not add up." Glenn C. Buchan, David Matonick, Calvin Shipbaugh, and Richard Mesic, *Future Roles of U.S. Nuclear Forces: Implications for U.S. Strategy* (Santa Monica, Calif.: RAND, 2003), 92. In this broader context of U.S. nuclear strategy (and assuming that these analysts are right), it is hardly conceivable that U.S. defense planners would stand idly by as China builds up its arsenal.

52. Department of Defense, "Annual Report to Congress: Military Power of the People's Republic of China 2009," 48, available at http://www.defenselink.mil/pubs/china.html.

53. Office of Naval Intelligence, "Seapower Questions on the Chinese Submarine Force," unclassified document obtained under the Freedom of Information Act by Hans M. Kristensen.

54. Stephen Saunders, *Jane's Fighting Ships* (Surrey, UK: IHS Jane's, 2009), 128; and Duncan Lennox, *Jane's Strategic Weapons Systems* (Surrey, UK: Jane's Information Group, 2009), 38.

55. Eleanor Keymer, *Jane's World Navies* (Surrey, UK: IHG Jane's, 2009), 84; and Lyle Goldstein and William Murray, "China Emerges as a Maritime Power," *Jane's Intelligence Review* (October 2004): 35. For other studies on the logic of a Chinese SSBN bastion strategy, see, for example, "Chinese Navy's Submarine Development Strategy," *Kanwa Defense Review*, July 1, 2005, 44–46,

FBIS-CHI-CPP20050801000242. A Japanese analyst speculated that China is propping up North Korea for fear that a collapse scenario would harm Chinese SSBN deployment options in the Bohai Sea, which is flanked by the Democratic People's Republic of Korea. See Junichi Abe, "Why China Does Not Want to See the Unification of the Korean Peninsula," *Sekai Shuho*, February 8, 2005, 54–55, FBIS-JPP20050203000035.

56. See 董其峰 [Dong Qifeng], 美国与苏/俄核潜艇发展战略对比分析 ["Comparative Analysis of U.S. and Soviet/Russian Nuclear Submarine Development Strategies"], 现代海军 [*Modern Ships*], no. 11B (November 2007): 34. The author claims that the Soviet Union's bastion strategy essentially rendered obsolete the antisubmarine defenses developed by the United States and its NATO allies in the Norwegian Sea and along the Greenland-Iceland-UK gap.

57. One Chinese analyst argues that geography is a major determinant of how countries design their SSBNs and associated deployment options. A long coastline directly facing the ocean and quick access to deep waters just off the shoreline are the ideal operational conditions for an SSBN. In an implicit reference to China, he observes that a country whose long coastal waters are part of the continental shelf may need to deploy submarines more than two hundred kilometers out to sea to find water deep enough for fleet boats to hide. He concludes that such geographic constraints would force the country to develop smaller SSBNs to operate in shallower sea-lanes and harbors. See 吴谐 [Wu Xie], 战略核潜艇设计方案简析 ["Zhanlue Heqianting Sheji Fangan Jianxi"], *Bingqi Zhishi*, no. 4 (April 2004): 53.

58. It is worth noting that the *Xia*-class SSBN is based at the Jianggezhuang Submarine Base, fifteen miles east of Qingdao on the Yellow Sea. For satellite imagery of the *Xia* at Jianggezhuang, see Thomas B. Cochran, Matthew G. McKinzie, Robert S. Norris, Laura S. Harrison, and Hans M. Kristensen, "China's Nuclear Forces: The World's First Look at China's Underground Facilities for Nuclear Warheads," *Imaging Notes* (Winter 2006), http://www.imagingnotes.com/go/page4a.php?menu_id=23. There is speculation that the Type 094 could be homeported at this facility, a location that might favor a bastion strategy.

59. Apparently referring to the lower forty-eight states, the Federation of American Scientists and the Natural Resources Defense Council point out that, "Even with a possible range of 5,095 miles (8,200 km), the JL-2 would not be able to target the continental United States from the Bo Hai Bay." However, a 5,000-mile range would allow China to target the entire states of Alaska and Hawaii as well as the critical node at Guam. Such a limited reach would still largely conform to China's minimalist doctrine. Kristensen, Norris, and McKinzie, *Chinese Nuclear Forces*, 85.

60. Chinese defense planners have devoted their attention (almost exclusively) to a Taiwan contingency since the 1995–1996 missile crises. In this broader strategic context of a more urgent security challenge, it seems unlikely that Beijing would place SSBN protection ahead of another expected confrontation over Taiwan. At the same time, however, it is important to acknowledge that the maritime capabilities developed to protect SSBNs in a Bohai/Yellow Sea bastion might play complementary roles in a Taiwan Strait crisis or war. Further, an SSBN fleet could very well play a more direct role in a Taiwan scenario should Chinese nuclear deterrence or coercion enter the equation. For an abstract, generic analysis of how nuclear weapons can deter great-power intervention on behalf of a client state, see 长缨 [Chang Ying], 浅谈核威慑的两个作用 ["Qiantan Heweishe de Liangge Zuoyong"], *Bingqi Zhishi*, no. 4 (April 2004): 51–52. Some U.S. analysts have speculated that an assured second-strike capability underwritten by a more survivable arsenal could embolden China to engage in nuclear brinkmanship, including a "demonstration shot" in-theater to dissuade U.S. and allied intervention in the Strait. Intriguingly, one article describes China's SSBN as an "assassin's mace" (*shashoujian* [杀手锏]) that can be employed to deter American and Japanese intervention in a cross-strait conflict. 高新涛 [Gao Xintao], 中国海军潜艇战略 ["Zhongguo Haijun Qianting Zhanlue"], 广角镜 [*Guang Jiao Jing*] (January 16–February 15, 2005): 69.

61. Toshi Yoshihara and James R. Holmes, "Command of the Sea with Chinese Characteristics," *Orbis* 49, no. 4 (Fall 2005): 677–694.

62. Christopher McConnaughy, "China's Undersea Nuclear Deterrent: Will the U.S. Navy Be Ready?" in *China's Nuclear Force Modernization*, ed. Lyle J. Goldstein and Andrew Erickson (Newport, R.I.: Naval War College Press, 2005), 44.

63. 刘江平 [Liu Jiangping], 海上挑战催生海军转型 ["Maritime Challenges Hasten a Naval Transition"], 海洋世界 [*Ocean World*], no. 8 (2007): 72.

64. Richard Fisher Jr., "Developing US-Chinese Nuclear Naval Competition in Asia," International Assessment and Strategy Center Web site, http://www.strategycenter.net/research/pubID.60/pub_detail.asp.

65. Ronald O'Rourke, *Navy Attack Submarine Procurement: Background and Issues for Congress* (Washington, D.C.: Congressional Research Service, May 20, 2009), 3.

66. The Chinese are quite aware of the ASW challenge. The permanent homeporting of *Los Angeles*–class SSNs at Guam has not gone unnoticed in China. For an in-depth Chinese analysis of Guam's importance to America's security posture in Asia, see 李文盛 [Li Wensheng], 聚焦关岛 ["Jujiao Guandao"], *Bingqi Zhishi*, no. 9 (September 2004): 15–19. One Chinese author argues that the PLA Navy must acquire its own ASW platforms to respond to such a shift in

U.S. naval posture in the Pacific. See 台风 [Tai Feng], 中国需要反潜艇巡逻机吗? ["Does China Need Anti-submarine Patrol Aircraft?"], 舰载武器 [*Jianzai Wuqi*], March 1, 2005, 70–75.

67. Oga Ryohei, "What the PRC Submarine Force Is Aiming For," *Sekai no Kansen*, July 1, 2005, 96–101.

68. A Chinese analysis argues that SSBN open-ocean patrols will not occur until the PLA Navy develops a more balanced force structure that includes aircraft carriers. Strategic nuclear submarines would then be able to operate in blue waters under the protective cover of carrier aircraft. "Heqianting yu Zhongguo Haijun," *Jianchuan Zhishi*, no. 306 (March 2005): 13.

69. 李杰 刘涛 [Li Jie and Liu Tao], 战略核潜艇发展的争论焦点及思考 ["Key Debates and Thinking about Strategic Nuclear Submarine Development"], 现代舰船 [*Modern Ships*] 11A (2008): 19.

70. For the most widely cited work on this issue, see Alastair Iain Johnston, "China's New 'Old Thinking': The Concept of Limited Deterrence," *International Security* 20, no. 3 (Winter 1995/96): 18–38.

71. Robert A. Manning, Ronald Montaperto, and Brad Roberts, *China, Nuclear Weapons, and Arms Control* (New York: Council on Foreign Relations, 2000), 47.

72. Stephen J. Hadley, "A Call to Deploy," *Washington Quarterly* 23, no. 3 (Summer 2000): 26.

73. For a range of potential technological breakthroughs in the future, see Stephen F. Cimbala, "Nuclear Weapons in the Twentieth Century: From Simplicity to Complexity," *Defense and Security Analysis* 21, no. 3 (September 2005): 279.

74. The depressed trajectory of SLBMs reduces their vulnerability to missile defenses and significantly stresses the response times of ballistic-missile-defense systems.

75. Jeffrey Lewis, "China and 'No First Use,'" July 17, 2005, http://www.armscontrolwonk.com/677/china-and-no-first-use.

76. Shen Dingli, "Nuclear Deterrence in the 21st Century," *China Security* 1 (Autumn 2005): 13.

77. For an American analysis of this point, see James Mulvenon, "Missile Defenses and the Taiwan Scenario," in *China and Missile Defense: Managing U.S.-PRC Strategic Relations*, ed. Alan D. Romberg and Michael McDevitt (Washington, D.C.: Henry L. Stimson Center, 2003), 58–60. The author postulates a thought-provoking scenario in which Taiwan unilaterally conducts offensive, conventional precision strikes against the mainland during a cross-strait conflict. Unable to determine the real source of these attacks, worst-case thinking could

lead Beijing to mistakenly conclude that Washington was exercising its preemptive option in a bid to disarm Chinese nuclear forces. At this point in the crisis, the PRC would face the same type of decision-making crossroad that Zhu and Shen identified earlier.

78. Rong Yu and Peng Guangqian, "Nuclear No-First-Use Revisited," *China Security* 5, no. 1 (Winter 2009): 85.

79. For an analysis of possible Chinese BMD countermeasures, see Andrew S. Erickson, "Chinese BMD Countermeasures: Breaching America's Great Wall in Space?" in *China's Nuclear Force Modernization*, ed. Lyle J. Goldstein and Andrew Erickson (Newport, R.I.: Naval War College Press, 2005), 77–88. For a Chinese overview of ballistic-missile decoy technologies, see 李文盛 [Li Wensheng], 漫话战略弹道导弹诱饵技术 ["Manhua Zhanlue Dandao Daodan Youer Jishu"], *Bingqi Zhishi*, no. 2 (February 2005): 28–31.

CHAPTER 7. SOFT POWER AT SEA

1. Confucius Institute Online, http://www.uri.edu/confucius/.

2. See Henry Steele Commager, *The Search for a Usable Past and Other Essays in Historiography* (New York: Knopf, 1967), 3–27. Commager's view of common history, traditions, and legends is consistent with scholarship on ethnonationalism. See, for instance, Ted Robert Gurr, *Minorities at Risk: A Global View of Ethnopolitical Conflicts* (Washington, D.C.: U.S. Institute of Peace Press, 1993); Benedict Anderson, *Imagined Communities*, rev. ed. (London: Verso, 1991); and Anthony D. Smith, *The Ethnic Origins of Nations* (Oxford: Blackwell, 1986).

3. Ronald L. Jepperson, Alexander Wendt, and Peter J. Katzenstein, "Norms, Identity, and Culture in National Security," in *The Culture of National Security: Norms and Identity in World Politics*, ed. Peter J. Katzenstein (New York: Columbia University Press, 1996), 33.

4. George Washington, "Farewell Address," in *George Washington: Writings* (New York: Library of America, 1997), 962–977. For a sampling of commentary on early America, see Alexander Hamilton, James Madison, and John Jay, *The Federalist Papers*, ed. Clinton Rossiter (New York: Penguin, 1961), esp. 77–84, 320–325; Thomas Paine, *The Thomas Paine Reader*, ed. Michael Foot and Isaac Kramnick (London: Penguin, 1987), 65–115; Alexis de Tocqueville, *Democracy in America*, trans. George Lawrence, ed. J. P. Mayer (New York: HarperPerennial, 1988), esp. 226–230; and Bernard Bailyn, *The Ideological Origins of the American Revolution* (Cambridge, Mass.: Harvard University Press, 1967), 55–93.

5. Samuel Flagg Bemis, *A Diplomatic History of the United States*, revised edition (New York: Henry Holt, 1942), 463–478. Bemis titled the chapter on the Spanish-American War and its aftermath "The Great Aberration of 1898."

6. See, for instance, Richard H. Collin, *Theodore Roosevelt's Caribbean: The Panama Canal, the Monroe Doctrine, and the Latin American Context* (Baton Rouge: Louisiana State University Press, 1991).

7. Reginald Stuart explores the "war myth" that the United States, throughout its history, has only embarked on moralistic crusades that culminate in total war. In reality, contends Stuart persuasively, the American Founders' thinking inclined strongly to limited wars of the kind envisioned by the Prussian strategic theorist Carl von Clausewitz. See Reginald C. Stuart, *War and American Thought: From the Revolution to the Monroe Doctrine* (Kent, Ohio: Kent State University Press, 1982), 182–194. See also Max Boot, *The Savage Wars of Peace: Small Wars and the Rise of American Power* (New York: Basic Books, 2002).

8. Jepperson, Wendt, and Katzenstein, "Norms, Identity, and Culture," 60.

9. John King Fairbank, "Introduction: Varieties of the Chinese Military Experience," in *Chinese Ways in Warfare*, ed. Frank A. Kierman and John King Fairbank (Cambridge, Mass.: Harvard University Press, 1974), 7.

10. Andrew Scobell, *China and Strategic Culture* (Carlisle Barracks, Penn.: Strategic Studies Institute, U.S. Army War College, May 2002), 3–4. For a fuller exposition of these views, see Andrew Scobell, *China's Use of Military Force: Beyond the Great Wall and the Long March* (Cambridge: Cambridge University Press, 2003).

11. See, for example, Alastair Iain Johnston, "Thinking about Strategic Culture," *International Security* 19, no. 4 (Spring 1995): 32–64; and Alastair Iain Johnston, *Cultural Realism: Strategic Culture and Grand Strategy in Chinese History* (Princeton, N.J.: Princeton University Press, 1995), esp. 1–31, 61–108.

12. Jepperson, Wendt, and Katzenstein, "Norms, Identity, and Culture," 33.

13. For a thorough review of the literature on strategic culture, see Jeffrey S. Lantis, "Strategic Culture and National Security Policy," *International Studies Review* 4, no. 3 (December 2002): 87–113; and Toshi Yoshihara, "Chinese Strategic Culture and Military Innovation: From the Nuclear to the Information Age" (Ph.D. diss., Fletcher School, Tufts University, 2004), 13–62.

14. For instance, international relations scholars of realist inclinations, most prominently Kenneth Waltz, contend that lesser powers tend to band together to counterbalance the rise of a new, potentially dominant great power. More recently, some scholars of Asian politics have declared that balance-of-power politics is primarily a Western phenomenon, and that the Asian system inclines less to balancing than to hierarchy. For an overview of the realist analysis, see Kenneth N. Waltz, "The Emerging Structure of International Politics," *International Security* 18, no. 2 (Fall 1993): 44–79; and Kenneth N. Waltz, *Theory of International Politics* (Reading, Mass.: Addison-Wesley, 1979). For a sample of other realist

analyses, see Aaron Friedberg, "Ripe for Rivalry," *International Security* 18, no. 3 (Winter 1993/94): 5–33; Richard K. Betts, "Wealth, Power, and Instability: East Asia and the United States after the Cold War," *International Security* 18, no. 3 (Winter 1993/94): 34–77; and Avery Goldstein, "Great Expectations: Interpreting China's Arrival," *International Security* 22, no. 3 (Winter 1997/98): 36–73. For a rejoinder to the realists, see David C. Kang, "Getting Asia Wrong: The Need for New Analytical Frameworks," *International Security* 27, no. 2 (Spring 2003): 57–85; and David C. Kang, "Hierarchy in Asian International Relations: 1300–1900," *Asian Security* 1, no. 1 (January 2005): 53–79.

15. Thucydides, *The Landmark Thucydides: A Comprehensive Guide to the Peloponnesian War*, ed. Robert B. Strassler, intro. Victor Davis Hanson (New York: Free Press, 1996), 43.

16. Johnston, *Cultural Realism*, 10.

17. Ibid., 10–11.

18. Charles Kupchan, *The Vulnerability of Empire* (Ithaca, N.Y.: Cornell University Press, 1994), 1–32.

19. Ibid., 5.

20. For the sake of avoiding clutter, we have avoided bringing strategic theory into this analysis. It is worth noting, nonetheless, that the notion of using strategic culture to amass public support for particular decisions is consistent with Carl von Clausewitz's notion of the "paradoxical trinity." Clausewitz proclaimed that wise statesmen must manage the government, the armed forces, and the people in order to maintain a cohesive war effort. Language and concepts derived from a society's traditions offer political and military leaders a mechanism to influence the citizenry, which the Prussian theorist depicted as the province of primordial passions. This conception of the public helps explain why political leaders can find it difficult to control public expectations they have created. See Carl von Clausewitz, *On War*, ed., trans. Michael Howard and Peter Paret (Princeton, N.J.: Princeton University Press, 1976), 89.

21. Jack Snyder, *The Soviet Strategic Culture: Implications for Nuclear Options* (Santa Monica, Calif.: RAND, 1977), 9.

22. Kupchan, *Vulnerability of Empire*, 5–6.

23. For the sake of analytical clarity, many analysts have confined strategic culture solely to the realm of military strategy. For instance, Alan Macmillan, Ken Booth, and Russell Trood maintain that if strategy "is allowed to mean more than the *military* dimension of *security*, then the word simply becomes synonymous with security, and so loses its special meaning. . . . In this event, *strategic* culture simply becomes synonymous with *political* culture. This, most will agree,

would not be helpful" (Macmillan, Booth, and Trood, "Strategic Culture," in *Strategic Cultures in the Asia-Pacific Region*, ed. Ken Booth and Russell Trood [New York: St. Martin's, 1999], esp. 10–11; their emphasis). One virtue of Charles Kupchan's analysis is that he does not limit strategic culture to military affairs but widens it to consider how states use diplomatic, economic, and ideological instruments alongside the military instrument. If we allow for the concept of grand strategy, we must allow culture to function at the grand strategic level. Alastair Iain Johnston makes a similar assumption. Colin Gray, despite sharp differences with Johnston in many areas, argues that culture provides "context" that suffuses all aspects of strategy-making, not just the military domain. And, in a similar vein, Toshi Yoshihara envisions a comprehensive "'hierarchy of strategy,' which is expressed as an interlinked set of preferences that flow from grand strategy to operations and tactics." See Kupchan, *Vulnerability of Empire*, 7–8; Johnston, *Cultural Realism*; Colin S. Gray, "Strategic Culture as Context: The First Generation of Theory Strikes Back," *Review of International Studies* 25 (1999): 49–69; and Yoshihara, "Chinese Strategic Culture," v, 89, 105.

24. Gray, "Strategic Culture as Context," 50. Gray is responding here to criticism from Iain Johnston, who has accused Gray's generation of theorists of postulating an unfalsifiable theory of strategic culture, among other sins. If strategic culture interpenetrates both ideas and actions, maintains Johnston in essence, then there is no way to measure it scientifically. He thus attempts to confine culture to the domain of ideas in an effort to measure its influence on actions. Gray's rejoinder: "Anyone who seeks a falsifiable theory of strategic culture in the school of Johnston, commits the same error as a doctor who sees people as having entirely separable bodies and minds. . . . We cannot understand strategic behaviour by that method, be it ever so rigorous" (ibid., 53). Agrees Ken Booth: "Theories in these subjects might become richer if less weight is given to 'rigour'" (Booth, "The Concept of Strategic Culture Affirmed," in *Strategic Power: USA/ USSR*, ed. Carl G. Jacobsen [New York: St. Martin's, 1990], 125).

25. Joseph S. Nye, *Soft Power: The Means to Success in World Politics* (New York: Public Affairs, 2004); and Joseph S. Nye, "Asia's Allure Lies in Soft Power," *Straits Times*, November 16, 2005.

26. Joseph S. Nye, "The American National Interest and Global Public Goods," *International Affairs* 78, no. 2 (April 2002): 238.

27. Chen Jian distinguishes usefully between "centrality" and "dominance" in Chinese political thought. He observes, "The Chinese collective memory of the 'Central Kingdom's' glorious past—remembered not just as the center of civilization, but civilization *in toto*—and the nation's humiliating experience in the modern age constituted a constant source for national mobilization in

the twentieth century." For Chen, then, China's ascent to great-power status need not involve territorial conquest or military domination. See Chen Jian, *The China Challenge for the Twenty-first Century* (Washington, D.C.: U.S. Institute of Peace Press, 1998), 4–8.

28. Thomas C. Schelling, *The Strategy of Conflict* (New York: Oxford University Press, 1963), esp. 21–52; and Thomas C. Schelling, *Arms and Influence* (New Haven, Conn.: Yale University Press, 1966), esp. 35–91. See also Jeffrey Z. Rubin and Jeswald W. Salacuse, "The Problem of Power in International Negotiations," *International Affairs* 66 (April 1990): 21–80.

29. On the Ming dynasty's turn away from the oceans, see, for instance, Valerie Hansen, "China in World History 300–1500 CE," *Education about Asia* 10, no. 3 (Winter 2005): 4–7.

30. For an account of China's naval efforts during the Cold War, see John Wilson Lewis and Xue Litai, *China's Strategic Sea Power: The Politics of Force Modernization in the Nuclear Age* (Stanford, Calif.: Stanford University Press, 1994).

31. Bernard D. Cole, *The Great Wall at Sea: China's Navy Enters the Twenty-first Century* (Annapolis, Md.: Naval Institute Press, 2001), 165–168; Jun Zhan, "China Goes to the Blue Waters: The Navy, Sea Power Mentality, and the South China Sea," *Journal of Strategic Studies* (September 1994): 180–203; and Alexander Chieh-cheng Huang, "The Chinese Navy's Offshore Active Defense Strategy," *Naval War College Review* 47, no. 3 (Summer 1994): 9–18.

32. See, for instance, David Hale, "China's Growing Appetites," *National Interest* 76 (Summer 2004): 137–147.

33. Taiwan is of course a complicating factor in China's emerging maritime strategy, but we consider it a neutral factor in the analysis presented here. Not only does the island sit at the center point of the first offshore island chain, potentially obstructing China's access to the Pacific high seas, it also sits astride sea-lanes connecting northern Chinese seaports with the Strait of Malacca and thence to suppliers of much-needed oil and natural gas. Either way, consequently, settling the Taiwan question on its terms will remain uppermost in the minds of China's leadership. See Toshi Yoshihara and James R. Holmes, "Command of the Sea with Chinese Characteristics," *Orbis* 49, no. 4 (Fall 2005): 677–694. For a contrary view, see Robert D. Kaplan, "How We Would Fight China," *Atlantic* 295, no. 5 (June 2005): 49–64. Kaplan prophesied that the PLA will indeed surge out eastward into the Pacific, as Liu Huaqing urged.

34. Edward L. Dreyer, "The Poyang Connection, 1363: Inland Naval Warfare in the Founding of the Ming Dynasty," in *Chinese Ways in Warfare*, ed. Frank A. Kierman and John King Fairbank (Cambridge, Mass.: Harvard University Press, 1974), 202–240.

35. Louise Levathes, *When China Ruled the Seas: The Treasure Fleet of the Dragon Throne, 1405–1433* (New York and Oxford: Oxford University Press, 1994), 73.

36. "Carry Forward Zheng He Spirit, Promote Peace and Development," *Renmin ribao* (People's Daily), July 13, 2005, FBIS-CHN-200507131477. See also the other installments in this series, published in the *People's Daily* on July 15, 19, and 20.

37. Editorial, "On Our Military's Historic Missions in the New Century, New Stage—Written on the 50th Anniversary of the Founding of '*Jiefangjun Bao*,'" *Jiefangjun bao*, February 17, 2006, FBIS-CHN-200602171477.

38. Bruce A. Elleman, *Waves of Hope: The U.S. Navy's Response to the Tsunami in Northern Indonesia* (Newport, R.I.: Naval War College Press, February 2007), 103–105.

39. 区肇威 [Qu Zhaowei], 医疗舰—中国施展软实力的海上平台 ["Hospital Ship: The Maritime Platform for China to Maximize Its Soft Power"], 现代兵器 [*Modern Weaponry*], no. 3 (2009): 14.

40. Elleman, *Waves of Hope*, 104.

41. 韦振华 [Wei Zhenhua], 郑和下西洋与中国的海洋文化 ["Zheng He's Expedition to the Western Seas and China's Oceanic Culture"], 珠江水运 [*Pearl River Water Transport*] 7 (2006): 144.

42. 朱广彦 [Zhu Guangyan], 唤醒600年沉睡的海权—郑和下西洋的纪念与反思 ["Awakening Sea Power from Its 600-Year Deep Slumber—Commemoration of and Reflections on Zheng He's Expedition to the Western Seas"], 党员干部之友 [*Friends of Party Members and Cadre*], July 2005, 19.

43. 王翔 [Wang Xiang], 对郑和下西洋和平外交政策的探究 ["An Inquiry into the Peaceful Foreign Policy of Zheng He's Expeditions to the Western Seas"], 中国水运 [*China Water Transport*] 4, no. 3 (March 2006): 12–13; and 云飞 [Yun Fei], 弘扬郑和精神 迈向海洋强国 ["Promote the Zheng He Spirit, Toward an Oceanic Power"], 珠江水运 [*Pearl River Water Transport*] 7 (2006): 152.

44. 周思敏 [Zhou Siming], 从儒家思想角度解读郑和下西洋 ["Interpreting Zheng He's Expedition to the Western Seas from the Angle of Confucian Thought"], 吉林工程技术师范学院学报 [*Journal of Jilin Teachers Institute of Engineering and Technology*] 22, no. 10 (October 2006): 29–30.

45. 饶咬成 [Xiao Yaocheng], 中国的海洋意识与海权现况 ["China's Oceanic Consciousness and the Current State of Sea Power"], 郧阳师范高等专科学校学报 [*Journal of Yunyang Teachers College*] 25, no. 5 (October 2005): 88.

46. 蔡一鸣 [Cai Yiming], 论郑和航海精神与我国和谐海洋观 ["On Zheng He's Seafaring Spirit and Our Nation's Harmonious Ocean Outlook"], 中国航海 [*Navigation of China*], no. 4 (December 2006): 3.

47. See, for instance, Kang, "Hierarchy in Asian International Relations," 53–79.

48. David Kang, *China Rising: Peace, Power, and Order in East Asia* (New York: Columbia University Press, 2007), 49.

49. Zheng Bijian, "China's 'Peaceful Rise' to Great-Power Status," *Foreign Affairs* 84, no. 5 (September/October 2005): 18–24; and Esther Pan, "The Promise and Pitfalls of China's 'Peaceful Rise,'" Council on Foreign Relations Web site, April 14, 2006, http://www.cfr.org/publication/10446/.

50. Speech by Chinese President Hu Jintao at the University of Pretoria on China-Africa Cooperation, "Enhance China-Africa Unity and Cooperation to Build a Harmonious World," February 7, 2007, available at http://www. internationalepolitik.de/.

51. Chen Jian and Zhao Haiyan, "Wen Jiabao on Sino-U.S. Relations: Cherish Harmony; Be Harmonious but Different," Zhongguo xinwenshe (China News Service), December 8, 2003, FBIS-CPP-20031208000052.

52. "Kenyan Girl Offered Chance to Go to College in China," Xinhua, March 20, 2005, FBIS-CHN-200503201477.

53. "Enlightenment Drawn from Global Worship of Confucius," *Renmin ribao*, September 29, 2005, FBIS-CHN-200509291477. Beijing's network of Confucian Institutes aims to popularize the teachings of Confucius and, in the process, further buttress China's soft power vis-à-vis its Asian neighbors. For more on China's use of soft power, see James R. Holmes, "'Soft Power' at Sea: Zheng He and China's Maritime Diplomacy," *Southeast Review of Asian Studies* 28 (2006), http://www.uky.edu/Centers/Asia/SECAAS/Seras/2006/2006TOC. html.

54. Yu Sui, "Peace Is Priceless in the Pursuit of Happiness," *China Daily*, August 14, 2006.

55. In Zheng He's day, notes one Chinese commentator in a riposte to the Pentagon's 2005 report on Chinese military power, the Ming dynasty "did not make use of its formidable national strength to extend its boundaries and territory; conversely, it extended and strengthened the Great Wall for its own defense. Furthermore, instead of establishing overseas colonies and plundering other countries, China's mighty fleet treated other nations kindly and generously but demanded little in return." Li Xuejiang, "U.S. Report 'The Military Power of the People's Republic of China' Harbors Sinister Motives," *Renmin ribao*, July 27, 2005, FBIS-CHN-200507271477.

56. State Council Information Office, "White Paper: China's Peaceful Development Road," Xinhua, December 22, 2005, FBIS-CHN-200512221477. See also Hu

Jintao, "Strengthen Mutually Beneficial Cooperation and Promote Common Development," speech at the Mexican Senate, September 12, 2005, Xinhua, September 13, 2005, FBIS-CHN-200509131477.

57. "See China in the Light of Her Development," speech by Premier of the State Council of the People's Republic of China Wen Jiabao, Cambridge University, United Kingdom, February 2, 2009.

58. See, e.g., "China Celebrates Ancient Mariner to Demonstrate Peaceful Rise," Xinhua, July 7, 2004.

59. Bruce Swanson, *Eighth Voyage of the Dragon: A History of China's Quest for Sea Power* (Annapolis, Md.: Naval Institute Press, 1982), 28.

60. The dimensions of the *baochuan* are a matter of some dispute. Ming histories report that the vessels were 440 feet long and 180 feet wide—a ratio that would make them so broad-beamed as to be "unresponsive even under moderate sea conditions," in the opinion of one modern analyst, Bruce Swanson. Swanson contends that the treasure ships more likely resembled the large junks put to sea in succeeding centuries, estimating their length at 180 feet. He further contends that ships with these dimensions would have been large enough to accommodate ship's companies of the size reported in the histories. Others, notably Louise Levathes, accept the figure from the histories. Either way, the treasure ships dwarfed the ships sailed by Zheng He's near-contemporaries, Christopher Columbus and Vasco da Gama. (Columbus' *Santa Maria* was all of 85 feet long.) See Swanson, *Eighth Voyage of the Dragon*, 33–34; and Levathes, *When China Ruled the Seas*, 19.

61. Swanson, *Eighth Voyage of the Dragon*, 34–36. In contemporary parlance, compartmentation—using watertight bulkheads to subdivide the interior of a ship's hull into many small compartments—restricts flooding to one or a few compartments. Barring major damage to the hull that breaches multiple bulkheads, a compartmented ship stands a good chance of withstanding "progressive flooding" that might sink a ship not so equipped.

62. Levathes, *When China Ruled the Seas*, 47, 50–52. On China's present-day "Malacca dilemma," see Ian Storey, "China's 'Malacca Dilemma,'" *China Brief* 6, no. 8 (April 12, 2006): 4–6; and Liu Jiangping and Feng Xianhui, "Going Global: Dialogue Spanning 600 Years," *Liaowang* (*Outlook*), September 8, 2005, FBIS-CHN-200509081477.

63. "China Launches Activities to Commemorate Sea Navigation Pioneer Zheng He," Xinhua, September 29, 2003, FBIS-CPP-20030928000052.

64. "Premier Wen's Several Talks during Europe Visit," Xinhua, May 16, 2004, FBIS-CPP-20040516000069. Wen sounded similar themes during a spring 2005

trip to South Asia. See Xiao Qiang, "Premier Wen's South Asian Tour Produces Abundant Results," *Renmin ribao*, April 13, 2005, FBIS-CHN-200504131477. On the extent of Chinese predominance in fifteenth-century Asia, see Roderich Ptak, "China and Portugal at Sea: The Early Ming Trading System and the *Estado da Índia* Compared," in Roderich Ptak, *China and the Asian Seas: Trade, Travel, and Visions of the Others (1400–1750)* (Aldershot, U.K.: Ashgate, 1998), 21–37.

65. "China Launches Activities," see note 61.

66. It is worth noting that Indians point out that Hindu kingdoms ruled the Indian Ocean before the Ming treasure voyages. While they are not as effective spokesmen for their maritime past as are the Chinese, Indians commonly point to their own grand seafaring past. The age of Hindu maritime supremacy ended a century before Zheng He's expeditions, however, leaving Indian maritime enthusiasts at a disadvantage vis-à-vis Chinese maritime diplomacy.

67. Hu Jintao, "Constantly Increasing Common Ground," speech to Australian Parliament, October 24, 2003, http://www.australianpolitics.com/news/2003/10/03-10-24b.shtml.

68. Intriguingly, Hu's questionable claims were based on Menzies' *1421*, an account deemed wildly speculative by most academic experts. Menzies claims, for example, that Zheng He reached American shores seventy years before Columbus. See Gavin Menzies, *1421: The Year China Discovered America* (New York: William Morrow, 2003); Hansen, "China in World History," 4–7; and Wang Gungwu, "China's Cautious Pride in an Ancient Mariner," *YaleGlobal Online*, August 4, 2005.

69. Chinese spokesmen have portrayed Beijing's contemporary policies, in particular peaceful development, as an extension of venerable Chinese traditions. To name one such spokesman, Xiong Guangkai, deputy chief of the PLA's General Staff, maintains that "China's persistently taking the road of peaceful development has historically inherited China's outstanding traditional culture and has also given important expression to the idea of peaceful diplomacy." During Zheng He's voyages, "what the Chinese nation disseminated to the outside world was the friendly heartfelt aspiration of peace, development and cooperation." See Xiong Guangkai, "Unswervingly Take the Road of Peaceful Development and Properly Deal with Diversification of Threats to Security," Xinhua, December 28, 2005, FBIS-CHN-200512281477.

70. Edward L. Dreyer, *Zheng He: China and the Oceans in the Early Ming Dynasty, 1405–1433* (Old Tappan, N.J.: Pearson Longman, 2006), xii.

71. Levathes, *When China Ruled the Seas*, 114–118; Frank Viviano, "China's Great Armada," *National Geographic*, July 2005, 41.

72. 吴伟兴 [Wu Weixing], 从软实力角度看近年来中国和东盟加强非传统安全合作的思考 ["Thoughts on the Strengthening of China-ASEAN Nontraditional Security Cooperation in Recent Years from a Soft Power Perspective"], 东南亚纵横 [*Around Southeast Asia*] (September 2008): 69.

73. 朱之江 [Zhu Zhijiang], 论非战争军事行动 ["On Non-War Military Operations"], 南京政治学院学报 [*Journal of Nanjing Institute of Politics*] 19, no. 5 (2003): 84.

74. 高月 [Gao Yue], 军事演习:非接触性对抗和政治较量 ["Military Exercises: Non-Contact Style Confrontation and Political Contest"], 舰载武器 [*Shipborne Weapons*], no. 11 (2005): 15–18.

75. Su Shiliang, "Persistently Follow the Guidance of Chairman Hu's Important Thought on the Navy's Building, Greatly Push Forward Innovation and Development in the Navy's Military Work," *Renmin Haijun*, June 6, 2009, 3, CPP20090716478009.

76. Quoted in Lu Xiang, "Navy Holds Meeting to Sum Up Experience in the First Escort Mission," *Renmin Haijun*, May 29, 2009, CPP20090702318002.

77. See 李大光 [Li Daguang], 亚丁湾护航—中国海军发展的新里程 ["Gulf of Aden Escort—New Milestone in the Chinese Navy's Development"], 国防科技工业 [*Defense Science and Technology Industry*] 1 (2009): 20; and 北军 [Bei Jun], 中国海军开赴索马里 ["Chinese Navy Bound for Somalia"], 海洋世界 [*Ocean World*] 1 (2009): 18.

78. 山东 王利文 [Shan Dong and Wang Liwen], 中国海军远洋护航意义重大 ["The Chinese Navy's Open Ocean Escort Mission Conveys Great Meaning"], 世界知识 [*World Affairs*], no. 3 (2009): 4.

79. See Li Daguang, "Chinese Navy Has Capacity to Fight against Piracy," *Wen Wei Po*, December 28, 2008, CPP20081225716007; and Lin Dong, "Global War on Terror Shifts from Land to Sea," *Zhongguo Qingnian Bao*, November 28, 2008, CPP20081128710011.

80. 李大光 [Li Daguang], 打击索马里海盗,中国展现负责任大国形象 ["Combating Somali Piracy, China Displays Responsible Great Power Image"], 生命与灾害 [*Life and Disaster*] 1 (2009): 23.

81. Wu Shengli, "Make Concerted Efforts to Jointly Build Harmonious Ocean," *Renmin Haijun*, April 22, 2009, 1, CPP20090615478011.

82. Jiang Zemin, "Enhance Mutual Understanding and Build Stronger Ties of Friendship and Cooperation," November 1, 1997, Harvard University, http://www.china-embassy.org/eng/zmgx/zysj/jzxfm/t36252.htm.

83. Joshua Kurlantzick, *Charm Offensive: How China's Soft Power Is Transforming the World* (New Haven, Conn.: Yale University Press, 2007), 10–11.

84. See for instance Kang, "Getting Asia Wrong."

85. See Evelyn Goh, "Great Powers and Southeast Asian Regional Security Strategies," *Military Technology* (January 2006): 321–323; and Denny Roy, "Southeast Asia and China: Balancing or Bandwagoning?" *Contemporary Southeast Asia* (August 2005): 311–312.

86. Bhaskar Balkrishnan, "China Woos Mauritius, Eyes Indian Ocean," *Political and Defence Weekly* 7, no. 41 (July 2009): 7–9, SAP20090731525005.

87. P. S. Das, "India's Strategic Concerns in the Indian Ocean," in *South Asia Defence and Strategy Year Book*, ed. Rajan Arya (New Delhi: Panchsheel, 2009), 96–100.

88. Gurpreet Khurana, "China-India Defense Rivalry," *Indian Defense Review* 23, no. 4 (July–September 2009), http://www.indiandefencereview.com/2009/04/china-india-maritime-rivalry.html.

89. Arun Prakash, "Indian Ocean: A Zone of Conflict?" in *South Asia Defence and Strategy Year Book*, ed. Rajan Arya (New Delhi: Panchsheel, 2009), 43–50.

90. M. K. Bhadrakumar, "Sri Lanka Wards Off Western Bullying," *Asia Times*, May 27, 2009.

91. For an Indian view of President Hu Jintao's rendition of the Zheng He narrative, see Sunanda K. Datta-Ray, "Frozen by China—India Has to Snap Out of Its Stupor if It Wants to Be a Force to Reckon With in Asia," *Hindustan Times*, January 8, 2007, 10, SAP20070108384011. Datta-Ray was a visiting senior research fellow at the Institute of Southeast Asian Studies, Singapore.

92. Thomas Mathew, "Mighty Dragon in the Sea," *Hindustan Times*, June 24, 2009.

93. G. Parthasarathy, "Challenges from China: India Faces Growing Hostility after 26/11," *Tribune,* March 19, 2009, SAP20090319378013.

94. Arun Kumar Singh, "Let's Prepare to Meet the Chinese in India's Ocean," *Deccan Chronicle*, February 20, 2009.

95. Walter Russell Mead, *Power, Terror, Peace, and War: America's Grand Strategy in a World at Risk* (New York: Alfred A. Knopf, 2004), 37.

96. China's ambition to dislodge America from its leading role in Asian affairs is already on display. In mid-December 2005, partly at Beijing's insistence, Asian nations held their inaugural East Asia Summit, a gathering that pointedly excluded the United States.

CHAPTER 8. U.S. MARITIME STRATEGY IN ASIA

1. Michèle Flournoy and Shawn Brimley, "The Contested Commons," U.S. Defense Department Web site, http://www.defense.gov/qdr/flournoy-article.html.

2. James R. Holmes and Toshi Yoshihara, "China and the Commons: Angell or Mahan?" *World Affairs* 168, no. 4 (Spring 2006): 172–191.

3. For the history of the 1986 strategy, we rely heavily on three compendia: John B. Hattendorf, *The Evolution of the U.S. Navy's Maritime Strategy, 1977–1986,* Newport Paper no. 19 (Newport, R.I.: Naval War College Press, 2004); John B. Hattendorf, ed., Newport Paper no. 30, *U.S. Naval Strategy in the 1970s: Selected Documents* (Newport, R.I.: Naval War College Press, 2007); and John B. Hattendorf, ed., *U.S. Naval Strategy in the 1980s: Selected Documents,* Newport Paper no. 33 (Newport, R.I.: Naval War College Press, 2008).

4. Carl von Clausewitz, *On War,* ed., trans. Peter Paret and Michael Howard (Princeton, N.J.: Princeton University Press, 1976), 136, 139.

5. Michael Handel, *Masters of War: Classical Strategic Thought,* 3rd ed. (London: Frank Cass, 2001), 117.

6. Samuel Huntington, "National Policy and the Transoceanic Navy," U.S. Naval Institute *Proceedings* 80, no. 5 (May 1954): 483–493.

7. Milan L. Hauner, "Stalin's Big-Fleet Program," *Naval War College Review* 57, no. 2 (Spring 2004): 87–120.

8. George W. Baer, *One Hundred Years of Sea Power: The U.S. Navy, 1890–1990* (Stanford, Calif.: Stanford University Press, 1994), 395, 398, 420, 422; Robert Waring Herrick, *The USSR's "Blue Belt of Defense" Concept: A Unified Military Plan for Defense against Seaborne Attack by Strike Carriers and Polaris/Poseidon SSBNs* (Arlington, Va.: Center for Naval Analyses, 1973).

9. Alfred Thayer Mahan, *Naval Strategy Compared and Contrasted with Principles and Practices of Military Operations on Land* (Boston: Little, Brown, 1911), 385, 391, 393, 397, 403, 441.

10. Sergei G. Gorshkov, *The Sea Power of the State* (Annapolis, Md.: Naval Institute Press, 1979).

11. George F. Kennan, "The Sources of Soviet Conduct," *Foreign Affairs*, July 1947, available at The History Guide Web site, "Lectures on Twentieth Century Europe," http://www.historyguide.org/Europe/kennan.html.

12. Norman Friedman, *The Fifty-Year War: Conflict and Strategy in the Cold War* (Annapolis, Md.: Naval Institute Press, 2000).

13. Hattendorf, *U.S. Naval Strategy in the 1970s,* 53–101.

14. James L. Holloway III, *Aircraft Carriers at War: A Personal Retrospective of Korea, Vietnam, and the Soviet Confrontation* (Annapolis, Md.: Naval Institute Press, 2007), 31.

15. William M. McBride, *Technological Change and the United States Navy, 1865–1945* (Baltimore: Johns Hopkins, 2000), 233.

16. Nathan Miller, *The U.S. Navy: A History*, 3rd ed. (Annapolis, Md.: Naval Institute Press, 1997), 273.

17. Hattendorf, *U.S. Naval Strategy in the 1970s*, 102–133.

18. Hattendorf, *Evolution of the U.S. Navy's Maritime Strategy*, 75.

19. "The Maritime Strategy, 1986," in Hattendorf, *U.S. Naval Strategy in the 1980s*, 203–258.

20. John J. Mearsheimer, "A Strategic Misstep: The Maritime Strategy and Deterrence in Europe," *International Security* 11, no. 2 (Fall 1986): 3–57. For a sampling of other commentary on the Maritime Strategy, see Robert W. Komer, "Maritime Strategy vs. Coalition Defense," *Foreign Affairs* 60, no. 5 (Summer 1982): 1124–1144; Barry R. Posen, "Measuring the European Conventional Balance: Coping with Complexity in Threat Assessment," *International Security* 9, no. 3 (Winter 1984–1985): 47–88; and Christopher A. Ford and David A. Rosenberg, "The Naval Intelligence Underpinnings of Reagan's Maritime Strategy," *Journal of Strategic Studies* 28, no. 2 (April 2005): 379–409.

21. Alfred Thayer Mahan, *From Sail to Steam: Recollections of Naval Life* (1907; repr., New York: Da Capo, 1968), 267–268.

22. Alfred Thayer Mahan, *Retrospect & Prospect: Studies in International Relations, Naval and Political* (Boston: Little, Brown, 1902), 8–12.

23. Carl Schurz, "Armed or Unarmed Peace," *Harper's Weekly Magazine*, June 19, 1897, 603.

24. Ivo H. Daalder and James M. Lindsay, "'For America, the Age of Geopolitics Has Ended and the Age of Global Politics Has Begun,'" *Boston Review*, February/March 2005, http://www.cfr.org/publication/9186/; and Ivo H. Daalder and James M. Lindsay, *America Unbound: The Bush Revolution in Foreign Policy* (Washington, D.C.: Brookings, 2003). For a sampling of similar views, see Joseph S. Nye, *Power in the Global Information Age: From Realism to Globalization* (London and New York: Routledge, 2004); and Michael Mandelbaum, *The Ideas That Conquered the World: Peace, Democracy, and Free Markets in the Twenty-first Century* (New York: Public Affairs, 2002).

25. Julian S. Corbett, *Some Principles of Maritime Strategy* (1911; repr., intro. Eric J. Grove, Annapolis, Md.: Naval Institute Press, 1988), 91–94.

26. For Corbett, concentration was a "kind of shibboleth" that obscured the lessons of British naval history. "Division," he maintained, was "bad only when it is pushed beyond the limits of well-knit deployment." Ibid., 131–132, 134.

27. Geoff Fine, "'Global Maritime Partnership' Gaining Steam at Home and with International Navies," *Defense Daily*, October 25, 2006, http://www.navy mil/navydata/cno/mullen/DEFENSE_DAILY_25OCT06_Global_Maritime_ Partnership_Gaining_Steam_At_Home_And_With_International_Navies.pdf.

28. U.S. Navy, Marine Corps, and Coast Guard, "A Cooperative Strategy for 21st Century Seapower" (Washington, D.C.: Department of the Navy, October 2007), http://www.navy.mil/maritime/MaritimeStrategy.pdf, 3.

29. U.S. Secretary of the Navy, ". . . From the Sea," September 1992, http://www. globalsecurity.org/military/library/policy/navy/fts.htm; U.S. Secretary of the Navy, "Forward . . . from the Sea," 1995, http://www.globalsecurity.org/military/library/policy/navy/forward-from-the-sea.pdf.

30. Karl Walling, "Why a Conversation with the Country? A Backward Look at Some Forward-Thinking Maritime Strategists," *Joint Force Quarterly* 50 (3rd quarter 2008), http://www.ndu.edu/inss/Press/jfq_pages/editions/i50/28.pdf.

31. Alfred Thayer Mahan, *The Influence of Sea Power upon History, 1660–1783* (1890; repr., New York: Dover, 1987), 76.

32. Ibid., 39, 53–54, 70–82.

33. Ibid., 38, 49, 68–69.

34. Ibid., 50.

35. Japan Ministry of Defense, "Defense of Japan 2009," Ministry of Defense Web site, http://www.mod.go.jp/e/publ/w_paper/pdf/2009/Part3-chap2.pdf.

36. Joseph S. Nye, "The American National Interest and Global Public Goods," *International Affairs* 78, no. 2 (April 2002): 238; and Eyre Crowe, "Memorandum on the Present State of British Relations with France and Germany, January 1, 1907," in *British Documents on the Origins of the War 1898–1914*, vol. 3, *The Testing of the Entente, 1904–6*, ed. G. P. Gooch and Harold Temperley (London: His Majesty's Stationery Office, 1927), 403–417.

37. Peter Dombrowski and Andrew C. Winner, "The U.S. Maritime Strategy and Implications for the Indo-Pacific Region," Paper presented to the Royal Australian Navy Seapower Conference, Sydney, Australia, February 2008.

38. U.S. Navy, Marine Corps, and Coast Guard, "A Cooperative Strategy," 4.

39. Ibid., 8.

40. Ibid., 13.

41. Ibid., 9.

42. Robert O. Work and Jan van Tol, "A Cooperative Strategy for 21st Century Seapower: An Assessment" (Washington, D.C.: Center for Strategic and Budgetary Assessments, March 26, 2008), 1–3.

43. Ibid., 4.

44. Huntington, "National Policy and the Transoceanic Navy," 483.

45. Work and van Tol, "An Assessment," 12.

46. Ibid., 20.

47. Ibid., 25.

48. Dombrowski and Winner, "U.S. Maritime Strategy," 11–13.

49. Andrew S. Erickson, "Assessing the New U.S. Maritime Strategy: A Window into Chinese Thinking," *Naval War College Review* 61, no. 4 (Autumn 2008): 36, 38–39; and Su Hao, "The U.S. Maritime Strategy's New Thinking: Reviewing the 'Cooperative Strategy for 21st Century Seapower,'" *Naval War College Review* 61, no. 4 (Autumn 2008): 70.

50. Wang Baofu, "The U.S. Military's 'Maritime Strategy' and Future Transformation," *Naval War College Review* 61, no. 4 (Autumn 2008): 62–64.

51. Ibid., 66. It is noteworthy that some American observers, notably Thomas Barnett, have likewise accused the Pentagon of cynically using China to whip up support for bigger defense budgets. Barnett declares that China has joined a realm of peace among the advanced nations. See Thomas P. M. Barnett, *The Pentagon's New Map: War and Peace in the Twenty-first Century* (New York: Putnam, 2004), 62, 108, 152, 169.

52. Lu Rude, "The New Maritime Strategy Surfaces," *Naval War College Review* 61, no. 4 (Autumn 2008): 58.

53. Ibid., 57.

54. 杜朝平 [Du Chaoping], 与狼共舞—美国"千舰 海军"计划于中国的选择 ["Dance with Wolves—America's 'Thousand-Ship Navy' Plan and China's Choices"], 舰载武器 [*Shipborne Weapons*] (December 2007): 25–26.

55. 李杰 [Li Jie], '千舰海军'的玄机 ["The Unfathomable 'Thousand-Ship' Navy"], 兵器知识 [*Ordnance Knowledge*], no. 2 (2007): 44.

56. 杨承军 孙毅 [Yang Chengjun and Sun Yi], 百星计划—快乐并痛着 ["The One-Hundred Satellite Plan—Joy with Pain"], 兵器知识 [*Ordnance Knowledge*], no. 8 (2007): 22; and Lu Desheng, "'100 Satellite Program' Might Not Work as Wished," *Jiefangjun Bao*, June 19, 2007, 5, OSC-CPP20070619702001.

57. Author discussions, Naval War College, Newport, R.I., August 8, 2008.

58. Quotations in this section come from an exchange of e-mail correspondence between James Holmes and Gurpreet Khurana, September 28–30, 2008.

59. Andrew S. Erickson, "New U.S. Maritime Strategy: Initial Chinese Responses," *China Security* 3, no. 4 (Autumn 2007): 45.

CHAPTER 9. WHO HOLDS THE TRIDENTS?

1. David A. Shlapak, David T. Orletsky, Toy I. Reid, Murray Scot Tanner, and Barry Wilson, *A Question of Balance: Political Context and Military Aspects of the China-Taiwan Dispute* (Santa Monica, Calif.: RAND, 2009), 126.

2. Ibid., 139.

3. Ibid., 131.

4. Ibid., 139.

5. Ibid., 140.

6. David A. Shlapak, David T. Orletsky, and Barry A. Wilson, *Dire Strait? Military Aspects of the China-Taiwan Confrontation and Options for U.S. Policy* (Santa Monica, Calif.: RAND, 2000), 56.

7. Ibid., xvi.

8. Ibid., 30.

9. Shlapak et al., *A Question of Balance*, 141.

10. Robert S. Ross, "The Stability of Deterrence in the Taiwan Strait," *National Interest* 65 (Fall 2001): 70.

11. Ibid., 72.

12. Robert S. Ross, "Balance of Power Politics and the Rise of China: Accommodation and Balancing in East Asia," *Security Studies* 15, no. 3 (July–September 2006): 372.

13. Robert Ross, "For China, How to Manage Taiwan?" *Forbes*, October 27, 2007.

14. Bernard D. Cole, *The Great Wall at Sea: China's Navy Enters the Twenty-first Century* (Annapolis, Md.: Naval Institute Press, 2001), 174.

15. Bernard D. Cole, "The Modernization of the PLAN and Taiwan's Security," in *Taiwan's Maritime Security*, ed. Martin Edmonds and Michael M. Tsai (London: Routledge, 2003), 72.

16. Bernard D. Cole, "The Military Instrument of Statecraft at Sea: Naval Options in an Escalatory Scenario Involving Taiwan: 2007–2016," in *Assessing the Threat: The Chinese Military and Taiwan's Security*, ed. Michael D. Swaine, Andrew N. D. Yang, and Evan S. Medeiros (Washington, D.C.: Carnegie Endowment for International Peace, 2007), 198.

17. Bernard D. Cole, "Right-Sizing the Navy: How Much Naval Force Will Beijing Deploy?" in *Right-Sizing the People's Liberation Army: Exploring the Contours of China's Military*, ed. Roy Kamphausen and Andrew Scobell (Carlisle Barracks, Carlisle, Pa.: Strategic Studies Institute, U.S. Army War College, 2007), 552–553.

18. Richard Sharpe, ed. *Jane's Fighting Ships* (Surrey, UK: Jane's Information Group, 1990), 79.

19. Michael G. Gallagher, "China's Illusory Threat to the South China Sea," *International Security* 19, no. 1 (Summer 1994): 181.

20. Christopher D. Yung, *People's War at Sea: Chinese Naval Power in the Twenty-First Century* (Alexandria, Va.: Center for Naval Analyses, 1996), 52.

21. Gerald Segal, "Does China Matter?" *Foreign Affairs* 78, no. 5 (September/October 1999): 29.

22. Bates Gill and Michael O'Hanlon, "China's Hollow Military," *National Interest* 56 (Summer 1999): 62.

23. Michael O'Hanlon, "Why China Cannot Conquer Taiwan," *International Security* 25, no. 2 (Fall 2000): 82.

24. Phillip C. Saunders and Scott Kastner, "Is a China-Taiwan Peace Deal in the Cards?" *Foreign Policy*, July 27, 2009, http://www.foreignpolicy.com/articles/2009/07/27/is_a_china_taiwan_peace_deal_in_the_cards.

25. Thomas J. Christensen, "Posing Problems without Catching Up: China's Rise and Challenges for U.S. Security Policy," *International Security* 25, no. 4 (Spring 2001): 5–40.

26. Cole, *Great Wall at Sea*, 184.

27. See Peter Lorge, *War, Politics and Society in Early Modern China* (London: Routledge, 2005), 89–90; Ralph D. Sawyer, *Fire and Water: The Art of Incendiary and Aquatic Warfare in China* (Boulder, Colo.: Westview, 2004); Peter Lorge, "Water Forces and Naval Operations," in *A Military History of China*, ed. David A. Graff and Robin Higham (Boulder, Colo.: Westview, 2002); David A. Graff, *Medieval Chinese Warfare* (London: Routledge, 2002), 131–135; David A. Graff, "Dou Jiande's Dilemma: Logistics, Strategy, and State Formation in Seventh-Century China," in *Warfare in Chinese History*, ed. Hans Van den Ven (Leiden, The Netherlands: Brill, 2000), 77–104; Billy K. L. So, *Prosperity, Region, and Institutions in Maritime China: The South Fukien Pattern, 946–1368* (Cambridge, Mass.: Harvard University Press, 2000); and Gang Deng, *Maritime Sector, Institutions and Sea Power of Premodern China* (Westport, Conn.: Greenwood Press, 1999).

28. Cole, *Great Wall at Sea*, 186–187.

29. Anthony Cordesman and Martin Klieber, *Chinese Military Modernization: Force Development and Strategic Capabilities* (Washington, D.C.: Center for Strategic and International Studies, 2007), 137.

30. Manu Pubby, "China Proposed Division of Pacific, Indian Ocean Regions, We Declined: U.S. Admiral," *Indian Express*, May 15, 2009, http://www.indianexpress.com/news/China-proposed-division-of-Pacific_Indian-Ocean-regions-we-declined-US-Admiral/459851.

31. T. A. Brooks, "Comments and Discussion," U.S. Naval Institute *Proceedings* 135, no. 6 (June 2009), http://www.usni.org/magazines/proceedings/archive/story.asp?STORY_ID=1898.

32. Robert S. Ross, "Myth," *National Interest Online*, August 25, 2009, http://www.nationalinterest.org/Article.aspx?id=22022.

33. Ibid.

34. Robert D. Kaplan, "America's Elegant Decline," *Atlantic*, November 2007, http://www.theatlantic.com/doc/200711/america-decline.

35. Michael I. Handel, *Masters of War: Classical Strategic Thought*, 3rd ed. (London: Frank Cass, 2001), 117.

 **Index**

About the Authors

Toshi Yoshihara is an associate professor of strategy at the Naval War College. Previously, he was a visiting professor in the Strategy Department at the Air War College. Dr. Yoshihara holds a PhD from the Fletcher School of Law and Diplomacy, Tufts University.

James R. Holmes is an associate professor of strategy at the Naval War College and a faculty associate at the University of Georgia School of Public and International Affairs. A former U.S. Navy surface warfare officer, he earned a PhD from the Fletcher School of Law and Diplomacy, Tufts University.

The Naval Institute Press is the book-publishing arm of the U.S. Naval Institute, a private, nonprofit, membership society for sea service professionals and others who share an interest in naval and maritime affairs. Established in 1873 at the U.S. Naval Academy in Annapolis, Maryland, where its offices remain today, the Naval Institute has members worldwide.

Members of the Naval Institute support the education programs of the society and receive the influential monthly magazine *Proceedings* or the colorful bimonthly magazine *Naval History* and discounts on fine nautical prints and on ship and aircraft photos. They also have access to the transcripts of the Institute's Oral History Program and get discounted admission to any of the Institute-sponsored seminars offered around the country.

The Naval Institute's book-publishing program, begun in 1898 with basic guides to naval practices, has broadened its scope to include books of more general interest. Now the Naval Institute Press publishes about seventy titles each year, ranging from how-to books on boating and navigation to battle histories, biographies, ship and aircraft guides, and novels. Institute members receive significant discounts on the Press's more than eight hundred books in print.

Full-time students are eligible for special half-price membership rates. Life memberships are also available.

For a free catalog describing Naval Institute Press books currently available, and for further information about joining the U.S. Naval Institute, please write to:

Member Services
U.S. Naval Institute
291 Wood Road
Annapolis, MD 21402-5034
Telephone: (800) 233-8764
Fax: (410) 571-1703
Web address: www.usni.org